This book is the first to offer a detailed analysis of Aristotelian and Kantian ethics together in a way that remains faithful to the texts and responsive to debates in contemporary ethics.

Recent moral philosophy has seen a revival of interest in the concept of virtue, and with it a reassessment of the role of virtue in the work of Aristotle and Kant. This book brings that reassessment to a new level of sophistication. Nancy Sherman argues that Kant preserves a notion of virtue in his moral theory that bears recognizable traces of the Aristotelian and Stoic traditions, and that his complex anthropology of morals brings him into surprising alliance with Aristotle. She develops her argument through close readings of major texts by both Aristotle and Kant, illustrating points of congruence and contrast.

While scrupulously focusing on textual details the book presents a dialogue between Aristotle and Kant that sheds light on contemporary debates about the importance in any account of moral judgment of general principles, on the one hand, and a grasp of particulars on the other. She also argues for the significant role emotions play in both the Kantian and the Aristotelian accounts of moral agency.

Making a Necessity of Virtue

Making a Necessity of Virtue

Aristotle and Kant on Virtue

NANCY SHERMAN
Georgetown University

CAMBRIDGE
UNIVERSITY PRESS

PUBLISHED BY THE PRESS SYNDICATE OF THE UNIVERSITY OF CAMBRIDGE
The Pitt Building, Trumpington Street, Cambridge, CB2 1RP

CAMBRIDGE UNIVERSITY PRESS
The Edinburgh Building, Cambridge CB2 2RU, United Kingdom
40 West 20th Street, New York, NY 10011-4211, USA
10 Stamford Road, Oakleigh, Melbourne 3166, Australia

First published 1997

Printed in the United States of America

Typeset in Palatino

Library of Congress Cataloging-in-Publication Data
Sherman, Nancy, 1951–
Making a necessity of virtue : Aristotle and Kant on virtue /
Nancy Sherman.
p.   cm.
Includes bibliographical references and index.
ISBN 0-521-56383-6 (hardcover). – ISBN 0-521-56487-5 (pbk.)
1. Aristotle – Ethics.   2. Kant, Immanuel, 1724–1804 – Ethics.
I. Title.
B491.E7S44   1996
179'.9 – dc20   96-26314
                                                CIP

A catalog record for this book is available from the British Library.

ISBN 0-521-56383-6 Hardback
ISBN 0-521-56487-5 Paperback

To Marshall, Kala, and Jonathan

Contents

Preface and Acknowledgments   *page* xi
Abbreviations and Notes on Translations   xiv

Chapter 1   A New Dialogue   1
1   The Framing Questions   5
2   Activity, Agency, and External Goods: Aristotle, the
     Stoics, and Kant   9
3   A Brief Overview   20

Chapter 2   The Emotional Structure of Aristotelian Virtue   24
1   Opening a Dialogue on the Emotions   24
2   The Alleged Problem with Emotions   28
3   How Emotions Figure in Morality   39
4   Aristotelian Emotions   52
5   Emotions and Their Relation to Choice   75
6   Cultivating Emotions   83
7   Cultivating Emotions Through Music and Tragedy   89
8   Virtue and Nonconflictual Emotions   93

Chapter 3   A Brief Stoic Interlude   99
1   Against Aristotelian Moderation   101
2   Stoic Therapy   107
3   Stoic Apathy and Kantian Antisentimentalism   116

Chapter 4   The Passional Underpinnings of Kantian Virtue   121
1   Some Background   121

Contents

2   Morality's Foundation and Moral Anthropology   127
3   Kantian Virtue   135
4   The Cultivation of Emotions as Supports for Duty   141
5   Virtue as a Structured Composite   158
6   In What Sense Are We Agents of Our Emotional
    Experience?   164
7   Respect as a Distinctive Moral Emotion   175
8   A Few Comparative Notes   181

Chapter 5   The Shared Voyage   187
1   Doing Things Together   188
2   Aristotelian Friendship and Shared Activity   199
3   Friendship and Its Place in Good Living   208
4   Wider Altruism   217
5   Kant and Friendship   224
6   The Ethical Commonwealth as a Social Goal   233

Chapter 6   Aristotelian Particularism   239
1   Brief Remarks on Practical Reason and "Habituated"
    Virtue   241
2   Aristotelian Particularism: A Start   243
3   Emotions as Evaluative   248
4   Perception and Intuitionism   254
5   Rules and Practical Insight   262
6   The Practical Syllogism Revisited   276

*Chapter 7   Making Room for Practical Wisdom in Kantian
         Ethics*   284
1   Some Roles for the Categorical Imperative   289
2   The Content of Maxims   294
3   Kantian Universalizability   305
4   Kantian "Reflective" Deliberation   311
5   Comparing Aristotle and Kant on Judgment and
    Deliberation   325

*Chapter 8   Perfecting Kantian Virtue: Discretionary
         Latitude and Superlative Virtue*   331
1   How Demanding is Kantian Virtue?   331

Contents

2   Imperfect Duties of Virtue: Latitudinarian and
      Rigoristic Readings   332
3   Superlative Virtue   350

Bibliography   363
Index   381

Preface and acknowledgments

This book began life in my final two years at Yale, and then grew to completion during the past six years at Georgetown. Its conception, however, was even earlier, for as I wrote the *Fabric of Character*, Kant's voice insistently pressed for inclusion in the discussion. It took many years to shape the conversation Kant would come to have with Aristotle. The themes I have settled on are those that I think are central to the debate, though by no means exhaustive. As readers will see, the debate is a reconstructed one. Careful attention is paid to the details of texts, but with an eye toward creating a shared discourse rather than a mapping of actual lines of transmission and debt. The felt need to bring Aristotle and Kant together in conversation has, of course, not been mine alone. With the flourishing of studies in the history of moral philosophy, others too have found points of intersection and contrast, which were often obscured in earlier, overly neat categorizations. I have profited from this general resurgence in history of philosophy studies as well as from the shifting interest in normative ethics toward taking a more serious look at texts and the complex stories they have to tell. In ancient ethics, I have learned enormously from the recent work of Julia Annas and Martha Nussbaum, and in Kantian studies, from Barbara Herman and Onora O'Neill's pioneering work. John Rawls's unpublished lectures on Kant, which I first heard in 1977, remain an inspiration and the source of my early interest in Kant's ethics.

Some parts of the book were developed earlier as published

papers, though in all cases they have been substantially altered or recast (I list those papers in the bibliography). Many of the themes of this book were presented in papers and seminars over the years at the APA Pacific Division session on Hellenistic emotions; the 8th International Kant Congress in Memphis; the University of Kentucky; Mount St. Mary's College; Johns Hopkins University; the Boston Area Colloquium in Ancient Philosophy at Brown University; Eastern Kentucky University as the keynote address at an NEH seminar; Rogers State College as an NEH scholar in residence; the socioeconomics conference at the University of California at Irvine; the Belgum Memorial Lectures, St. Olaf College; University of Virginia; the workshop on Kantian ethics at the University of North Carolina; the APA Pacific Division session on the virtues of common pursuit; the University of Maryland; Bryn Mawr College; the University of Arizona; the University of California at Santa Barbara. In addition, I have taught graduate seminars on the themes of the book at Georgetown University, Johns Hopkins University, and the University of Maryland. I am deeply grateful for the patience and helpful criticisms of all my students and discussants on these various occasions.

Initial research for this book was supported by a Mellon Fellowship awarded by the Whitney Humanities Center at Yale and an American Council for Learned Studies (1987–88). I have subsequently received a Mellon Summer Fellowship (1992) and generous summer grants from Georgetown. Additional leave time and a sabbatical in the fall of 1995 have enabled me to finish the project. Georgetown has been a most congenial and nurturing atmosphere for working on this volume, and I am thankful to my colleagues for creating that environment. Special thanks to my chair, Wayne Davis, who has supported my work in many ways and who has done much to cultivate the congeniality of community at Georgetown.

Many individuals have read parts of the book at various stages and I am truly grateful for their many comments and general encouragement over the years. My "particularist" wish is to acknowledge just how all these various individuals helped to support the overall project, but I fear that would take me into a lengthy discourse that in the end would be more a personal musing than a public record of debt. Consequently, I shall revert to somewhat impersonal lists, but my gratitude is anything but impersonal. Special thanks go to Julia Annas, Martha Nussbaum, Jerry Schneewind, Owen Flanagan, Richard Kraut, Alisdair Mac-Intyre, Michael Slote, Onora O'Neill, Tom Hill, Terry Pinkard, and Geoff Sayre-McCord, who have read large portions of the book in its penultimate stages. I also owe much thanks to Alisa Carse, who read the final manuscript in the context of a seminar we taught together on Kantian ethics. I am deeply grateful also to Marcia Baron, Henry Richardson, Adrian Piper, Andy Reath, Aryeh Kosman, Maggie Little, Alfonso Gómez-Lobo, Dan Robinson, Natalie Brender, Jonathan Dancy, Aaron Ben Ze-ev, Paula Gottlieb, Jay Reuscher, and Marcelo Boeri for their comments on particular chapters. I hope I have not inadvertently omitted any names. In addition, I wish to thank two anonymous reviewers. A different sort of gratitude goes to Michael Friedman, conversations with whom have taught me something about the lived life of philosophy. My family – Marshall, Kala, and Jonathan – have patiently shared the daily life of this book with me. With terrific love, and much gratitude for their patience and companionship, I dedicate this work to them.

Abbreviations and notes on translations

ARISTOTLE

DA	*De Anima*
EE	*Eudemian Ethics*
MA	*De Motu Animalium*
Meta.	*Metaphysics*
MM	*Magna Moralia*
NE	*Nicomachean Ethics*
Phys.	*Physics*
Poet.	*Poetics*
Pol.	*Politics*
Rh.	*Rhetoric*

Note: Unless otherwise stated, translations are from Jonathan Barnes, ed., *The Complete Works of Aristotle*, the Revised Oxford Translation, vols. 1 and 2 (Princeton: Princeton University Press, 1984). Also, I replace "noble" with "fine" as a translation of *to kalon* and, when appropriate, replace "man" with "person." I have consulted with the following other editions:

Armstrong, G. Cyril, tr. 1969. *Magna Moralia*. Cambridge, MA: Loeb Classical Library, Harvard University Press.

Hicks, R. D. 1976 reprint. *De Anima*. New York: Arno Press (Cambridge: Cambridge University Press, 1907).

Irwin, T. H., tr. 1985. *Nicomachean Ethics*. Indianapolis: Hackett.

Nussbaum, Martha C. 1978. *Aristotle's De Motu Animalium.* Princeton: Princeton University Press.
Racham, H., tr. 1944. *Politics.* Cambridge, MA: Harvard University Press.
　1971. *Eudemian Ethics.* Cambridge, MA: Loeb Classical Library, Harvard University Press.
Woods, Michael, tr. with commentary. 1982. *Aristotle's Eudemian Ethics.* Oxford: Oxford University Press.

KANT

Anth.   *Anthropology from a Pragmatic Point of View*
DV   *The Doctrine of Virtue,* Part II of *The Metaphysic of Morals*
G   *Groundwork of the Metaphysic of Morals*
KpV   *Critique of Practical Judgment*
KrV   *Critique of Pure Reason*
LE   *Lectures on Ethics*
Rel.   *Religion Within the Limits of Reason Alone*
(Other works by Kant are cited in unabbreviated form.)

I have quoted from the following translations of Kantian texts:
Anthropology from a Pragmatic Point of View, tr. Mary J. Gregor. 1974. The Hague: Nijoff.
"Conjectural Beginning of Human History," tr. Emil L. Fackenheim. 1963. In *Kant on History,* ed. Lewis White Beck. Indianapolis: Bobbs-Merrill.
Critique of Practical Reason, tr. Lewis White Beck. 1956. Indianapolis: Bobbs-Merrill.
Critique of Pure Reason, tr. Norman Kemp Smith. 1965. New York: St. Martin's Press.
Doctrine of Virtue, Part II of *The Metaphysic of Morals.* tr. Mary J. Gregor. 1964. Philadelphia: University of Pennsylvania Press.
Groundwork of the Metaphysic of Morals, tr. H. J. Paton. 1964. New York: Harper and Row.
"Idea for a Universal History from a Cosmopolitan Point of View," tr. Lewis White Beck. 1963. In *Kant on History,* ed. Lewis White Beck. Indianapolis: Bobbs-Merrill.
Lectures on Ethics, tr. Louis Infield. 1963. Indianapolis: Hackett.

"Perpetual Peace," tr. Louis White Beck. 1963. In *Kant on History*, ed. Lewis White Beck. Indianapolis: Bobbs-Merrill.

Religion Within the Limits of Reason Alone, tr. Theodore M. Greene and Hoyt H. Hudson. 1960. New York: Harper & Row.

"What Is Enlightenment," tr. Lewis White Beck. 1963. In *Kant on History*, ed. Lewis White Beck. Indianapolis: Bobbs-Merrill.

A note on citations: References to Kant's texts are to the pagination in the Prussian Academy edition of *Kants gesammelte Schriften*. Where the translation I have used does not have running paginations from the Academy edition, I have supplied the Academy paging followed by the page in translation. When quoting from the *Lectures on Ethics* (LE), I cite only the page in translation, as this work is not included in the Academy edition.

THE STOICS

E-K	Edelstein-Kidd edition of Posidonius. 1972. Cambridge: Cambridge University Press.
Ep.	Seneca, *Epistulae Morales*, vols. 1–3, tr. Richard Gummere. 1917–22. Cambridge, MA: Loeb Classical Library, Harvard University Press.
Fin.	Cicero, *De Finibus Bonorum et Malorum*, tr. H. Rackham. 1921. Cambridge, MA: Loeb Classical Library, Harvard University Press.
Ir.	Seneca. *De Ira (On Anger)*. In *Moral Essays*, vol. 1.
L and S	Long and Sedley, *The Hellenistic Philosophers*, vols. 1 and 2. 1987. Cambridge: Cambridge University Press. (In those cases where I cite "L and S," I use their translation of the fragment.)
SVF	Von Arnim, *Stoicorum Verterum Fragmenta*, vols. 1–4. 1986. New York: Irvington.
TD	Cicero, *Tusculan Disputations*, tr. J. E. King. 1964. Cambridge, MA: Loeb Classical Library, Harvard University Press.
Arius	In Stobaeus, *Eclogae Physicae et Ethicae*, vol. 2, ed. C. Wachsmuth. 1884. Germany: Wiedmannos.

Other texts and translations I use are:

Diogenes Laertius, vols. 1 and 2, tr. R. D. Hicks. 1972. Cambridge, MA: Loeb Classical Library, Harvard University Press.

Plutarch, *Moralia*, vol. 6, tr. W. C. Helmbold. 1939. Cambridge, MA: Loeb Classical Library, Harvard University Press.

Seneca, *Moral Essays*, vols. 1–3, tr. John W. Basore. 1928–32. Cambridge, MA: Loeb Classical Library, Harvard University Press.

Chapter 1
A new dialogue

Recent moral philosophy has seen a revival of interest in virtue, and with it a striking, if often implicit, dialogue between Aristotle and Kant. To think of Kant as an exponent of virtue may seem to some readers itself novel and not easily associated with the Kant familiar to discussions of justice and rights. Certainly Kant's conception of virtue is in important ways distinct from Aristotle's, and Kantian texts are correctly thought of as a locus for modern discussions of autonomy and respect in a way that Aristotle's texts simply are not. But all the same, Kant, great admirer of the Stoics that he was, preserves the notion of virtue in his moral theory in a manner that bears recognizable traces to the Aristotelian tradition to which the Stoics themselves react. It is important to appreciate from the start, however, that Kant's reaction to the Stoics is complex and different in different periods of his writing. To cast Kant as the harsh "duty philosopher," unsympathetic to human emotions, and to see this as a Stoic inheritance would be misguided. For it has not been adequately appreciated that Kant develops a complex anthropology of morals – a tailoring of morality to the contingent features of the human case – which at times brings him into surprising alliance with Aristotle and his project of limning an account of human excellence. Still, there remains the crucial distinction between Aristotle and Kant – that for Kant, moral anthropology rests always on a foundation of pure morality, on a conception of the autonomy of reason that can

1

be stripped, for the most part,[1] from the constraints of the human case. To establish a metaphysic of morals where reason alone is the source of moral authority remains a constant goal, even when the more focused interest is in developing an account that applies to humans. For Aristotle, there is nothing but the human case and its inescapable finitude.

Of course, there is no simple lineage between Aristotle and Kant, and a full historical reconstruction would require winding our way through the thicket of terms and technical coinages in which the various traditions are tangled. To some limited extent, this kind of work is unavoidable, especially if one is to preserve the theoretical integrity of the Aristotelian and Kantian frameworks. But for the most part, this is not a study of the evolution of various philosophical concepts, or a garnering of texts to show ancestral debt or deviation. What is exciting about the present debate between the Aristotelians and Kantians is the fertile discussion of substantive topics. These discussions have far-reaching range, touching on: the place of procedures and rules in an account of morality; the role of external goods in a conception of what is morally worthy; the place of emotions in moral character; the relation of justice to virtue; the nature of human perception and judgment in discerning moral salience; and the value of friends in the best human life. The illumination of each theory by the other has been crucial for revitalizing our understanding of each, as well as for a renewed discussion in moral philosophy in general.

Rapprochement can be dangerous, however, especially when it obscures important demarcating lines. To a certain extent this has happened in the present debate, with the rush to mutual accommodation eclipsing the structural and foundational integrity of each theory. One aim of the present work is to restore the distinctive theoretical structures of each tradition within a dialogue that nonetheless acknowledges some shared terrain. Of course, it would be naïve to think that two philosophers working from different traditions and historical periods could carry on a discussion about character, moral judgment, praise and blame, and the

---

[1] I explore this qualification in Chapter 4, sec. 2.

like, that shared as much in common as, say, the debate internal to ancient ethics itself. Aristotle conducts a conversation with Socrates and Plato, and the Hellenists in turn with their predecessors that rest on shared conceptions which we simply do not expect to find linking Aristotle and Kant. Much of ancient ethics is indeed a debate devoted to recording subtle moves in an ongoing, dialectical conversation among its many participants. To read Cicero is to be reminded of just how rich and detailed these conversations are, and of the common framework in which they often take place. Aristotle pioneers the dialectical tradition, prefacing each of his discussions with a review of the opinions of the many and wise, preserving what is best in these as he develops a systematic account. To bring Aristotle and Kant into a conversation of the ancient sort, with the hope of a similarly unified framework, would be a fantastical goal.

But all the same, we must not overstate the distance between Kant and the ancients. As a well-educated *philosophe* of the eighteenth century, Kant viewed his own work as dialectically engaged with the ancients. The Latin Stoics were well known in eighteenth-century Europe, and Kant was deeply influenced by them. But he was familiar also with the broad lines of the earlier virtue theory of the Greeks. Classical antiquity could be exploited against Christianity while still leaving room for the Enlightenment's new face of modernity. As Peter Gay so beautifully reminds us, "Even in East Prussia classical currency was valid coin: Kant did not find it necessary to identify the phrase, *sapere aude* [dare to know], which he had suggested as a motto for the Enlightenment, as a Horatian tag. . . . Antiquity was anything but esoteric: it was inescapable."[2] Thus, Kant was self-aware of his historical predecessors and in sympathy with important parts of the ancient tradition of virtue. His own distinctive contributions cannot be underestimated, but by his own telling, the account of virtues owes clear debts to "the ancient moral philosophers, who pretty well exhausted all that can be said upon virtue."[3] Just what the debt was, will be our task to understand. But at very least we have Kant's own blessings in taking up a dialogue between him-

[2] Gay (1966), 39, 40.   [3] Rel. 24n./20n.

self and Aristotle. As part of such a conversation, common themes will be explored both as shared terrain and as separate moments plucked from their larger respective theories. Equally, subtle differences in emphasis will be noted alongside instances of thematic overlap. For what is figure in one theory, may be at most background in another. All this should be recorded as moments in a nuanced conversation that is honest about the differences and not overly partisan in defending the often competing views.

In many ways the conversation is already being conducted in contemporary debates about the place of virtue in morality, in discussions of the role of character versus rules, in the comparison of eudaimonistic conceptions versus action-centered accounts, in worries about the importance of affect and human gesture in an account of human morality. But these debates often lose their vitality when they are removed from the texts. The loss is not simply one of historical accuracy; often, the textual account of a moral conception enables us to see that distinctions are more subtle than we initially thought, that apparently exhaustive alternatives turn out not to be so, that, not surprisingly, real positions are often more interesting and rich than their cardboard analogues.

Parallel to the contemporary debate has been a rejuvenation of interest within the history of moral philosophy itself, most dramatically in Kantian scholarship. Our understanding of Kant's moral philosophy has become considerably adjusted as more of Kant's ethical corpus is translated and discussed within the Kantian secondary literature. The overly restrictive focus of the *Groundwork* and the second *Critique,* and their often disparaging remarks on the contingent dimensions of human morality, are undercut somewhat by the views of the *Doctrine of Virtue, Religion Within the Limits of Reason Alone,* the *Lectures on Ethics,* and the *Anthropology from a Pragmatic Point of View,* where more of the details of the human case and the special features of human sensibility are filled in. As a result, we have a much clearer picture of the project of the anthropology of morals, and its companion role to an *a priori* grounding of morality. On the ancient side, Aristotelian ethics continues to attract those seeking alternatives to narrowly conceived utilitarian or deontological conceptions. And within ancient scholarship itself, a renewal of energy, much of it in work directed toward the Hellenistic period, has opened up vistas to Aristotle and Plato, as well as to Kant and his relation to the Stoics. The dialogue that ensues in this study owes much to contemporary work in ancient and Kantian moral philosophy as well as, of course, to nonhistorical debate that sheds important light on Aristotelian and Kantian views.

1 THE FRAMING QUESTIONS

With these brief words of introduction, I consider the way Aristotle and Kant each frame their conception of moral inquiry. What questions structure a work like the *Nicomachean Ethics* or Kant's *Metaphysic of Moral* ? Here, no doubt, we will tread over familiar ground, but a general review will prepare us for some more comparative remarks. We can begin with Aristotle.

Aristotle, like Socrates and Plato before him, and the Stoics after, begins his inquiry with the question, What is a good and happy life for a human being? In their terms, What is *eudaimonia* (happiness)? What are its parts and structure of parts? Is it a life of civic achievement and active public service; of living with family and friends in pursuit of common ends; of pleasure and excitement; of theoretical reflection; of prosperity and health or freedom; of possessing and exercising virtuous character? Aristotle's well-known answer is that the best human life will require at its center the exercise of virtue, or excellent human (social) functioning. Virtues are character states that dispose us to respond well to the conditions of human life through both wisely chosen actions and appropriate emotions. To live a good life requires acting from such states. But the activity requirement itself presupposes a certain measure of prosperity and luck. That is, the good life owes much to agency and effort, but also it owes something to good fortune. Simply to act from virtue in a noncramped way requires that the world be in some way hospitable to one's intentions. In a sense, virtuous activity cannot be purely internal but must have some outward success in the world, and this requires propitious conditions as well as external resources or goods. But in addition,

5

the fully good life will require external goods, such as friendship, enjoyed for their own sake and not merely instrumental to virtue. So, Aristotle will argue, the presence of friendship adds something to happiness in its own right, and its loss or absence mars it. On the Aristotelian view, then, virtue and subsequent questions of how we ought to act toward self and others arise within the more fundamental question of human well-being. Reflection about the good life is the context for a study of the virtues and for assessment of the moral conduct of one's life.

Kant, as is well known, repudiates a conception of human good as foundational to morality. The pivotal concern is no longer the assessment of a good life (subject as it is to the vagaries of human nature and, on the Aristotelian view, good fortune), but one of an intention or maxim of action, with criteria for such assessment grounded in the shared operations of reason. The goodness of intention makes direct appeal to the authority of reason and to requirements for its respect and preservation as it is embodied in rational agents. We come to virtue not through inquiry into human flourishing, but out of an interest in knowing the attitude that accompanies properly justified moral judgments. Central to this view will be that such judgments, or reasons, must be those that others could hold or assent to as rational agents. Thus, the question of morality is severed from that of happiness, and the foundation of morality becomes autonomously constructed reasons that issue from our legislative capacities. We shall have much to say about aspects of this transition, but it is very much emphasized in the coming pages and chapters that this transition away from human nature to the authority of autonomous reason is not absolute. Full virtue requires not only adherence to legislative reason, but also the habituation of a supportive empirical character. As we shall see, Kant insists that we have duties to cultivate our emotions so that we can act from principle with the right affective engagement with others. In a sense to be explored, Kantian virtue becomes naturalized. An understanding of Kantian morality is incomplete without an understanding of his conception of moral anthropology.

But even if Kantian moral anthropology edges us closer to the terrain of ancient ethics, is there not this substantial difference between the ancient and modern projects – that a eudaimonistic ethics, such as Aristotle's, rests on a form of ethical egoism, which is distinctly absent in Kantian ethics? For is it not the case that in Aristotelian ethics the pursuit of a final end is the pursuit of one's own good? Is it not *my* happiness that I am after? Do not the virtues ultimately redound to pursuit of self-interest?

This well-worn modern charge of ancient ethics as essentially egoistic has been recently addressed by Julia Annas in *The Morality of Happiness*. Her view is that while ancient ethics may be formally and thinly egoist (i.e., an inquiry "structured around the question of what will best promote *the agent's* happiness"),[4] substantively it is not so, since once specified, the final good will include virtues that are other-regarding and that are so in a non-instrumental way.[5] Thus, her view is that, on the whole, ancient eudaimonistic ethics can escape the kind of schizophrenia she thinks characterterizes Epicurus's position. On that view, an agent posits her final good as pleasure, where this is construed as her own pleasure. Suppose such an agent, Annas argues, discovers she can best fulfill this goal by benefiting others for their own sake. But then while that agent bears in mind that she is helping her friends for their own sake as an intrinsic good, another part of her mind is aware that the point of all this activity in the first place is simply to obtain pleasure for herself.[6] The claim is that Aristotelian eudaimonistic ethics can escape precisely this sort of egoism. As Annas puts it, there is no incompatibility in positing as a final good *my own happiness* and positing as a primary constituent of that final good acting toward others out of genuine altruistic regard. "There is no reason *prima facie,* why the good of others cannot matter to me independently of my own interests, just because it is introduced as something required by my final good."[7] And part of the reason there is no conflict, she claims, is that *eudaimonia* is not antecedently specified in the Aristotelian inquiry. Its content is left indeterminate.

---

4 Annas (1993, 291; italics hers).
5 See, e.g., 223.
6 Annas (1993, 241). See Kraut's (1995) helpful discussion of this, though I disagree with his criticism. See note 8 below.
7 Annas (1993, 127).

The point cannot be that *any* porous sketch of the final good requires specification along nonegoistic lines.[8] Rather, it is that the *formal* starting point of my own happiness need not restrict the selection of contents and that the contents Aristotle himself specifies do in fact include virtues that are noninstrumentally concerned with others' well-being. Though such concern is part of my good, when I help others for their own sake, it is not further mediated by some independent concern that it be in my interest.

Although Aristotelian eudaimonism can find room for genuine altruism, there is still an issue between Aristotle and Kant on just how, within the conception of right action, one fully takes into account the interests of others. Kantian ethics holds that the voice of others is essential to one's own principled moral reasons. According to one formula of the Categorical Imperative, to act permissibly is to act on maxims that others similarly circumstanced could endorse; according to another, it is to act in such a way that those who are the recipients of your actions could endorse your ends. The focus for moral inquiry becomes, Am I exempting myself? Am I duly acknowledging the agency of others? In a perspicuous way, the emphasis is on the standing of others in my world of action. In a more positive way, too, I must promote others' agency for their own sake and, in consideration of their agency, stand guard against policies of mutual neglect. The foundation point of morality becomes the shared and equal reason of persons. The construction of general moral precepts starts from this thought. Now, there is no comparable move in Aristotelian ethics. Aristotle just accepts, in a commonsensical way, that noninstrumental regard for others is a requisite form of the virtuous

---

[8] On this, see Richard Kraut (1995), who has argued against Annas on two grounds – that the indeterminacy of *eudaimonia* is irrelevant to the argument for establishing a nonegoistic view of happiness, and that Annas's denial of *eudaimonia* as substantively egoistic would fare better if she recognized that the final good each person pursues is not merely her own good but the good of human beings in general. I think he is right on the first point. But regarding the latter, while it is true that the eudaimonistic inquiry is about the best human life and not just a life that happens to suit me, at the same time the inquiry is meant to be Socratic and as such, a personal reflection about how *I* ought to live. To pursue Kraut's suggestion further, we need to know just how considerations of objective well-being can at once be practical reflections about one's own case.

activity that constitutes the human good; it is not reflection on our shared status with others that grounds that point or, in general, grounds considerations of how I ought to live. Of course, there is some notion of shared reasons. So, for example, the rational determinations of the *phronimos* (the person of practical wisdom) are not meant to be reasons isolated from the view of others. On the Aristotelian scheme, they serve as a model and inspirational focus. But for an agent to look to the projected choices and responses of a *phronimos* is still not the same as asking if others, similarly circumstanced, could endorse my choice and reasons. The constraint to act as others *could* is simply absent. This is to mark a bold but, I think, accurate contrast with Kantian doctrine. As our study unfolds, some of the other traditional contrast points between Aristotelian and Kantian ethics will turn out, however, to have softer contours. At very least, the conversation between Aristotle and Kant is considerably more nuanced than the usual cartoonish comparisons would have us believe.

2 ACTIVITY, AGENCY, AND EXTERNAL GOODS: ARISTOTLE, THE STOICS, AND KANT

A central theme in the ancient discussion of *eudaimonia* is the place of external goods in a conception of happiness. By and large, ancient theorists argue for the centrality (dominance, in some cases, sufficiency, in others) of virtue in the *eudaimōn* life. But throughout the texts, difficult questions soon arise as to the impact on such a life of goods that are external to one's control but that seem intuitively to be part of a life worth living. At issue is the role of luck or fortune, and the vulnerability of a good life to circumstances beyond one's own effort. Kant's rejection of *eudaimonia* as the focus of moral inquiry and his attempt to protect moral agency from the conditions of external success represent repudiations of important aspects of Aristotle's project. I now briefly consider some of these themes in order further to situate Kant's inquiry relative to Aristotle's.

On my interpretation of Aristotle's view, happiness is a structured, mixed good; its constituents are virtuous activities and external goods, the latter being subordinate to the former.[9] Thus, the formal criteria of the highest human good – that it be ultimate, complete (comprehensive), and humanly self-sufficient[10] – point to a conception of happiness that will include goods beyond our control. In part, this result has to do with the fact that Aristotle regards virtuous *activity* as more complete than virtuous states that remain unactualized.[11] And virtuous activity requires, in an unequivocal way, external goods. It requires goods beyond our own control to be used as instruments, as well as objects and occasions for realizing our activity. But external goods have other roles, too, in the good life. Some external goods are intrinsically valuable and their loss can spoil happiness:

> Yet evidently, as we said, it [happiness] needs the external goods as well; for it is impossible, or not easy, to do fine acts without the proper equipment. In many actions we use friends and riches and political power as instruments; and there are some things the lack of which takes the lustre from [or ruins] happiness,[12] as good birth, satisfactory children, beauty; for the man who is very ugly in appearance or ill-born or solitary and childless is hardly happy, and perhaps a man would be still less so if he had thoroughly bad children or friends or had lost good children or friends by death.[13]

[9] I take virtuous activities in the happy life to include the excellent exercise of theoretical reason, or contemplation. See Sherman (1989, 94–106). Richard Kraut (1989) argues lucidly for an alternative interpretation in which there are two clear answers Aristotle offers to the "what is happiness" question. On the best answer, happiness consists in just one good: namely, the excellent exercise of the theoretical part of reason. On the second best answer, it consists in the exercise of practical virtues such as courage and magnanimity. Some individuals may be capable of the best kind of life; others, of the second best. I cannot explore our different interpretations here except to note that on my view, the civic life can itself leave room for philosophical activity.

[10] NE 1097a25ff.

[11] NE 1095b31–1096a2.

[12] I replace the Revised Oxford Translation's "blessedness" with "happiness," as I take the argument to require that *to makarion* in this context be roughly synonymous with *to eudaimōn*. See note 21 below.

[13] NE 1099a32–b5.

The underlying emphasis on activity is connected with Aristotle's metaphysical view that a potential state becomes more fully realized and complete as it takes on a more determinate form. Thus, wood *qua* proximate material is a potentiality that becomes more fully actualized when the carpenter, through his craft, shapes the material into a chair. Similarly, virtue is a state of potentiality more fully realized when it is determinately expressed in concrete activity.[14]

But beyond this metaphysical position, the emphasis on activity is meant to appeal to some broad consensus – that we think a life worth living is an active one, that part of its value has to do with an engagement in the world marked by a sense of zest and energy.[15] A life of *having* virtue, but not *living* it, spent in quiescence or inertia, would not appeal to us in the same way. Thus, a virtuous Rip Van Winkle, his goodness frozen in sleep, seems a feeble model of good living. Like Sleeping Beauty, lying in wait under a glass lid, there is something deeply unfulfilling about such a model of passive beauty and goodness: "Possession of excellence seems actually compatible with being asleep, or with lifelong inactivity, and, further, with the greatest sufferings and misfortunes; but a person who was living so no one would call happy, unless he were maintaining a thesis at all costs." [16] In all this, the epistemological point has some bearing too – that we can't know another's virtue except by inference from its expression in various kinds of external activity, choices, and conduct. We depend upon manifest activity and affect to grasp the fineness of character. Conceptually, too, character is, on Aristotle's view, deeply connected to a reliable and steady pattern of activity. It is not a dormant inner state but a reliable way of responding to a wide range of external and internal conditions. Virtue is a state of character connected with choice and action (a *hexis prohairetikē*).

---

[14] On the idea of *teleion* (complete) as what is complete both in the sense of comprehensive and most fully realized through actualization, see NE 1129b30–31.

[15] One argument given for including friends in a good life is that they help sustain our activities and energize our projects (NE 1170a4–12).

[16] NE 1095b32–96a2.

But even if we could make conceptual sense of a notion of character independent of action, Aristotle's claim is that what is humanly best is not in possession but in use, in confrontation with
the determinate conditions of existence. *Eudaimonia* is *eupraxia* –
good activity:[17]

> With those who identify happiness with excellence or some one
> excellence our account is in harmony; for to excellence belongs
> activity in accordance with excellence but it makes, perhaps, no
> small difference whether we place the chief good in possession
> or in use, in state or in activity. For the state may exist without
> producing any good result, as in a man who is asleep or in some
> other way quite inactive, but the activity cannot; for one who
> has the activity will of necessity be acting, and acting well. And
> as in the Olympic games it is not the most beautiful and the
> strongest that are crowned but those who compete (for it is
> some of these that are victorious), so those who act rightly win
> the fine and good things in life.[18]

But what of virtuous effort that is active but that nonetheless
results in impeded or unfree activity? There is the contrast suggested earlier, between quiessence and activity. But in addition
there is the notion of striving and effort that is interior yet highly
active. Does exertion of this sort count as fine action, achieving
the end of what is fine and good? Or must one have, in addition,
sufficient external goods – adequate health, freedom, some material comfort, and friends – so that one can begin to set one's
choices in action that meets the world? (This is indeed a serious
question for Aristotle, deeply connected with the candidacy of
contemplation for the best life. For in assessing whether contemplation is a viable candidate, Aristotle often asks whether a
life devoted to its pursuit would be a suitably active life, and as
active as a life of the more exteriorized action characteristic of
virtuous activity in the *polis*.)[19] Aristotle's analogy with the Olym-

---

[17] NE 1098b20–22; Pol. 1325a22, b14; 1325a40.

[18] NE 1098b30–1099a5.

[19] Pol. 1325b16ff; NE 1177a20ff. In NE X6–8, Aristotle talks about the life of
theōrētikē energeia but restricts terms *praxis* and *to prattein* to political and ethical life. In *Politics* VII.3, intellectual activity is called a kind of *praxis*.

piast, in the preceding quotation, is important. The Olympiast, injured before the competition and relegated merely to imagining himself competing in the race, has failed to achieve his end in some important sense. As Aristotle puts it, only those who compete are crowned. Similarly, the person committed to good living cares that action ensues and that one's efforts enable one to act. If one is tortured on the wheel, all the good intentions in the world aren't sufficient to achieve the end of virtuous action. Effort, fully frustrated, does not count as good activity in the fullest sense.

Yet the matter is complex, for there are other passages in which Aristotle suggests that fine activity is safer than this and less vulnerable to fortune. Similar to the tone of *Groundwork* I, these passages in *Nicomachean* I seem to maintain that the truly virtuous agent can act well however cramped the circumstances and niggardly the gifts of fortune. The fineness of action is captured in doing what one can. We must turn to the passages in question to make the best sense of Aristotle's dialectical moves here. With an interpretation in hand, we can in due time compare it to Kant's position on virtue and its relation to happiness.

There are a number of passages to garner. At NE I.9 1099b17–24, Aristotle says that on one view, happiness is regarded as widely available (*polukoinon*7), because its primary component, excellence or virtue, is a "matter of study and care" more than mere chance. Aristotle goes on to endorse this view by appeal to our values – that it would strike a false note (*plēmmeles*) if we were to leave something as important as happiness to fortune alone. He continues, in NE I.10, that happiness is not easily dislodged; for its primary component, virtuous activity, is an enduring and stable good, manifest even in great misfortune. The virtuous person "will bear the fortunes of life most finely and altogether suitably (*emmelōs*), if he is truly good and foursquare without reproach."[20]

He qualifies that frequent and great misfortunes can, nonetheless, "crush and spoil" one's happiness,[21] "bringing pain and impeding activity." "Yet even in these, what is fine shines

---

[20] NE 1100b19–22; my own translation.
[21] For further discussion of this passage (NE 100b27–28), and for *to makarion* as synonymous with *to eudaimōn*, see Nussbaum (1986, 329–36).

through, when a person bears with good temper many great misfortunes, not through insensibility to pain, but because he is noble
and great-souled [*megalopsuchos*]."[22]

> And if activities control life, as we have said, then no happy
> person could ever become miserable; for he will never do acts
> that are hateful and mean. For the truly good and wise person,
> we presume, will bear the fortunes of life becomingly and from
> the resources he has will always perform the finest actions he
> can.[23]

At face value, the passages argue that even virtuous *activity* can
get by with little. The hallmark of true goodness and wisdom is
durability and flexibility in expressing one's virtue finely, whatever the resources. What is required is resourcefulness, however
meager the supplies.[24] Frequent and severe reversals can eat
away at one's happiness, perhaps by frustrating one's good intentions or hampering one's output, or simply by bringing pain or
hurt that must be borne alongside the daily work of doing good.
But so long as there can be *some* exercise of the appropriate virtues, there is fineness in one's actions. The truly good and wise
person cannot become wretched or morally dispicable (*athlios*).[25]
And this supports our intuitions, Aristotle contends. Ideally, we
want the central part of good living to be something that is within
our control, and not left to the wind.[26] We expect it to be tolerably
stable.

But Aristotle never unambivalently embraces this stoic ideal in
the way that the Stoics themselves will. He is well aware that
some of the reversals that cramp external output can be so severe
and chronic as to gnaw at even the best person's interior. There
are hardships that don't sit at the surface. Revealingly, he uses

---

22 NE 1100b30-b33; my own translation.
23 NE 1100b33–1101a3; my own translation.
24 Though note, when the *technē* analogy is used, Aristotle stresses that a crafter
cannot perform her craft without the proper material, and that the better the
material, the *finer* the product (Pol. VII, 1326a4).
25 NE 1101a1–6.
26 NE 1099b18–25.

terms of pollution and spoilage to describe how happiness is vulnerable to tragic reversals.[27] Thus, though some deprivations merely prevent *full* realization of virtue, others undermine its very sustenance.[28] Our children may die the victims of senseless violence, our freedom may be taken away, we may lack what to eat or find ourselves without adequate health care or shelter. If we are truly good and virtuous, then we may still act with decency, without becoming moral wretches. But these kinds of deprivations, especially when they are chronic and multiple, can dig deep, even in the lives of the virtuous. They may not stay at the surface ready to blow away like a change of wind. Poor health and inadequate resources to remedy it can leave permanent scars on what we can do for ourselves and others. Something inside may spoil such that even the most resolute get flattened. It takes a long time, Aristotle says, to reverse these kinds of blows and a long run of continued, favorable luck.[29] Time and good fortune can heal, but slowly. The point of these remarks is that as enduring as virtuous character is, and as varied and resourceful as its capacity for fine exercise can be, Aristotle, unlike the Stoics, never unequivocally holds the view that virtuous agency is invulnerable to fortune. Virtue is more stable than other kinds of goods, but it is not fully exempt from the same kinds of forces that undo one's happiness.

Notoriously, in *Groundwork* I, Kant characterizes the moral sphere by a certain indifference to external goods and consequences:

Even if, by some special disfavour of destiny or by the niggardly endowment of step-motherly nature, this will is entirely lacking in power to carry out its intentions; if by its utmost effort it still accomplishes nothing, . . . even then it would still

27 See 1099b2, 1100b28; on this, see Nussbaum (1986, ch. 11, esp. 337) and White (1992, 76n).
28 Conversely, I would argue, propitious conditions are not just further determinants added on to virtue; they are essential to keeping virtue alive in the first place.
29 NE 1101a11–13. See Irwin (1985c).

shine like a jewel for its own sake as something which has its full value in itself. Its usefulness or fruitlessness can neither add to, nor subtract from, this value.[30]

But the claim, even here, in this forceful passage, is a restricted one – that the ground of morality and the conception of moral worth are protected from the impact of external goods, while happiness, of course, is not. Moreover, this claim about the ground of morality is itself compatible with the view that particular moral precepts and duties arise in response to the contingent features of human life – that is, a policy of benevolence to the fact that we are finitely rational agents limited in our self-sufficiency, prohibitions on deception to the fact that we can use our reason in perverted ways. Virtue is strength in adhering to legislative reason in the face of risks and vulnerabilities that routinely threaten it. In this sense, morality has its source in autonomous, practical reason, but its particular content is tailored to the finitude of human life. As it is often conceived, virtue is fortitude against contrary inclinations. But equally, on Kant's view, virtue draws its strength from human powers necessary for the full practice of morality. So, for example, we have duties of virtue to cultivate affective sensitivities required to recognize morally relevant features of our environment and engage with others in humanly effective ways. As such we have derivative duties to cultivate our animal and social natures in ways that support a good will. So Kant's view is not that moral agency is a function of disembodied reason, with all the features of our embodied life thrown into some isolated pursuit of happiness. Rather, his theory requires a conception of moral agency that draws upon the resources of our human powers.

Still, the Kantian separation of human well-being (or happiness) and morality must not be minimized. The distinction can best be understood as a response to nagging difficulties the Stoics faced in trying to establish the goodness of virtue as separate from the goodness of externalities and outcomes.[31] Briefly, the

---

[30] G 394.
[31] As my study concerns primarily Aristotle and Kant, I do not attempt to disen-

A new dialogue

Stoics identify morality with happiness. Only what is fine, that is, morally praiseworthy, is good.[32] And happiness as the most complete good simply is fineness. Even so, they worry about whether external goods can in any way enhance happiness – whether, that is, such goods can be of positive value, additive to happiness, as Aristotle holds, or whether they are indifferents that, given our natural constitution, may be selected or preferred[33] rather than dispreferred, though not, properly speaking, "chosen" as a proper part of happiness. For "to choose" is reserved for objects that are truly good. Generally speaking, the Stoics will opt for the second position: The preferred indifferents are goods with which the virtuous person should be concerned but which do not themselves add to our happiness; for virtue, alone, on the Stoic view, is sufficient for happiness. They go on to illustrate the point with a series of metaphors. To try to enhance one's happiness by adding the value of the indifferents would be like adding a drop of honey to the Aegean Sea – it makes it no sweeter; or it would be like trying to enhance the illumination of the sun with the light of a lamp – it makes it no brighter.[34] Like the additive value of these other goods, the indifferents add nothing to the illumination of virtue. Still, the Stoics are often criticized for ending up with a pluralist position little different from Aristotle's, since they seem to acknowledge that they would select a life of virtue plus a preferred indifferent over a life of virtue without it.[35] In their own defense, they argue happiness is a sum of uniform parts; putting external advantages inside happiness would be adding something dissimilar to it – like adding apples to oranges.

tangle the various strands in the Stoic tradition. Rather, I am content to show general trends that mark the transition between Aristotle and Kant. I take this up explicitly in Chapter 3.

[32] See, e.g., Cicero, Fin. 3.11–14. For a good, general discussion, see Irwin (1986).

[33] To this end, they coin the words *ta proēgmena* and *ta lēpta* ("the things preferred" and "the things selected") to distinguish the "selection" of the indifferent goods from goods that are more properly *haireton*, or "chosen." For some discussion, see Diogenes Laertius 7.101–3; Sextus Empiricus, M 11.64–67 (SVF 1.361); Stobaeus, 2.84,18–85,11 (SVF 3.128); for a collection of fragments, see Long and Sedley (1987, sec. 58).

[34] Fin. 3.45; 4.29 ; 5.71; Seneca, Ep. 92. 5–6; 92.17; see Irwin (1986, 237).

[35] Fin. 3.43–44 ; 4.30–31; Irwin (1986, 238–42).

Ultimately, the therapeutic goal of the Stoics is to persuade practitioners that external goods lack important value, even though they may still be of rational concern. A life with other things besides virtue is *not* "more desirable," reports Cicero in *De Finibus*, but only "more worth taking" than a life of virtue and virtue alone" (where again the term "taking" bears the deflationary force of merely preferring as opposed to "choosing" what is good).[36] Still, the view is counterintuitive:

> Suppose a man to be at once blind, infirm, afflicted by dire disease, in exile, childless, destitute and tortured on the rack; what is your name, Zeno for him? "A happy man," says Zeno. A supremely happy man as well? "To be sure," he will reply, "because I have proved that happiness no more admits of degrees than does virtue, in which happiness itself consists."[37]

Now, in a parallel way, Kant wants to leave external goods and results outside the arena of what we *unconditionally* value. This is in part for reasons original not with him but with Socrates, namely, that external goods can be misused and are not unconditionally good without guidance from elsewhere.[38] On a traditional Kantian view (elements of which we will assess in Chapter 4), external goods come to constitute a different kind of value, related to our natural constitution but not adding to our moral worthiness. They do not enhance moral worth, just as, analogously, the Stoics had held that external goods added to virtue do not enhance virtue, or *a fortiori*, on their view, happiness.

Kant's thought is familiar from the first few paragraphs of the *Groundwork*: "It is impossible to conceive of anything at all in the world, or even out of it which can be taken as good without qualification, except a *good will*." Kant goes on to list constitutional goods – talents of the mind (intelligence, wit, and judgment) and qualities of temperament (courage, resolution, constancy of purpose) – as well as more external gifts of fortune (power, wealth, honor, health, and even happiness), as needing the guidance of a good will. The good will guides their right use.

[36] Fin. 4.20.   [37] Fin. 5. 84.
[38] *Euthyphro* 280e3–281e-5; *Meno* 87e3–88e2.

"Without the principles of a good will they become exceedingly bad." It "sets a limit to the esteem in which they are rightly held."[39]

It is important to appreciate that by rejecting the idea that there is just one overall end and that it is identical with virtue, Kant hopes to find a more comfortable place for external goods and outcomes than the Stoic revisionist view of happiness allowed. By breaking the identity of virtue and happiness, he carves out a separate niche for happiness: happiness is the achievement of desired ends and the pursuits of ends of self-interest, such as wealth and power; virtue or what is morally worthy is good willing – that is, effort constrained by principles of practical reason. Virtue is subject to control, he wants to claim, in a way that happiness, ultimately, is not. Through this separation of value, Kant hopes to avoid both the Stoic counterintuitive claim that what we select for our natural advantage is unrelated to our happiness as well as the position that motivates such a reaction – that external goods weigh into our happiness in the very same way that virtuous agency does.

Thus, the idea of a unified life, aiming at one thing, composite (as it is for Aristotle) or uniform (as it is for the Stoics), is something Kant, for the most part, gives up. The qualification is important. For there is, of course, the Highest Good, a composite that self-consciously harkens back to the ancient scheme. But Kant wants to maintain strict regulation of one good by another, of duty regulating consequential reward. Still, at times there is some throwback to the idea that the expectation of reward may itself motivate our virtuous action. Thus, in Kant's early writings there are glimmers of a theological eudaimonism, and glimpses of the idea that moral motivation gets its push from the rewards of divine justice.[40] But by and large the Highest Good is a composite good intended to have a clearer ordering of goods than articulated in Aristotle's system.[41]

[39] G 393–94.
[40] Cf. KrV A813/b841 ; Allison (1990, 69–70).
[41] For Aristotle's own clear statements about virtue ordering the use of external goods, see Pol. 1323b7–11; 1323b15–19; 1325b7.

Kant's push inward to will and agency as the locus of moral focus can often strike a sympathetic chord with our own modern sensibilities. In contrast, to focus as Aristotle does on the fineness of good *living* seems to undermine the value of our own contributions, putting them at the mercy of a hospitable and well-endowed world. However, it is not clear, at the end of the day, if Kant is able to exempt inward virtue from fortune in the way that in his more Stoic moments, he wishes to. As seen in the discussion of Aristotle's views earlier, effort and fortitude can themselves be weakened by long and persistent hardship, such as ill health, enduring poverty, or the ravages of war. Similarly here, in the case of Kant's views, it is not simply that these contingencies can effect the *fruit* of a good will; it is that they can weaken the will itself. Granted, this may be rare where true virtue is found, for here the ability to show fortitude against the most extreme contrary forces may be its hallmark. But in less hallowed but still noble cases, effort can be gnawed at by the very strength of the opposition, and courage and fortitude can weaken despite our most fervent desires to hold on.[42]

These considerations about the vulnerability of moral capacities raise more general questions about the nature of Kantian moral agency. In particular, can full Kantian moral agency be conceived independently of a comprehensive notion of habituated, empirical character? In the actual circumstances of moral practice, can the capacities for legislative reason function independently of the supportive structures of emotion and affective sensibility? In the course of these pages, I shall argue "no," claiming that Kant himself situates virtue within a complex discussion of moral psychology in which that fuller notion of character is brought to bear.

3 A BRIEF OVERVIEW

At this point it might be helpful to offer a brief overview of the material to follow. But I should anticipate that I have been selec-

---

[42] In Rel. 36/31, Kant explains this in terms of an improper ranking of our incentives.

tive in my treatment of Aristotelian and Kantian themes; thus, for example, I do not talk about the thorny problems of Kant on freedom and its relation to Aristotle's conception of voluntary agency.[43] Nor do I address the impact of Kantian ethics on liberal theories of justice and this in relation to recent trends in developing a thicker, Aristotelian-based theory of justice and well-being.[44] The absence of themes such as these should signal neither their lack of intrinsic interest nor importance in a fully comprehensive treatment. But as always, one must make choices, and given the particular narrative I wish to pursue, attention to these themes would divert me from my course.

Specifically, this book is about the role of emotions and practical reason in each theorist's account of virtue, though on the whole I direct greater attention to the place of emotions in moral character, for I believe inquiry in this area has been sorely neglected. The study begins with Aristotle's view of the place of emotions in the practice of virtue and, most generally, with his belief that emotions are susceptible to moderation and transformation. These views were intensely criticized in the Hellenistic period, and in Chapter 3, in a brief interlude, I consider Stoic arguments for extirpation of the emotions and their notion of therapeutic change. The Latin Stoic influence on Kant is profound and deep, and in this chapter, I chart some of these debts. But signficantly, and surprisingly, Kant endorses the natural advantage of emotion for morality in a way that in the end, I argue, aligns him more closely with Aristotle than with the Stoics. In

---

[43] We can note that in contrast to Kant's preoccupation with incompatibilism (i.e., the thesis that both determinism is true and that freedom to do otherwise is required for moral imputation), Aristotle simply takes it for granted that there are external events in the world that are contingent (that could have been otherwise), and argues from this back to causes that are also capable of being contingent or otherwise. So he *assumes* that there are events produced without necessitation, that they can turn out otherwise, and that if this is so, they are caused by agents that are themselves capable of voluntary agency. See Broadie (1991, ch. 3) for a helpful discussion on Aristotle in relation to determinism. For recent discussions on Kant on freedom, see Allison (1990) and critiques of Allison in Guyer (1992) and Ameriks (1992).

[44] On Aristotelian-based theories of justice, see Nussbaum (1988b, 1990b) and Sen (1993).

Chapter 4, I turn to Kant's moral anthropology and its general relation to the project of grounding morality in reason. I show the considerable textual support for a place for the emotions in Kantian virtue, though I argue that Kant's views on these matters are riddled by a pervasive ambivalence about the emotions and lack of systematization in his discussion of them. Kant's familiar teeter-totter with the emotions is perhaps most apparent in his views about friendship, which I take up in conjunction with Aristotle's views in Chapter 5. Here I explore the general value of "doing things together" and argue that Aristotle's theory insists upon, in way virtually negelected by modern moral theory, the importance of shared activity and its place in moral development. Still, Kant's critical vantage point is important here – his conception of respect as independent of affiliative attachment points out the clear limits of Aristotle's restriction of altruism to those with whom we share a context.

In Chapters 6, 7, and 8, I shift my focus to notions of practical reason and moral perception in the accounts of Aristotle and Kant. Traditionally, Aristotle's conception of practical wisdom as a matter of judging the particulars is contrasted with an account of Kantian moral judgment as either rule-based or procedural. So whereas within Aristotelian ethics the moral moment is generally conceived of as a narrative process of judging the particular shape of a case, within Kantian ethics the moral moment is conceived as the moment of insuring that one's judgment can function as a principle, either via its relation to subsumptive rules or a testing procedure. While there are elements of truth in this picture, the picture is too simple. In Chapter 6, I argue that Aristotelian particularism is not intuitionistic, if by that we mean that judgments of particulars are immediate and untethered to either discursive capacities or rules. Both play a limited role in Aristotelian judgment. The rules that enter are certainly not Kantian-like maxims turned into universalized principles, but in Chapter 7, I argue that the procedure of testing one's maxim by constructing law may not best characterize Kantian deliberation itself. Granted, such a procedure has some role in reconstructing the presumptive rules that stand as background norms shaping moral judgment. Nevertheless, in the case of hard moral choices, where usual guidelines do not help us to know what to do, it is probably not deliberation by universalization that makes most sense, but a more informal method of reflective deliberation whereby we sharpen and assess the values implicit in background norms. Here Kant and Aristotle move closer together again. But there is a contrastive note on which I conclude. While the apparent absence of perfect, juridical duties in Aristotelian ethics is often noted, what is less frequently noted is just how unclear Aristotle is about how much "latitude" we have in fulfilling what is right and fine. In some of Aristotle's formulations, it sounds as though hitting the mean is a matter of hitting a bull's-eye, with little room for discretion. Kant, of course, makes great use of the notion of discretionary judgment in his notion of imperfect duties. But then the question raised, in Chapter 8, is just how minimal or demanding Kantian virtue becomes.

Chapter 2
The emotional structure of Aristotelian virtue

1 OPENING A DIALOGUE ON THE EMOTIONS

In this chapter I, set the stage for a dialogue between Aristotle and Kant on the subject of the emotions and their place in morality. On a traditional reading of both authors, the contrast is drawn along the following lines: On an Aristotelian account, virtue is expressed not merely in fine action but in fine emotions as well; both action and emotion are morally praiseworthy aspects of character. Kantian theory, in contrast, locates moral merit narrowly in duty-motivated action, with emotions or feelings often viewed as detracting from, or at least not adding to, what is morally meritorious. I adhere to the general lines of this Aristotelian sketch, while breaking from the Kantian one. In place of the traditional Kantian account, I argue for the importance of a composite conception of virtue which includes cultivated emotions that support moral interest. This interpretation pays heed to the grounding of morality in practical reason, and to the interface of practical reason with our affective natures. That is, I take seriously the Kantian moral project as a project both in the metaphysics of morality and in moral anthropology – in the grounding of morality and in the application of morality to the specific conditions of human nature, including our emotional natures. We shall come to this in Chapter 4. For now, the focus will be principally on Aristotelian virtue. Our task will be to understand how emotions figure in moral character and in what sense we can be held responsible for them. In what sense are they up to us? In what sense can they be said to be fine?

Putting aside interpretive questions for the moment, the general issue of the role of the emotions in morality is complex, in part because of our own general ambivalence toward emotions, which is reflected on the practical and theoretical levels. In everyday life emotional experience is often little understood and all too often viewed pejoratively as an enemy of the reflective and rational life. Important parts of our emotional lives remain private and often unarticulated. Sometimes this is reflected along gender lines, but not always. Although emotions are frequently given free rein in our literary transports as both children and adults, we often remain puzzled about how to bring our fantasy and imaginative wanderings back to the emotional core of our nonliterary lives.[1] Moreover, we tend to think of emotional experience narrowly, in terms of peaks and valleys rather than of a wider range that includes not only highs and lows but also subtle shades of movement that color our waking lives. As a result, when we turn to the role of emotions in morality, we bring to bear only a narrow band of our emotional inventory, often putting the emphasis on the pathological or obsessive. Kant himself sometimes thinks of emotions in terms of these intractable misfits, as passions that possess us or as affects that storm us unaware,[2] though as I have already indicated, his view is far more complex. What needs to be emphasized now is that Aristotle does not cast emotions in this way or view them as inhibitors of reason. Although Aristotle does not always exploit the full explanatory force of his own account of emotions, or adequately adumbrate an account of emotional development, he does argue forcefully for the central importance of emotions in healthy and virtuous living.

On the theoretical plane, conceptions of emotions in philosophy and psychology have also tended to sunder emotions from

---

[1] For a discussion that argues for literary experience as a "school" for the emotions, see Nussbaum (1990a) and my discussion of her book in Sherman (1994a). Cf. Kenny's early suggestions (1963) that the emotions elicited in fiction reading are only "counterfeit emotions."
[2] *Anth.* 251ff.

morality. The Cartesian mind–body split has cast a shadow long into the early part of this century, with emotions often conceived of as inner feels, outward behaviors, or drives.[3] In each case, emotion is to some degree cut off from more complex mental representation. Though there are many strands in the Freudian legacy,[4] emotion as drive occupies a central place within most stages of that theory. As drive, emotion is characterized primarily in terms of quantitative units of energy ("quanta" that form part of what Freud views an "economic" theory of the psyche).

Aristotle's writing represents a clear alternative to these positions. The path we find clearly articulated in Aristotle's *Rhetoric* is a theory of the emotions in which emotions are object-directed and constituted by thought contents that are evaluative.[5] Emotions are not feels or drives, but cognitively rich, mental states. This is not to deny that emotions will have affective elements, and

---

[3] These are broad trends only. Kenny (1963) criticized the "sensation" view of emotion in an important early work. In experimental psychology, Averill (1974, 1976) has emphasized a social constructivist view of emotion, and Lazarus (1966) has also emphasized the cognitivist foundations of emotions. Within psychoanalytic discourse, the object-relations theory marks a clear break from the Freudian drive model and its emphasis on emotion as the release of physiological tension. Here the work of Fairbairn (1952), Klein (1975), Sullivan (1953), and, more recently, Kernberg (1976) is important. For an overview of trends in object relations, see Greenberg and Mitchell (1983). On the Freudian notion of discharge and its physiological symbolism, see Brenner (1982). It is important to note that within the classical Freudian framework, emotions come to attach to objects, most visibly during the period of early childhood, but Freud saw this more as an instrumental way of discharging drive than as a constitutive feature of emotions themselves.

[4] See Sherman (1995a) for the connection of psychoanalysis and philosophical accounts of moral and emotional development. For a comprehensive discussion of the connection between Freud's theory and ethics, see Wallwork (1991).

[5] For contemporary cognitive views of the emotions in experimental psychology literature, see Averill (1974); Frijda (1986); Lazarus (1966); and Parrott and Sabini (1989). For philosophical accounts, see Davis (1987, 1988); de Sousa (1987); Gordon (1987); Greenspan (1988); Lyons (1980); Oakley (1992); Roberts (1988); Solomon (1973). A significant contribution to the discussion comes from psychoanalytic object relations theorists. For an excellent review of the field, see Greenberg and Mitchell (1983).

in some cases motivational (or desiderative) elements as well.[6] But the cognitive element is central for the overall identity of the emotion, and both affect and desire are, as we shall see, incomplete without reference to particular evaluations or construals constitutive of the emotion. In the ethical and political writings, emotions figure as an important element in virtuous conduct, deeply linked with capacities for choice and wise judgment. Indeed, Aristotle insists that emotions are not stray features of moral motivation or optional aesthetic trim, but are a necessary and reliable constituent of virtue and its actualization. Still, Aristotle's assumption that emotions play an important role in morality faces initial challenges, particularly from moderns bred on a work such as Kant's *Groundwork of the Metaphysics of Morals*, which often seems to pose the divide between emotions and reason in the harshest and most exclusive terms. In what sense does Aristotle's conception of emotions in general, and his conception of the cultivated emotions of virtue, in particular, take us beyond the familiar view that emotions just happen to us, without the engagement of our agency or rational capacities? In what sense are emotions states for which we can be held responsible? These questions are central to our understanding the moral significance Aristotle places on the emotions.

This chapter divides as follows: I begin, in Section 2, with some general worries about introducing emotions into an account of morality, address the objections, and then, in Section 3, sketch in a more constructive way the significant roles emotions play in the moral life. Although I refer to Aristotelian and Kantian accounts in these early sections, by and large my remarks remain at some distance from the texts. The aim in these early sections is to provide something of a survey of the phenomena (*tithenai ta phainomena*), a culling of the views of the many and wise, as Aristotle would put it, to serve as a springboard for a more systematic adumbration of Aristotle's own views. In Sections 4 through 8, I turn more directly to the texts as I discuss Aristotle's account of

---

[6] For a very useful, broadly Aristotelian account, see Oakley (1992).

the emotions, the sense in which their cultivation is a part of moral development, and their role in the structure of virtue.

2 THE ALLEGED PROBLEM WITH EMOTIONS

From an intuitive point of view, emotions are both central to morality, and yet problematic. They are central because as moral beings we care not only about how we *act* but also about how we *feel* – what our emotional moods are, as well as our attitudes and affects. The point is not that emotion is internal and action external, for both action and emotion have exterior moments that point to deeper interior states, linked with character. It is that emotions tend to grab hold of dimensions of life and to express them in ways that are distinctive and important. They present themselves as modes of *registering value* (e.g., what is dangerous or beneficial, needy or attractive, disturbing or insulting) and modes of *communicating value* that are important to our interactions with others and our engagement in their well-being. On this second characterization, they express *attitudes.*

The inclusion of emotions as part of what is ethically important faces notorious problems, however. In a familiar series of objections, often embodied in a traditional reading of Kant (though not exclusive to it), emotions are viewed as the enemy of both reason and morality. They are the foe of agency and control, representing our passive sides. The stories and beliefs wrapped up in our emotional experiences are those we cannot always trust in calmer and more reflective moments. We can summarize these objections briefly for the moment. First, there is the problem of *partiality:* Emotions may respond to what is morally salient, but in an overly partial and selective way, fastening on evidence that is too restrictive, or unrelated to the rightness and wrongness of the action. As such, emotions do not allow us to take up the sort of impartial or universal point of view required of morality. They are not a way of responding to the claims others make on us simply in virtue of their rational agency. This overlaps with a narrower objection often made within Kantian ethics – that emotions connect only

accidentally with moral interest.[7] For with merely emotional motivation, there will only be an accidental relation between the
agent's reasons for having acted and what makes the action right.
Again, the claim is often put in terms of the *contingency* of
emotions – that we can be committed to the moral wrongness of
some action, say that of betraying a patriot to a tyrant for gain,
independent of any contingent features of our emotional makeup.
As Kant himself puts the objection in the *Groundwork,* emotion
does not provide the ground for a criterion or rule; at best it can
conform with moral law but this conformity is itself "too contingent and precarious" to exclude "actions which transgress" the
law.[8] So, it has been argued, sympathy is morally blind, for we
can sympathize with the criminal as well as the victim, sympathy
itself being neutral with regard to moral approbation or
condemnation.[9]

In addition, there is the alleged *unreliability* of emotions as
moral motives. As it is often explained, emotions exhibit *excess*
and *are capricious,* too "on again/off again" to provide stable motivation for moral action. They cannot be counted on to be there or
counted on to last. Even if they start out strong, they can peter out
into a whimper, especially if new interests and new temptations
take the foreground. In addition to these internal instabilities,
emotions are also unreliable sources of motivation in that nature
and nurture cannot be counted on to distribute them evenly in all
persons. Again, these objections are familiar parts of Kant's writings.[10] Stepmother nature can be all too niggardly, the *Groundwork* warns. And virtue, if too dependent on habituated emotions,
Kant tells us elsewhere, "is neither armed for all situations nor

---

[7] Herman (1993, ch. 1) develops this theme.

[8] G 390. Also see Guyer for remarks from the *Reflexionen,* 6902, "feeling has no
rule, it is therefore changeable and fickle," as it appears in Guyer (1993, 340).

[9] Here we can object to Herman's related example (1994, 4–5) – in which
through sympathy a kind soul ends up helping a burglar carrying a bundle
out of the Museum of Fine Arts – by noting that the motive of duty, just like the
motive of sympathy, without practical wisdom, is blind.

[10] Guyer (1993, 338–44) neatly divides up the first two objections as (1) the
unreliability of inclination as providing a *criterion* for what duty requires and
(2) its unreliability in providing a *motive* for conformity to what is required by
such a criterion; cf. LE 36.

adequately insured against the changes that new temptations could bring about."[11]

Furthermore as "passions" or states that we undergo and suffer (from the Greek *paschein* – to be affected or suffer), emotions are *involuntary* happenings endured with little intervention or consent. They can easily overcome us, like the weather. Unlike action or belief, they appear to be exempt from direct willing. We cannot will to feel, in the same way we can will to believe or will to act.

Finally, emotions are typically attached to objects and events that are *beyond our control*. Through emotions, we invest importance in what we cannot control or master or make permanent: loved ones die, friends turn on us, attachment to status and security comes undone by sickness and old age. The implicit objection is that emotions make us *vulnerable* and *threaten our self-sufficiency*. Emotions involve caring about certain objects or events (positively or negatively), and this makes us vulnerable to their presence or loss. To give importance to emotions is to embrace vulnerability. This is a recurrent theme in Stoic ethics, as we shall see in Chapter 3.[12]

Summing up the objections, there is (1) the *partiality of discrimination* through emotion and *accidental nature* of emotion's connection with what is right, (2) the *unreliability of emotion as motive*, often explained in terms of emotion's *excess* or *caprice*, (3) the *involuntarism* of emotion, and (4) the *vulnerability* that comes from emotional attachment to objects and that threatens self-sufficiency.

These are familiar objections well entrenched in the literature and rooted in doctrines going back to the Stoics. Increasingly they are being countered by philosophers of many stripes, including Kantian defenders.[13] We will be exploring Kant's more com-

---

[11] DV 383–4. See also G 425.
[12] See especially Kant's views about friendship and his emphasis on the vulnerability of being a friend (DV469–74; Rel. 33/28). I discuss the topic of friendship in Kantian ethics in Chapter 5.
[13] See Baron (1984), Blum (1980), Herman (1993), Nussbaum (1986), Oakley (1992), Stocker (1976, 1987), Williams (1981).

prehensive views in the next chapter, but for the moment we can meet these charges in a broadly Aristotelian way, pointing out *en passant* places of convergence and divergence in my interpretations of Aristotelian and Kantian views. The more thoroughgoing exchange awaits the systematic development of their views in the chapters that follow.

Aristotle meets the objection about the partiality of emotion in the following way: He concedes that emotions may sometimes stubbornly attach to slender evidence or have too selective a focus. But he insists that their unresponsiveness to *certain* reasons does not entail that they do not rest on reasons *at all*, or that in a fundamental way, they are intractable. Emotions, on Aristotle's view, have firm cognitive foundations and rest on appraisals. Those appraisals are not immune to reflection or criticism, and neither are the emotions they ground. This is not to deny that the process of developing more rational and morally supportive emotions is a slow one, with more resistance and inertia than are likely to be involved in the change of belief alone. Nonetheless, Aristotle does not exclude the transformation of emotion from an overall process that engages reason.

That emotions pick and choose may not be all that troubling for morality. Granted, where partiality involves inappropriate emotions of bias or parochialism, then, like prejudiced beliefs, these emotions need to be controlled or transformed. But many forms of emotional selectivity are permissible and even to be encouraged. Kant himself argues the point. In *The Doctrine of Virtue* he states that the positive duty of beneficence must always be carried out by humans, who by their nature are finite and subject to limitations of time and resources.[14] Deliberation about the particulars – for example, whom to help and when and where – must rely materially on emotions and the information they provide us about urgency and moral salience. They are an essential source of information. True, the report of the emotions may not be final or decisive, or on their own give us justifying reasons for the rightness or wrongness of actions.[15] But even so, emotions can

[14] See DV 451–52 for the constraints on beneficence.
[15] Note, in this regard, that the duty motive may also not be decisive without

mark a moral occasion, as well as through their very selectivity help us negotiate the moral "play-room" (*Spielraum*) in which we have latitude for discretionary judgment. In this sense, while emotions may not be necessary for grounding morality per se, they do appear necessary for putting it into practice.

But this still leaves intact Kant's more fundamental claim concerning the partiality of emotions. This is that emotions themselves cannot yield an adequate determination of what it is morally right to do; however helpful they may be to morality, they cannot provide a universally valid criterion or principle. Another way of making the point is that emotions such as compassion, sympathy, friendship and the like are responses to persons *in situ* and depend upon likes and dislikes, attractions and repulsions, however judicious and regulated these can become. Kant claims there is a more fundamental moral response to persons in virtue of which we acknowledge the unconditional value of a person, whatever the contingencies of their circumstances or our own. In an obvious way, any discussion of this must await full examination of the terms of Kant's own theory. Only then can we see how Kant reconciles this claim with his own acknowledgment of the moral importance of emotions. For the moment, we can begin to see that Kant's objection to the emotions is not an outright denouncement of their moral utility, but a claim about their inadequacy in grounding a moral practice that requires us to take a fundamental moral interest in all persons, regardless of circumstances.

The second objection concerns the reliability of emotions as motives. Assuming we know what the right thing is to do, can emotions reliably motivate us to do it? Just how emotions are motives within an Aristotelian account of the virtues is something we shall come to. But if reliability is the sticking point, then Aristotle's likely response would again be to remind us that it is *cultivated* (or *habituated*) emotions, not immediate impulses, that are a part of virtue.[16] And part of what is to be cultivated is

adequate information from practically wise judgment. Put simply, one cannot act finely from the motive of duty without proper discernment of the case.

[16] NE 1103a14–18, 1105b19–1106a4.

strength as well as sensitivity to the variety of circumstances in which specific emotions, such as generosity, kindness, fear, or pity, are important responses. Few of our potentialities stand us well in their raw or untutored state. So, too, virtue, on the Aristotelian view, is not natural virtue but, rather, the developmental product of a slow and steady habituation of natural receptivities where habituation, at all stages, requires the engagement of practical reason, itself conceived of developmentally. We have the susceptibilities "to receive virtue by nature, but they are made perfect by habit" and by practical wisdom.[17]

Here a comparison with Kant is important. On the Kantian view I shall defend, Kant himself distinguishes between "immediate" inclinations and the "practical" emotions cultivated as supports for duty. These latter require a process of habituation much like that to which Aristotle points. In the Kantian case, emotions are shaped by reason and, in particular, by the normative values reason itself generates. Moreover, on a proper comparison of the reliability of emotions as motives with the reliability of the duty motive, it should be pointed out that the duty motive itself needs to be cultivated within a project of character habituation if it is to be properly internalized and readily summonable. There are a few points to note here. First, to act from duty is to act from a grasp of justificatory reasons that are properly internalized. In this regard, the Categorical Imperative is not always best thought of as an external procedural method to be appealed to when there are deliberative questions. A more plausible view of it is as a source of normative values that shape routine moral judgment and that can be appealed back to for further specification in hard choices. Second, to act from duty is to be responsive to principles as well as particulars. Linking Kant and Aristotle arm and arm, the motive of duty operates well only when it is informed by practical wisdom. We return to both these points in Chapter 7.

In the third objection, certain emotions may be involuntary, being more similar to compulsion and physical disease than to intention. And these may warrant pardon or pity.[18] But emotions,

---

[17] NE 1103a25; 1144b30–32.
[18] The *Eudemian Ethics* is more explicit in separating out involuntary cases of

Aristotle argues, are varied and complex phenomena, and many are subject to a considerable degree of consent and self-governance, even if all not always or in all circumstances. More generally, passivity need not imply involuntarism. Emotions are ways of being affected but are also ways of coming to assent to certain beliefs and construals. They are not just passive transports but are often active aspirations of imagination and belief. Though individuals cannot typically will to feel certain emotions at a moment's notice, they can choose to cultivate certain emotions over time as a significant part of developing moral character. More crucially, many *actions* and *activities* we care about cannot themselves be willed at a moment's notice either. They take preparation, and the planning and execution of sub-ends. We can't do philosophy at the snap of a finger. But we can snap a finger just like that. Nor can we read a foreign language without training. The cultivated emotions of mature character are more like complex activities than basic acts.[19] They require practice and the development of related capacities. To a limited degree, Kant agrees on this point.

The vulnerability of the emotional life to contingent events and objects – to the vicissitudes of accident and loss as captured in the fourth objection – is a more complex matter. Traditional Kantians do not worry about the contingent aspects of the moral life, viewing them as problems for happiness and not morality. That is, fulfillments and satisfactions of desire and emotional investment affect one's chances for happiness, not the goodness of one's moral will. Opening remarks in the *Groundwork* about the good will and its freedom from stepmother nature and her consequences push in this direction.[20] However, this is a limited view

---

emotional motivation, e.g., cases of compulsion. "Hence, many regard love, anger in some cases, and natural impulses as involuntary, as being too strong for nature; we pardon them as things capable of overpowering nature" (EE 1225a20–23; see NE 1111a35ff, and 1136a9).

[19] See Oakley (1992) for further discussion of this point. Perhaps "snapping a finger" is not the best example, since young children often do have to set out to learn even this skill. But the point should be clear enough.

[20] G 394.

of Kantian ethical theory. On a more comprehensive account of Kant's ethical writings, virtue is a progress that depends upon the development of contingent natures. The motive of duty, within a full conception of moral character, gains support from cultivated emotions at the same time that it stands ready to oppose those that are contrary. Thus, where depression or anger stand in the way of moral requirements to help, duty stands ready to fill the void.[21] But at the same time, one has a duty to cultivate emotions so that on the whole they better promote the moral life. In the case of Aristotelian character, in contrast, moral motives are themselves partially constituted by emotions, and goodness as well as happiness rest centrally in the state of one's emotions. There is no separate, invulnerable source of motive (such as Kant's pure practical reason) from which morality can issue. So, for example, grief arising from tragic loss can deprive one of happiness, and also of goodness, as in the case of Medea's evil pawning of her own children as the result of her jealous rage against Jason. The inner core of character, and not simply the external conditions of happiness, can get corrupted by emotional states.[22] Kant's view is that moral corruption results from our own choices, but even then, it is a perverse *ranking* of motives, not a virus, that *infects* the moral motive (or capacity for duty) itself:

> The distinction between a good man and one who is evil cannot lie in the difference between the incentives which they adopt into their maxim . . . but rather must depend upon *subordination . . . i.e., which of the two incentives he makes the condition of the other.* Consequently man (even the best) is evil only in that he

[21] See the famous sympathy example at G 398. Herman (1993, ch. 1), but not Guyer (1993), holds that duty is the only morally worthy motive. My own view, which I take up in Chapter 4, is closer to Guyer's.

[22] I take this as a part of the force of the remarks at NE 1099b2 – and also the force of Aristotle's claim in the *Rhetoric* (1389b13–90a24) that the elderly can suffer degradation of character as the result of an accumulation of untoward experiences. But Aristotle is notoriously dialectical in his account of the role of external goods in happiness. At NE I.8 (1100b33–1101a8) he downplays the role of external goods in happiness, suggesting that the "truly good and wise person" (much like the Stoic sage) is one and the same as the happy person.

reverses the moral order of the incentives when he adopts them into his maxim.[23]

The relevant point is that "the reversal of the ethical order of the incentives" does not itself penetrate the moral or legislative source. For Aristotle, there is no part of the soul that in a comparable way can remain invulnerable.

We shall say more about the specific roles emotions play in the moral life. But it is important to note that from a eudaimonistic perspective such as Aristotle's, emotions chart some of the same terrain that ethical inquiry into the good life does.[24] Put briefly, emotions register the importance of certain concerns and objects in our lives. They are powerful modes by which we record that something is valued or not, and worth keeping with or avoiding. They indicate this not from an impartial point of view, but from my own corner of the world, from the point of view of what matters to me. Thus, it is because I care about certain features of self that threats against these give rise to anger, because I am attached to a friend that I grieve at her departure, because I value my work that I await its fruits with hope and feel joy when I succeed and disappointment when I fail. In this way the emotions reflect in a concrete and immersed way the values that reflective inquiry marks more abstractly. Within the dialectical process of specifying the constituents of the good life, the readings of the heart might be seen as filling in the gaps left by the more programmatic, outlining moments of the inquiry.[25] In a broad way, emotions are thus part of the same dialectical project of registering what is valued, and of recognizing that what is valued, including *eudaimonia* itself, can be threatened or lost.

But it may be objected that this is just what emotions do badly. They give us readings *too* immersed in the moment, too heated, too fresh with discovery, too partial and selective. They bring in

---

[23] Rel. 36/31.

[24] Nussbaum (1996) develops the idea of a eudaimonistic conception of emotions in her Gifford lectures on the emotions.

[25] So Aristotle tells us ethical inquiry makes claims that hold only for the most part (*hōs epi to polu*), leaving time and effort as co-partners of the process: NE 1094b19–27; 1098a22.

bodily responses in a conspicuous and uncontrolled way – send our heart racing, cause us to go all clammy, make us violent and headstrong. All this distorts our own more judicious readings of what we care about. The whole point of ancient inquiry into the good life, from Socrates onward, is to reflect calmly and circumspectly about one's own practices. It is to bring to bear the intellect and the kind of global grasp that practical wisdom affords. Granted, ancient ethical reflection is a deeply practical pursuit, undertaken by those already committed to the notion that it makes a difference to one's practices. It is never simply an intellectual exercise pursued for its own sake, at an arm's distance from practice. But even so, ancient ethical inquiry is reevaluative and reflective, and in this regard, the objection goes, it is very different from readings of the heart. Again, it may be granted that the subject matter of an inquiry into the good life is excellent living in the conditions of human finitude. As such, a preeminent concern is the pervasiveness of flux and human reaction to it – to the fact that attachment can turn to loss, that political freedom can turn to enslavement, that happiness can be reversed. And that, too, there are renewals – fresh beginnings, new births, new objects of value entering one's life. It is just these comings and goings that emotions register so palpably, with riveted attention. But the objection, now, is that emotions register all this too intensely – missing the forest for the trees. Love overwhelms, crowding out other voices, grief can make the whole world go black. Emotions may share a similar eudaimonistic perspective with other cognitive modes insofar as they register matters of importance. But what they lack is precisely the balance of a less passionate gaze.

This is a familiar but still important line of objection that an Aristotelian defense of the emotions cannot easily dismiss. It is an objection that is in its own way, as we shall see, Aristotle's own. We shall return to it in various forms. At the moment, we can begin to see that similar worries arise when we turn to the notion of moral character and its affective structure. The Aristotelian view is that emotions, in general, can be harmonized with the judgments of practical wisdom. The orectic part of the soul (which is the *seat* of the emotions) is *alogon* – not irrational but nonrational, in the restricted sense that it lacks its own source of

37

authoritative rationality. Even so, the emotions proper to it are cognitive-laden capacities that cannot operate without some form of ratiocination. That part of the soul "shares in reason," as Aristotle is at pains to explain, and in a derivative sense can be said to have reason.[26] Moreover, with proper training the emotions and appetites proper to that part of the soul can be made to listen to and "obey" the more reasonable and circumspect judgments of the authority of the rational part.[27] They are responsive to reason and can be shaped by it. The ideal end state is a state of transformed and schooled emotions that support the judgments of practical wisdom. Whereas the *enkratēs* (the continent person) controls herself with regard to emotions that fall short of a mean state, the *sōphrōn* (the temperate one) has emotions that are internally in a mean state. We stand well with regard to the emotions, in other words, are truly virtuous and temperate, when emotions are transformed in this deep manner and not merely suppressed or controlled.

Yet, and here is the force of the earlier objections, an individual for whom the emotional life is important and a deep feature of character may simply not be able to cool the heat of emotion or recast affect in a way that always keeps up with wise intention or choice. So, for example, deep attachment to love objects, of the sort that Aristotelian *philia* within the good life requires, may make us more vulnerable to grief or disappointment. At a given moment, these emotions may crowd out other affects that the exercise of specific virtues here and now demands. Thus, while we may be able to bring ourselves to *act well* when we are psychologically down, we may not be able to muster the *right affect*. Or if we do, it may lack authenticity and the right kind of deep connection with praiseworthy character. The underlying point is that to value the kind of investments the emotions make *and* to be *agents* of our emotional lives in the way we seem to be agents of other aspects of our moral character may be a tall order. It may demand more control than even well-moderated and cultivated emotional experience easily allows. We return to some of these objections

[26] NE 1102b25–26, 1103a1–2.   [27] NE 1102b31.

later, but for now they give us a taste of the challenge Aristotle faces in giving emotions their due.

Before turning to the texts in which Aristotle takes up his account of the emotions, I want to outline in a positive way some of the roles emotions play in the moral life. A few of these were hinted at earlier in the defense against objections, but now they can be taken up in a slightly more systematic fashion. My remarks in Section 3, however, are still rather general, with more exegetical study of the texts to follow. The intent now is to formulate some intuitive views about the role of emotions in morality so that we can draw on these as background, as we turn to Aristotle and later to Kant.

3 HOW EMOTIONS FIGURE IN MORALITY

We can begin with something of a survey of the role of emotions in morality. As already suggested, emotions play a crucial epistemic role in the moral life in their function of recording information. We can think of them as *modes of attention* enabling us to notice what is morally salient, important, or urgent in ourselves and our surroundings.[28] They help us *track* the morally relevant "news." In the case of grief, what is salient is that humans suffer and face loss; in the case of pity, that they sometimes fail through blameless ignorance, duress, sickness, or accident; in the case of empathy, that they need the express support and union of others who can understand and identify with them; in the case of love, that we find certain individuals attractive and worthy of our time and devotion. Moreover, emotions draw us in in a way that demands (and sometimes rivets) our attention, putting to the top of

---

[28] On the general issue of moral salience, see Blum (1980); Dancy (1993); Herman (1993, ch. 4); McDowell (1979); Murdoch (1970); Nussbaum (1986); Sherman (1989). Something like this role of the emotions is noticed by Descartes, too, but primarily in terms of an account of the objects that *cause* different emotion, without attention to the intentionality of the emotions. So, he notes, objects that move the senses cause "diverse passions in us . . . because of the diverse ways in which they may harm or help us, or in general be of some importance to us" (Article LII of *The Passions of the Soul*).

our priority orderings thoughts or actions regarding these matters. We focus with intensity and impact, making inferences that
might not otherwise have arisen or be thought of in as compelling
a way.[29] Emotions thus prepare us for moral deliberation and
choice. They serve as epistemological tools helping us to mark the
moral occasion. Without the report of the emotions we would
often be hard-pressed to know which occasions require our min-
istrations or, having established such occasions, how best to help.
Through emotions we pick up subtle information that simply
may not be accessible to us otherwise. In this sense, emotions are
an essential source of information. It may also be that the kind of
information they deliver, clothed as it is through the medium of
emotion, is itself essential to the process of decision making.[30]

It should become clear that emotional sensitivity is more than a
purely perceptual or cognitive matter. Of course, emotions work
through perceptual and cognitive pathways as well as through
other modes of sensitivity. There is no special sensory or cognitive
organ dedicated to emotional sensitivity; it relies on the others.
We fear for ourselves or others by what we think and imagine, as
well as by what we see, hear, smell, touch, or perhaps even taste.
Although vision (perhaps for evolutionary reasons) often seems
to be in the lead in bringing us the news of what is important in
our surroundings,[31] at least in earliest infancy, it is touch (a proxi-
mal rather than distal sensory modality) that is the important
mode of affective communication. Being comforted "at a distance" comes a little later (e.g., as when the exploring child settles
for being attentively watched or smiled at rather than held).[32] But
the general point remains that emotions do not reduce to the
exercise of sensory modalities or cognitive functions.

In addition to their role as modes of attention, emotions play a
role in *communicating information* to others. They are modes of
responding. Putting the two together, emotions become modes

[29] De Sousa (1987).
[30] For suggestions here, see Damasio's experimental research (1994) on the way
we depend on emotional information for coming to decisions.
[31] See Kivy's (1990) interesting remarks on the "interpretive" aspect of seeing in
relation to the other modalities.
[32] Greenspan (1989).

both for *receiving* information and *signaling* it. Through emotions we both track and convey what we care about. Focusing on the second role now, manifest affect and attitude are often taken to convey morally relevant information, including important aspects of our moral character, for example, that we value certain persons, are hurt by the prejudice of others, are moved visibly by certain calls for help. Who we are and what we hold as important are reflected in our emotional attitudes and expressions. This emotional display may be verbal as well as nonverbal, in the latter case, a matter of what some have called gestural articulation, important in early childhood but in our adult relations as well.[33] True, sometimes these less controlled emotional expressions, through facial gestures and vocalization, betray what we wish *not* to show – that we are in fact hurt, annoyed, or have become impatient; that we feel slighted even though we know the injury was not intentional. The gap between how we would like to respond spontaneously and how we in fact do may not be to our liking. Who the real self is becomes something of a conflict, and sometimes a matter for defense. Others, too, may feel uneasy by the perceived lack of congruence, not sure what to trust, vulnerable to the looks and glances that prey on their own emotions. These sorts of issues once again raise challenges to the program of including emotions in an account of moral character. This will be discussed in Section 5 of the present chapter when we consider just how we are or can be "in charge" of different aspects of our emotional lives.

For the time being, however, it seems uncontroversial that the presence of certain affects and, conversely, their absence can be morally significant. To take one example, helping action that is emotionally flat may simply not be received in the same way as action conveyed through more positive, affective expression. As recipients, we may judge that it lacks what is important for our well-being – namely, that others be engaged with us here and now, and that they view that kind of attention and engagement as itself important. Of course emotional tone is not always to the

---

[33] The term is Stanley Greenspan's (1989); he has done extensive research on the reciprocal communication of affect in parent–infant interactions.

point. If someone is bleeding profusely, then helpful action might simply be action aimed at stopping the bleeding, whatever its emotional tone. The communication of emotion is neither here nor there. But there are clearly other cases where it matters, and matters a lot. It typically matters in how we comfort a child, how we volunteer services to a student, how we show our willingness to help a colleague who needs our resources. The point of helping in many of these cases is to reassure another that we care – to show patience, availability, considerateness, empathy. Here, the quality of the emotional interaction is inseparable from the act of helping. In the case of a parent or teacher, it is part of how we define the notion of assistance. Mutual aid is in these cases partly emotional tenor. And this may be conveyed by the kind of affective, gestural articulation that we spoke of earlier. We may feel another's attentional devotion because of a smile, or a laugh, or a twinkling eye, or a long and intense gaze. Conversely, we may sense another's disapproval through gaze breaking or a stolid glance, flitting motions, head shaking, or flat intonation. All are signs of how we are being taken by others.[34] Moreover, they form a part of our conduct that action and conversation considered more narrowly systematically exclude. They seem to be something we care about when we appraise character and reflect on how persons express their moral commitments and concerns.

---

[34] This is plainest in infants who depend upon gaze and smile for reassurance of love. By tracking smiles they learn to reciprocate in kind, making play a matter of dialogue through preverbal gestural articulation. Moreover, Greenspan (1989) has observed that parental expression of emotion at the earliest stages of a child's life (4–8 months) may figure crucially in how a child comes to differentiate her own affective proclivities and ultimately, learn self-control. In caregiving environments where there is active and expressive feedback, children learn to identify their needs and dependencies. By reading parents' faces, they come to know when and where danger lurks and when and where emotions need trimming. In contrast, in those environments where there is little reciprocal feedback, where parents are "poker-faced," children tend to show more deficits in affective differentiation and control. Without the proper cues from others, they tend to lack the kind of early warning system that helps them to recognize and control their own responses. For further discussion of emotional expression, see Darwin (1872); Ekman (1973, 1982).

We have been considering emotions as *modes of attending and signaling value*. Regret figures interestingly as an attitude that signals certain values. In particular, it can be seen as an attitude that signals not so much what a person has done, as what a person has *not* done and how she responds to not acting. It might be worthwhile pausing for a bit to explore this emotion, since it is has been the focus of some discussion in recent moral philosophy that bears on our own concerns about the expression of character through emotion.[35] Cases of regret often involve moral conflicts where an agent is faced with two competing claims that conflict not logically but contingently, here and now in the circumstances of the world. Both claims cannot be effected. To do one is to leave something of equal moral weight undone. Though in such circumstances one may, practically speaking, make a choice, the choice is not necessarily rational or justified. The sensitive agent is aware of a "moral remainder," which is experienced emotionally as regret (or in Bernard Williams's term, as "agent-regret"). It indicates that though one may not be at fault for failing to meet a claim, one nonetheless feels some degree of responsibility. Its presence tells us something additional about the agent's moral character, over and above how and what she chooses. It signals an awareness of the complexity of the moral life and difficulty of making wise choices in constrained circumstances.

In other cases of moral conflict what is required is not merely that a claim go unheeded, but that an agent actively do something base in order to promote the competing claim. To free my family held hostage by a tyrant, Aristotle tells us, I may have to agree to perform a heinous act.[36] To allow the naval ships to set sail,

---

[35] Williams (1973, 1981). Baron (1988) explores Williams's discussion of agent-regret, arguing that the notion may help us avoid too minimalist a conception of responsibility.

[36] For a valuable discussion of moral conflict as it is treated by Aristotle in his notion of mixed actions in NE III.1, see Stocker (1990, ch. 3). In NE IX.4 Aristotle suggests that internal conflict and regret will plague the bad person, but not the good one. However, it is not at all clear that Aristotle has in mind here regret caused by the kinds of conflict he discusses in NE III.1, namely, those in which doing what is best still leaves undone other compelling claims. Rather, in NE IX.4 he has in mind the kinds of conflict caused by *akrasia* or

Agamemnon must violate his duty to his daughter. These are cases of dirty hands – cases where an agent must harm to help, kill innocents to save other innocent lives, violate one unqualified duty to fulfill another. The deontological considerations that might prohibit such actions are not my present concern. Rather what interests me is this more limited point: Assuming that under certain conditions a "dirty" action *is*, practically speaking, required, the agent who experiences no regret or loss in performing such an action seems to lack an adequate moral appreciation of the complexity of the circumstances. This is not to say all agents must face these or lesser conflicts with a tortured soul. Even in conflict cases, there may be no question in an agent's mind about what course of action must be taken. But still, though there is no ambivalence, there may be loss. And not to feel that loss (expressed through sorrow or grief or regret) is to fail to take seriously a moral claim. It is to assume that the claim can be wiped out by an act of mental balancing. But the point of regret is that it marks a cost that is not canceled out by a corresponding benefit. In this sense, conscientious deliberation and decision making do not exhaust everything that matters in the expression of moral character. To make a decision yet not to feel any residue from an unmet claim that tugs with equal moral force may be the sign of a morally deficient character.

It might be argued in reply that regret of this sort is morally commendable in only a secondary way, insofar as it sensitizes an agent to the sorts of claims that "typically" can be fulfilled by action. Though in a conflict situation I may violate a duty, my regret signals that typically I can fulfill that requirement and am aware of the force of the duty. The claim would be that the moral value of regret is ultimately parasitic upon action. It plays the role so many other emotions play of marking an occasion for moral action. The only difference is that it alerts us to a *type* of occasion, not a particular token that may here and now cue action. However, this reply does not go far enough. For even apart from the contribution to prospective action, there is a dimension of moral

weakness in general. I am grateful to Paula Gottlieb for helping me to clarify this.

44

character revealed directly by the emotion. The presence of regret tells us that this claim *does* matter here and now – that one is responding to present need, however one goes on to formulate an appropriate intention next time around. Just as those future intentions to act will reveal character, so does the emotion now. They both have their common source in character. Put another way, regret is a way of showing commitment (what you care about) when action is impossible. As such, it is a mode of response, valuable in its own right apart from any contribution it makes to future action.

In making this point, I do not deny that there is a likely psychological correlation between recognizing a claim that must be left undone and acting on that sort of claim in the future, when circumstances are more favorable. Moreover, even in the cramped circumstances of conflict, regret may issue in some measure of compensatory action here and now. Yet, still I want to make the stronger claim that even if the practice of regret leads to no "payoffs" in present or future action, an agent who experiences regret at having to leave a claim undone because of competing claims exhibits an important feature of moral character. What is valuable is not that she loses sleep, feels tortured inside or emotionally wrought on the outside. It is not sentimentalism that is at stake, nor self-punishment. Rather, it is that she is able to appreciate and emotionally express concerns that are here and now relevant. She has a kind of moral vision and communication of that vision in affective expression. And this is not reducible to a disposition to action, narrowly construed.

We have spoken thus far of emotions as modes of *attending* and *conveying* value, largely in the context of others and our external surroundings. But emotions are also important for coming to know ourselves. They can record and convey value to ourselves. Here, the *revelatory* function of emotions is especially important. They can *disclose* information that we might not have been aware of independent of experiencing those emotions.[37] So, for example, I might not be aware how deeply I feel about a distant

---

[37] See Stocker (1996) for an insightful discussion of this point, and also for a more general discussion of the epistemic capacities of emotions.

cousin's suffering were it not that I find myself overwhelmed by feelings of sorrow when I dwell on his circumstances. The valuation that the emotion reveals, in some sense, takes me by surprise. I suggested that this disclosing power of emotions plays an important role in the project of self-knowledge, a project, which on both Aristotelian and Kantian views, is central to the cultivation of virtue. On the Aristotelian view, the arena for self-knowledge typically will be within friendship, and in particular, what Aristotle calls "character" or "virtue" friendships.[38] Such friends know each other intimately and share a mutual interest in living a critically reflective, good life. But in addition, they spend their days with one another in a way that promotes the candid flow of emotions and evaluative information those emotions contain. On the Kantian view, the duty to self-knowledge is something of a "meta-virtue" underlying all virtues. As Kant puts it, "the first command of all duties to oneself" is to know oneself – to know one's heart.[39] Principal here will be keeping vigil over one's own attempts at self-deception. Significantly, Kant takes radical evil to be not so much a matter of following the temptations of contrary inclination, but of veiling such inclination in rationalizations that escape reason's own survey.[40] But here too, emotions will be of important epistemic advantage insofar as they can disclose, with some reliability, moral commitments and conflicts. Presumably, Kant's notions of a "happy" and "melancholic" heart play this role. They reveal deeper, moral attitudes.[41]

We can appreciate the connection between the revelatory aspect of emotions and the pursuit of self-knowledge in more general ways. Here, we can learn something from depth psychology.[42] On that view, a present emotion can transport us to past

---

[38] NE IX.9; see Cooper (1980) and Sherman (1989, ch. 4).

[39] DV 441.

[40] Rel. 57/50. I say more about this in Chapter 4, Section 4.

[41] See, for example, DV 484–85.

[42] I mention Freudian depth psychology to point out what I take are commonsense, Proustian sorts of uses of emotion to prod memory. The theory of repression, to which my remarks are related, is a complicated subject that Freud, as is well known, revised his views on many times. Perhaps most

similar emotions, and with the experiencing of those past emotions, we can come to disclose to ourselves the evaluations and construals that are implicit in those relived emotions. This is the work of *affective memory*. Through the probes and prods of present thought and feeling, we build bridges to the past, viscerally feeling once again the hurt and sting of old loss, or the shame of childhood failure and perceived defeat. It is not just that we feel pleasure or pain. Rather, we are in the presence of a concrete emotion and the story it tells. In psychoanalysis the recapitulation of patterns of emotional response through transference onto an analyst is intended to be a way of feeling emotions at a detached level. The patient restages at the same time as she watches and interprets. The underlying ideology is that affective remembering and reliving of past emotional experiences in this manner can be liberative, for by exposing what is often defensively hidden some of the very need for those defenses, expressed in anger or perhaps self-shame, begins to crumble. Thus one tries to understand the source of present disabling emotions by freeing them from their primitive roots. On most versions of this view, the goal is not to remove the patient from the vulnerabilities of emotion, as the Stoics might argue. Rather, the hope is to make possible a way of experiencing even the vulnerabilities of emotions in a less crippling and less self-destructive way.

In this process, emotion is both the subject of self-knowledge (in virtue of what it discloses) and the medium (because it facilitates the disclosures). The memory of emotionally powerful experiences is reawakened in reexperiencing those affective episodes, and awakened in a way that cannot be achieved by knowing in a detached way that such and such happened or by even viewing in a purely cognitive way the relevant scenes on the visual screen of the mind. So one remembers the majesty of a beloved aunt – how she charmed one as a child, how the books and paintings in her house were part of her magical aura, how monumental it all was, with all that emotionally charged information disclosed by

fascinating is his revision of his view of the role of repression in the production of anxiety. See Freud (1894, 1896, 1917, 1926).

47

being in the grip now of the relevant emotions. Once again, the epistemic advantage of emotion as medium seems to be its peculiar ability to make vividly present the objects of its evaluative focus. The evaluations are disclosed in a way that puts our nose right into the matter, in a focused and riveted way.

There is a danger in our discussion so far of thinking of emotions as primarily instrumental – as epistemological tools whose value is primarily in terms of accessing and conveying antecedent valuings.[43] They come to be mining tools that dig up and reveal what we already care about. To use a different metaphor, they are a kind of radar. But this distorts things, and misses much of the character of emotion. The operations of emotions themselves often *create some of what is valued* and also *are valued intrinsically* even in their exercise as instruments. To take the first point, emotions do not always reveal what we already care about, but can themselves invest with value otherwise neutral states of affairs. The point is clearest when we think about the kind of "halo effect" loved or admired ones have over our lives.[44] What we associate with our loved ones often becomes charged with our original attachment to them, so that new things come to take on value for us. At work is a kind of transference that is a familiar part of certain identificatory emotions, such as emulation, respect, and love.[45] The limited point now is that attachment emotions, characteristic of love or friendship, create new objects of care or fear for us. This role of emotions will have crucial importance in moral development, and in learning in general. We learn best from those with whom we can identify and from those whom we value positively. This underlies Aristotle's view that *philia* is the central arena in which character development takes place.

There is a second point. Granted, the expression of emotion reveals old values and creates new ones as well. But even aside

[43] I am indebted to Stocker's (1996) discussion of this point.

[44] A simlar point may be made about negative valuing, and may be at the heart of insidious forms of discrimination. See Piper (1990).

[45] Aristotle himself (Poet. IV) emphasizes the importance of identification (or *mimēsis*) as a learning method, and combines this in the books on friendship with the importance of an empathetic, responsive relationship as a context for learning.

from these contributions, experiencing emotion itself bears value. A world without humor, laughter, playfulness, flirtatiousness, as well as aggression and fear, would simply be impoverished, let alone unrecognizable as human. Simply to be an emotional creature and to live with others on an emotional plane (in a life that engages our emotions and in which emotions are part of the social fiber) is an intrinsic part of living humanly. We prize that way of experiencing self and others, apart from whatever else it leads to. Certainly, on the Aristotelian view, a *eudaimōn* life is a life lived emotionally, and part of what is valuable is just realizing oneself through emotions. We express our excellent functioning through both action *and* emotion, and these expressions are valued in their own right.[46] The point is perhaps intuitively clearest in the case of friendship. We simply value the emotionality of a shared life. As Aristotle puts it, "there are some things the lack of which takes the luster from happiness."[47] Friendship is such a thing. Without it, happiness would be seriously marred, hopelessly less complete.

There is a final role for emotions and one probably most emphasized in connection with morality. This is the role of emotions as *motives*. Emotions can move us to action. They are *motivational*. We act *out of* compassion, *out of* friendliness, *out of* sympathy. In this role, emotions are reasons for acting. Both Kant and the Stoics cast suspicion on the moral significance of this role, arguing for the unreliability of this sort of motivation for moral action. Kant also clarifies that emotions themselves do not directly motivate action, but in a more mediated way, ground maxims of actions. That is, emotions present themselves as registering reasons for actions; they are incentives that we as agents can then choose or "take up" as reasons. We shall return to the motivational aspect of emotion,

---

[46] NE 1109a23.

[47] NE 1099b2–6; see also 1100b25–28 for another formulation of external goods, such as friendship, as noninstrumentally valued within the good life. For an excellent summary discussion of external goods, in terms of both their instrumental and their noninstrumental roles, see Annas (1993, 378–84). She draws on the earlier essays of Irwin (1985c) and Nussbaum (1986), as well as that of Cooper (1985), who denies external goods noninstrumental value. For a good general discussion of external goods in Aristotelian *eudaimonia*, see White (1992).

in the discussions that follow in this chapter and in our study of Kant. Here, I should note that I have emphasized the other roles because by and large they are obscured by an exclusive focus on the moral significance of emotion as motivation. One benefit of pointing out these other roles, is that even if Kant accords duty the privileged role of moral motive, he still can leave room for emotions to play these other roles in a complete account of moral practice.

We have now outlined a number of pervasive functions of the emotions in moral life. We can sum up by saying that emotions are sensitivities that (1) help us to *attend to and record* what we care about (in both a positive and negative sense). They are *modes of recording values.* (2) Furthermore, they assist us in *signaling* those valuings to both ourselves and others. They are *modes of conveying and expressing values.* (3) As a part of these last two capacities, they can *reveal* values we were previously unaware of (i.e., record and convey them). They are *modes of disoclosing values.* (4) In some cases, they help to *establish* what we value or detest, rather than merely track or reveal antecedent valuings. They are *modes of establishing values.* (5) Additionally, emotions can be *valued for their own sake,* simply as important ways of living a full, human life. They are *intrinsically valued.* (6) Finally, emotions *motivate* action. They provide impetus for action. They are *motives for action.* In a variety of ways, I shall refer back to these various roles in discussing Aristotelian and Kantian virtue. Separating out these various roles is important for appreciating that the moral significance of emotions is underestimated if we restrict emotion to simply the role of motivating action.

A few loose ends should be tied up before we proceed. Emotions, it can be said, often expose us to the rawer side of ourselves and others. Through emotions, we are exposed to, and expose, our underbellies. But this suggests a certain candor on the part of emotions that we are not always in control of. To what degree are our feelings, and how we express them, "up to us?" If our joy is expressed in a smile or other physical gesture, are these behavioral options that we choose, or reflex reactions that are barely conscious? How broad is the range of alternatives between these two points? Are shrugs of the shoulder and laughing eyes (i.e., motor movements) no more nor less controllable than shivering or blushing (i.e., visceral responses)? In the case of the emotions themselves, in what sense are they a matter of constitutional temperament? In what sense can an emotional disposition be up to us, in what sense can a given occurrence? These are important questions, which tug at the heart of any discussion of virtue theory that introduces the emotions. They are questions we will need to raise in addressing the moral theories of Aristotle and Kant.

Throughout this study, we should also bear in mind that emotion is not a univocal thing, but refers to mental states with considerable range and diversity. Certain emotions have an intensity that seem to make us succumb to their pull. Passionate love may have moments like this, in which the vertigo of the experience eclipses calmer control. We are not necessarily victims, like those picked up by the wind and tossed about. But part of the euphoria of the experience comes precisely from abandoning resistances and letting go. This, of course, may be a choice. But once we assent, for a limited time at least, it is as if we become more possessed than possessor. (The contemporary issues of date rape revolve around these themes.) Blake warns us of possible consequences in *Songs of Innocence*:

> To be in a passion you good may do.
> But no good if a passion is in you.

Other emotions may be more readily responsive to coaching. But even here it may be more a matter of prior training than of being able to effect a change at will, in a moment's notice. Negative emotions such as anger, jealousy, or envy typically come under careful social vigilance, with attempts made to narrow the gap between what is "reasonable" given the logic of anger or jealousy and what, given a moral or social stance, "ought" to be expressed and perhaps even felt. Again, emotions can be shallow and headstrong, just as they can be deep and honest. Some are marked by conspicuous physiological signs, others not. Some are inertial, others pass before we can come to know or identify them. Some return regularly, rooted in more primitive drives, others seem fresh and original, unmet in past lives. Some wound deeply, others only graze us, the knife never plunging into our core. But

51

in all events, in a moral theory that takes emotions seriously and that aims at being practical, it is reasonable to expect awareness of their diversity, and where appropriate, provisions for their training.

At this point we should have some idea of the different points at which emotions might enter the moral life and how they might begin to figure in an account of moral character. Along the way I have signaled various problems that will have to be faced regarding how we can be held responsible for our emotions, and praised or blamed for those aspects of character that appeal to them. With this as background, it is finally time to turn to a more systematic consideration of Aristotle's views on the emotions and their place in his account of virtue.

4 ARISTOTELIAN EMOTIONS

What are emotions? What kind of account of emotions does Aristotle proffer? Where do we look for such an account? Here we stumble on an odd fact. For all the emphasis in Aristotle's ethical works of the importance of emotions in a conception of mature moral character, we find no systematic analysis of emotions in those works. Where we think we might come across them – say, at the end of Book I and in Book II of the *Nicomachean* where Aristotle begins to introduce a discussion of excellences of character as excellences of the orectic part (i.e., the part that houses the emotions) – the only analysis we find is that emotions (*pathē*),[48] such as appetite, anger, fear, and confidence, are connected with ("accompanied by") pleasure and pain.[49] Just what to make of the point in the local context is unclear. Earlier in Book II, Aristotle offers other general *endoxa* connecting virtue with pleasure and pain (e.g., that virtue has to do with "right pleasures and pains," and that we become virtuous through the punishing and reinforcing effects of these pleasures and pains). But these remarks seem to shed little light on the specific role of pleasure and pain *within* emotions. Aristotle also makes the general point in this book that

---

[48] Generally, I translate *"pathē"* as "emotions," though where other terms, such as "passions" or "feelings," fit the context better, I use them.
[49] NE 1105b21–23.

emotions will not themselves be states of character (*hexeis*), though states of character will be ways of standing well or badly toward the emotions. Again, we are not told more about the structure of emotion or about how emotions are internally transformed when we stand well toward them. This is odd. Given Aristotle's view that virtue is a way of hitting the mean with regard to both action and emotion, we would expect an analysis of emotion in the ethical writings somewhat comparable to the analysis we find of action and choice.

In the *Rhetoric*, Book II, we find an extensive treatment of the emotions that goes some way to filling in the lacuna. The task of this manual is to make available to the orator an account of various emotions, including the specific sorts of beliefs that are connected with particular emotions. What emerges there is an account of the emotions in which evaluations or appraisals play an important constitutive role. Whether Aristotle's rhetorician can be viewed as relying on mostly popular *endoxa* or psychological theories,[50] the result seems to move us toward the kind of analysis that is conspicuously absent in the ethical writings and that is crucial for understanding the affective structure of virtue. As we said earlier, Aristotle's account is distinct from a number of alternatives that find clear expression in the first half of this century in experimental psychology as well as philosophy. It will be helpful to delineate briefly these views in order to mark their contrast with Aristotle's account.

The first is the commonsense view in which emotion is thought to be an irreducible quality of feeling or sensation. It may be caused by a physical state, but the emotion itself is the sensation we feel when we are in that state. It is a felt affect, a distinctive feeling, but not something that is *about* something else. The view quickly falters, however, when we realize that emotions on this view become no more than private states, feel like itches and

[50] On this, see Cooper (1993), Nussbaum (1994, ch. 3), and Striker (1996), whose plausible view is that although the rhetorician need not be an expert in psychological theory, he should know the true results of the theory. As such, as she puts it, "what we should expect to find in the *Rhet.* is not science or philosophical theory, but theory-based results."

53

tickles, inaccessible to identification in terms of propositional content (i.e., mental representation of what they are about).

A second view, associated with William James and Carl Lange,[51] is that emotions are proprioceptions of visceral or behavioral movements. They are an awareness of bodily changes in the peripheral nervous system. We are afraid because we tremble, angry because of the knots in our stomachs, not the other way around. The view, though rather counterintuitive, nonetheless captures the idea that emotions, more than other mental states, seem to have conspicuous physiological and kinesthetic components. These often dominate children's and adults' reports of their emotional experiences. They dominate the literary, too. Consider in this vein the lines of Sappho:

> When I see you, my voice fails,
> my tongue is paralyzed,
> a fiery fever runs through my whole body
> my eyes are swimming,
> and can see nothing
> my ears are filled with a throbbing din
> I am shivering all over . . .[52]

Literary history, social convention, and perhaps evolution conspire to tell us this is love. But even here it is not hard to imagine that what is described could be dread or awe, or perhaps mystical inspiration. The general point is that even well-honed physiological feelings do not easily identify specific emotions. Proprioceptions of our skin tingling or our chest constricting, or our readiness to flee or fight, underdetermine just what emotion we are feeling. Many distinct emotions share these features, and without contextual clues, and thoughts that dwell on those clues, we are in the dark about what we are experiencing.[53] The chief burden of the work of Cannon was to show that emotional affects are virtually identical across manifestly different states.[54]

---

[51] See James and Lange (1884).
[52] As quoted by de Sousa (1987, 50), who makes a similar point.
[53] Schacter and Singer (1962).
[54] Cannon (1927).

A third view steps outside the privacy of the mind, locating emotions in behavior.[55] On this general view, emotions are modes of readiness to act or, in Freud's early idiom, discharges of tension. Support for this view comes from the fact that we often experience emotions as excitations in need of release,[56] and we often describe emotions in terms of dispositions to concrete behavior: "I felt like hitting him," "I could have exploded," "I wanted to spit," "I wanted to be alone with him, wrapped in his embrace." Yet the action tendency view seems at best a partial account of emotion. The basic issue here is not that some emotions, such as apathy, inhibition, and depression, seem to lack clear activation modes, whereas others are more a matter of the rich movement of thought, so well depicted, for example, in Henry James's novels. It is, rather, that emotions are about something (internal or external) that we represent in thought. As such they have propositional content. Their identity depends on that content.

This takes us to Aristotle's view. At the heart of his account is the view that emotions are *about* something that we represent in thought. Emotions are intentional states. As such they have cognitive content. They are identified by that content, by what we dwell on, whether it be fleetingly or with concentrated attention. Equally, these states can be beliefs or just musings and construals only slenderly based on "objective" evidence. Such an account need not exclude other features of emotion, such as awareness of physiological and behavioral response or felt sensations. The claim is that these, when present, are dependent on cognitive (i.e., descriptive and evaluative) content, and are directed toward that content.

The fact that Aristotle's account falls within the *Rhetoric* has heuristic import. The rhetorician's task is to persuade the jury by

---

55 Skinner (1953). Also Arnold (1960) and Frijda (1986, 71): "'Action tendency' and 'emotion' are one and the same thing." We might include the later Wittgenstein and Ryle in this list.

56 In this regard, there is similarity between behaviorism's push outward and the classical Freudian notion of the release of drive, although Freud was by no means offering a behavioral account that reduced the mental to outward movement.

argument and disputation. He must tell his audience the right
stories if he is to influence their emotions in desired ways,
carefully crafting his arguments so as to produce the intended
emotional responses. The claim is that emotions are produced by
evaluations, but also, more strongly, that emotions are partly constituted by them. That is, it is not just that certain antecedent
evaluations typically cause certain emotions. Rather, the connection is a conceptual one. Anger would not be anger without
thoughts that I was unfairly injured.[57] Fear would not be fear if
there weren't some mental content of a threat or danger. Indeed,
Aristotle is insistent that closely related emotions, such as contempt, spite, and insolence, are differentiated not by their "feels"
but by their distinct evaluative focuses.[58]

Like the tragedian's job in Aristotle's *Poetics*, the orator's is to
describe characters and their actions in concrete ways such that
they arouse sympathetic identification. Thus it is through discursive methods that the rhetorician, like the skilled writer, works on
the emotions, changing the heart by changing belief. It is these
changes of heart that will in turn inspire the right thoughts and
action – in the case of the courtroom, a ballot cast in the right way.
"When people are feeling friendly and placable, they think one
sort of thing; when they are feeling angry or hostile, they think
either something totally different or the same thing with a
different intensity."[59] Still, the primary lesson of the *Rhetoric* is not
about the motivational force of emotion, but about its cognitive
and, more specifically, evaluative foundation. To feel hostile or
friendly, indeed to feel specific emotions in general, is to take
oneself to have *reason* to feel one way or the other; the rhetorician's task, if he wishes to elicit emotions, is to persuade his
listeners that they objectively have such reasons. Note that Aristotle's concern here is not with whether certain emotions are in
general those one *ought* to feel as one lives the good life, or with
whether the beliefs that ground specific emotions are *true*. The
inquiry is not normative, but descriptive: to supply the orator

[57] See Oakley (1992) for a related discussion.
[58] Rh. 1378b14.
[59] Rh. 1377b30.

with the circumstantial and conventional beliefs and evaluations that structure specific emotions so that those emotions can be elicited as required in the courtroom. Toward this end, Aristotle says, the orator will need to know the states of mind (*pōs diakemenoi*) of those affected by specific emotions, the objects toward which those emotions are directed (*tisin*), and the evaluations or appraisals about those objects (*epi poiois; dia poia*) that produce the emotion.[60]

What we shall see emerging is the view of an object of emotion as not simply something pointed to or behaviorally signaled, but something that appears to an agent in a certain way and that can cause emotion in virtue of that intentional representation. Emotions involve a kind of judging. I am angry *at him* because (*I believe or imagine*) he injured me. More specifically, the judging is about the goodness or badness of what I take to have happened.[61] Thus anger requires an *evaluation* that one has been unjustly slighted by another; fear, that there is imminent harm or danger that can destroy us; shame, that certain events in which we are involved are a discredit to us. Pleasure or pain is intentionally related to the evaluation. Generally speaking, pleasure or pain, on Aristotle's view, is itself a judging of something good or bad.[62] Emotion is a kind of pleasure or pain, as Aristotle often puts it,[63] in that it is a more determinate form of such judgment. In some cases, emotion can lead to a reactive desire that may inspire action. This figures prominently in Aristotle's definition of anger. "Anger," Aristotle tells us, "is a desire [*orexis*] accompanied by pain toward the revenge of what one regards as a slight toward oneself or one's friends that is unwarranted."[64]

Emotions, thus, are complexes that include evaluations and affects (or feelings of pleasure and pain), and that in some cases, though not all, lead to desires to act. In the following paragraphs I

---

60 Rh. 1378a22–24; 1379a10–12.
61 The notion of appraisal occurs in contemporary cognitivist psychology literature as well; see Arnold (1960); Frijda (1986); Lazarus (1966).
62 See DA 431a8–10.
63 See the NE II discussion where Aristotle generally refers to cultivated emotions as right pleasures and pains.
64 Rh. 1378a30–32.

take up these various elements. Getting clearer about these will better help us locate the points at which emotions may be subject to control and, in this regard, appropriate as a foundation for virtue.

We can begin with the notion of evaluations. Aristotle suggests that the evaluations constitutive of emotions are about matters important to us. In the case of fear, he says it is "great" pains or losses or what has "great" power of destroying us.[65] Similarly, we are not likely to grieve if we lose a pencil, though may if what is lost has sentimental value or is something we view as nonfungible. But does Aristotle hold that it is actually beliefs that ground emotions, or can it be cognitive attitudes that are weaker than strict belief, for example, imaginings or construals, that we dwell on without concern about "objective truth?"[66] Earlier, we noted that emotions are often characterized by a partiality in what we take in as relevant. There seems to be a certain laxity in the standards of evidence. Aspects of reality may be disregarded or under- or overvalued, and attention focused on slender probabilities. There may be a selective gaze that long outlasts its "objective" warrant, a way of representing things that settles for a certain antiquity and archaism of view. Emotions are prone to a certain atavism, as Ronald de Sousa has put it, or "spillover" in Pat Greenspan's terms, from past judgments where there was either warrant for belief or at least a greater fit between emotion and perceptual evidence.[67] Familiar sorts of examples point to this inertial aspect of emotion. For example, I may be anxious about my daughter's safety while at the same time I believe she is home safe; or I may fear spiders, though I know that most spiders I am likely to encounter are harmless; or I may become livid with my two-year-old for what I see as a kind of lying, though I know, intellectually, that he is engaged in only the playful pretend of a toddler who can't yet distinguish between lying and make-

[65] Rh. 1382a24; 29.
[66] For contemporary warnings against a strict judgmentalist account of emotion, see Davis (1988); Greenspan (1988); Stocker (1987).
[67] De Sousa (1987); Greenspan (1988).

believe. On Aristotle's view, are these cases that show the emotion to be grounded in something that falls short of belief, something we are not ready to grasp by belief? I believe so, but we need to tread carefully here.

It is very tempting to bring in Aristotle's notion of *phantasia* at this juncture. The subject of *phantasia* (loosely translated as "imagining" or "appearing" though wider than our use of those terms) is complex and full examination of it would take us deep into Aristotle's philosophy of mind.[68] But most briefly, we can make the following programmatic points. *Phantasia* is a function of perceptual and cognitive capacities related to what we often think of as "interpretive" seeing or, in a Wittgensteinian idiom, "seeing as." In this sense it is not just a registering of perceptual input but a "thinking about it" in a certain way (a "seeing the face in the cloud" type of phenomenon). In some cases *phantasia* is associated with conditions of nonveridical perception. In this sense, a *phantasia* may not correctly represent the objects in one's perceptual field. So, for example, a *phantasia* of the sun as being six inches in diameter (as big as my hand) will stand in need of correction by our knowledge of its true size and the tricks of perspective.[69] We cannot accept the *phantasia* or "appearing" with conviction (*pistis*),[70] or, put differently, we can't take *phantasia* as veridical, on faith, for we know how often we are deceived. We might think of the cognitive content of emotions in this way. For while emotion involves intentional focus and construal, its construals do not always bear the evidentiary warrant of full-bodied belief. A further attraction is that *phantasia* is an inclusive capacity that characterizes human (adult and infant) as well as animal cognitive functions. Characterizing emotion through *phantasia* would thus allow Aristotle to ascribe emotions in more than a merely metaphorical way to children in their early developmental stages as well as to animals. This would extend his general approach, explicit in the *De Motu Animalium,* of viewing human

---

[68] See Modrak (1987); Nussbaum (1978); for a related discussion of the broader theme of Aristotelian intentionality, see Caston (1992).
[69] DA 428b2–3.   [70] DA 428a19–22.

intentionality as part of a larger, "common" story (*peri tēs koinēs aitias*) about the intentionality of animal motion.[71]

However, there are various problems with an approach that makes *phantasia* central, especially in the technical way it is understood in the more psychological treatises. For a start, Aristotle himself in the *De Anima* stipulates that *phantasia* is insufficient to ground emotion. In believing something is truly fearful, we engage the emotions and come to feel fear. In merely having the *phantasia* of what is fearful, we may become physically aroused or excited but not experience the emotion itself.[72] Still, there may be little reason to take this as a rigid constraint once we turn to the *Rhetoric*, which is, after all, a popular work not intended as lectures on psychology or the philosophy of mind. This signals the more general point that any easy fluidity between the two works may be problematic. This also applies to how we are to understand *phantasia* itself. The term is used infrequently in the *Rhetoric*, although forms of the verb *phainesthai* occur repeatedly in the definitional accounts of the various emotions, for instance, anger is pain at an "apparent" injury (*phainomenēn oligōrian*), pity is pain at "apparent" destructive evil (*phainomenōi kakōi phthartikōi*).[73] Throughout, the verbal form is used to signal the idea of a "perceived" harm or benefit, with the emphasis on intentionality – on how things *appear* to an agent, on how an agent *appraises* things. The more technical notion of *phantasia* developed in the psychological writings, of a representational function that falls short of full belief or conviction, is not emphasized. Indeed, in the *Rhetoric*, Aristotle regularly interchanges *phainesthai* forms and other cognitive words for thinking and believing, without drawing any

[71] MA 698a1–5.
[72] DA 427b22. See also MA 703b5ff., where Aristotle says that an arousal response, such as palpitation or an erection, may be caused by *phantasia* without the command of thought. Aristotle's point is that such arousals are not voluntary actions. In the *De Anima* he seems to want to say they are not emotions either.
[73] Rh. 1378a30; 1385b13; 1383b15, etc. The term *phantasia* appears at 1382a21–23 in the definition of fear (and also in the definition of anger at NE 1149a30), but the *Rhetoric* definitions of the other emotions rely on verbal forms of *phainesthai*. I am indebted to Martha Nussbaum (1994, ch. 3), for her discussion of related issues.

implicit attention to a technical contrast that might be at work.[74] He does not seem to be especially interested in the issue of evidentiary warrant and the possible inadequacy of *phantasia* on this score.

Perhaps this should not surprise us in a manual about forensics. The task of the *Rhetoric* is to guide the orator in constructing arguments and exhortations that elicit specific emotions. To do this, the orator must persuade, bringing his listener to accept a story, even if in a cooler moment it is rejected by circumspect judgment. To grip the listener in a riveted way is the challenge. To persuade the listener that things *appear* in a certain way, here and now, is the task. The actual objectivity of the evidence is not directly at issue. More generally, introducing *phantasia* is not meant as a way to discredit the descriptive and evaluative content of emotions, or to show that they can be any less compelling to an agent than warranted beliefs.

To sum up, Aristotle is well aware of cognitive states that fall short of strict belief. This slot is filled by Aristotle's technical notion of *phantasia*. As I have suggested, in our own contemporary discussions of the emotions these weaker propositional attitudes are introduced to deal with the problem of casting emotions as cognitive yet in conflict with beliefs to which we give fuller endorsement. However, Aristotle, at least in the *Rhetoric*, is more concerned with showing that the cognitive states constitutive of emotions can *grip us* and earn *confident mental acceptance*, independent of whether there is sufficient strength of evidence for assenting "objectively" to something's being the case. Even when there is inadequate, objective evidentiary warrant, we still can give a *compelling* kind of acceptance through emotions.

With this in mind, we can return to my fearing for my daughter's safety even when I believe there are no longer any lurking dangers. How does Aristotle account for this inertial aspect of emotions? Relying on the account in the *De Anima*, he might argue that what I feel is only the vestige of fear, some residue or

---

[74] So, for example, the definition of fear (Rh. 1382b32ff.) employs the term *phantasia,* but then moves on to the verbs and verbal forms of "to think" and "to expect."

shadowy fear, an arousal caused by *phantasia* in the technical sense but not by belief. It is not really emotion because it is not based on belief. But turning to the central account in the *Rhetoric,* he would most likely argue that it is not just vestigial fear that I feel, but genuine fear because in a certain way I really *do not accept* that all dangers are removed (however aware I am of the slim probabilities or distortion of my view). I am still in the grip of the old story, at least for the moment, or when I am caught off guard and find my thoughts dwelling where they will. This is to acknowledge that my beliefs and *phantasia* are unstable. I go back and forth telling and believing different stories, in the grip of fear and free from it, depending on which story line I embrace (consciously or not) at a given moment. It is a kind of oscillation, a fading in and out of competing views, each of which seems to hold sway for a short while. Aristotle does not develop this sort of account to the extent the Stoics do. But there seems to be sufficient evidence in the *Rhetoric* to point us in this direction. The upshot is that cognitive states that fall short of strict belief may ground emotion. Although they may lack evidentiary warrant of the sort that characterizes belief, we no less strongly feel compelled by them.

Turning now to a different issue, but one that still relates to the evaluative element of emotions, it is often said that objectless emotions present a counterexample to an intentional account such as Aristotle's. In such cases, we may feel a generalized sense of fear or anxiety, directed at no object in particular. Moods, similarly, are vague, *about* nothing in particular. With depression, the world seems to go black, infecting everything with its bile yet being about nothing except perhaps the existential condition. Although Aristotle does not discuss these sorts of cases,[75] I think many of them (though not all) can be accommodated within a broadly intentional theory such as his. A large group of such emotions, it can be argued, are intentional even though their objects are indefinite and vague. Thus, I may experience a generalized sense of fear and have the thought that some danger looms, without being more specific about my fear and without being able

---

[75] The Stoics, however, speak of *melancholia* regularly.

to peg it onto any determinate external object. What my evaluation is about is indefinite. But still, we might say it is *about* something, something I cannot articulate. That is to say, we could
imagine it having a propositional object, for example, "I am afraid
about something I can't quite describe." In some cases, that propositional content acts as place holder for a future, more determinate,
evaluation. At that point, of course, we might want to say we
have a different emotion, but still, one that may be thought of as
having evolved from the earlier emotion.

Emotions also may have definite objects that nonetheless mask
underlying emotions whose evaluative contents are not easily
accessible. Pride in one's excellence in certain areas may cover for
"unfelt" shame in deeper, more occluded domains. If and when
the affective component of shame comes to be felt, it may again
have only an indefinite evaluative object – that it is about me or
someone related to me. Only after further self scrutiny may a
more precise evaluation be articulated.[76] Once again, I am not
suggesting that Aristotle touched on these sorts of cases. My
claim is only that the kind of theory he is proposing can make
some sense of these phenomena, and that as an explanatory
schema it covers a wide band of emotions. In an interesting way,
Plato is more open to candid discussion of what we might now
call unconscious emotions. We are told in the graphic discussion
of the soul in *Republic* IX that sometimes in sleep, wild appetites
resist slumber, sallying forth to indulge in incest and other foolish
fantasies. "You are aware that in such case there is nothing it will
not venture to undertake as being released from all sense of
shame and all reason."[77] These emotions are stirrings bared to
thought only under its slumbering veil.

The types of emotions that have vague or occluded intentional
focus should be distinguished from what Pat Greenspan has
called more purely "objectless sensations" and which in Aristotle's terms, might be classified with the arousals and excitations

---

[76] Some psychoanalytically oriented thinkers have speculated that these emotions are "unconscious" in part because they are originally stored in memory
prelinguistically. See Greenspan (1989).
[77] *Republic* 571d.

(palpitations and erections) that fall short of proper emotion.[78] These kinds of examples often are taken to be counterexamples to an intentional theory of emotion, but I suggest that they are not, in fact, emotions. As an example of an "objectless sensation" Greenspan suggests the feeling of edginess induced by too much coffee. This sort of feeling may come to be directed at some object, but initially, at least, it is visceral without being intentional.

I now turn to a different aspect of the emotional complex, namely, the affect or feel constitutive of emotions. Thus far the affective element of emotions has been described as intentionally directed toward a constitutive evaluation. When I am angry, I feel pain at the thought that I have been insulted. But this way of putting matters is not always explicit in Aristotle's formulations. Sometimes he says pleasure and pain "accompany" or "follow" (*hepesthai tina hēdonēn*) an emotion, or, alternatively, that a particular emotion is "with" (*meta*) pleasure or pain.[79] Yet the notion of accompaniment is too weak to do the work Aristotle intends. For in that role pleasure could be merely a symptom or coincident of emotion, something that in principle could lack any intentional connection with the grounding evaluation. Consider the shame I come to feel from a gaffe made in a sensitive social setting. Here, the pain is directed *toward* the thought that I may have blundered before others whom I care about. The pain does not simply "accompany" the awareness that I may have socially erred. It is intentionally focused on that awareness. *That,* in an acute way, is what I am pained *about.* In other formulations, however, Aristotle is aware of just this point, making explicit the intentionality of affect through the preposition *epi.* Pity is a painful feeling *directed at,* or *toward* (*epi*) the appearance of someone suffering,[80] indigna-

---

[78] DA 427b22; MA 703b5ff. Greenspan (1988). Here we might also want to put conditions such as panic syndrome, which some researchers regard as chemical disturbances lacking (at least at moments of onset) even indefinite, intentional focus.

[79] For example, *meta lupēs* at Rh. 1378a30; *hepesthai tina hēdonēn* at Rh. 1378 b1; *holōs hois hepetai hēdonē ē lupē* at NE 1105b23. More general remarks about the various kinds of connections among pleasure and pain and virtue come in NE 1104b4–1105a16.

[80] Rh. 1385b12.

tion is pain *at* (*epi*) unmerited good fortune,[81] and similar formulations hold for envy and emulation. Thus, in his more careful formulations, Aristotle seems to regard affect not as some free-floating sensation but as intentionally connected with the evaluative focus of the emotion.

It is also worth noting that, in contradistinction to a theory such as that of William James, Aristotle is not particularly interested in locating awareness of the affect of emotion in specific physiological sensations. In the case of anger, Aristotle does write that there is a boiling of blood around the heart, and presumably the feel of such boiling.[82] But awareness of this is not essential to experiencing the pain of anger and is not mentioned among the elements of anger in the *Rhetoric* definition. Moreover, Aristotle is sensitive to the general point that a felt affect or arousal symptom does not adequately distinguish emotions. Contempt, spite, and insolence each involve pain, though these emotions are differentiated not by any peculiar pain but by the constitutive evaluations toward which they are directed.[83] Moreover, the affect of an emotion can change with a shift in the evaluative focus of that emotion. This seems clear in the case of love. In its simplest moments, love can be bittersweet, infused with both the giddy pleasure of vertiginous romance and the pain of vulnerability. Similarly, the exaltation of winning a race may be characterized both by a heady rush of joy and by a febrile tension of near loss. It is to Aristotle's credit that in his paradigm analysis of anger, the mix of pleasurable and painful affect is carefully preserved: There is pain at perceived injury and pleasure in the prospect of revenge. We often tend to classify emotions as "negative" or "positive" on the basis of predominant feel, and many of Aristotle's definitions (anger aside) focus on one affect or the other. Even so, we need to be mindful of the more subtle mixtures that make up specific emotions, and the quickness of even a flash of emotion in switching from one affective pole to another as the constitutive, evaluative focus shifts. In this sense, many emotions might more usefully be thought of as complex *systems* of emotions, with evaluations and felt affects that vary across them.

---

[81] Rh. 1386b16–17.   [82] DA 403a15-b1.   [83] Rh. 1378b10ff.

There is a final element in the account of Aristotelian emotion that needs discussion: the desiderative element of emotion. In what sense is emotion a motive for action? On this subject, Gisela Striker has recently laid bare the interesting contrast that whereas Book I of the *Rhetoric* stresses the role of emotions primarily as motivational (as kinds of irrational desire [*alogos orexis*]), Book II of the *Rhetoric* stresses instead an epistemic role for emotions, whereby emotions are primarily ways of evaluating and taking in information about one's surroundings.[84] The early motivational analysis, with its emphasis on *epithumia* and *thumos,* appetite and spirit, looks backward to a Platonic division of the soul; the epistemic account of emotions looks forward to the Stoics. Whatever the contrast between the two treatments in the *Rhetoric,* it is striking how relatively unimportant the desiderative role for emotions is in the central treatment in *Rhetoric* II. We are thrown off guard if we take the opening definition of anger to serve as a general template for all the emotions that follow. For Aristotle seems to define anger as having three elements – the *phantasia* that someone has injured you without warrant, the pain accompanying that evaluation, and a desire for revenge. If we standardize the account (as Justin Oakley recently has),[85] then an emotion involves an evaluation, an affect, and a desire. Some of the emotions Aristotle takes up do have desiderative elements mentioned: Spite involves a desire to thwart one's opponent, insolence, a desire to speak and act in ways that will cause shame to another. Emulation and envy are also taken up as actional: "Emulation makes us take steps to secure the good things in question," "envy makes us take steps to thwart our neighbor for having them."[86] But when we turn to calmness, confidence, shame, and pity, the actional components are not included. And more strikingly, the discussion of fear leaves out the "flight" response we so commonly associate with that emotion. Now, some of the reason for this absence may be simply local. The orator's primary interest is in "regarding whom" and "for what reasons" a person can be put in a "certain state of mind." There is no denying that emotions can motivate action as well as further thought. Why else would the orator be

---

[84] Striker (1996). [85] Oakley (1992). [86] Rh. 1388a35-b1.

interested in arousing them? But the orator's task aside, Aristotle seems to be making the very reasonable claim that the desiderative aspect of emotion can be absent in an account of emotion in a way the cognitive and affective elements of emotion simply cannot. Surely, a tragic audience can experience pity and fear without even an inhibited desire to act from those emotions. Fear requires the thought of something threatening and the feeling of pain directed at that construal; pity is the perception or thought that someone has suffered undeservingly and the response of pain directed at that evaluation. On the Aristotelian view, we do not have a proper emotion without these affectively charged cognitions. The popular behavioral view of emotions as "action-tendencies"[87] misses this point.

When we turn to the role of emotion in Aristotelian virtuous character, the motivational dimension of emotion also need not be as central as it is often made out to be. But this will take some explaining. For to some degree, the orthodox Kantian tradition in morality has gotten philosophers used to thinking of emotions as primarily motivational. The famous example in the opening of the *Groundwork,* in which skepticism is cast on the moral worth of sympathy, takes up sympathy as motivational. It is an inclination that can haphazardly lead to the morally right action. But since it is unreliable as the basis of a motive, either because some have it and others don't, or because some have it but can't always summon it when they need it, morality needs to find a more secure foundation in duty. If we are truly moral, we do something because it is right, irrespective of whether we are inclined to do it by emotion. If the action is overdetermined, and the result of mixed motivation, then doing it because it is right must still be sufficient for the action.

In some sense, the motivational role of emotions can become uninteresting in an Aristotelian account as well. For if a character is truly habituated with emotions that are not in conflict with one's judgments of what is best, then it might be argued that *that* state of nonconflict is sufficient for acting on one's judgments of

---

[87] See, for example, Arnold (1960).

what is right.[88] Does one need supportive emotion as well for the judgment to be effective? Isn't the important work being done by one's judgment that the action is fine and not by any positive emotions, in addition? Doesn't an additional requirement that positive emotion be there to motivate the action become either too stringent, or otiose? As the Stoics charge, the thought of virtue and duty alone is sufficient.[89]

One way out of this problem, and a way of reemploying emotion within virtue, is to acknowledge that the very judging that some action is right, that is, the work of practical wisdom, typically involves the epistemic capacities of emotions. Emotional sensitivities are ways of *tracking* the morally relevant "news." What is salient with grief is that humans suffer and face loss; with pity, that they sometimes fail through blameless ignorance, duress, sickness, or accident. The *Rhetoric* II emphasis on emotions as evaluations of events as good or bad stresses this epistemic and evaluative capacity of emotions. Of course, when we relate this capacity to moral judgment and choice, it needs to be emphasized that the news the emotions bear is not indefeasible, nor is it all that is required for choice. Part of what emotions do is alert us to possible *occasions* for moral choice, as well as to information we might not notice were we to look on stripped of emotional engagement. From here we may go on to deliberate, in those instances where a deliberative question is raised. But more fundamentally, to make use of the evaluations contained in the reports of the emotions in no sense precludes further discussion about the accuracy of the information on particular occasions. I take it that this is simply part of the general descriptive and critical process required for wisely judging what is salient in a particular case. Although Aristotle sometimes is read as suggesting that the wise person can see (or be sensitive to) what is relevant in a flash, it makes more sense to think of "seeing aright" as itself a process continuous with the discursive and deliberative capacities of practical reason. On this view, as I describe it in

---

[88] Annas (1993, 64) raises this issue; I discuss it further in my review of her book in Sherman (1995d).

[89] See Nussbaum's (1994, 412) discussion of the Stoic "motivational argument."

Chapter 6, the perceptual model of practical reason emphasized in Book VI of the *Nicomachean* (and I am including here the role of emotions as ways of seeing) and the deliberative model emphasized more in Book III become intertwined.

It might be too stringent to say that a necessary condition of any act of moral judgment requires that the proper emotions be engaged. I do not argue for such a strong claim. Even so, I think part of our resistance to a claim about the role of emotions in moral judgment has much to do with a misconception of emotions as always intense and strongly felt, rather than as the subtle shades of coloring they often are. Still, it is a separate question just what motivational role emotions that have served as epistemic sensitivities will have. It would be peculiar to think that someone who felt compassion for a person in distress and who decided to act generously, in part on the basis of that report of the emotions, was not in any way *moved* by the emotion. Emotions just often do seem to have "energy" or a desiderative component, we might say. But I think the crucial point is that in the case of virtue there is a decision to act because it is judged as the right thing to do, in this way, at this time, toward this person. To say, in addition, that we are moved to act by feelings can seem to leave the feeling dangling, unattached to the moral choice, in a way that it is not when we say that part of our very recognition of the moral occasion and of the rightness of the action depended on the emotion.

But these remarks on the internal motivation of virtuous judgment aside, and assuming that in some cases we do act "from" or "out of" an emotion, what kind of account of emotional motivation does Aristotle give? One way of framing the question is to ask whether emotional motivation falls under the general schema of the practical syllogism. Is emotional motivation, for Aristotle, essentially a case of acting from a pro-attitude (emotion being, in this case, the specific form *orexis* takes in the major premise of such a syllogism) combined with a belief (as expressed in the minor premise)? (Note that emotion may also figure in the minor premise, giving us, as I have emphasized elsewhere, perceptual information about specific particulars relevant for choice, for instance, that *this* person is needy or *this* option is attractive to me. Emotion is a mode of attending what is salient. However, I am now fastening on the desire component of emotion – as in anger's desire for revenge; it is this component that locates emotion in the major premise, even if emotion figures too in the minor premise.)[90] The syllogistic schema implies purposiveness: I do *x* in order to promote *y*. I cross the street in order to visit my neighbor. Similarly, I strike Felicity in order to satisfy my anger.

But this way of thinking about the acting out of emotion may be too rational and not in fact descriptive of how we sometimes *do* act from anger. We often do slam doors and storm out of rooms, even when no one is around to notice. We act impulsively, without any strategy at all. "Anger must always be felt toward some particular individual," Aristotle says, and someone that can be "aware of our anger," that is, an individual, like Callias or Socrates.[91] Presumably he means there is something irrational in wreaking damage on an inanimate object. Kicking the cabinet door while no one watches or punching a pillow in the privacy of one's room, are not, on Aristotle's view, paradigm cases of acting from anger.[92] Defacing a photograph of an ex-lover comes closer to the mark, for here at least there is symbolic aim.[93] But still, these cases of anger don't really aim (effectively or not) at revenge. They are ways of venting – ways of letting it out. They are reactive more than purposive, even though they involve voluntary actions.[94] They are certainly not the involuntary responses of the viscera.

[90] For the syllogism as representing the "movers" of desire and belief, see DA 433a9, MA 700b17–19. Accordingly, at MA 701a25 Aristotle refers to the major premise as the premise of the "good" and the minor premise as the premise of the "possible." Cf. NE VII.3 for the idea of the major and minor premises as "universal" and "particular." For further discussion of the practical syllogism, see Sherman (1989, ch. 3); for a recent critique, see Richardson (1994).

[91] Rh. 1378a35; 1380b25; 1382a5.

[92] Compare Wittgenstein's remarks here: "When I am angry about something, I sometimes beat on the ground or against a tree with my cane. But I do not for that matter believe that the earth is guilty or that beating is of any help. I ventilate my anger. And all rituals are of this sort" (quoted in Solomon 1973).

[93] I once read in the paper that when Jerry Brown was asked by a supporter to autograph a picture of him in which Clinton also appeared, he first scratched out Clinton's face.

[94] Perhaps Aristotle's distinction between what is "merely voluntary" and what is "prohairetic" might be useful here; see NE III. 2. But Aristotle wants to

Consider in this vein my tousling my lover's hair *out of* affection.[95] Do I do it *in order to* show my affection? Sometimes "yes," sometimes "no." The answer is "yes" when there is doubt in the air or need for affirmation. I make a point of expressing my affection in that way. But other times, I do it for no reason at all. Or, I might flippantly say, because I want to. The same might go for kissing. "Why did you kiss me?" my son might ask. "Because I felt like it," I might reply.

These examples seem to contrast with Aristotle's standard example of voluntary action schematized under the practical syllogism. I drink in order to slake thirst with the belief that there is something quaffable nearby. Or, again, if I am not thirsty, I drink in order to enjoy the robust orange flavor, with the thought that this drink holds out such promise. Whether or not conscious, there is a purposiveness to my action to which I can assent to if questioned. Even if I say, "I drank the juice for no reason at all," if pressed, there is presumably some pleasure I expect to get from drinking. In that sense, it is rationalized by some further end. But this is different from my reply to my son, "I kissed you *because* I felt like it." Granted, this may be elliptical for *"because* I love you" or *"out of* affection." This is something of a reason, but the reason is not *in order to express my love.* The kiss just is my expression of love. The "because" ends with what the kiss symbolizes. I don't think of it, at least on this occasion, as a good I (even subliminally) intend here to promote. As Rosalind Hursthouse puts the matter, it is "not that the agent does the action *in order to* express the emotion, but rather qua expression of emotion."[96]

---

explain all voluntary motion by the practical syllogism, and I am here suggesting that some ways of "expressing" emotion may seem inappropriate for this kind of explanation.

[95] The example is Hursthouse's (1991).

[96] Hursthouse 1991. Dan Robinson has suggested that the case of my kissing my son is no different from the standard thirst-slaking case, and so does not challenge the practical syllogism model. If I kiss my son as a habitual mode of gratification, then the "because" is answered by the pleasure the action secures. But my point is that kissing or tousling hair is, in some cases, not *in order to* secure pleasure or express affection. Instead, in these cases, the action just *expresses* the emotion.

Still other cases of emotional motivation are more like *acting on emotion* than acting *out of emotion*, at least in the sense that the expression "acting on emotion" suggests less of an impulsive and more of a controlled or deliberative response. In such cases, coming to feel anger may be viewed as an opportunity for learning how to act from the emotion in constructive and socially appropriate or adaptive ways. One works out ways of *dealing* with one's emotions, ways, as agents, of responding to one's more impulsive urgings. Desires such as those for revenge join with beliefs about how *best* to act on those desires. The conclusion is a reasoned decision. "Best" may have a moral flavor to it, but not necessarily. One may act *on* one's anger in ways that deflect it or, again, in ways that sweeten and deepen it. The point is that one responds, with some deliberateness; one creates an agenda of what to do when in the grip of an emotion. One becomes a practical agent who can exercise a certain amount of choice about how to act on emotions and how, in general, to stand toward them.

Imagine in this vein a child's mounting frustration at being tagged regularly as "it" in a tag game. Just when he is ready to tag other kids, they get to base. When he does succeed in tagging someone else, he is not fast enough to get to base himself. He becomes "it" yet again. The frustration leads to anger that he's being unfairly picked on, and to angry behavior in the form of abusive language and physical hitting. These responses are seen as ways of getting back, ways of punishing the perceived antagonists. Yet over time and with coaching, he learns to react in more toned-down ways. He comes to see that there are more acceptable ways of registering his anger. He can renegotiate with other players the rules for "safe" time, eliminate the tag-back move, limit how many times in a row a player can be "it." There is a range of alternative outlets for venting his frustration. Trying these out runs parallel to an exercise in instrumental reasoning. The child is looking for some effective but "appropriate" way of satisfying the urgings of an emotion. After time, these ways may themselves serve to subdue the emotion, changing perceptions and evaluations that ground the emotion itself.

I have spoken largely of negative emotions as presenting themselves as registering reasons for action. But positive emotions, too, can be excitatory. They are not always or typically calm states. True, some will be just that, Aristotle reminds us, as when we are free from pain, or feel inoffensive pleasure or even the expectancy of reasonable hope. But other positive emotions can pressure action, with responses that range from reactive and expressive to strategic. To jump for joy is to release excitement, just as to start out of fear is. A scream of ecstasy vents tension, as does a scream of fear. Romantic love is notorious for its driven activity, for its headstrong "pressuring" for relief, and for its loquaciousness. But while its intensity often pressures impulsive actions, another side of love fosters creativity, opening up vistas and new arenas for action that were once shut from view. This again may have deep explanations having to do with the lifting of defenses, and with the role of identification and transference of value that comes as a part of important relationships. I cannot explore these matters here, although Aristotle's own remarks about the important place of *philia* within human development are suggestive in this regard. The general point for now is that emotional motivation takes many forms, and that among these responses some may mark a creativity and depth of vision that takes us some way from unmediated, primitive impulse.

At this point we can begin to see the broad compatibility between an Aristotelian account of the emotions and an account of the moral significance of emotions, along the lines limned in this chapter's Section 3. Emotions are not blind sensations, but judgings of what we take to be good and bad in the world. They track salience in virtue of making evaluations about the world. These evaluations may present reasons for action. Moreover, through emotions we convey to others not just that we are in pleasure or pain, but that we care about something in particular, or are the sort of person who takes certain things to be important. We convey and record determinate information through our emotions.

Of course, those who hold a sensation theory of the emotions might also see a close connection between certain kinds of evaluations and the emotion as feeling. They could argue that certain beliefs typically cause those kinds of affects.[97] But insofar as the

[97] For a good discussion of this argument, to which I am here indebted, see

connection is not conceptual but merely contingent, it could be, on such a view, that while fear is typically caused by something appearing threatening, on other occasions that same feeling could be experienced without having that characteristic thought or, indeed, any cognition paired up with that affect at all. For it is the feel alone that constitutes the emotion, and anything it is associated with is purely contingent. Thoughts, such as that nectarines are mottled red, could be connected with fear, so long as the feel is characteristic. The Aristotelian view of emotions as intentional not only is inherently more plausible but gives a more natural account of how emotions track salience. Emotional responses are responses to intentional objects. They represent something about how we see the world. Thus, fear is conceptually a matter of responding to what we take to be a threat, anger, to what we see as an injury, and so on. We read the news, in part, by reading our emotions. If our emotions are just feels, then reading emotions will give us little more than the feel, even if the emotions are contingently connected with certain types of evaluations. These matters will be important when we come to take up Kant's analysis of emotions.

Here, we should appreciate that Aristotle himself, in talking about the affective structure of virtue (as for example, in *Nicomachean Ethics* II), does not outline these various ways in which emotions are morally significant. In a sense he simply assumes they will play a pervasive role in the active life of virtue. His view, briefly for now, is that virtuous character states are the developmental product of habituated emotions combined with and informed by practical reasoning. When we actualize character, we do so through expressing both fine emotion and fine choices. My suggestion is that we best understand the full significance of emotion in the expression of character when we separate out the various roles as we did earlier. My present claim is that Aristotle's own analysis of emotions, as put forth in the *Rhetoric*, gives broad support for these roles.

Oakley (1992, 22). Descartes seems to hold this sort of view of emotion as sensations caused by belief. See note 28 above.

5 EMOTIONS AND THEIR RELATION TO CHOICE

Aristotle holds that we are morally assessed not only for our actions, but for our emotions as well. Both can be praiseworthy and blameworthy, both fine and shameful, both determinable according to the mean. Among other things, I take this to mean not merely that we are held in esteem or disesteem for our emotions (i.e., admired or condemned), but that, in many cases, though not all, we can also be credited and blamed for our emotions. That is, in many cases we are held morally responsible for them.[98] But in what sense, on Aristotle's view, can we be held responsible for our emotions? In what sense are they "up to us?" In what sense are they related to choice?

For some philosophers, the alleged involuntarism of the emotions is, as we have said, connected with their passivity. If the emotions are passions (modes of being affected), then the correct attitude toward them is helplessness or resignation. They are phenomena beyond our control and deliberate choice. Passive with regard to our emotions, we are responsible neither for them nor for the actions to which they may lead. Indeed, passions become sources of excuses. Remarks such as "I couldn't help it, I was

[98] This is a complicated matter. No doubt the practices of praising and blaming are also educative attitudes. They are ways of pointing out exemplary and defective behavior, and ways of exhorting and deterring. Also, recent discussions of the important role of luck and external goods in Aristotle's writings well indicate that Aristotle is simply not as preoccupied as a modern, such as Kant, in fully separating out luck and passivity from the sphere of moral agency. Still, at such places as NE 1109b30, for example, Aristotle makes it clear that he means to link praise and blame with the voluntary. It is also worth noting that the Revised Oxford Translation is misleading here. That translation reads, "Since excellence is concerned with passions and actions, and on voluntary passions and actions praise and blame are bestowed." More literally Aristotle says, " Since excellence is concerned with passions and actions, and on that which is voluntary, praise and blame are bestowed." Aristotle would be reluctant to think of emotions as voluntary, though as I argue Section 5, above, he does think they are nonetheless subject to choice in a more indirect way. For a contemporary discusion of different forms of moral assessment of emotion, and a comparison with assessment of action, see Oakley (1992, ch. 5).

fuming with anger" "imply that passivity abnegates responsibil-ity."[99] The theme of the passivity of emotion is notorious in tradi-tional Kantian ethics, and an impetus for locating virtue in the direct exercise of the will.

To what extent does the *Nicomachean Ethics* distance itself from this modern picture? Aristotle's term for the emotions is *pathē*, coming from the verb *paschein*, to be acted upon, in other words, to suffer. It refers to a state or condition of the soul resulting from something acting upon it, and contrasts with *poiein* (to make) and *prattein* (to do). The term *pathē* is closely related to another form – *pathēmata* – which in earlier writers refers to what is experienced by way of the misfortunes and calamities that befall one. In the *Nicomachean Ethics*, Aristotle explicitly emphasizes the passivity of the emotions, and the literal sense that they are ways or modes of being acted upon. "In respect of the emotions [*ta pathē*] we are said to be moved [*kineisthai*]."[100] "By capacities I mean the things with respect to which we are capable of feeling these [emotions], of being angry or being pained or feeling pity" (*orgisthēnai, lupēthēnai, eleēsai*).[101] In the case of the first two emotions, the grammar explicitly indicates a passive state, a state of being acted upon.

Passivity is not linked here to involuntarism. But just how and if emotions are related to choice is not made explicit either. In-deed, in the discussion from which I have been drawing in *Nic-omachean* II.5, Aristotle contrasts passions or emotions with states of character, claiming that states of character, not emotions, in-volve choice (they are a *hexis prohairetikē*) and that, again, states of character, not emotions, are the objects of moral praise and blame.[102] This contrast seems perplexing since emotions, as we have been saying, along with actions, are the modes by which

---

[99] See Solomon (1973, 1984) for an attack on this position, and critiques of Solomon in Gordon (1987) and Roberts (1984); see also Peters and Mace (1962). Solomon's argument accepts the inference that if emotions are passive, then they must be involuntary. His solution is to deny the premise. Emotions, he argues, are not passions but kinds of actions. As actions, they are within the domain of our responsibility. Gordon and Roberts deny that passivity entails involuntarism. This is essentially Aristotle's position.

[100] NE 1106a6.   [101] NE 1105b25.   [102] NE 1106a2; 1106a8–9.

virtuous states of character are expressed, and virtues involve choice precisely in the sense that they can be expressed in ways that are deliberate and chosen.[103] It is true, intuitively speaking, we do not choose to express our character through emotions in quite the way that we choose to express it through action. Aristotle might be intending by these comments in *Nicomachean* II.5 to restrict choice to only those realizations of virtue through action. But this would be peculiar at best, since we are told repeatedly that both emotion and action fall under what is praiseworthy or blameworthy in character. The two modes, action and passion, seem to go together. And the sense in which moral accreditation is applied to them is not differentiated. In the case of generosity, the Aristotelian agent chooses finely when and toward whom and from what sources to give money, but also is the sort of person for whom affect and manner bespeak liberality. Generous feelings motivate the action, but also, insofar as those feelings are settled and not in nagging conflict with others, they are conveyed in attitude as well. The full expression of character is subject to what seems to be univocal moral assessment: the virtuous agent hits the mean with regard to both emotion and action; the virtuous agent's actions and emotions are fine (*kalon*). There seems to be univocal use of the evaluative terms.

But still there is something odd in putting this point through the notion of choice. For even if emotion and action both express character, they are not subject to choice in the same way. Action seeks to bring about some apparent good through beliefs about available means and constituents of desired ends. In the case of many actions that are routine, we no longer have to go through any explicit sort of reasoning. Even so, there is purposive promotion of an apparent good. We take a strategic or instrumental stance that can be explained in terms of a belief and desire state. Emotion, in contrast, does not itself necessarily involve a choice to promote some good. Rather, it is a sensitivity to events and objects that hold importance to us. It is a way of being affected, a way of noticing and reacting, but not itself a way of doing. As we have seen, emotion may go on to inspire action through a desiderative

---

[103] The problem is posed in roughly this way by Kosman (1980).

element. But this motivational aspect of emotion does not exhaust emotion or give us license to think of emotion as little more than a composite belief and desire that lead to a chosen action. Action clearly involves choice of an apparent good; emotion is a way of judging an apparent good.[104]

Despite these points, Aristotle is nonetheless pointing to an important way that the emotional structure of character involves choice, and consequently, an important way in which we do choose how to express our character through emotions. What is fundamental here is the notion of habituating good character. The choice is in cultivating or habituating emotions so that they will become reliable resources for the many roles emotions play in the moral life. Through education, we choose the "condition" of our emotions, choose to transform or cultivate them, as part of the process of forming our states of character or *hexeis*. We choose to bring about, ultimately, certain emotional consequences by actions we take. Put this way, choosing emotions involves an education of consciously shaping emotional capacities and refining them into more discerning sensitivities. To choose emotions, on an Aristotelian view, is to choose to cultivate them. Thus, it is not that we can always will a given episode of emotion but, rather, that we can develop a state of character that shapes emotional capacities as an enduring resource of character. Through certain efforts that are within our control we can learn to regulate our emotions, as well as more robustly transform them. As a result of this pattern of choice, emotions become not raw impulses or capacities, but socialized modes of response. They are influenced by choice over time, even if they are not a matter of choice at any moment. That is to say, in the establishment of character there are few shortcuts. What is required is a gradual process of refinement and control of one's more primitive emotional responses. It is of course true that a good deal of early learning involves the choices and guidance *of others*. Aristotle, in particular, is one to emphasize that parents' early reciprocation and interaction with children is crucial for character development, and he stresses repeatedly, as we shall see, the irreplaceability of early emotional habituation

---

[104] See DA 431a8–10.

within the family. But even where there is strong guidance and choice from outside, as in the early childhood years, Aristotle still holds that the child's own cognitive and affiliative efforts contribute significantly to the shaping of emotions. Aristotelian habituation is never a mindless process, but one that must engage the learner's critical efforts from the start.[105] On the whole, his remarks on virtue can be understood in a profound way as charting a developmental course whereby the transformation of one's emotional nature becomes increasingly, over time (with the accumulation of experience and the growth of practical reason), more one's own responsibility and choice. This is consistent with a theory emphasizing that the good life is valued principally not because of what happens to us, but because of one's own effort, achieved through "study and care." "To entrust to chance what is greatest and most fine would be a very defective arrangement"[106] Similarly, to think of emotions as merely natural accidents, or merely accidents of others' training, would be to abdicate responsibility for a part of the good life over which one can have considerable influence.

Aristotle continues with these general considerations about the status of emotions in the *Nicomachean* II.5 account. That which is neither within the range of our control nor subject to praise and blame is the *unqualified* or *simple* capacity to be affected emotionally (*dunasthai paschein haplōs*).[107] This is a natural capacity or disposition (*dunatoi men esmen phusei*) and is quite distinct from being good or bad, which "we become not by nature" but by habituation.[108] The former is the capacity to feel fear, delight, hatred, friendliness, or gentleness unconditionally, without respect to the circumstances, the degree, or the object. It is affective susceptibility, more or less the same for all.[109] But as we have just

---

[105] Relevant here is Aristotle's interesting observation (Phys. 184b12–13) that the very young child first calls all men "father," and all women "mother," then quickly learns to discriminate. See also the Poet. IV on early learning through *mimêsis*.

[106] NE 1099b17–24; 1095b26.   [107] NE 1106a7–8.   [108] NE 1106a9.

[109] Absent in this discussion is any notion of constitutional differences of temperament. Contrast Pol. VIII, where there is discussion of different emotional temperaments, notably along class lines.

said, Aristotle indicates that there is a further developmental and social story to be told here – that within the context of important relations to others, children come to feel emotions in increasingly more differentiated and selective ways, gradually arriving at the full intentionality characteristic of adult emotion and, in the best of circumstances, characteristic of mature virtue.[110] That is, the stable condition of feeling specific emotions finely – in the right way, in the right circumstances, for the right reasons – marks the cultivated emotional tendencies constitutive of virtue.

Still, Aristotle's conception of habituating the emotions (and its connection with choice) might seem limited in an important way. On the Aristotelian view, character development (*ethismos*) is largely a matter of early education. The bulk of the work is done early on under the tutelage of teachers and elders and within the context of early family life. What comes later is more a matter of refinement and stabilization than true character change. Granted, as we have been arguing, this early process will be a dynamic and interactive one, with natural *philia* the privileged context for reciprocal love (*antiphilēsis*) and mutual care (*eunoia*). The interactive process will engage cognitive capacities, and depend upon a child's active contributions, at the earliest stages. Explanation and reasoning will be introduced appropriate to the cognitive level of the learner. In this sense early habituation is neither mindless nor passive. Still, what takes place at a young age makes all the difference. "It makes no small difference, then, whether we form habits of one kind or of another immediately from youth; it makes a very great difference, or rather *all* the difference."[111] And if one

---

[110] See NE VIII.12 and Pol. II.1 for a sketch of the development of the attachment relation in natural *philia;* also Sherman (1989, chs. 4 and 5). Aristotle interestingly includes as a part of the NE account the idea that children's love for parents requires the development of intentional capacities for focusing on objects: "Children love their parents only after time has elapsed and they have acquired understanding or perception" (1161b25–8). On developmental remarks about intentionality and the discrimination of objects, see Meta. 980a20–27, Phys. 184b11–12, Poet. 1448b4–12, Rh. 1371b9–10. It may be, as some researchers now think, that intentional capacities for discriminating objects are importantly connected with the formation of object ties to parents or caregivers (Shapiro and Stern 1989).

[111] NE 1103b23–25; cf. 1104b12; 1105a1–6; 1095b5–8.

lacks this proper beginning in the right pleasures and pains, there is little hope for change. Moderation and transformation of the emotions depend upon establishing the right states of character early on.

> For he who lives as passion directs will not hear argument that dissuades him, nor understand it if he does; and how can we persuade one in such a state to change his ways? . . . The character, then, must somehow be there already with a kinship to excellence, loving what is fine and hating what is base.[112]

Indeed, Aristotle's own lectures, though practical, are, as we have said, intended for an audience already trained in good character. "Anyone who is to listen intelligently to lectures about what is fine and just . . . must have been brought up in good habits."[113] "The soul of the student must first have been culti-vated by means of habits for noble joy and noble hatred, like earth which is to nourish the seed."[114] It is not simply that otherwise listeners will not be converted. It is that his lectures are not designed as a therapy that *can* convert or catalyze substantial, adult character change. To be sure, Aristotle maintains that character is deepened and refined by deliberation and ethical reflection of the sort his lectures are meant to inspire. Laws, too, will play a crucial role in later character training, and are meant "to cover the whole of life." "It is surely not enough that when they are young they should get the right nurture and attention; since they must, even when they are grown up, practice and be habituated to them [i.e., the laws]."[115] Friendship and community will also have a powerful place in the maintenance of good character, providing the kinds of dynamic interactions important for emulation, and the continuing transmission of values. But profound character change is not something Aristotle ever really envisions as a possible moment of adult life. It is certainly not something that philosophy as argument can undertake. "It is hard, if not impossible, to remove by argument the traits that have

[112] NE 1179b26–29.   [113] NE 1095b3–6.   [114] NE 1179b24–26.
[115] NE 1180a1–4.

81

long since been incorporated in the character."[116] The path of early childhood holds the key for good character.

 The view of philosophy as therapy that can reconstitute character will await Stoic treatment.[117] At the heart of their program is adult reeducation of the soul. The adult committed to virtue must and can transform her soul through practical stratagems that involve philosophical belief as well as behavioral practices. As Cicero puts it, one must row the "oars of dialectic" in order to cure the diseases of the soul, especially irrational passions. For Aristotle, in contrast, transformation and control of the emotions depend primarily upon early habituation. The moderate character is formed at youth. Psychogogy (a leading forth of the soul) is for the young.

I shall return to this point and its implications for conceiving of virtue as an ongoing, developmental process. At present, however, we still need to consider in greater detail the habituation and control of emotion as a part of character formation. How do we refine emotions and make them more discriminating and less impulsive? Just what do we do to our emotions such that it makes sense to credit us for expressing our emotions well? Aristotle famously tells us that action leads to the corresponding character states. We become just by doing just actions, and temperate by acting temperately.[118] But in what sense does this take us beyond character conceived of narrowly as a disposition to act? In what sense does it take us to character as manifest also in emotion? What do we do, and choose to do, in order to cultivate certain emotions?

In taking up these questions, I shall have to wander from the texts, since Aristotle is silent on many of the details. Perhaps this has to with what was mentioned earlier – that those he invites to listen to his lectures are already well habituated. The training by which emotions are regulated and transformed is largely behind them. The task at hand is to deepen their understanding of what constitutes the good life in a way that enlightens, more than profoundly transforms, their habits of good living. But whatever the

---

[116] NE 1179b15ff.
[117] See Chapter 3; see also Nussbaum (1994).   [118] NE II.4.

reasons for the spottiness in detail, I take myself to be limning an account that is in keeping with the spirit of his theory.[119]

6 CULTIVATING EMOTIONS

Common parlance includes a host of locutions which presume that emotions are "up to us" in various ways. Thus we exhort ourselves and others by such phrases as "pull yourself together," "snap out of it," "put on a good face," "lighten up," "be cheerful," "think positive," "keep a stiff upper lip." In many instances, what we are being implored to do is to take on the semblance of an emotion so that it can "take hold" and rub off on our inner state. Practice as if you believe and you will believe. As Ronald de Sousa puts it, "earnest pretense is the royal road to sincere faith."[120] Sometimes we "pretend" through behavioral changes – through changes in facial expressions, body gestures, and vocalizations that evoke in us a changed mood.[121] If we are fuming, relaxing our facial muscles, ungnarling our fingers, breathing deeply and slowly may put us in the frame of mind to see things in a calmer light. We try to inhibit the present emotion by inhibiting the physiognomic or physiological responses that typically accompany it. The James–Lange theory may be in the background here, and its notion of proprioceptive feedback from expression. Something like this may undergird Aristotle's notion of becoming by doing. Putting on the look of an emotion may introduce into our thoughts the evaluations that typically constitute such emotions.

Some of these suggestions involve nuancing an emotional state from outside in – trying on more luxuriant smiles as a way of trying to become more loving. But equally, a newly felt emotion

[119] I supplement the account of habituation also in Sherman (1989, ch. 5), where my specific concern is to show the cognitive structure of habituation. In the present section, I am more interested in detailing the cultivation of emotion, apart from more general issues of the cognitive nature of practice and habituation.
[120] De Sousa (1988).
[121] See Ekman (1973, 1982); Goffman (1959); Izard (1977).

may demand a new look, a concrete and stable realization for oneself and others to behold. Here the nudging works from inside out, though still it is the facial or gestural expression that coaches the emotion. Thus, we can fuel the flames of an emotion by allowing it bodily expression. To weep may intensify our grief, or simply bring us to acknowledge its presence. There are yet other sorts of actions I might take that are not a matter of body language or putting on a new face. I may fail to talk myself out of love, discovering that only when I change locales do the old ways begin to lose their grip. Other times, it is more trial by fire: staying put and exposing myself to what is painful in order to become inured. The process involves desensitization. Again, these various behavioral and expressive methods give some force to the Aristotelian idea of becoming by doing.

But of course we would expect that on an Aristotelian view emotional changes require not merely facial or behavioral alteration but an evaluative change (a change of the evaluative or cognitive content of emotion); moreover, that behavioral or expressive changes really prepare us for changes at this level. But if this is so, then there are more direct ways to alter emotions through changes of perception or belief. A child frightened by goblins she sees in her room may be comforted by an adult who turns on the lights, and shows her that what she took to be goblins were just the shadows cast by her beloved stuffed animals. When the lights go out again, she sees the silhouettes differently, as part of a friendlier, cozier scene. A patient depressed by the possibility of relapse might be reminded of the statistics in her favor and the steady progress she has made to date. Seeing things in a new light, with new emphases and stresses, can help allay fear. We shift the gestalt, recompose the scene. In a different vein, anger at a child may subside when one focuses less on minor annoyances and more on admirable traits. In other instances, experiencing emotions is a matter of giving inner assent to a thought – of allowing oneself to dwell on certain fantasies or stories and the emotions they structure. Many of these cases include discursive methods that involve persuasion or simply pointing out how things look from a different point of view. The evaluations that are a part of emotion are exposed and reassessed for their reasonableness.

Mental training might also follow a more methodical and introspective model. One can learn to attend carefully to the onset of certain emotions and the way one's mind tends to move from one perceived object of importance to another. Through this kind of watchful mindfulness, an agent can become aware of the beliefs that ground particular emotions, and intentionally try to reject those she thinks are irrational either on prudential grounds (for example, they cause me discomfort) and/or epistemic grounds (they are not adequately warranted).[122]

Aristotle has little familiarity with this more introspective mode of mental training. But interestingly, we don't see indications in his ethical writings of the more garden variety approach of trying to change emotions through revision of underlying evaluations and thoughts. The absence is curious, given his explicit emphasis on persuasion and discursive methods in the *Rhetoric*, as ways of changing emotions. Why don't we find a similar emphasis in the ethical writings? Some of the explanation may be, as we said earlier, that ethical cultivation of the emotions is reserved by and large for the young. Aristotle's point might be that although habituation engages their cognitive capacities, children often learn how to differentiate and control emotions more in the context of doing (e.g., playing) than in the context of explicit self-reflection or argument. To be sure, persuasion will be at work at the earliest stages of moral development in countless forms (e.g., exhortations to see things this way or in this light, to see the advantage of this approach rather than that). This is underscored by the language of *Nicomachean* I.13, which analogizes the lower part of the soul's compliance to reason with a child listening to the exhortations of her parent. And again in the division of the soul in

---

122 I have in mind the kind of intentional change of belief that is part of certain Buddhist practices, but that also seems to characterize Stoic therapy. Mental control involves a *wish* to change beliefs for therapeutic reasons, such as reducing suffering and anxiety. But the process also involves extensive *philosophical* therapy, whereby one seeks epistemic evidence for these new beliefs. See Guenther (1989); Thera (1986); Thurman (1984, 1990).

I.7, the rational soul is divided up into two parts, one that is obedient and can be persuaded by reason (*epipeithes logōi*) and another that more properly possesses reason and issues theoretical and practical discriminations.[123] Even though the formal apparatus is in place, Aristotle doesn't go into detail about how persuasion and discourse can change emotions. In this sense, he doesn't exploit the rich cognitive *Rhetoric* account for a model of emotional development. Again, maybe he thinks the analogy between the courtroom and the developmental sphere doesn't quite hold. In the ethical works, Aristotle is thinking about *character* change, changes of emotional tendencies and patterns, not just the provocation of this or that discrete occurrence of emotion. As such, character development requires deeper and broader forms of persuasion than those that characterize courtroom oratory. What is required for ethical training are more subtle methods of persuasion that are at work, for example, when children identify with role models, adopt their patterns of seeing and doing, share in activities that support certain objects of attachment and value, learn ways of response through reciprocal interaction in play and in general, through the mutual flow within strong affiliative bonds. Here what is trained are patterns of reaction rather than an accidental or isolated response. To abstract some primarily intellectual or forensic method from these exchanges would be to tear the cognitive part of character change away from its affective and social fabric. Aristotle seems right to resist that move, especially in the context of early education. Character excellence depends upon habituation and experience, as he puts it, not abstract intellectual instruction (*ek didaskalias*).[124]

But still, we would expect to see some development of the point that emotions can be deepened and changed through discourse and persuasion (of the more embodied varieties already mentioned), and yet we don't find this explicitly argued for in the ethical writings. We don't see Aristotle taking up the idea that emotions can be transformed by gradual transformation of their evaluative contents. We don't see him arguing that adults can revise or reform their emotional dispositions through a thor-

---

[123] NE 1098a4–5.   [124] NE 1103a14–18.

oughgoing reflection on the patterns of evaluations constitutive of them. The implicit *Rhetoric* idea that there are evaluative construals that ground our emotions, and that revision of these can work toward substantive change of our emotional lives, is not something explicitly adumbrated in the ethical writings. The question is, does Aristotle think adults cannot significantly change emotional habits, or did he simply not systematize his views, in the way, say, the Stoics do by taking adult therapy of the emotions to be their primary and explicit concern? Their claim is that as adults we must reevaluate not merely *what* we emotionally invest in, but *that* we invest at all.

We shall say more about this in the next chapter, but a few words are relevant here. Briefly put, according to Stoic doctrine, emotion just is judgment. It is a cognitive assent, an embracing or a commitment to a presentation, typically expressed linguistically through a proposition. However, for the Stoics, emotions are by definition defective and in error. They are assents to false valuations about objects in the world. Given that these evaluations are attachments to what is impermanent in the world, they can lead to disturbances and anxiety that ultimately destabilize the pursuit of happiness. To remove this threat, the Stoics recommend extirpation through philosophical therapy. Extirpation works on the assumption that emotions can be treated by radical changes of belief through persuasion and philosophical enlightenment. For if emotions are no more than misappropriation of belief, then they should be treatable by a method that works essentially at the level of belief. Persuasion and argument should be able to grab hold of these beliefs entirely, without remainder. Accordingly, the Stoics propose philosophy as a spiritual therapy that cures the diseases or passions of the soul.

The attraction of the Stoic view rests in its powerful description of the anguish of the engaged emotional life. Emotions depend on attachment, (that is, investing objects with importance and care), yet objects of attachment are never perfectly stable. Abandonment, separation, failure, and loss are the constant costs of love, effort, and friendship. The more tightly we cling to our investments, the more dependent we become on what is uncontrolled and outside our own mastery. Self-reproach and persecution are often responses to lack of control. In our relations with others, the same clinginess of emotions can lead to overstepping what is appropriate, just as it can lead to exclusionary preferences and partialities.

Aristotle is certainly not open to the Stoics' more radical form of adult reeducation aimed at extirpating emotional investment. For he doesn't see the vulnerability to which the emotions expose us as an inherent evil. Even so, his own account of moderation can be viewed as compatible with the general idea of emotional therapy that the Stoics develop. The absence of explicit discussion in the ethical treatises of the idea of character development as requiring emotional changes through changes in evaluations does not mean there isn't room for such a story in a more worked-out version of his view. Nor does the account of habituation preclude this.[125] We can reconstruct the point in the following way. Aristotle tells us, for example, that hitting the mean with regard to anger requires a sensitive judgment regarding toward whom, for what reason, and in what circumstances it is reasonable to feel anger.[126] But certainly we would expect capacities for control and sensitive response not to be a static matter as we reach adulthood. Each occasion of a miss or near miss is occasion for self-observation about what was going on, and what really was at stake. If one gets too angry about a remark made toward oneself, then one may have to reconsider just why one overreacted and got so easily bruised. This seems to be an obvious part of the perfection of virtue and an important way in which the emotional structure of virtue is constantly being informed by our reflective capacities. "Being good strictly speaking requires practical wisdom"[127] in the sense now that critically reflecting on one's life brings one back regularly to the status of one's emotional responses and their adequacy in supporting our finest judgments. Commitments to generosity unsupported by feelings of sympathy for others or pity at their plight point to a need for emotional remediation. We are always examining our lives, Aristotle sug-

---

[125] My view of habituation as critical (1989, ch.5) would be highly compatible with this view.
[126] NE 1109b15ff.   [127] NE 1144b29–31.

gests in *Nicomachean* I, with an eye toward a target that can guide practice.[128] More discerning and adequate emotions are part of the practical goal. My claim is that with proper adjustment of Aristotle's remarks in the *Rhetoric*, we learn something more about how it is that we might effect emotional change in a way that is more than merely a matter of control or suppression.

7 CULTIVATING EMOTIONS THROUGH MUSIC AND TRAGEDY

We need briefly to take up a further element in Aristotle's view about how we bring emotions under our control. This concerns his notion of musical education in *Politics* VIII and his view of the cultivation of the emotions implicit in appreciating the dramatic tragedies. Here we can see a more explicit educative application of the points raised in the *Rhetoric*. This complex subject deserves thorough treatment in its own right,[129] a task I cannot take on now. But given the importance of *mousikē* to the ancient conception of character development, a few words are necessary.

Very briefly, musical modes for the ancients were taken to express specific emotional moods or temperaments. The view finds expression in the accounts of education in the early books of the *Republic* as well as the *Laws;* the more formal aspects of the theory are developed extensively by Aristoxenus. The general view emerges in *Politics* VIII.

> Rhythm and melody supply imitations of anger and gentleness, and also of courage and temperance, and of all the qualities contrary to these, and of the other qualities of character, . . . as we know from our own experience, for in listening to such strains our souls undergo a change . . . Even in mere melodies there is an imitation of character, for the musical

128 NE 1094a25.
129 For a general discussion of the political and ethical role of ancient music education, with a focus on Aristotle, see Lord (1982). For a useful sourcebook of ancient texts on music, see Barker (1984). On tragedy and the emotions, see Belfiore (1992) and Halliwell (1986, 1992). For a helpful discussion of different ethical themes relating to Aristotle's *Poetics*, see the anthology edited by Rorty (1992) on the *Poetics*.

modes differ essentially from one another, and those who hear them are differently affected by each. . . . The same principles apply to rhythms.[130]

Modes are mimetic, in other words, expressive of specific characters, in virtue of their evocative powers. Just as in our own idiom the minor key is often said to evoke a sense of sadness or grief, similarly the ancient modes were believed to have comparable, conventionally structured, effects – the Dorian mode evoking restraint; the Phrygian, enthusiasm and passion; the Mixolydian, sadness and gravity. There may be some evidence that Aristotle thought that the evocative power of music had to do with a listener's perception of musical movement as corresponding to the perceived movement of certain emotions. Particular patterns of sound, with their specific tension and resolution, might resemble specific passional states of character. But given that music was often thought of as lyrical (a poem set to music or accompanied), evocative effect also depended to a great degree on the expressive content of language. It is not insignificant in this regard that the *aulos* is viewed as an inferior educational instrument by both Aristotle and Plato precisely because it doesn't leave the mouth free for vocal song. Thematic content of poems was matched to specific modes, and in cases where there were no words, there still was a conventional association with specific literary themes.

For our purposes, what is significant about musical *mimēsis* is that its cultivation of emotion seems to be via a process that engages cognitive capacities. Elation and alert spirit might be intentionally directed toward some thought of military triumph, calm and moderate restraint, toward thoughts that dwell on temperate character. To identify with music through *mimēsis* is to identify with a theme it represents and captures in a charged way. In this sense, music provides an important context for cultivating the rudiments of general classes of emotions. Obviously these contexts or "paradigm scenarios" (in Ronald de Sousa's terminology) are limited and not fine-tuned enough to stand emotions well on their own. Further refinement will depend on the attach-

[130] Pol. 1340a19ff.

ment and reciprocation of emotion within the family, as well as within other nonmusical contexts where richer discriminations and evaluations are required. But even within the musical context, emotions might be more or less differentiated depending on the detail of the literary representation captured by the lyric poem. The salient point for our purposes is that musical *mimēsis* involves a way of coming to feel certain emotions that does not merely work from behavioral and expressive cues. It requires coming to have certain cognitive and evaluative beliefs about themes or objects.[131] Of course, this account of music's relation to emotions may not sit well with us as modern listeners of purely instrumental music. For we may want to hold that the emotion felt by a listener attending to a piece of instrumental music is cognitive and intentional (i.e., directed at the music), precisely in a way that is not structured by narrative or, indeed, by any linguistic cues. However, this is not the place to develop such accounts.[132] What is important for our purposes is that ancient music is largely associated with narrative and lyric. As a medium for training the emotions, it does so through something like a *persuasive telling of the story*, which allows the listener to become immersed in that object of attention. But just how this works is not something Aristotle pursues, nor can we.

Similar issues are raised in Aristotle's treatment of tragedy, and in particular, his view of the role of the spectator in coming to feel the tragic emotions of pity and fear. I shall be most brief here, as I have discussed these subjects elsewhere.[133] But this much can be said now. Attending the tragedies is part of adult training of characters, and so it is here that we seem to find Aristotle's recognition of the point that emotions can be cultivated in significant ways even once we are beyond the impressionable years of childhood. Moreover, the process of coming to feel these emotions involves acceptance of certain beliefs. In the case of feeling pity, it is believing that a character similar to ourselves has suffered undeservingly or at very least disproportionately to the tragic choice

---

131 See Sherman (1989, 181–83) for related discussion.
132 See Kivy (1984, 1990).
133 See Sherman (1992) on tragic mistakes; also Lear (1992) on *katharsis*.

she has made. In the case of fear, there is a more visceral identification with the impending danger and loss, and the enormous
impact such loss will have on any reasonable future. Like the
rhetorician, the tragedian provokes emotions through persuasive
words. He constructs a plot, a series of probable events that in this
case gains the listener's acceptance and willing immersion into
the imaginary world of the drama.

Aristotle, like Plato, is well aware of the power of the tragic
emotions and their ability to hold sway long after the festival has
ended and the audience emerges from its mystery. But his argument with Plato is that this is no reason for censorship. For what
tragedy evokes are emotions that need schooling and expression,
not extirpation. The tragic emotions are emotions that transport
us to the heart of *eudaimonia* and to the proper human reaction to
the limits of intelligent choice and to the disasters the wisest and
best intentions can bring. They are emotions not restricted to
make-believe or the "counterfeit,"[134] but emotions deeply connected to ways of attending what is important in our own lives.
Here the work of imagination, or *mimēsis*, brings us to what matters on stage, and at home. And it does this not by raw feel or
congruent mood, but by engagement in thought and
representation – by allowing us to rehearse in our minds whether
some outcome is deserved or not, given what we believe about
the character and the merits of a hemmed-in choice. Moreover,
the thoughts and emotions they ground are not left behind in the
theater but persist long after as probes for our own self-
understanding and as models for our own immersed reactions.
Thus, we seem to have in the theater the kind of program for
working on the emotions that Aristotle envisioned in the courtroom.[135] And we seem to have it within the context of ethical
education, since attending the tragic festivals was a civic and
religious matter for the Greeks, not merely recreation. Along with
music, it was a crucial part of the cultivation of character. Perhaps

[134] The term is that of Anthony Kenny (1963) who seems to express ambivalence
about reintegrating these emotions into nonliterary contexts.
[135] For an interesting comparison of Aristotle's view of evoking emotions
through persuasive rhetoric in the law courts and tragic drama on the stage,
see Eden (1986).

here is our evidence that adult cultivation of emotion, through persuasion and belief, was something Aristotle took seriously.

8 VIRTUE AND NONCONFLICTUAL EMOTIONS

We have discussed in some detail the constitution and cultivation of Aristotelian emotion with an eye toward how emotional affect can be praised as somehow accessible to an agent's influence. The questions have concerned agency. In Aristotle's idiom, how is emotion related to choice? This has taken us back to a review of habituation and to considerations about persuasion and its role in transforming the evaluative contents of emotions. We have seen that early on in the *Nicomachean*, Aristotle records the role of persuasion in training the emotions, most notably in his formal division of the soul into two parts: a part that issues practical reasons, and another part that is responsive to those reasons. But his own remarks about habituation do not dwell on this process of persuasion or, more generally, on a process of emotional change through an examination of the thoughts that emotions contain. His own emphasis is more on becoming by doing – habituation through action. By turning to Aristotle's *Rhetoric*, I have suggested ways to fill in Aristotle's account of emotional cultivation so that it is in keeping with the place left open in the *Nicomachean Ethics* for persuasion and a more discursive process.

But there is one final issue to take up, that of the overall Aristotelian goal of moderating emotions so they can be brought in line with the best judgments of practical reason. On Aristotle's view, a person whose emotions are truly responsive to reason is not merely inhibiting conflicting emotions, but *lacks* those contrary pulls. The pleasure Aristotle speaks of so often as the sign of virtue is precisely the pleasure that marks absence of conflict and struggle. "We must take as a sign of [character] states the pleasure or pain that supervenes on acts; for the person who abstains from bodily pleasures and delights in this very fact is temperate, while the person who is annoyed at it is self-indulgent."[136] The elabora-

[136] NE 1104b3–11.

tion of this in the analysis of supervenient pleasure in *Nic-omachean Ethics,* Book X, also emphasizes that the agent who experiences true enjoyment in the exercise of her capacities is in the best condition possible. Pleasure "completes an activity" "as the bloom of youth does on those in the flower of their age" when both an agent is an excellent condition and external conditions are optimal.[137] In the case of virtue, the excellent condition of the agent is presumably a harmony of emotion with judgments of what is best and fine.

Aristotle suggests this as a goal of virtue and as embodied in the idealized figure of the *phronimos.* Even if we think Aristotle concedes that few actually reach this goal, nonetheless, he takes it as a *human* goal, not a divine goal in the way he sometimes views a life devoted to contemplation.[138] (If a life of contemplative activity is the first-best life, the virtuous life, including well-ordered emotions, is already the second best.) But still it might be argued that Aristotle's overall optimism for transforming emotions into medial states, nonconflictually responsive to right judgment, may be a bit naïve. In raising these objections we return again to some of Kant's own deep worries about the emotions, often inspired by the Stoics. The worry is that even when emotions have been well cultivated and directed at appropriate values, Cupid's arrow sometimes strays to those whom we know cannot requite our love, attachment sometimes becomes a bit too possessive, grief outlives what we think are reasonable limits, anger may swell up before it can be nipped in the bud. Even for those whose emotional tenor is by and large even and calm, there may be moments of experiencing awkward and inappropriate extremes. Similarly, we may stop tears at old hurts with a sense that the hurt is final and over, though we know deep down that it is over only for now – until the next time, whenever that comes. Of course, there may be incremental progress toward bringing emotions within our purview and agency. We can become wiser about our choices and more apt in our feelings. But if we continue to invest importance in certain objects such as friends and material security, or honor and fame, then we remain vulnerable to the emotional

[137] NE 1174b14–75a2. [138] NE X7–9.

excesses to which those investments can lead and to the hurts and losses that lie beyond our control. If we allow emotions a place in our lives, then we allow ourselves *to be struck* suddenly and unawares by objects that catch our attention. We allow ourselves to be touched, to be drawn in, to be engaged in a riveted and absorbed way. In a certain way, we assent to being passive. For we give up a certain amount of self-mastery in order to be able to live in a way that is susceptible to the emotions. This is precisely what our friends and acquaintances may value when we help in a way that expresses emotions – we show a presence and engagement, a willingness to be drawn in and follow their nuanced lead. We are open to the moment. But this very openness can be a sacrifice of control and a willingness to be affected by what the global judgment of practical wisdom may not always endorse. It is a willingness to be affected in a way that may not allow us to regain control quite so easily.

This may have consequences for the stability of virtue. For if virtue is a way of standing well toward the emotions, then *that* evaluative stance may not always be able to bring emotion round in a way that still preserves what is best and most characteristic in emotion. Good character must be reliable and stable – *monimos kai bebaios*. But grounded in the emotions, virtue may not be perfectly firm and stable, but instead subject to some of the flux inherent in emotional experience and in the objects of emotional focus. Again, virtue requires emotional engagement and affect – pity and fear, love and mourning, as these are appropriate attitudes toward others with whom we interact. But these emotions don't turn on and off in the way that planned actions begin and finish. Rather, they linger, sometimes outliving their welcome, no longer cohering with our judgment of what is best.

Of course, it can be argued that Aristotle is not blind to the moral importance of conflicting feelings, especially in the case of hard or tragic choices where there is no clear, right judgment, and any choice among the alternatives will reasonably be met by regret at what is left undone or grief at the evil one may have to do. Such are the instances of mixed actions Aristotle documents in *Nicomachean* III.1, where "it is difficult to abide by our decisions." These are the cases that strain a human soul, where wholeheartedness would characterize only the insensate. So, too, the virtue of courage, so prominent in Aristotle's account of the virtues, itself requires a psyche in which a choice to do what is fine, for example, to put oneself in danger's way for the sake of the *polis* – sits side by side with fear of the real dangers and pain at the potential losses. "The more he is possessed of excellence in its entirety . . . the more he will be pained at the thought of his death."[139] Still, Aristotle's view seems to be that these are special arenas. In many of the other arenas of human conduct, in areas, for example, that concern bodily appetite and sexual longing, matters are settled, and emotions and desires can be more easily cultivated to support judgments of what is best.[140] To some extent this may be true. Yet even here, I am suggesting, we may still feel the force of the view that conflict is never fully or once and for all resolved – that so long as we engage emotionally and feel the draw of emotional pulls, what we think is best and how we emotionally react may require some negotiation. Although *reducing* internal conflict may be a crucial part of moral development, an idealized characterization, even of the mature moral *psyche*, as one that *lacks* conflict seems superhuman and, indeed, to pull against some of the inherent subversiveness of the emotions. Kant is undoubtedly impressed by precisely this point and canonizes the role of duty to address the problem of conflict and contrary pull.[141] Aristotle is more impressed by the plasticity of emotion and on the face of it, more sanguine about the possibilities for psychic harmony.

But if the picture of psychic unity may have to be somewhat relaxed, then so, too, the requirement that the virtuous response *always* be a matter of seeing what it is right to do and desiring to do in a wholehearted way. A Kantian perspective reinforces the commonsense point that we can't always rely on our emotions. Contrary inclinations can pull us astray; positive feelings are not always there when we need them. Aristotle's response, of course,

---

[139] NE 1117b1–20.

[140] See Hardie (1977) on this point.

[141] See the interesting discussion of Loewald (1980, ch. 23) on the Freudian notion of conflict as never fully resolvable.

is that feelings aren't so capricious and unreliable, especially if we take seriously a project of habituation. They can be trained to be there, and psychic unity is a plausible goal.

Yet, as we have just seen, this still may be asking a lot of emotion, and denying something about its inherent nature. We cannot always have the right emotional resources at hand or be absent conflicting ones. Inhibitory control may sometimes be more within our reach, or at least a reasonable fallback, even for the reasonably virtuous. Again, it may be enough simply that we not have conflicting emotions, and not always the more positive feelings. Can't we act generously because it is the right thing to do, even if we can't now summon generous feelings that would motivate the action?[142] Don't we need the fallback of something like principle – of acting because it is right, even though our reason for acting may not have as an incentive positive, support-ive emotion? Aren't there times when this is sufficient for express-ing virtue?

On a most natural reading of Aristotle's ethics, he would prob-ably answer "no" to the last question. Virtue demands appropri-ate emotional expression, and such a response may simply lack it. But there is an important qualification that demands an airing and that may possibly weaken the force of that "no." If we take seriously the remarks of Section 3, then emotions can be seen as playing an effective role in virtue in more ways than simply at the motivational level. In addition to being motivational, they are morally useful because they serve various epistemic functions. So, for example, it may be in virtue of effective emotional sen-sitivities that I am alerted to an incident of inequity or need, even though I then go on to act generously in less than a wholehearted way. The point is that it is not an all-or-nothing story. There is latitude for how emotions are expressed in character excellence. In virtue of certain roles emotions serve, they may be actualized finely, that is, in the right way, toward the right persons, in the right circumstances, even though motivationally, when we go on

---

142 The question is raised by Annas (1993, 63–66). The discussion that follows is meant as a response to her Stoic criticism of Aristotelian virtue. See also my comments in Sherman (1995d).

to act, we may still be conflicted. Aristotle doesn't develop this sort of point, though his remarks about emotions as evaluative give little reason for thinking that the motivational role of emotion will exhaust the role of emotion in virtue. It may be our own modern gloss, perhaps an intuitive one but one also inspired by Kant's separation of duty motives from motives based on inclination, that brings the motivational role to the fore. But, as we shall see, Kant himself is not unaware of a broader set of functions for emotion, and appeals to it in striking ways.

Chapter 3

A brief Stoic interlude

Stoic views on the emotions represent a pivotal transition between the Aristotelian and Kantian accounts of virtue. Of course, Stoic views are complex and by no means embody an homogenous doctrine. There are significant differences articulated in the early Stoa, as well as between it and its later, Roman manifestation. The later Stoics are often criticized for lacking the theoretical rigor and philosophical interest of the earlier Stoa. I, myself, am not particularly sympathetic to this criticism. True, the later Stoics often present their philosophical views in a homey way with an eye to therapy, but their concern to see ethical inquiry as a practical subject matter puts them squarely in the Socratic tradition. In this vein, they follow closely the example of Socrates, who demanded of his interlocutors that they submit for cross-examination not merely *entertained* beliefs, but those that they *sincerely lived by*. In extending the project of moral therapy, the later Stoics make an invaluable contribution to ethical inquiry.

Before discussing this contribution, it will be helpful to sketch very schematically the relevant lines of the Stoic transition. For our purposes, what is most important is the Stoic objection to Aristotle's account of the passions and their role in his account of virtue. By isolating reason as the exclusive ground of morality, the Stoics pave the way for Kant's rational grounding of morality. Moreover, their account of nonmoral goods (the so-called preferred indifferents) and the relation of these to the moral good foreshadows Kant's own distinction between the nonmoral and the moral. Finally, their distinction between diseased *pathē* and reason-based or enlightened emotions (*eupatheiai*) provides, if not the actual source of Kant's own distinction between pathological and practical emotions, at least an important early analogue. For these reasons, then, some familiarity with Stoic views will stand us well in charting the passage from Aristotle to Kant on the emotions. (I emphasize it is only a very broad familiarity that we now pursue. For a more scholarly examination of Stoic views in fine detail, I direct readers to the recent work of others.[1] Thus the brevity of this interlude should not be read as a negative comment on the intrinsic importance of Stoic views. Nor should it be seen as minimizing the importance of the ancient Stoa's critique of Aristotle or the Latin Stoic influence on Kant's thinking. This is far from my intent. Whereas the Stoic critique of the peripatetics has been the subject of considerable recent scholarship within ancient philosophy, the Stoic influence on Kant remains poorly documented in contemporary exegesis.[2] The area remains a crucial one for future research, and one that is at long last accessible given recent advances in Hellenistic scholarship. Because of the broader purposes of this narrative, however, such a project cannot be undertaken here, though I hope to point us in the direction of some fruitful inquiries.)

---

[1] For excellent recent works that cover different strands of Stoic ethics, see Annas (1993), Brunschwig and Nussbaum (1993), Cooper (1995), Forschner (1985), Inwood (1985, 1986), Irwin (1986), Long (1983), Mistis (1986), Nussbaum (1994), Schofield and Striker (1986), Striker (1996), Taylor (1987). Also, extremely helpful are the commentaries of Long and Sedley (1987) that accompany their collection of Hellenistic fragments. For slightly older but helpful work, see Long (1974) and Rist(1969, 1978a).

My own understanding of the Stoics texts has profited from the weekly meetings of our Greek reading group at Georgetown during the summer and fall of 1995. Fond appreciation is due Richard Bett, Marcelo Boeri and Alfonso Gómez-Lobo, with whom I worked on the extract of Arius Didymus in Stoabeus as well as other Stoic texts collected in Long and Sedley. I also wish to thank Brad Inwood, who shared with me an unpublished translation of Arius's text.

[2] A notable exception in the English speaking literature is Seidler (1981a, 1981b, 1983).

1 AGAINST ARISTOTELIAN MODERATION

As noted in the last chapter, the Stoics object to Aristotelian virtue on the grounds that emotions (*pathē*) are not the sorts of mental states that can be controlled or moderated. (Indeed, on their rendering of the term, *pathē* become, by definition, defective and irrational states.[3] As such, the term has a far narrower focus than it does in Aristotle's usage. But though *pathos* comes to be used as a term of art, I will continue to translate it as "emotion" or "passion" in order to preserve the important dialogue the Stoics intend to have with Aristotle on the general subject of the emotions.) Thus, a persistent Stoic criticism is that the emotions have a life of their own and an intensity and excess (*hormē pleonazousa*) that defy easy access and regulation. As Seneca puts it, "they begin, grow, and run riot."[4] Trying to stop a passion is like trying to stop a runner in full speed. The motion outsteps the command. The oft-cited analogy is from Chrysippus:

> When someone walks in accordance with his impulse, the movement of his legs is not excessive but commensurate with the impulse, so that he can stop or change whenever he wants to. But when people run in accordance with their impulse, this sort of thing no longer happens. The movement of their legs exceeds their impulse, so that they are carried away and unable to change obediently, as soon as they have started to do so. Something similar, I think, takes place with impulses, owing to their going beyond the rational proportion. The result is that when someone has the impulse he is not readily obedient to reason.[5]

The runner analogy suggests the image of inertial motion: Once passions are activated, they can't easily be reversed. Even well-trained passional dispositions can easily regress to their old

[3] In the Latin writers, *pathos* becomes *morbus* – a diseased state.

[4] Ir. 2.4.

[5] Galen, *On Hippocrates' and Plato's Doctrines* 4.2.10–18, part (SVF 3.462, part) = L and S 65J; I have modified the Long and Sedley translation very slightly by adding "readily" in the last sentence; the phrase is *mē eupeithōs echein*.

ways and remain there with a kind of atavism. So, for example, though one may be generally gentle, disappointment at an unexpected and significant loss may unleash a torrent of anger; so too a physical pain may rob one of one's more usual good cheer. Conflicts between judgments of how one ought to feel and how one actually does feel and behave easily set in. There may be regression but also, as the analogy suggests, inertia – a feeling of being stuck in a repeating pattern, unable to heed reason.

Given these excesses, emotions, it is argued, are an unreliable source of motives for virtue. Following earlier remarks (in Chapter 2, Section 2), we can call this *the unreliability objection*.[6] Connected with this objection are related complaints – that emotion's storminess may result in its petering out well before it can motivate an action, or if the emotion is available, it may be too reckless to motivate morally judicious action:

> So anger begins with a mighty rush, then breaks down from untimely exhaustion. . . . Its first blows are fierce; so serpents when they first crawl from their lair are charged with venom, but their fangs are harmless after they have been drained by repeated biting. Consequently, not all who have sinned alike are punished alike, and often he who has committed the smaller sin receives the greater punishment, because he was subjected to anger when it was fresh.[7]

The general criticism, which emerges from these texts of Chrysippus and Seneca against an Aristotelian theory of virtue, is that a policy of moderation cannot reliably govern and educate the emotions. States of character that express emotions can come unhinged, with emotions unresponsive to both habit and reason. What is demanded, they argue, is the more radical solution of extirpation. Seneca makes this clearest in the case of anger, but the point is meant to be general: "The enemy must be stopped at the very frontier." "Let us be rid of it altogether," rid of anything "which needs to be controlled with anxious care."[8] Since it is only

---

[6] Nussbaum labels it the "argument from excess" (1994, 394).

[7] Seneca, Ir. 1.17.

[8] Ir.1.8; 2.13; on the seriousness (albeit implausibility) of the claim to extirpate, see Nussbaum (1994, ch. 10).

as adults that we are truly capable of emotions (for emotions are a corruption of the reasoning capacities that only adults have), it is only as adults that we are capable of extirpating them and of weaning ourselves from values other than virtue.

Here we come to a second criticism of the emotions, *the vulnerability objection* (also anticipated in Chapter 2). The Stoics hold that emotions are ways of investing importance in externals, which are subject to loss and which, as such, make us vulnerable and threaten our stable well-being. So, for example, when we love we also fear losing what we love on the grounds that a loved one or the love of a loved one matters to our well-being. When we pity someone who has suffered a natural disaster, it is because we place value in having certain external goods and view the deprivation as a true loss of happiness. When we feel anger at an unwarranted insult, it is because we are attached to certain views of ourselves that are easily threatened. In essence, emotions involve attachments to objects that are contingent and highly unstable. But since true happiness is a self-sufficient good, the Stoics argue that both emotions and the goods to which they attach cannot be part of happiness. In this sense, emotions involve false evaluations. They lead us to pursue as choiceworthy goods that are in fact not genuine parts of our good. It is virtue alone, as perfection of our reason, that constitutes our happiness. Thus, the Stoic view is that virtue alone is sufficient for *eudaimonia*. It is the only proper object of choice and is wholly constitutive of happiness. Everything else – health, wealth, reputation, friendship are indifferents, albeit "preferred indifferents." To value them as true goods, important to one's happiness, is just to have false views about the good. The indifferents may be "selected" in a good life, but they are not parts of the goodness of that good life or even contributors to its happiness. Untutored, we live a life of emotion cleaving to values other than virtue; as Stoics, our salvation is in learning how to detach from false goods.

We shall come to this therapy in a moment. But first we should briefly review the more theoretical elements of the Stoic account of the passions, as it undergirds Stoic therapeutic methods. Generally speaking, the Stoics identify passion with judgment or opinion. Thus, Arius Didymus refers to the view in his report that "in the case of all the soul's passions, when they [the Stoics] call them 'opinions,' 'opinion' is used instead of weak supposition,"[9] and again Andronicus adverts to the view in his Stoic catalogue of the passions: "Distress is . . . a fresh opinion that something bad is present"; "pleasure . . . is a fresh opinion that something good is present."[10] The view is repeated by Cicero: "Distress is a newly formed belief of present evil"; "delight is a newly formed belief of present good." He summarizes: "The act of belief we have included in all previous definitions they hold to be a weak acquiescence."[11]

The conception of passions as cognitive falls within the orthodox Stoic doctrine of a monistic rational soul. Within this monistic psychology, passion has its home in the seat of reason even though it is itself a misappropriation of that faculty. It is an erroneous and persuasive judgment to which assent is given. Thus, by definition, passions are delusive states. They are errors in evaluative belief. Plutarch's summary is helpful here:

They suppose that the passionate and irrational part is not distinguished from the rational by any distinction within the soul's nature, but the same part of the soul (which they call thought and commanding-faculty) becomes virtue and vice as it wholly turns around and changes in passions and alterations of tenor character, and contains nothing irrational within itself. It is called irrational whenever an excessive impulse which has become strong and dominant carries it off towards something wrong and contrary to the dictates of reason. For passion is vicious and uncontrolled reason which acquires vehemence and strength from bad and erroneous judgment.[12]

9 Stobaeus 2.88, 22–89, 2 (SVF 3.378, part) = L and S 65C. See Stobaeus 2.90, 7–18, for a weaker formulation in which belief (or opinion) is a cause of emotion and not identical to it. For different views on the relation of emotion to belief, see Galen, *On Hippocrates' and Plato's doctrines* 4.3.2–5 (Posidonius fr. 34, part) = L and S 65K.
10 Andronicus, *On Passions* 1 (SVF 3.391, part) = L and S 65B.
11 TD 4.15
12 *On moral virtue* 440E-441D = L and S 61B.

Underlying the theory of the unified soul is the belief that there is no irreducible conflict of the sort that requires fundamentally separate soul parts, as we find in *Republic* IV.[13] To both grieve and not grieve for a lost loved object is indicative, on the Stoic view, not of different soul centers but of oscillating beliefs about what is worthy and not worthy of our attention. Careful observation of the phenomena, they argue, reveals not so much domination of reason or passion by the other but shifting beliefs, sometimes volatile and transient, that push us from one pole to another. "Every passion is a fluttering."[14] In general, passions are a "fluttery ignorance" that lead to an unstable soul.[15]

The placement of passion in the rational soul has clear implications for stilling these oscillations. For if passions are through and through reason-based states, then they should be reformable through a method that works specifically on beliefs. If they are no more than aberrant forms of judgment, then persuasion and argument can grab hold without remainder. Granted, discouragement and encouragement through argument must work in deep ways. It is philosophy as *therapy* and not as Aristotelian lecture or even Socratic dialogue that is required; as we shall see, at the heart of such therapy is constant self-watchfulness and comprehensive belief reform. But part of the reason for faith in this therapy rests precisely on the psychological theory – that without separate and potentially conflicting soul parts, there are no deep structural reasons for viewing conflict as inescapably rooted in our own way of processing the world. Appetites are no longer conceived of as desires that necessarily regress at weak moments to more primitive original states, or fears and sorrows as states that must

---

[13] See Inwood (1993) for a rejection of Platonic (and Posidonian) dualism in Seneca and an argument for Seneca's orthodox, monistic view of the soul. Still, on Inwood's view (174ff.), Seneca constructs a criterion of rationality for the passions (namely, susceptibility to change by a conscious and voluntary rational decision) narrower than that constructed by the earlier Stoics (namely, expressibility or reliance on *lekta*).

[14] Stobaeus 2.88, 12.

[15] See Inwood (1993) for an interesting discussion of the nature of this oscillation within a monistic soul.

always preserve vestigial objects of attachment. The therapy of reason, working in conjunction with a theory of the soul, replaces the original objects of the impulses with those that truly accord with nature (*kathēkon*) and are appropriate (*oikeion*). The evaluative discriminations of the first impulses thus do not live on, nor are there permanent and separate dwellings in the soul for those impulses to take refuge in and continue battle.

The Stoics' thoroughgoing cognitivism does not prevent them from trying to capture the conspicuous physical feel of emotional experience. Passions are a "fluttering" (*ptoia*) of the soul marked by "shrinkings" and " stretchings," by "contractions, cowerings, tearings, swellings, and expansions."[16] The characteristic charge of certain emotions is referred to in terms of the "freshness" of belief (*prosphaton*), indicative less of actual recentness than of emotion's inertial capacity to make the sting or zing of even old hurts and pleasures seem new.[17] As Cicero puts it in interpreting Zeno's term, passion retains its power of being "vigorous" (*vigeat*), and its "greenness" (*viriditatem*).[18]

More systematic than the peripatetics, the Stoics divide passion into four primary sorts – appetite (*epithumia*), fear (*phobos*), pleasure (*hedonē*), and distress (*lupē*). Appetite and fear are prospective and are constituted by positive and negative appraisals about prospective goods and "bads"; pleasure or distress are constituted by the "fresh beliefs" that arise when we are already in the grip of those appraisals.[19] From these basic four passions derive a broad range of common emotions, including under appetite, various forms of aggression and longing; under fear, astonishment, shame, and confusion and dread; under pleasure, self-gratification and enjoyment at other's misfortunes; under

---

[16] Stobaeus 2.88, 8–90, 6 (SVF 3.378,389, part) = L and S 65A; Galen, *On Hippocrates' and Plato's Doctrines* 4.3.2–5 (Posidonius fr. 34, part) = L and S 65K; Stobaeus 2.88, 22–89, 3 (SVF 3.378, part) = L and S 65C; Galen *On Hippocrates' and Plato's Doctrines* 4.2.1–6 (SVF 3.463, part) = L and S 65D.

[17] Stobaeus 2.88, 22–89, 3 (SVF 3.378,part) = L and S 65C; Diogenes Laertius 7.116 (SVF 3.431) = L and S 65F.

[18] TD 3.75.

[19] Stobaeus 2.88, 8–90, 6 (SVF 3.378, 389, part) = L and S 65A; TD 4.11–12.

distress, malice, envy, jealousy, grief, annoyance, and sorrow.[20] Thus, we are reminded once again that the Stoic identification of passion with judgment is not meant to compromise the range and complexity of ordinary emotional experience. Whether their full revision can, in fact, preserve that complexity will be discussed shortly, in Section 3.

2 STOIC THERAPY

Since the Stoic view is that reason is the sole source of virtue, passions, as perversions of reason, can have no place in virtuous motivation and wise judgment.[21] They need to be rooted out through a cure that will involve a thoroughgoing denial of judgments to which voluntary, but faulty, assent was formerly given. It is "emotional therapy," to use the title of Chrysippus's book, that is required if the pathological attachment to external goods is to be overcome and virtue and happiness achieved. The reform of belief is at the deepest level. What is required is to come to believe that what lies outside the self and is external to one's true nature or reason are not proper objects of importance. Attachments to wealth, fame, friends, health, noble birth, beauty, strength, and so on must accordingly be severed and these objects recognized as having no intrinsic value or place in happiness. Happiness is what is in accord with nature, and these goods can never be secured in a way that allows what is truly proper (*kathēkon*) to one's nature, namely, reason, to prevail. In short, passions, as attachments to external goods, undermine self-sufficiency. "The man who would fear losing any of these things cannot be happy. We want the happy man to be safe, impregnable, fenced and fortified, so that he is not just largely unafraid, but completely."[22] Removing oneself from investment in these contingencies – from the graspiness and possessiveness of wanting what lies beyond control – will thus be a crucial step toward equanimity, but only to

---

[20] Stobaeus 2.90, 19–91, 9 (SVF 3.394 part) = L and S 65E; TD 4.15–22.
[21] This is qualified somewhat by the doctrine of *eupatheia*, which I discuss at the end of this chapter. I argue that these so-called wholesome emotions are emotions in name only.
[22] TD 5.40–41 = L and S 63L.

the extent to which that removal is part of the larger project of perfecting one's nature, or reason. More cosmically, we are parts of a larger universe of god and nature, designed as species to conform to that universal nature through the perfection of reason. Virtue is a *homologia* (a consistency of reason) achieved within the individual in its obedience to reason's command, and within universal nature in its conformity to Zeus's reason. "God introduced man as a student of himself and his works, and not merely as a student but also as an interpreter of these things. . . . [In our case] nature ended at studying and attending to things and a way of life in harmony with nature. See to it then that you do not die without having studied these things."[23]

The cure by argument and exhortation must ultimately penetrate philosophical beliefs. That is, the therapy is philosophy; the diseased passion is a false belief; the cure is a discursive method that leads to true and reasoned belief about what is of value or worth in the world. However, therapy probes deep philosophical beliefs only gradually by first gaining access through more superficial layers. Thus, the psychogogy is highly systematic, as good therapy must be. It goes deeper and deeper incrementally as the patient becomes more and more receptive to its truths. The incremental method is perspicuous in *De Ira*.[24] A brief study of parts of the text helps illustrate that method as well as some general features of Stoic therapy.

Seneca is asked by Novatus to instruct him on how anger can be allayed. He starts not with the cure, however, but with reminders of just how maladaptive anger can be. The initial step is to paint its external signs – the hideous distortions of pyrotechnic rage:

> His eyes blaze and sparkle, his whole face is crimson with the blood that surges from the lowest depths of the heart, his lips quiver, his teeth are clenched, his hair bristles and stands on end, his breathing is forced and harsh, his joints crack from writhing, he groans and bellows, bursts out into speech with

[23] Epictetus, *Discourses* 1.6.12–22 = L and S 63E.
[24] I owe thanks to Martha Nussbaum for her suggestion to me that the *De Ira* proceeds in an incremental way.

scarcely intelligible words, strikes his hands together continually, and stamps the ground with his feet . . . it is an ugly and horrible picture of distorted and swollen frenzy – you cannot tell whether this vice is more execrable or more hideous.[25]

The mood is set. The patient feels the turbulence and disfunctionality of anger. The notion of anger as lack of conformity to one's nature is prepared. But further strategies are required. For though anger may be contrary to nature, it nonetheless may be useful. From here, Seneca goes on in more didactic fashion to argue against its utility. Desire for vengeance, inspired by anger, may go against the dictates of justice, just as anger's call for arms may lack the endurance of courage directed by reason. "There is in anger, consequently, nothing great, nothing noble, even when it seems impassioned, contemptuous alike of gods and men." So ends the first part of the teaching. From this text we can see that skills in transforming emotions need not be restricted to the courtroom, where Aristotle sometimes seems to confine them,[26] but have a place in individual, moral therapy. Here the Stoic doctor exhorts the patient, suffering from diseases of the soul, to see the disvalue of those passions and the need to come to search for alternatives. The method of persuasion becomes a form of psychic treatment.

The therapy continues in the second book with conscious acknowledgment that Novatus must now descend into narrower and drier matters. Here theory must enter. But Seneca deliberately begins with the theme of voluntarism – that the surrender to anger is volitional. For from the start, the message to Novatus is that he is in control, that it is his assent to an impression that results in the impulse that constitutes his anger: "These processes are impossible unless the mind has given assent to the

---

[25] Ir. 1.1.

[26] An important qualification is in order here. The argument can be made that Aristotle extended the methods of rhetoric (and the manipulation of emotions) beyond the courtroom to the theatre. See Eden (1986) for comparisons between the *Poetics* and *Rhetoric*. On the tragedian's arousal of cathartic emotions, see Belfiore (1992), Golden (1962), Halliwell (1986), Lear (1992), and Nussbaum (1986). I take up the general topic in Chapter 2, Section 7.

impressions that moved it."[27] The patient is thus directly introduced to philosophical theory; it is not kept hidden as a secret
metier, exposure to which might somehow overly intellectualize
the process. All the same it is introduced gradually, the first lesson
being that one is responsible for one's condition, and ultimately
for one's cure.

The way is now paved for the curative tonics of Book III. These
must be adjusted to the individual, but there are general points
that hold. We must understand that attachment to money, competition, and false pride incite anger. Once that proclivity exists it
spreads and is regularly displaced onto other objects: "You will be
angry first with this man, then with that one; first with slaves,
then with freedmen; first with parents, then with children; first
with acquaintances, then with strangers."[28] We must guard
against these false projections by watchful observation of our
behavior and by meditative reflection at the close of each day. In
the *Epistles*, Seneca himself adopts the practice of closing each
letter with a thought for the day. Ask yourself: "What bad habit
have you cured today?" We are told to rehearse certain key
thoughts, for example, that the lust and ambition of others are a
matter of natural disease and weakness to be met by therapy
rather than by reactive anger or faultfinding. We are reminded
regularly of the fruits of mental industry and the strength of
willpower. "Nothing is so hard and difficult that it cannot be
conquered by the human intellect."[29] We are told to watch the
signs of anger welling in our own breasts, so that we can nip it in
the bud and short-circuit any routine reaction.[30] We are told to
keep fixed in our minds that the unexpected can happen so that
we will have less to fear or cling to.[31] Carefully choose friends, we
are urged, who are tranquil so that their mood and good cheer
will spread.[32] There are thus practical and mental stratagems for
supporting the deeper philosophical ideology that passion is a
matter of our own assent to false goods. This is the central belief
that must always give meaning to these practices.

[27] Ir. 2.1.   [28] Ir. 3.28.   [29] Ir. 2.12.   [30] Ir. 2.29.
[31] Plutarch, *On Tranquility of Mind*, 469, in *Moralia*.   [32] Ir. 3.8.

Cicero, in the *Tusculan Disputations*, makes it even clearer that all the various curative exercises must hang on the deeper understanding and redescription of emotional experience. This does not prevent him from reviewing the more specific strategies. Among these are methods for withdrawing attention from what is painful, for reminding oneself of the losses one can expect in life, for being prepared, as Anaxagoras was when, according to the story, he said upon hearing of his son's death, "I knew that I had begotten a mortal,"[33] for being aware of the importance of timing in administering one's counsel. But just as the phrase "You are not the only one" (*Non tibi hoc soli*) has limited effect to pull the mourner out of her deepest grief,[34] so, too, these methods of coaxing and badgering have little purchase without the deeper philosophical revision that the objects to which the passions attach lack real worth. This is the keystone belief, and failure to grasp it is the real cause of suffering. The strategies work only to the degree to which this belief informs the practice.[35] Cicero, like Seneca, seems to be pointing to a form of bootstrapping. As Ronald de Sousa has put it elsewhere, "sometimes we bestow real value on some prospect, just by choosing it."[36] In this case, by believing certain assumptions about emotions we succeed in transforming them. Like the edge given by self-confidence in competitive situations,[37] acceptance of the terms of the therapy goes some way to constituting its success. "Philosophy claims that she will succeed: only let us consent to her treatment."[38] Thus Cicero knew long before Freud that therapy cannot work without at least the initial resistances broken. The deeper work of philosophical therapy, "pushing the oars of dialectic,"[39] as Cicero puts it, rests on this initial consent.

The practical nature of this philosophy is abundantly clear, and its contrast with the thinness of Aristotle's remarks about emotional change, and habituation in general, is striking. Despite Aristotle's keen intent on producing *practical* lectures about good living, he offers little by way of concrete exercises one can under-

---

[33] TD 3.30.   [34] TD 3.79.   [35] TD 3.81–82.   [36] De Sousa (1987, 237).   [37] De Sousa (1988, 324).   [38] TD 3.84.   [39] TD 4.9.

take in the habituation process. His own lectures are a dialectical specification of the more general components in the good life, and there is reason to believe that practical wisdom in the concrete case will also be a matter of deliberative specification.[40] Through such a process, one revises and changes broader ends and commitments. But there are limits to how much change one can make given the stubbornness of habit and the starting points from which one revises. In contrast, the Stoic ideology is that few vices are beyond cure, and that character transformation, through adult reeducation, is possible. But it is important to remember that as practical as Stoic philosophy is, it does not work exclusively or primarily at the level of superficial incantation or exhortation. To repeat over and over that "there is nothing to fear/grieve/hate, etc." of course doesn't work. If the bulk of Stoic therapy were at this level, their optimism for extirpating emotion would be no less naïve than Aristotle's optimism for moderating it. The therapy indeed is meant to go far deeper, teaching that what one fears is not a genuine danger, that what one hopes for not a genuine good, that love objects are fungible, and that anger is not an expedient for justice or courage. The behavioral how-to's are constantly undergirded by a philosophical instruction in what is of genuine and lasting value in the world. And this, on the Stoic view, is virtue grounded in reason.

But we might still ask, How is *that* lesson internalized rather than merely intellectually comprehended? How does one embrace and commit oneself to that evaluative system in a way that is experiential and not merely doxastic? How does it radiate and permeate through all one's practice? The temptation is to say that one embraces it through the emotions or passions, but this option is, of course, not open to the Stoics. Emotions just are beliefs. Granted, *apatheia* is supposed to be *eupatheia*, a wholesome kind of passional state where there is neither total inertia nor the sharp contractions of emotional surges. But still, how do we explain the sort of vitality and resonance by which we come to know things in the heart and not merely the head? Can the experience of "knowing through the emotions" be preserved without the emo-

---

[40] See Richardson (1994) for an account of this process.

tions? The issue is not a terminological or locational one. It is a matter of being able to capture the phenomena.

Yet it is here that the Stoics seem weakest. There is at the one level, philosophical revision. And at the other, surface psychogogy. But it is not clear how the two really combine to effect the deep character change the Stoics envision. A brief contrast from other kinds of psychotherapy might be instructive here. As discused in Chapter 2, in psychoanalysis the recapitulation of patterns of emotional response through transference onto an analyst is intended to be a way of seeing at a detached level. One relives memories affectively, tapping the past by congruent emotions in the present. As one accesses past beliefs and emotions, they can be examined without secondary defenses, and looked at with some measure of honesty. As in Stoic therapy, the removal of ignorance is key, and in both theories this is meant to bring with it an untying of the knots that form when emotions blindly cling to objects whose role or importance is not understood. For Freud, the intended result is non-neurotic emotions, for the Stoics, *apatheia* or indifference to the vicissitudes of what lies outside self control. But what one fails to see in the Stoics is how philosophical appreciation of the nonimportance of external goods works through consciousness at a sufficiently deep level to induce practical indifference. We may come to believe that all that matters is what is within one's rational control, and that this is the ground of enduring virtue and happiness. But what is comparable in the Stoics to the Freudian experiential awakening to such a discovery. Is the fact that emotions are taken away as a medium of discovery itself the handicap?

Another contrast comes from a very different kind of therapy implicit in certain aspects of Buddhism. One could point to many superficial similarities between Buddhism and Stoicism. Both view the attachment and blindness of emotion as a defilement, and see wisdom as a state of calm removed from the vortex of desire. The philosophical underpinnings, though, are diametrically opposed. At the foundation of Buddhism is a belief in the impermanence of substantial existence, including, most fundamentally, the self. Whereas Stoicism narrows but tightens the boundary around self, Buddhism removes it entirely. This is not the place for detailed exposition, nor do I have expertise.[41] For our purposes, the relevant issue is how a philosophical ideology can inform consciousness and character in a way that influences conduct. In what sense does the philosophy bootstrap? What is crucial here is that the metaphysical regestalt takes place at the subliminal level. Through meditative practice, the student is taught to watch dispassionately the thoughts and emotions that fill and empty the mind, including especially those that still yearn and crave for attachment to false goods. The skill is to watch in a way that releases those thoughts and lets them pass without engagement. The meditator learns how not to be dragged into the conversation of one's own mind. The stream of consciousness passes, and one may identify the various states, but more as a way of letting them pass than as a way of taking up their defense. Thus, meditation is a mode whereby one can watch rather than engage, and calmly release the object of focus rather than pursue or invest. It provides a stance of detachment to be adopted in nonmeditative moments where the temptations and attractions of the material world often press in with more intensity. Unlike Stoic reflection at the end of each day, this reflection is not simply a recording of one's acknowledged faults and perfections, but itself a practice of stilling and disengaging from delusional attachments. It is a way of cleaning out the recesses into which those attachments may still hide. In a very strained way there is some resemblance to Freudian free association here. But whereas the point of free association is to track historical lineages, and so recover the historical self from deep repression, the point of meditative watchfulness is ultimately to release from that very self or ego.

There is no doubt that this sort of meditative practice is meant to blend with the particular metaphysical views of Buddhism, in particular selflessness. But whatever this harmony of method and content, what is important for our discussion is that here is a method, distinct from that of the Stoics, that aims to still the mind

---

[41] I am deeply grateful to Michael Friedman for helping me to understand Buddhist practices and doctrines and their connection to some of the themes of this chapter.

and sever it from attachment to objects that are viewed (for different reasons) as having no intrinsic value. Moreover, it is a method alert to the tricks and habits of the mind, and so may gain purchase where more superficial methods of character change fail.

But the contrast with Buddhism is important in another regard. According to Buddhism, all objects of attachment, be they external goods or one's own self and rational capacities, are potential sources of disquiet. The Stoics, in contrast, seem to exempt reason from jealous attachment. But why should this be so? For the retreat to the stronghold of reason, as foundation for virtue, might itself be a source of psychic anxiety. Though the well-cured Stoic may no longer be attached to changing goods outside the self, she will be deeply and supremely committed to the value of reason as authoritative, and thus prey to an attitude of control and mastery toward the world. At its extreme, it can be a jealous kind of view, in which reason is perceived as indomitable and capable of vanquishing all folly and suffering. The sober truth, of course, is that humans lack perfect rationality and their rational capacities are themselves subject to the decay that comes with physical frailty. We are not gods, even though perfection may bring us increasingly in line with what is divine and universally rational. Commitment to the rule and mastery of reason may paradoxically be a kind of anxious control of the very sort the Stoics wish to avoid. Learning to let go and adopt true dispassion may be a therapy that the soul committed to the power of reason cannot take.

This sort of point was not entirely lost on one Stoic. Posidonius seems to be aware that the Stoic position can in principle make reason, as well as the external goods, objects of emotional attachment. As such, both can become "hostages to fortune."[42] But the Stoic response to this seems to be merely stipulative: that passion has as its objects external goods, not reason. The wise man will simply not fear for its loss or long for its presence. Clearly, the revision does not take us very far.

---

[42] Fragment 164 E-K, 266D. I am grateful to Nussbaum (1994, 378) for bringing this passage to my attention.

3 STOIC APATHY AND KANTIAN ANTISENTIMENTALISM

We have outlined the Stoics' departure from Aristotelian views regarding the emotions. In summary, the Stoics propose a more extreme cognitivism than Aristotle offers. They go on to outline a thoroughgoing philosophical therapy that, while giving some indication of the practical ways we can transform emotions, becomes in their own hands a method of radical extirpation of emotions. In the name of self-sufficiency, they eliminate the excesses and vulnerabilities of emotions, while forfeiting the advantages emotions can offer to a theory of virtue, including, presumably, the epistemic advantages a cognitive theory of the emotions, such as their own, so readily exposes. But what can we now say of the relationship between Stoic doctrines on the emotions and Kantian views? The next chapter develops a full account of Kantian views on the emotions, but here several issues can be introduced. We can begin with Kant's famous embrace of the Stoic sage, captured well in the following passage:

> The Stoic showed a noble cast of mind when he had his Sage say: I want a friend, not that he might help me in poverty, sickness, imprisonment, etc., but rather that I might stand by him and rescue a man. But the same Sage, when he could not save his friend, said to himself: what is it to me? In other words, he repudiated imparted suffering.[43]

I have more to say about this passage in Chapter 4. But for now, we can ask: Is the embrace of Stoic apathy to be taken as a rejection of soppy sentimentalism, or of sentiment itself? Indeed, is Kant's frequent use of Stoic rhetoric a genuine endorsement of the Stoic radical position on the emotions? I do not believe so. I believe Kant uses the Stoic sage both to support an attack against sentimentalism and then to reinstate the emotions in purified or "practical" form. But we need to take up these matters with some care, returning first to a more careful look at the Stoic texts.

[43] DV 456. See Baron's (1995 a, ch. 6; 1995b) helpful discussion of this passage and Sherman (1995e) for comments on her discussion. I discuss the passage further in Chapter 4, sec. 4.

As we have said, the Stoics urge extirpation of the emotions, on the grounds that emotional attachment threatens the self-sufficiency required of *eudaimonia*. Apathy is freedom from *pathē* or passion. But some of the texts might be read as suggesting that the aim of therapy is something slightly less than outright extirpation of all emotional experience. The aim is not *apatheia* but, rather, *eupatheia*, good feeling.[44] *Pathē*, as we have said, divide into four types: those that fall under appetite, pleasure, fear, and distress. After Stoic therapy and a deep appreciation of the true object of value, hygienic emotions, according to this modified view, are supposed to emerge from the original *pathē*, free, we might say, of their toxic valuations. They represent, allegedly, a mode of affective experience wholly liberated from clinginess and vulnerable attachment.

> They say there are three good feelings, joy [*chara*], watchfulness [*eulabeia*], wishing [*boulēsis*]. Joy, they say, is the opposite of pleasure, consisting in well-reasoned [*eulogon*] swelling [elation]; and watchfulness is the opposite of fear, consisting in well-reasoned shrinking. For the wise man will not be afraid at all, but he will be watchful. They say that wishing is the opposite of appetite, consisting in well-reasoned stretching [*orexis* – desire]. Just as certain passions fall under the primary ones, so too with the primary good feelings. Under wishing: kindness, generosity, warmth, affection. Under watchfulness: respect, cleanliness. Under joy: delight, sociability, cheerfulness.[45]

The idea now is that the sage can enjoy "safe" emotions, always obedient to reason's authoritative valuations. Such emotions are thoroughly "rationalized," becoming in a foolproof way *eulogon*, or well reasoned. Whether these facsimiles are really anything like emotions is a significant problem. I doubt that they can be. Indeed, the Stoics seem to appreciate the point in noting that there is nothing that survives the revision that corresponds to distress and its subtypes of pity and sorrow. That is, there are only

---

44 It is noteworthy that there is no reference to *eupatheia* in Arius.
45 Diogenes Laertius 7.116 (SVF 3.431) = L and S 65 F; see TD 4.12–14: *constantiae* corresponds to *eupatheiai*.

three "good feelings." The thought probably is that there is no sanitized or disturbance-free way of feeling distress. But the worry can be generalized – there is no absolute guarantee of freedom from disturbance in experiencing the other allegedly "wholesome" emotions. If they are emotions, they, too, can catch us off guard and threaten our control. To aim for a fully disturbance-free state of *eupatheia* is, in effect, to aim for *apatheia*.

These Stoic worries about safeguarding happiness from reversal are not Kant's own concerns in casting his view back to Stoic apathy. His worries are not about the attachment of sentiment to unstable externals,[46] but about sentimentalism, and grand but ineffectual emotions. He imports the ancient Stoic sage not to restage the Stoic revision about what *eudaimonia* will contain, but as we shall see in the next chapter, to fight against the sentimentalism he finds in the eighteenth-century air.[47] Conversely, the ancient Stoic sage is not particularly worried about grand but morally impotent affects, but *is* worried about how living emotionally could rob one of *eudaimonia*. That is the whole reason for emotional therapy. Kant, in severing virtue from *eudaimonia*, doesn't share this worry. By and large, he lets happiness (as he understands the notion) fall where it may, and hopes that in the progress of virtue, reason can adequately moderate emotion, more along Aristotelian lines.

But we can say a little more about the Stoics and Kant. The distinction between diseased *pathē* and the enlightened emotions, or *eupatheiai*, provides, if not the actual source of Kant's own distinction between pathological and practical emotions, at least an important early analogue.[48] Kant, of course, does not subscribe to the Stoic view of emotions as judgments. As such the distinction between pathological and practical emotions is not a matter of false versus reasoned evaluations, as it is for the Stoics, but

---

[46] Kant, of course, does retain the unreliability objection that the Stoics articulate.
[47] To some degree, the Roman Stoics (particulary, Seneca in *De Clementia*) may have been doing something similar in their use of the ideas of the ancient Stoa. See Baron (1995b), who draws the connection.
[48] In not requiring that practical emotions be fully disturbance free, Kant may be articulating a notion that is more stable than the corresponding Stoic notion of *eupatheia*.

more a matter of passive versus active and controlled, affective responses.[49] There is this more substantial difference: In the case of the ancient Stoics, the presence of the "revised" emotions (*eupatheiai*) may be truly peripheral – a nominal and formal "add-on" to soften the austere edges of the sage's rational virtue. We shall see that Kant's rhetoric sometimes suggests practical emotions will serve a similar purpose, "dressing virtue to advantage," as he puts it in the *Anthropology*. Here there is a sense of emotions as mere window dressing. But as I shall argue, in his ample, non-Stoic moments, Kant relies on the emotions as a substantive part of his account of virtue, and as a part of the account of what we have a duty to cultivate. Anticipating the discussion in Chapter 4, we can put the accommodation in this way: Following the Stoics, Kant grounds virtue in reason and, like them, sees little need for the motivational role of emotions in morality. As the Stoics might put it, *contra* Aristotle, the virtuous person acts generously because it is the right thing to do, without having to summon extra emotional feelings to motivate the action.[50] Duty will function similarly. But while Kant makes this claim about the motivational role of emotion, he does it without forfeiting the advantage of emotion's evaluative function. And in this sense, as Stoic as his rhetoric often is, I shall argue that he in fact allies himself with the commonsense view (and Aristotle's too), that emotions are simply too epistemically useful to forsake them. The Stoics, in rejecting emotions entirely, forfeit any such advantage.

What then of a more genuine Kantian apathy? As I argue in the next chapter, the apathy Kant is most interested in is not absence of emotion, but absence of sentimentality and *tyrannizing* emotions (in his terms, agitations and passions). This is the state of

49 Note at Anth. 236 Kant adapts Stoic terminology suggesting that only certain emotions – here, sensitivity rather than sentimentality – will involve a voluntary assent. ("Sensitivity is a power or strength by which we grant or refuse permission for the state of pleasure or displeasure to enter our mind, so that it implies a choice. On the other hand, sentimentality is a weakness by which we can be affected, even against our will.") On the Stoic view, all emotions involve assent, even if it is assent to a false valuation. This is central to their view of our moral responsibility for emotions.
50 On this point, see the discussion at the end of Chapter 2.

moral mental health and equanimity of the truly virtuous agent. The Stoics' "saving notion" of *eupatheia* aside, Kant's project of moral anthropology suggests that he had no comparable interest in making virtue lean of emotion.[51] He saw the natural advantage of emotion, even in a morality whose authority must ultimately rest in reason. Still, it is by a strange twist of inheritance that he did not avail himself of the shared ancient view that emotions are not brute sensations, but states that have evaluative content. This might have made it easier for him to let go of certain rhetoric against the emotions and appreciate even more fully just how reason's project can work through the emotions.

[51] See esp. Rel. 58/51.

Chapter 4

The passional underpinnings of Kantian virtue

1 SOME BACKGROUND

In preceding chapters we have begun to consider Kant's position on the emotions[1] and their place in his conception of morality. We have warned repeatedly that Kant's familiar castigation of the emotions is part of a more complex story he has to tell, which it is now time to explore.

Kant's position on the emotions is no simple matter. But in many ways it can be understood through the lens of the Enlightenment. Like many members of what Peter Gay has called the international family of *philosophes*,[2] Kant was an appreciative and well-educated reader of antiquity, and in particular of the Latin Stoics.[3] There is a clear dialectical engagement with the Stoics in his writing, and many of his more familiar views about the emotions echo that identification. What is emphasized in these views is a self-governance by reason that would be undermined by undue reliance on emotion. Under Stoic tutelage, he often tags the

---

[1] Kant does not have a single term to refer to emotion. For what we generally classify as emotions, he uses the various terms *Gefühl* (feeling), *Affekt* (emotional agitation), and *Leidenschaft* (passion). When I am talking about Kant's discussion of a specific variety of emotion, I signal the point, but in general I use the term "emotion" to refer to the general grouping.

[2] Following Gay (1966), I use the term to refer to the Enlightenment's international family of philosophers rather than to just its French members.

[3] For recent studies, see Seidler (1981a,1981b,1983).

emotions as maladies in need of spiritual healing.[4] And like the good doctor so familiar in Stoic philosophy, Kant outlines a nosology of different manias with recommendations for their cures. Again, following Stoic tradition, a therapy that emphasizes the authority of reason is crucial for reform.[5] However, Kant typically stands in two worlds, with one eye toward antiquity and another toward the nearer horizon. What is closer at hand is the view that emotions can be a salutary part of our nature; they are an inescapable part of our psychology that can be linked to taste and aesthetics, and to our humanity as well as our happiness. Although Kant is the Enlightenment figure who gives reason its firmest foundation, he is nonetheless part of a historical milieu in which sentiment and sympathy had their fair proponents and in which many a tear was shed in the act of kindness and compassion. Emotions were in the air; they were celebrated and cultivated parts of everyday rhetoric, even if excessive displays might expose one to the risk of being branded mad or irrational.[6] Kant repudiates much of the sentimentalism of his day, though leaves a clear place for sentiment.

Under the Scottish Enlightenment, of course, emotions become the systematic foundation of the moral life, and compassion and sympathy the medium of judicious judgment. Hume, too, engages in a dialectic with the Stoics that reveals his own ambivalence about grounding morality in human sentiment and, ultimately, in the contingencies of human nature: "I wish from my Heart," he wrote to Francis Hutcheson, " I could avoid conclud-

---

[4] Anth. 251, 253; DV 457.

[5] See Nussbaum (1994) for a development of the idea of Stoic therapy of emotional states.

[6] As Peter Gay so well documents, many of the *philosophes* directed their passion toward the ancients and expressed it in the erotics of reading them: Diderot says, "After reading Seneca, am I the same man I was before I read him? That's not so – it can't be so." Rousseau was known for his idealizing the ancients. But he was not alone. A lesser-known figure of the period, Alfieri, says that as a young man he came upon Plutarch and his record of the lives of Caesar, Brutus, Cato, and others. "I wept, raved, and fell into such ecstasies that if anyone had been in the next room he would have called me insane. Every time I came to any of the great actions of these famous persons, my agitation was so extreme that I could not remain seated. I was like one beside myself" (Gay 1966, 47).

ing, that since Morality, according to your Opinion as well as mine, is determin'd merely by Sentiment, it regards only human Nature & human Life."[7]

Although Kant's central preoccupation in moral theory is also the human case, unlike Hume, his march is intended to move beyond the "capital" of human nature[8] to a foundation for morality safely outside human contingency. The distinction between a metaphysics of morality and an anthropology is meant to capture this division between an *a priori* grounding and the specific circumstances of the human case. Kant introduces emotions, not as part of the ground of morality but as a part of moral anthropology, or what we would call moral psychology. Here the old-fashioned project of virtue – of habituating character including its passional underpinnings – finds a place. Still, I shall urge care in understanding this distinction and the relation between the two parts of the project. A central part of my argument in the coming pages is that at a systematic level, Kant's anthropology is a part of his *full* moral theory in ways that are often not acknowledged.

The point I now stress is that both Stoic as well as more positive, contemporary views about the emotions are part of Kant's implicit tutelage. To focus exclusively on either his harangues against irrational passions or his seeming eulogies of what nature has given us, distorts the fuller picture. Both poles are in his account. At his best, his self-conscious task is to explain how the emotions are morally important and yet posterior to the foundation of morality in reason. In this sense, though emotions are the stuff of our embodied rational natures, their value is always conditional, supporting rather than grounding morality.

However, there is a third line of inheritance that Kant brings to bear on his account of the emotions. This is his Pietist background. In grounding morality in reason, Kant certainly rejects much of the sentimentalism and emotional intensity of his religious upbringing. However, not all aspects of the Pietist emphasis on the emotional life are expunged. In particular, Pietist insistence on coming to know one's own soul, not simply through

---

[7] As quoted by Gay (1966, 65) from Hume's letter to Hutcheson, March 16, 1740.
[8] This is Hume's famous phrase at *Treatise*, intro. (xx).

good deeds but through emotional attitudes and affect, is recast in Kant's own notion that good cheer and contentment are the outer signs of a good will. Although Kant is insistent that it is a happy, not melancholic heart that is the true sign of goodness,[9] he allows that some negative feelings such as disgust may have their place in revealing an individual's sincere struggle with sin. Generally speaking, Pietism undergirds Kant's view that morality requires conscientious first-person assessment. But more specifically, Kant's Pietist background may suggest to him the importance of introspecting *through* the medium of the emotions. The emotions may disclose important information about one's moral state.

I must caution, though, that these remarks about background influence are meant as no more than that. They are simply sketchy stage notes to set in place Kant's views. My concern is not to demonstrate decisive historical influence or debt, but merely to signal broad, background trends. My more systematic claim is that Kant's teeter-totter with the emotions can be best understood with Aristotle's view in the background. But here again my interest is not a historical one about debt or transmission. It is not clear that Kant read Aristotle directly, even though he is deeply familiar with the broad lines of ancient eudaimonistic theory. His own theory is meant to stand as a critique of it.[10] Still, even this conceptual lineage is not my present concern – which is the moral significance of emotions in Kantian ethics. My claim is that we can grasp in a sharper way the significant contours of Kant's views through a broad dialogue with Aristotle on this subject. Reciprocally, through the vantage point of Kantian ethics, Aristotle's own views becomes clearer.

---

[9] See DV 484–85 and Anth. 331–33 for the general notion that cheer rather than contempt for the species is the appropriate response to human struggle against evil. On the "gloomy soul," see Campbell (1987, 126ff.). On Pietist writings, see Erb (1983; 1989).

[10] I take this to be the unmistakable force of the opening pages of the *Groundwork*: The unconditioned goodness of the good will replaces ancient conceptions of what is ultimately good in the pursuit of good living. As such, Kant does not do away with the concept of the good in his theory of morality but makes rational agency the candidate that best fills that slot. For a defense of this claim and for a view that Kantian ethics has been mischaracterized as deontological, see Herman (1993, ch. 10).

Chapter 2 set out in some detail Aristotle's conception of virtue and its affective structure. At important junctures, it pointed to traditional Kantian criticisms of a conception of virtue rooted in the emotions. If upon closer inspection it turns out that Kant is more receptive to the emotions playing supporting roles in morality, then what are those roles? More generally, how do emotions figure in his account of virtue? Will they be part of virtue? Will they be morally estimable? How will Kant's account differ from Aristotle's?

One way of setting the problem of this chapter is to reflect back on the *Groundwork* and contrast it with a theme that runs through *The Doctrine of Virtue*. It has long bothered readers of Kant's *Groundwork* that Kant takes himself there to be reconstructing ordinary morality, and yet assigns no moral worth to emotions that support morality. The issue becomes more complicated in the face of a growing acknowledgment that in later works, such as *The Doctrine of Virtue*, Kant recognizes the duty to develop emotions as a part of our duties of virtue. We have a duty to habitutate empirical character and, in some sense, a duty to diminish the merely accidental natures of our nature. Our agency extends deeply to the cultivation of our passional selves. Thus, according to *The Doctrine of Virtue*, our end-setting capacities (i.e., rational agency) are sustained and developed by the setting of obligatory ends and sub-ends. These require the cultivation of our natural powers and receptivities in ways that empower our agency. Included among these receptivities are emotions. The question then arises, Are these cultivated emotions now candidates for moral worth?

On one leading view, the assignment of moral worth for the performance of a dutiful action does not entail that inclinations cannot be present.[11] It is simply that they cannot ground one's reasons for performing that action. They cannot be the agent's motives for acting. Moral interest must guide one's will, and this is not rooted in emotional motivation. But it is important to note that the *Groundwork* has in mind primarily inclinations that are *immediate* or *impulsive*. The *Groundwork* famously opens with a

[11] Herman (1993, ch. 1)

discussion of the unconditioned goodness of a good will and the claim that only dutiful action guided by its principles has moral worth.Actions motivated by *immediate* inclinations, however in conformity they may be with duty, lack moral worth. To act honestly because it is the best policy for doing business fails, in an obvious way, to embrace a moral motive. But so, too, on Kant's view, is acting from genuine, but immediate, sympathy for another's well-being "without any further motive of vanity or self-interest."[12] Kant suggests that the inadequacy of sympathy has to do again with its accidental connection to moral interest. Sometimes it may succeed as a criterion for doing what is dutiful, but sometimes not.[13] In a broader way, he views it on its own as a nonmoral motive that falls under the principle of self-love or happiness. Not only does this minimize the positive roles inclinations play in moral practice, it leaves to the side the question of whether *cultivated* virtuous emotions are themselves to be viewed as falling outside moral motivation. Yet elsewhere, Kant takes the cultivation of emotions as a central focus and suggests that hand in hand with the strengthening of duty as the motive for doing what is dutiful (and morally permissible) is cultivating emotions to support duty's work. Virtue requires both. In this chapter I review some of these texts and propose a conception of moral character in which emotions responsive to the constraints and ends of duty come to be viewed as morally estimable.

Kant's overall discussion of the emotions and their relation to virtue is episodic, but still there is more to draw from than most commentators have noted. Some of the important treatments are in the later works – in *The Doctrine of Virtue* (1797), in *Religion Within the Limits of Reason Alone* (1793), and in *Anthropology from a Pragmatic Point of View* (1798). But also there is a substantive discussion in the *Critique of Practical Reason* (1788), written only three years after the *Groundwork*.[14]

---

[12] G 398.

[13] See Oakely (1992, ch. 3) for an argument that this objection can be directed against the duty motive itself.

[14] Also the *Critique of Judgment*. The connection of this with the treatment of the emotions in the ethical writings has been discussed admirably by Paul Guyer. The last chapter of his (1993) book focuses more exclusively on the treatment

Before turning to the emotions we need first to review the relationship Kant envisages between a metaphysics of morals and its accompanying anthropology. This should stand us well for appraising the more specific case in which emotions are central to the practice of human morality. Second, we need to situate Kant's notion of virtue within his general moral theory.

2 MORALITY'S FOUNDATION AND MORAL ANTHROPOLOGY

The *Groundwork* is notorious for its warnings against mixing the *a priori* foundation of morality with contingent features of the human case. Morality, as Kant puts it, cannot depend "on the special nature of human reason."[15] The familiar tone is set in the following passage:

> Nevertheless such a completely isolated metaphysic of morals, mixed with no anthropology . . . still less with occult qualities (which might be called hypophysical), is not only an indispensable substratum of all theoretical and precisely defined knowledge of duties, but is at the same time a desideratum of the utmost importance for the actual execution of moral precepts. Unmixed with the alien element of added empirical inducements, the pure thought of duty, and in general of the moral law, has by way of reason alone (which first learns from this that by itself it is able to be practical as well as theoretical) an influence on the human heart so much more powerful than all the further impulsions capable of being called up from the field of experience that in the consciousness of its own dignity reason despises these impulsions and is able gradually to become their master. In place of this, a mixed moral philosophy, compounded of impulsions from feeling and inclination and at the same time of rational concepts, must make the mind waver between motives which can be brought under no single princi-

of emotions in the ethical works. For a symposium on his book, see the discussions of Ameriks (1995), Guyer (1995), and Sherman (1995c).
[15] G 411–12.

ple and which can guide us only by mere accident to the good, but very often also the evil.[16]

Kant's emphasis here is twofold. First, he is concerned to discuss the issue of motivation: We can act on principle without the inducement of inclination, without, that is, feelings generated by a source other than the principle of our legislative agency (i.e, the Categorical Imperative). As Kant states the point earlier in the *Lectures on Ethics,* moral principle can itself serve as a *motive* or "mainspring" for the performance of our obligation.[17] Second, moral principle also serves as *criterion* or norm for determining moral obligation. And his point just quoted is that emotions do not do nearly as well in this capacity. They "can guide us only by mere accident to the good" but very often lead us to what is evil. The argument, a variant of one regarding the external goods often made by Plato and later the Stoics,[18] is that emotions do not ground a principle that itself connects us with the right-making features of an action. So, the claim here is that emotions are neither central to our formulating principles of action, nor required as a mainspring for executing action once we determine what is right. They serve poorly both as norms and as motives.

Certainly what is most salient about this *Groundwork* passage is its tone. Reason "despises" inclination. A mixed moral philosophy makes the mind "waver" without direction as to why an action is right or wrong. But tone aside, the underlying message is that a *metaphysics* of morality cannot be mixed. The *authority* of morality (as criterion for what is right and motive for executing the judgments that ensue) must come from reason alone.

---

[16] G 410–11; cf. DV 216–17.

[17] LE 36; see DV 387. I am indebted to Paul Guyer's general discussion (1993, 338–44), in which he distinguishes between "moral principle as a *criterion* of what duty requires and moral principle as a *motive* for conformity to what is required by such a criterion."

[18] See, for example, *Meno* 87c-88a, *Euthydemus* 280e, *Gorgias* 467e for the idea of "intermediates" as things that sometimes participate in the good, sometimes in the bad, and sometimes in neither. For Stoic views, see Diogenes Laertius 7.101–3 = L and S 58 A, as well as also the other fragments cited by L and S in sec. 58, "Value and indifference."

However, in his later writings Kant is far clearer that we can still preserve an unmixed metaphysics of morality while allowing moral anthropology a proper role. Moral theory as a whole includes both, and as such, becomes something of a "mixed moral philosophy." On this view, practical reason, not natural sensibility, will remain the source of morality's constraints. It is always the conception of free practical agency that grounds our fundamental moral norms. But the "actual execution" of moral principles, or full moral practice itself, relies on the resources of a supportive empirical nature. Moreover, our particular moral principles generated by practical reason are themselves tailored to the embodied human case. So, for example, beneficence appeals to the fact of our limited rational agency and the need for social interdependence as remedy. Put generally for the moment, the generation of our specific duties from the fact of our rational nature requires contingent premises that tailor rational agency to human vulnerabilities and powers. An understanding of what limits and threatens rational agency and what human powers support it are essential for the articulation of our duties. Kant elaborates the general point in the Introduction to *The Metaphysic of Morals*. In a most significant way, his remarks take us beyond the harsher, more exclusionary rhetoric of the *Groundwork*.

> But just as a metaphysic of nature must also contain principles for applying those universal first principles of nature as such to objects of experience, so a metaphysic of morals cannot dispense with principles of application; and we shall often have to take as our object the particular *nature* of man, which is known only by experience, to show in it the implications of the universal moral principles.[19]

The point that emerges here is that to direct the moral project toward the human condition is not necessarily to jeopardize its *a priori* grounding. Put differently, Kant is not worried here, in this work written in 1797, twelve years after the *Groundwork*, that a focus on human nature will undermine the source of morality in reason. What remains *a priori* is that action must respect free

---

[19] DV 216–17.

practical agency and the ultimate value of a person as an author of her own reasons and actions. Kant often takes this idea to be best expressed through universalizability: Others must be able to accept and act on maxims at the same time I do. In this regard, I am one among others in a community of lawmakers, each capable of acting on reasons that could become universal laws that everyone could follow. The legislative form respects each person's fundamental, practical agency. But when and how a maxim might threaten practical agency, and, more fundamentally, what the special nature of our practical agency is, such that it can be *fully* empowered, is itself an applied matter.[20] To grant this is not to "find" morality in practice. It is to constrain practice by what has been set as morally important in advance of it.

Indeed, Kant himself would be the first to concede that the Categorical Imperative, as opposed to the moral law, is itself an anthropological construct. It addresses the problem of moral law for a finitely rational agent who can be aware of that moral law and yet oppose it because of inclination. This is the standing occasion for an imperative.[21] Like virtue, the Categorical Imperative is situated in a field of rational players who are not holy. "Human morality in its highest stages can still be nothing more than virtue."[22] The Categorical Imperative constrains; virtue, as we shall see, is fortitude in meeting its demands. But what is human-oriented about the Categorical Imperative is not simply that it is formally designed for beings who might will contrary to moral law. Substantively, too, as we have been saying, it generates norms by reference to our finite brand of rational willing and the specific conditions of finitude and vulnerability that characterize

---

20 For Kant's own suggestions that an appendix regarding applications of the Categorical Imperative would be a part of the "complete exposition of the [moral] system," see DV 468–69. See also Buchanan (1977), Gregor (1963), Herman (1993, 230–36), O'Neill (1989), and Sedgwick (1988). Gregor discusses the issue in terms of the "schematization" of the moral law.

21 KpV 32–3. It is also the standing occasion for the feeling of respect, which I take up in Section 7. Notably, respect, like the Categorical Imperative, is not appropriately ascribed to the divine will; see KpV 72–73. For an interesting discussion of the anthropological and social aspects of Kant's moral theory, see Robinson and Harré (1994).

22 DV 383.

our lives. Thus, the very adaptation of the moral law to the notion of the Categorical Imperative (and its specific formulae), and the generation through these of specific perfect and imperfect duties that are juridical and ethical, all, at various levels of specificity, depend upon material assumptions that pertain to us as embedded humans. So, in a formal and most general way, as humans we need constraints and ends (i.e., "oughts") imposed on our will. This is the bare idea behind a Categorical Imperative. But in a more substantive way, the duties that result will meet the challenges of our specific condition – that we are prone to deception, that our desires can be excessive, that self-interest may inappropriately outweigh other-regard, that we cannot achieve our ends alone, without social cooperation, and, too, that we have certain natural powers and receptivities that can be cultivated to meet these challenges. Thus, in both the bare notion of the Categorical Imperative and in its application in a system of duties, *a posteriori* elements applicable to the human case enter moral theory. We shall see also that another level of anthropology is sandwiched between the bare idea of the Categorical Imperative and its results. For the contradiction tests by which the Categorical Imperative produces its results also depend upon *a posteriori* elements.

We can appreciate these points as we turn to duties of beneficence and nondeceit. Beneficence is classified by Kant as an imperfect, ethical duty. It is *imperfect* in that it proposes an end or policy whose fulfillment is wide in latitude. It is *ethical* in that its sanctions are internally, and not legally, enforceable. What is significant for our present discussion is that it is a substantive moral principle not for any rational agent, but specifically for human beings whose rational capacities happen to be finite and who therefore need the collaborative assistance and resources of others. A maxim that seeks to gain self-advantage by denying mutual aid is incoherent in the universalized world of that maxim because the agent of such a maxim will be denied what she needs for effective *human* willing.[23] The universalized maxim violates or

---

[23] See the distinction between what is often called the contradiction in will and contradiction in concept interpretations of the Formula of Universal Law at G

"contradicts" her will in the sense of failing to supply what is required for the human brand of free practical agency. It is thus because of our finite human condition that a policy of mutual disinterest is impermissible, and its opposite, beneficence, morally required. In this sense, beneficence requires appeal to the contingent fact of our non-self-sufficient wills. We contradict our wills by a maxim of nonbeneficence insofar as we deny a standing fact about them. The duty to gratitude returns to this same point – that we need to keep alive conditions of beneficence in the face of our limited self-sufficiency. The general point is that ethical duties, as applications of the constraining power of the Categorical Imperative, are attempts to preserve our peculiar brand of finite agency.

The duty not to lie might be thought to fare better as a prohibition against any rational being, irrespective of contingent limitations.[24] Although lying to self or others can be an issue only for beings who lack full transparency, still the wrongness of lying, in contrast to that of nonbeneficence, might be thought of as appealing to only our rational natures and not to any contingent feature that marks our special brand of rationality. This seems to be Kant's point when he takes up deceitful promising as a breach of universalizability. To make a deceitful promise in a world in which everyone does is simply conceptually incoherent; it is a contradiction in conception. It is inconceivable, irrespective of any practical limitations on our wills.[25] But this doesn't get it quite right. Even the conceptual incoherence of universalized false promising depends upon facts of our human nature – that we remember false promises, for example, and are unprepared to trust those who have made them in the past. In other ways, too, it can be argued that a maxim of lying frustrates the peculiar *practical* rational agency we have as humans.[26] It may be conceptually

---

424. I am here referring to a maxim that reveals a contradiction in will.

[24] Unlike the duty of beneficence, it is a perfect duty, though like beneficence, it is an ethical duty because it falls under a general end of self-perfection enforceable by internal rather than external sanctions (DV 429–31; LE 118.)

[25] G 422.

[26] See Korsgaard (1985) on interpreting the Formula of Universal Law as based on a test of practical consistency. She calls this the "practical interpretation."

incoherent for humans, constituted as we are, to lie in a world of liars, but also the lie won't work to get you what you want, because again, the contract of language, upon which human interaction depends, has been ruptured. In such a world, it is *practically* incoherent to use lying as an efficient means. There is no ride upon which to be a free rider.[27] But the very idea of practical incoherence of this sort depends upon a feature of our finite rational natures: that to achieve our ends we humans must work through stepwise instrumental means. We reason instrumentally in time and space, and in this presumably differ from gods and angels whose will, we tend to think, can be their immediate command. To point out a practical contradiction in an agent's action requires that we are already working with a test that applies specifically to those who bring about ends instrumentally.

The general point I wish to stress is that the metaphysic of morals makes its transition into anthropology early on. The work of "application" is already embedded in the very notion of

---

27 It should be noted that I am not here arguing that this is the only or necessarily best way to interpret the impermissibility of lying, or that it adequately exposes what is *morally wrong* with these maxims. In this regard, Barbara Herman has noted an important problem with the practical interpretation of the Formula of Universal Law: essentially, that it flags as morally problematic (i.e., produces as false prohibitions) coordination and timing maxims that depend upon taking advantage of knowledge of other individuals' schedules or habits. In so doing, it fails to distinguish free riding from coordination. In booking a tennis court on Sunday at ten a.m. when I know others will be in church, I "take advantage" of the existing practices, but not unfairly. See Herman (1993, 138–43). She suggests that trying to correct this result by adding a publicity requirement, such that people wouldn't mind "our taking advantage of their . . . patterns of behavior," does not itself explain why satisfying that requirement *shows* the moral permissibility of the maxim (see 227n). I, like Herman, believe we can get at the wrongness of lying more directly through the Formula of Humanity, and the duty to treat self and others not merely as means but always at the same time as ends-in-themselves. Lying is a violation of duties to self in that it perverts the purpose of our rational natures and the basis of our status as ends-in-themselves; it is a violation of duties to others in that it forces the will of another in the basic sense of denying that agent the opportunity to consent. Even more basic, it violates the fundamental social contract, which speech represents and in which a language user implicitly agrees to engage. In this basic sense, it manipulates. I take up these issues further in Chapter 7.

the Categorical Imperative and its contradiction tests, and more substantively, is its appeal to empirical premises in grounding specific, normatiave principles. The passage cited earlier distinguishing a metaphysics of morals and a moral anthropology underemphasizes this point:

> A metaphysic of morals cannot be based on anthropology but can be applied to it.
>
> The counterpart of a metaphysic of morals, the other member of the division of practical philosophy in general, would be moral anthropology. But this would concern only the subjective conditions that hinder or help man in *putting into practice* the laws given in a metaphysic of morals. It would deal with the generation, propagation, and strengthening of moral principles (in the education of school children and of the public at large), and other such teachings and precepts based on experience.[28]

But this misses the force of Kant's own fuller theory. Substantive moral principles and duties of end (and not merely more applied "precepts" taught to children) are themselves a "putting into practice of the laws given in a metaphysic of morals." Moreover, the derivation of duties is itself constrained by the idea of a Categorical Imperative whose tests of consistency are informed, to a varying degree, by the human case. The duties that result represent ways of fortressing our finite rationality in the face of yet further conditions of finitude – such as our mortality, and our capacities to be hurt, deceived, tempted, and coerced.[29] Especially worrisome, Kant holds, is our capacity for rationalization – for here we use reason against itself in an attempt to escape its own self-vigil. Rationalization is reason's own corruption of itself.[30]

[28] DV 217.

[29] See Barbara Herman's (1993, 205) notion of "situated" agency.

[30] Rel. 38/33–34. Indeed, in the *Religion*, Kant argues that radical evil is a matter not so much of yielding to contrary inclination, but of yielding to contrary inclination carefully veiled in rationalization: "This dishonesty by which we humbug ourselves . . . constitutes the foul taint in our race." Not surprisingly, Kant makes "the first command of all duties" the duty to know yourself, DV 441.

However, our main focus in this chapter is the emotions. At what point do they enter the anthropology of morals? I have said throughout that Kant has an underappreciated account of the virtues. What is Kant's account of virtue and how do emotions figure in it? In what follows I shall counter the standard interpretation that emotions are a merely accidental feature of moral practice that has little systematic and positive value in the moral life. In a preponderance of texts, Kant argues that we have a duty to cultivate emotions so that they can become a pervasive part of the supportive structure of virtues. So, for example, by schooling our sympathy in certain ways rather than others, we use the receptivities of our nature to support the virtue of beneficence. In this and similar ways, emotions become a morally effective part of virtue. Still, it might be argued that Kant ultimately marginalizes the emotions by viewing them as expressions of our merely *passive* selves, which as such fall outside our practical agency. But I believe this misrepresents matters greatly. For although emotions are part of our "nature," Kant's considered view is that our nature, and emotions as part of it, can be cultivated by the will. In this sense, they are not beyond the influence of practical freedom or moral agency. Indeed, cultivated emotions become an important expression of the dominion of practical reason. Like the ancients, Kant views the cultivation of human nature, or our natural perfection, important evidence of the effect of our practical agency on our natures.

3 KANTIAN VIRTUE

Before we can focus on the role of emotions in virtue, we need to understand Kant's conception of virtue and its place within his own systematic framework.[31] The notion of virtue is discussed most extensively in Part II of *The Metaphysic of Morals*, entitled *The Doctrine of Virtue* (*Tugendlehre*). Part I of *The Metaphysic of Morals* is devoted to *The Doctrine of Law* and concerns juridical duties; Part II, or *The Doctrine of Virtue*, is devoted to ethics and to those duties that "do not come under external laws" but are, rather, internally

---

[31] For a very useful overview of Kant's account of virtue, see Gregor (1963).

sanctioned.[32] Kant explains the difference as follows: "What essentially distinguishes a duty of virtue from a juridical duty is the
fact that external compulsion to a juridical duty is morally possible, whereas a duty of virtue is based only on free self-
constraint."[33] Of course, juridical duties, too, can be done from
internal sanction, that is, from the spirit of duty, rather than from
fear of external sanction.[34] But ethical duties cannot, conversely,
be legally enforced. Ethical duties thus have to do with character
(the term "ethical" comes from the Greek term for character,
ēthos). The Kantian conception of virtue lays specific stress on the
notion of strength of will, or fortitude, in obeying an internal
sanction:

> Now the power and deliberate resolve to withstand a strong
> but unjust opponent is *fortitude (fortitudo)*; and fortitude in rela-
> tion to the forces opposing a moral attitude of will *in us* is virtue
> (*virtus, fortitudo moralis*). So the part of the general doctrine of
> duties that brings inner, rather than outer, freedom under laws
> is a *doctrine of virtue*.[35]

Kant indicates here that virtue will be a matter of self-control
against pervasive obstacles, such as the objects of inappropriate
desire or temptation. As he says a few lines later, "virtue is the
power to master one's inclinations when they rebel against the
law."[36] The emphasis here is on inhibitory control; what comes to
mind is the popular view, often associated with Kant, of duty
triumphing over inclinations. What is absent – at least in these
remarks – is the more Aristotelian notion that fully mature virtue
rests not merely in control, but in transforming desires so they no
longer rebel. However, I suggest that Kant leaves room for this
picture of virtue as well, and that this emerges in a more comprehensive study of his account.

Even so, it is important to note early on that Kant is less optimistic than Aristotle about the possibility of overall transformation and psychic harmony. Indeed, the centering of Kant's theory
around duty is testimony to this: Duty marks the enduring conflict between morality and inclination, and to some degree, moral-

[32] DV 379.   [33] DV 383.   [34] DV 383.   [35] DV 380.   [36] DV 383.

ity and happiness.[37] Aristotle simply does not view conflicts between the judgment of what is best and desire as either so pervasive or enduring. As we have said at the end of Chapter 2, he is
optimistic about the possibility of overall psychic harmony and
views right feelings as a steady and reliable part of virtue. But
there is this further point of comparison: Like Kant, Aristotle
holds that virtue involves practical reason. As part of its functions, such reason – our own and that of others – guides the
habituation of character and the choice of how to "stand well"
with regard to emotion and appetite. Kant develops the connection between virtue and practical reason in a new way. Virtue is
fortitude in acting on reasons that may oppose contrary inclinations and that conform to standards of moral accountability generated by practical reason itself. What is new in the Kantian account is not so much the idea of acting on reasons or choices that
incorporate some and oppose other particular inclinations.[38] As I
have just implied, something like this is already implicit in Aristotle's notion of standing well toward appetites and passions. The
notion of *prohairesis* as deliberative choice that "decides upon"
(literally, "takes before others") certain appetites and emotions as
motives may be an expression of something like the general idea
embodied in the Kantian notion of acting on a maxim or reason.[39]
But however similar or not a maxim and *prohairesis* are,[40] what is
certainly new is that our reasons for action must meet standards
that appeal to the very nature of our practical reason. These include the universalizability feature of our reason giving (that
what is a reason for me could be a reason for others similarly
circumstanced), the fact of our autonomy (that we are ultimately

---

[37] Though, of course, the doctrine of the Highest Good is meant to reduce that
conflict in the long run, given the postulate of immortality, KpV 122–24.

[38] On the notion of "taking up" or "incorporating" an inclination into a maxim,
see Rel. 27/23. See the helpful discussions by Allison (1990) and Reath (1989)
and more general discussion of the deliberative standpoint by Hill (1973,
1985).

[39] For a general discussion of *prohairesis*, see Charles (1984, 137–42); Sherman
(1989, ch.3).

[40] See Chapter 7, where I further explore this comparison in light of a more
extensive examination of the notion of a maxim.

the authors of our own ends and must assent to ends to which we contribute), the fact of our humanity (that we violate our rational nature when our reason giving is manipulated or coerced), and, finally, the fact that we are a part of a community of other rational agents, a Kingdom of Ends (in which we are equal to others in sharing all these capacities). Virtue is that attitude of will, that fortitude, in acting on reasons that preserve these features, embodied as they are in the various formulae of the Categorical Imperative. On the Aristotelian view, although practical reason is the backbone of virtue, it is never understood as an internal source of law or a source of autonomy, humanity, and community in the sense that Kant requires.

I said earlier in this section that ethical duties, such as duties of virtue, involve *internal governance.* They are not externally sanctioned as juridical duties are. But also, they involve the *prescription (duties) of ends* as broad policies, wide in requirement. Duties that are wide in this sense are imperfect, in contrast with perfect duties that more narrowly prescribe or proscribe specific types of actions. Kant does allow for perfect ethical duties, such as prohibitions on suicide, gluttony, and lust, as well as prohibitions on lying, avarice, and servility. However, these themselves fall under more general duties of end, enforceable by internal sanction. The most general ends, or duties of virtue, are the ends of one's own perfection and the happiness of others. Here we see an attempt to separate self-regard and other-regard in a way that is not as sharply drawn in Aristotelian theory. And with this distinction between self and other comes an asymmetry of duties: On Kant's view we must promote our own perfection and, especially, our own moral perfection as this regulates the pursuit of our perfection in general. But we cannot undertake such a project for others, for it would be a violation of their very status as free moral agents.[41] In promoting their happiness, we leave to them the setting of their own ends, including the general end of their moral perfection.

One thing to notice here is that these general duties to self and others lead to derivative duties constitutive of their fulfillment. In

---

[41] DV 385–86.

this regard, Kant, unlike Aristotle, intends his theory of virtue to be a "doctrine of ends" that sets out in a systematic way a hierarchical system of duties. True, Aristotle conceives of *eudaimonia*, or happiness as a *structured* system of ends, and holds that the good life requires grasping the intelligibility of one's ends as they figure in some ordered whole. This is made explicit in the opening chapters of the *Nicomachean Ethics*. Ethical inquiry, he argues there, just is reflection about the whole of one's life in a way that can reveal the nesting and interlocking of ends. Certain pursuits make sense only in the light of other pursuits (bridlemaking in terms of horsemanship, for example),[42] and these ultimately for the sake of happiness. Still, when we turn to the actual adumbration of the primary components of *eudaimonia* – namely, the virtues – there is never an attempt to systematize rigidly these or their subparts in hierarchical fashion. In Kant's theory, we do find such an attempt. There are duties of virtue and subduties, all ultimately requisite for promoting the fundamental value of a person, either in self or other, as a free practical rational agent. Virtue is formally strength of will; the duties of virtue are the substantive duties of end and their subduties, which manifest in concrete ways the attitude of promoting rational agency in self or others.[43] In the case of self, promoting one's own rational agency

---

[42] NE 1094a6–16.

[43] Natalie Brender (in correspondence) has remarked to me that while Kant discusses plural *duties* of *virtue,* he less often says there are distinct *virtues.* Her claim is that this shift in terminology is an attempt to emphasize the aesthetic presentation of virtue as a unitary *whole.* I quote her helpful comments: "In at least two places [Kant] declares that talk of the virtues is really a figurative way of gesturing at aspects of virtue which must be presented in all its unitary splendor by philosophers to attain maximum affective results (Anth. 295; DV 406). I think that it is important to acknowledge his point (at DV 406) that what we unavoidably think of as multiple virtues are really the multiple objects of a unitary virtue, in order to appreciate his later point (at Anth. 295) that philosophers are culpable in failing to present an adequate aesthetics of morals." I note, though, that at DV 383 Kant uses both the notions of plural "virtues" (*verschiedene Tugenden*) and plural "duties of virtue"; in the context of this passage, the two terms seem to be very close in meaning. Both are distinguished from a unitary ground of moral choice – a "virtuous attitude of will" (*tugendhafte Gesinnung*).

is a matter of self-perfection; in the case of others, when we contribute to their morally permissible ends of happiness, we are valuing their rational agency as it is embodied in their choice of ends. In both cases, there is a clear pyramidal structure with free practical agency at the pinnacle. Aristotelian theory does not present virtue in this ordered way, even though, as with Kant, Aristotle holds that our peculiar function of rationality is at the center of an account of virtue.[44] Nor does Aristotle's theory sharply distinguish between ends specifically directed at self versus others, in the way that Kant's theory of the duties of ends does. Of course, generosity is clearly other-directed, whereas temperance, in the paradigmatic case, is directed toward self. But though Aristotle is, for the most part, keen to preserve this distinction as part of commonsense usage,[45] still he does not use it as an organizing principle for the division of virtue as Kant does. There is not the same pyramidal structure of virtue that stems from the unconditioned value of rational agency itself.

In analyzing the derivative system of duties that flow from general ends, we can begin to see Kantian virtue as something more than merely self-control and mastery, and as involving, in addition, the positive cultivation and development of human nature. Granted, Kant often talks about virtue as fortitude and strength *against opponents* (e.g., "*Virtue* is the strength of man's maxims in fulfilling his duty. We can recognize strength of any kind only by the obstacles it can overcome, and in the case of virtue these obstacles are the natural inclinations").[46] But these sorts of remarks need to be understood in a qualified way, first, as making an epistemic claim about the conditions in which virtue is most perspicuous, and second, as describing one, but not all, of the ways in which virtue is manifest. Virtue, as we shall see, is manifest equally in the positive transformation of our natures, including our emotional receptivities. It is now time to turn to that account.

---

[44] See the famous function argument at NE 1098a3ff.

[45] See Annas (1993, 240–90) for the connection between self-love and other-love in Aristotle's theory.

[46] DV 394.

4 THE CULTIVATION OF EMOTIONS AS
SUPPORTS FOR DUTY:
THE DOCTRINE OF VIRTUE

As we have just said, in *The Doctrine of Virtue,* Kant conceives of virtue as the strength of a person's commitment (maxim) in fulfilling her duty. It is the strength of obeying an internal sanction in the performance of ethical or juridical duties. Kant familiarly suggests that virtue may be most perspicuous in fortitude against contrary inclinations.[47] But the power and mastery of a will governed by morality is also manifest, he insists, in the transformation of our sensuous natures by that will into states that positively support it. Realizing the full capacity of such a will involves transforming our animal nature in ways that align with morality. "Man has a duty of striving to raise himself from the crude state of his nature, from his animality and to realize ever more fully in himself the humanity by which he alone is capable of setting ends."[48] Briefly put, our humanity is the capacity to set ends, or adopt reasons for action.[49] The perfection of our humanity (or a good will) involves choice guided by reason's own principle, in other words, the Categorical Imperative.[50] But perfection also involves working up our natures to support that principle. Kant puts it as follows:

> When we say that man has a duty to take as his end the perfection characteristic of man as such (of humanity, really), we must locate perfection in what man can bring into being by his actions, not in the mere gifts he receives from nature; for otherwise it would not be a duty to make perfection an end. This

[47] DV 380; 394.
[48] DV 387.
[49] See DV 392.
[50] In Herman's terms, as primary motive in the case of performing required action and as constraint ("motive of duty as a limiting condition") in the case of doing what is morally permissible. An attitude of virtue can be expressed in both functions of the Categorical Imperative, as the spirit that motivates doing what is ethically or juridically required, or that regulates nonrequired actions such that they are not in violation of what is required. Actions that are candidates for moral worth are only those that are morally required.

duty must therefore be the *cultivation* of one's powers (or natural capacities). . . . At the same time this duty includes the cultivation of one's *will* (moral attitude) [*sittlicher Denkungsart*] to fulfill every duty as such.[51]

Here Kant is anticipating a bifurcation of the duty to one's own perfection into the duty of natural perfection and the duty of moral perfection. The duty of natural perfection, Kant says, involves the transformation of certain powers. Kant has in mind primarily "powers of mind, soul, and body," as "means to all possible ends." Powers of mind, he specifies later, as involving understanding and reasoning; powers of soul as involving capacities of "memory, and imagination and the like"; and powers of the body as involving our animal stuff whose maintenance is required for our "animal vigour."[52] Surprisingly, Kant does not list here emotional capacities as among the natural powers that subserve our duty to moral perfection. Whatever the reason for the absence,[53] it is quickly remedied. For we do find explicit and extended appeal to the notion of cultivated feelings as among the resources we need to rely on in fulfilling our other obigatory end, namely, the promotion of the happiness of others. It becomes systematic in the discussion of that end that we have derivative duties to cultivate feelings, such as sympathetic joy and sorrow, as ways of realizing beneficence and other sub-ends of that general duty. As Kant says,

> Sympathetic joy and sorrow . . . are really sensuous feelings of a pleasure or pain . . . at another's state of happiness or sadness (shared feeling, feeling participated in). Nature has already implanted in man the susceptibility for these feelings.

---

[51] DV 386–87.

[52] DV 445. Kant's division of powers of mind, soul, and body contrasts with the standard Aristotelian division of goods into goods of the soul, goods of the body, and external goods. Virtue has to do with the goods of the soul; health and strength would be bodily goods that promote virtue and may be intrinsically valuable, though not themselves a part of virtue. External goods would be such things as wealth and office, which also promote virtue but which are not intrinsically valuable.

[53] Guyer (1993, 376) attributes this to Kant's borrowing of Wolffian categories of natural perfection.

But to use this as a means to promoting active and rational benevolence is still a particular, though only a conditioned, duty.[54]

Once we get this far, it is easy to see that the cultivation of such feelings becomes part of an underlying project of natural perfection that supports our moral perfection and its application to both self and others.

But to return to the earlier quote about moral perfection, Kant adds to it a few lines later, that as a human being one has a duty of cultivating one's will "to the *purest* attitude of virtue, in which the law is the motive as well as the norm for his actions and he obeys it from duty."[55] What stands out here is that at the same time we are to develop our talents and emotional capacities as part of virtue (and so conceive of virtue along the ancient model of an empirical project of character habituation), we are nevertheless to develop a *purer* attitude of virtue that is grounded in and responds to the rational nature of persons as end setters and moral legislators. It is this moral interest – that is, interest in acting from moral principles for their own sake – that guides our will, as criterion and motive, in the performance of dutiful and permissible action. So we need to cultivate our natural receptivities and the like to support our capacity to act from autonomous principles, but the latter remains, in the purest sense, the source of morality. All this seems to diminish the role of emotions again. Does Kant's expansion of the notion of virtue, in the end, amount to little?[56]

I don't think so. Kant can be seen as reiterating the claim that the ultimate ground of the moral project must rest in the *authority* of reason, without denying that natural receptivities can be shaped by and respond to that authority. On this interpretation, it is more the authority of the moral law than its purity or even sufficiency for motivation that is key.[57] But Kant can go further.

---

54 DV 456; italics omitted.
55 DV 387; italics added.
56 Later (in Section 7) I take up Kant's view that our legislative agency can on its own give rise to the practical interest of respect.
57 Something like this view was suggested to me by Barbara Herman.

He might also be seen as arguing that this responsiveness to morality, as rooted in the rational nature of persons, flourishes best in someone who has cultivated emotional capacities. The emphasis in *The Doctrine of Virtue* is on *who* will act in morally worthy ways from a pure attitude of virtue. And the thought is that what we can do to increase our chances to be part of that pool, is to cultivate emotions that do not battle with our duty motive and that positively promote it. Such emotions are not themselves expressive of the purest attitude of virtue in that they are not the ultimate source of *adequate* reasons for doing what is required or for determining what is morally permissible. But they are a layer of character that can, nonetheless, best support moral motivation.

As such, it becomes important to understand what this supportive structure could be like. To a certain extent the claims represent attempts to come to grips with the suggestive remarks Kant makes in the first chapter of the *Groundwork*:[58]

> Some qualities are even helpful to this good will itself and can make its task very much easier. They have none the less no inner unconditioned worth, but rather presuppose a good will which sets a limit to the esteem in which they are rightly held and does not permit us to regard them as absolutely good . . . They are far from being properly described as good without qualification (however unconditionally they have been commended by the ancients).[59]

The passage makes no mention of specific emotional dispositions. Under consideration in the extended text from which this is drawn are talents of mind (intelligence, wit), qualities of temperament (such as courage, resolution, and presumably moderation and self-control), and gifts of fortune (power, wealth, honor) all of which are described as conditional goods requiring the regulation of a good will, or will motivated by duty. In passing, it is worth noting that some of these goods (e.g., power, wealth, and honor) are much like Aristotelian external goods, in that they are instrumental and subordinate to genuine virtue; others, courage – for

---

[58] An earlier and somewhat different formulation of this supportive structure is in Sherman (1990).

[59] G 393–94.

example – are viewed by Aristotle as themselves virtues, in that if genuine, they must already be regulated by right reason.[60] If we widen Kant's list to include cultivated emotions, as Kant allows more explicitly in other works, then even this opening passage of the *Groundwork* gives us a framework for understanding how such emotions can play a supportive role in the functioning of the mature moral agent.

But what are the roles emotions might play on such a view? Not surprisingly, some of the roles we limned in Chapter 2, Section 2, as plausible parts of a reconstructed Aristotelian account, find a home in the Kantian account as well. In what follows, I want to review these general roles and the supporting Kantian texts.

First, emotions serve as *modes of attention* that help us to track what is morally salient as morally salient in our circumstances, and thus locate possible moments for morally permissible and required actions.[61] Sympathy, for example, draws us to occasions of distress or need. We attend in a charged and alert way, taking in what detached reason or perception might miss. Like all feelings, these inclinations need to be cultivated to serve morality well. We have natural susceptibilities to feel others' pleasures and pains, Kant says.[62] We need to cultivate these – visit the debtors' prisons and sickbeds – in order to orient these sensitivities appropriately, in this case, toward circumstances of need and poverty that are potential occasions for beneficence.

> We have an indirect duty to cultivate the sympathetic natural (aesthetic) feelings in us and to use them as so many means to participating from moral principles and from the feeling appropriate to these principles. – Thus, it is our duty: not to avoid places where we shall find the poor who lack the most basic essentials, but rather seek them out; not to shun sick-rooms or debtors' prisons in order to avoid the painful sympathetic feelings that we cannot guard against. For this is still one of the

[60] See Pol. VII.1.
[61] For suggestions of this view, see Herman (1993, ch. 4). I discuss the point in connection with Aristotle in Sherman (1989, ch. 2).
[62] DV 456.

145

impulses which nature has implanted in us so that we may do what the thought of duty alone would not accomplish.[63]

The point is that the thought of duty alone is insufficient to provide information about which objects and circumstances require our moral attention. Given a practical interest in the moral law and its spheres of justice and virtue, we still require further information about when and where and how to deploy our practical interest. And such information is often provided through the emotions. Capacities for grief prime us to notice human mourning and loss; capacities for compassion, to notice that others suffer in ways that often seem undeserving. Emotions present information not in indefeasible ways, but in ways that are a start for morality. Moral agency is a truncated notion if it begins with choice rather than in what we frame as the circumstances relevant for choice. And emotions play a role in what we record. It would be pointless to forgo the advantages of this capacity in tracking the morally relevant "news."

The notion that emotions are modes of attending moral salience may also have application to the duty of self-knowledge, which Kant maintains underwrites all our duties of self-perfection.[64] Emotions can turn inward to alert us of our own inner states, to help us to read, as he says, our own heart. As such, they may be thought of as mediums by which we can become more aware of our thoughts and motives. Here, as we have said before, emotion may have a *revelatory* aspect, *disclosing* a care or valuation (associated with that emotion) that we might otherwise not have been aware of. Of course, there is no privileged access here, nor infallibilism. Deception and rationalization are among the ways reason works against itself. This is a steady part of our condition and, as he puts it, part of our radical evil.[65] But the emotions may offer a way of acknowledging the proceedings of the inner tribunal that we fail to notice when we take up a cooler view. Here I have in mind Kant's many statements that the pleasure of virtue provides a palpable way of recording for us the fact

---

[63] DV 457.   [64] DV 441.
[65] See Rel. 38/33–34; 57/50; 33/28.

of our own virtue, just as melancholic gloom may point to unresolved conflict.[66]

Second, not only do we read circumstances through the emotions, but we *respond* through them. Manifest affect is a vehicle or *mode for conveying* moral interest. Through emotions, we communitcate or *signal* moral interest to others in ways tailored to particular circumstances and needs. I take it that this is implicit in Kant's claim that benevolent feelings are a means for fulfilling our duty of beneficence. The interpretive emphasis is now not on locating moral salience through the emotions, but on doing what is right with the right sort of emotional attitude. Kant does not emphasize this claim in the way that Aristotle does, but there is more to his remarks than has typically met the commentator's eye.[67] As Kant sometimes puts it, emotion is a "garment that dresses virtue to advantage." The general point comes across clearly in the following passage from the *Anthropology*:

> No matter how insignificant these laws of refined humanity may seem, especially in comparison with pure moral laws, anything that promotes sociability, even if it consists only in pleasing maxims or manners, is a garment that dresses virtue to advantage, a garment to be recommended to virtue in more serious respects too. The *cynic's purism* and the *anchorite's mortification of the flesh,* without social well-being, are distorted figures of virtue, which do not attract us to it. Forsaken by the graces, they can make no claim to humanity.[68]

Kant does not speak directly of the emotions here, though he is explicit in a parallel passage in *The Doctrine of Virtue*. "Pleasantness in our relations with others, good-naturedness, mutual love and respect" are ways in which "we associate virtue with the graces, and to effect this is in itself a duty of virtue."[69] Emotions of this sort *intensify and enhance* the content of moral principle. Certain actions come to include their attitudinal components, presenting virtue in a more palpable and agreeable way. They make

---

[66] See the famous note to Schiller, Rel. 23–24n/19n; also, see DV 484–85 on the ethical ascetic.
[67] Baron (1984) develops this interpretive point in her lively criticism of Stocker.
[68] Anth. 282.   [69] DV 473.

more attractive a morality that in its purer form may gain few adherents. This is to emphasize the related educational dimension of Kant's point.[70] Virtue has an educative role. What is to serve as a model of virtue must be practically and pedagogically sound. Virtuous character must be something we could admire and be encouraged to be like. An attractive aesthetic of virtue recommends the life of virtue to both agent and beneficiary, and stably reinforces its value within the community.[71]

This is the positive way of making the point. But Kant's remarks about the *aesthetic* of emotion betray a characteristic ambivalence. Indeed, in the above passage from *The Doctrine of Virtue,* he goes on to say that the emotions are "only small change" or literally, "mere fashion" that forms the outer semblance of virtue. The point now seems to be that emotions are mere decorative flourish; they *enhance* morality, but only as ornamental trim. They are little more than window dressing, their absence leaving the core of morality unmarred. Elsewhere, too, he suggests that emotions provide only a *faute de mieux* morality. They constitute an early stage of moral development, a provisional morality, to be superseded when reason is mature enough ultimately to take the reins. "It was still wisdom on nature's part," Kant remarks in the *Anthropology,* "to implant in us the predisposition to sympathy, so that it could handle the reins *provisionally,* until reason has

[70] For the notion of virtue as a moral ornament (a *moralische Zutat*), see DV 464, though Kant does not specifically refer here to the affective element of the virtues.
[71] See "Conjectural Beginnings of Human History," 113. Although Kant emphasizes the importance of aesthetics in conveying virtue toward others, he warns against settling for mere semblance in ourselves: "We must value even the semblance of good in others" but "the semblance of good *in ourselves* . . . we must ruthlessly wipe away: we must tear off the veil with which self-love covers our moral defects" (Anth. 153). Cf. Anth. 244. Also, note that the remarks about the educative value of emotional aesthetics contrast with Kant's more austere remarks in the *Religion* and *Groundwork,* in which he emphasizes the educative importance of a "pure " example of virtue as a role model for children: Rel. 48/44; G 411n; G 427n. For an excellent present-day clinical discussion of the place of conveying emotions to children as part of early moral development, see Greenspan (1989, 36).

achieved the necessary strength."[72] One needn't look far for yet other remarks that marginalize the emotions. They are there in number, often side by side with an acknowledgment of the moral benefit of emotions. This is part of Kant's familiar teeter-totter with the emotions. It is part of the highly rhetorical style he resorts to when discussing them. But when Kant is being systematic, his negative attitude toward the emotions can best be understood as part of a contrast in which he pits the conditional value of emotion against the unconditional goodness of the moral motive. On this Kantian view, affability, sympathy, and the like gain their moral value derivatively. In the person who constrains her actions and does what is dutiful in response to the requirements of the moral law, they provide attractive, indeed human, ways of expressing that interest. However, in and of themselves, apart from their role in a structured conception of character (grounded in legislative reason), they do not convey moral concern; for in and of themselves these emotions are not specifically responses to our rational agency and the claims that flow from that. Significantly, Kant recognizes that emotion *can* respond to this fact. Respect he takes to be such an emotion, and we shall come to his discussion of it shortly. It is a feeling that registers and expresses the purest moral concern toward the person as a rational agent, and thereby author of the moral law. Still, other more context-specific emotions, though not morally "responsive" in the same pure way, are nonetheless an indispensible part of moral practice by connecting us palpably with human circumstance and by giving us a medium for conveying that connection to others. They are responsive to the *conditions* of morality, if not to what *grounds* our morality.

Third, and finally, emotions play a motivational role. The question, of course, for the Kantian is, Do they play a role as *moral motive* ? For we can regard emotions in their other two roles as

---

[72] Anth. 253; see also 254. The Stoic echoes here are clear. On the Stoic view, reason sets in late; in addition, the Stoics hold that we don't have genuine emotions until we have mature reason. Kant rejects the second part of the claim because he rejects the Stoics' cognitive account of the emotions.

merely supportive – as supporting the motive of duty – by helping us locate what is morally salient and then helping us express
our morally required actions in a humanly engaged way, and we
can do this without thereby claiming that the moral action is itself
done out of emotion. Rather, duty, or acting on principle, remains
the moral motive. That is, on the Kantian view, as a morally
motivated agent, what grounds my reason (for not betraying the
patriot to the tyrant for gain, say) is not compassion I happen to
feel, but that such action is wrong, and wrong because it manipulates another's rational agency. Emotional motivation is nonmoral. On some views, nonmoral motivation may be present, but
all the same, it is not the locus of the morality, or moral worth, of
the action.[73]

But there seems to be something arbitrary about allowing emotions a role in virtue which nevertheless precludes a morally motivational role, especialy once we come to view the emotions that
are a part of virtue as cultivated emotions, responsive to the authority of reason as the ultimate source of moral values. Presumably the restriction has to do with Kant's claim that reasons based
on emotion are only *accidentally* connected with the rightness of
action. But suppose compassion could be cultivated so that to act
from it involved a concern for the rightness of action and for the
claims others make on one in virtue of their agency. And, too, that
in acting from compassion, we could distinguish needs that ought
to be satisfied from those which ought not to be satisfied. On such
a view, a maxim grounded in compassion would seem to have
moral content, and moral worth. Compassion would no longer be
merely accidentally connected with morality.[74] One might object
here that it is reason that is still doing the discriminative work,
and that compassion could never be so thoroughgoingly responsive to reason that it, so to speak, could fully internalize moral
principle. There may be something to this point. Our compassion
may extend to circumstances wider or narrower than our morally
justified reasons for beneficence. *On its own*, it may not lead us to

---

[73] See, for example, Herman (1993, ch. 1).
[74] I am grateful to Andy Reath for helping me formulate the point.

the moral import of the "news" it records or lead us to actions that are responsive to moral claims. But still, as something of a compromise point, we might want to hold that when acting from compassion is properly regulated by concerns for the rightness of action, then that fully, emotionally embodied response is morally worthy.

We have sketched two plausible roles for the emotions within the Kantian account of moral agency and, in a more speculative way, have entertained a third. Regarding these roles (which capture epistemic, attitudinal, and motivational functions), Kant can be seen as arguing for an Aristotelian-like view in which emotions are natural advantages that enable full moral agency. But more needs to be said about Kant's rhetoric against the emotions, especially if we are to take seriously his more positive remarks. For if Kant is somewhat Aristotelian in the views just discussed, there are strands that pull him away from faith in the emotions. In particular, there is the constant worry about ineffectual emotion, or sentimentalism. As stated in Chapter 3, Kant imports the Stoic sage and his practice of apathy as part of his arsenal against sentimentalism. So, for example, consider the following passage from *The Doctrine of Virtue*, which, strikingly, appears just after Kant's positive remarks about cultivating sympathy:

> The Stoic showed a noble cast of mind when he had his Sage say: I want a friend, not that he might help me in poverty, sickness, imprisonment, etc., but rather that I might stand by him and rescue a man. But the same Sage, when he could not save his friend, said to himself: what is it to me? In other words, he repudiated imparted suffering.[75]

And another, from the *Lecture on Ethics:*

> If in such a case there is no way in which I can be of help to the sufferer and I can do nothing to alter his situation, I might as

---

[75] DV 457. On this passage on Kant and Stoic apathy, see Marcia Baron's insightful discussions (1995a, ch. 6; 1995b) and Sherman (1995e) for comments on them.

well turn coldly away and say with the Stoics: "It is no concern of mine; my wishes cannot help him."[76]

Kant's point seems to be this: If emotion cannot accompany beneficent action or somehow be aimed at conspicuous material results, then its communication is morally pointless. It is to be repudiated. But the immediate objection, of course, is that sometimes the communication of emotion *just is* the point. It is materially *how* we are beneficent, in an effective way. Indeed, often it is not one's place to act but, rather, one's place to be empathetic – to listen and be concerned without taking up action. It might not be because one cannot do anything else – as in the quoted passage – ("When he could not save his friend, [the Sage] said to himself, what is it to me?") – but because anything else one might do, except listen with concern, might preempt the friend's own choice and her own autonomy.

Put differently, the question is whether communication of emotion can "alter the situation," and Kant doesn't elaborate. But it seems a commonplace point that a show of empathy, for example, when more interventive action either can't be taken or is out of place, is itself a way of actively sharing in another's ends. Tenderly telling an ailing parent at a nursing home who looks forward to the cheer of daily visits, "I know how important it is to you that I come visit and I wish I could, but my work schedule is inflexible this week," seems something more than an ineffectual communication of feeling. Nor is one simply informing another of one's priorities. Rather, there is the intention of letting the other know one is sympathetic to her needs, and supportive in a circumscribed way. Of course, in many cases, the repetition of these sorts of phrases in a life that shows little else by way of altruism begins to ring hollow. But short of that wider assessment of an agent's track record, such phrases ought not in themselves be ruled out as ways of responding to others' needs. They are ways of letting others know their needs have been recorded. To deny this is to deny that empathy is a morally important and morally crucial form of response.

[76] LE 200.

This sort of point isn't entirely missed by Kant. He suggests, for example, that the duty of gratitude must show both sensitivity (*Zärtlichkeit*) and the cordiality of a benevolent attitude of will (*Innigkeit der wohlwollenden Gesinnung*).[77] And in this context he concedes that "even a mere heartfelt benevolence [*herzliche Wohlwollen*] on another's part, without material results, deserves to be called a duty of virtue."[78] It is still *active* gratitude, he goes on to say. In this way Kant may come close to conceding that a maxim of beneficence is not morally idle even if its only point is to communicate emotion.

The general point is that Kant wants to repudiate sentimentalism, not sentiment. At bottom, his worry seems the reasonable one, that indulging sentiment can sometimes be more a matter of self-absorption than altruistic engagement in the social world. The problem is that Kant is not always effective in making the point, as the above passages about apathy attest. The bias of his age comes out further when he says in the *Anthropology* that the shedding of tears is effeminate; tears are sobs that make "disgusting music." Sorrow expressed through them is to be pardoned, not encouraged, and then only if it is a glisten in the eye, not a fallen teardrop, and again only if there is nothing else one can do – "only if it comes from generous but helpless sympathy."[79] We might find more apt his remarks on remorse – that in suffering remorse "we consider our list of debts cancelled merely by it (our penitence) and so spare ourselves the redoubled effort toward improvement that reason now requires."[80] But the most effective and humorous statement I can find against maudlin sentiment is conveyed not by Kant, but by Boswell in his *Life of Johnson*. And I think it pins down Kant's worries to a tee: Boswell tells the story of one "affected man," John Gilbert Cooper by name, who upon learning that his son at a nearby school in London was ill, was "in such violent agitation, on account of the indisposition of his son" and so anxious to see him that the only comfort he could find was in deciding "to write an Elegy." His sensible companion, Mr. Fitzherbert, "satisfied . . . of the sincerity of his [friend's] emo-

---

[77] DV 456.   [78] DV 455; italics omitted.   [79] Anth. 255–56.   [80] Anth. 236.

tions," slyly said to him " 'Had you not better take [a] post-chaise and go to see him' " at once?[81]

But does Kant's railing against romantic sentiment in this Boswellian manner prevent him from appreciating that emotional expression can be an important way we communicate moral concern, even apart from action? My claim has been that it does not. In addition, to our earlier remarks about the role of emotions in Kantian virtue, a few further remarks should suffice for now. First, as we have said before, Kant's views regarding the emotions at some level bear the marks of his Pietist background. True, Kant rejects much of the emotional fervor of his religious upbringing, but not all aspects of the Pietist emphasis on the emotionality of the moral life are expunged. The Pietist insistence on coming to know one's own soul not simply through good deeds, but through emotional attitudes and affect, is recast in Kant's own notion that good cheer (*ein fröhliches Herz*)[82] (in contrast to Pietist melancholia) are the outer signs of a good will. Second, in language ironically reminiscent of the opening of the *Groundwork*, Kant is insistent at the end of *The Doctrine of Virtue*, in the section entitled "Ethical aescetic," that duty done without emotion has "no inner worth" (*keinen inneren Wert*) and only with emotion can it become "meritorious and exemplary" (*verdienstlich und exemplarisch*).[83] Third, in a casuistical discussion in *The Doctrine of Virtue*, Kant suggests that to do without benevolent feelings, even were their purpose not actively to promote beneficence, would be to rob the world of a great moral ornament (*einer grossen moralischen Zierde der Welt*), a "beautiful moral whole" valuable "in its full perfection" and as such, "required for its own sake."[84] Here the claim is somewhat clearer that the aesthetic of morality is not just a decorative flourish, but a fuller realization of moral virtue. Morality is marred and less complete if it lacks this dimension. Kant might also be seen as arguing that benevolent feelings are valued intrinsically, as a morally fine thing, even apart from their promotion of the motive of duty (though presumably they must still be conditioned by it, within a structured conception of character). Finally, to recall our earlier point, "sensitivity" and a

---

[81] Boswell (1934, 149 and note).   [82] DV 485.   [83] DV 485.   [84] DV 458; cf. 464.

"heartfelt benevolence" are themselves conceived by Kant as a proper part of a virtue of end, such as gratitude.[85] In short, although Kant invokes Stoic apathy, it is not to rehearse the radical Stoic belief that emotions must be extirpated. Rather, on Kant's view, it is sentimentalism that is the enemy. Conceived in this way, Kant's Stoic rhetoric becomes considerably deflated. His alliance with Aristotle's commonsense view – that emotions are important for virtue – remains, for the moment, relatively undisturbed.

Several other implications follow from this Kantian conception of the moral significance of emotions. Although there is a tradition of viewing the feelings connected with virtue as primarily captured by the notion of the derivative pleasure of an unconflicted commitment to morality, the above discussion suggests that a conception of the emotions along these lines will be far too thin.[86] Effective moral agency requires cultivated *ordinary* emotional sensitivities *to record and express* the demands of morality in context-specific ways. The Stoic idea that Kant rehearses, that duty alone is sufficient for doing what is right (and that this, on the Kantian view, yields pleasure), may eliminate a role for emotions as moral motives, but it does not eliminate a role for emotion in the other functions we have discussed. To fill in these functions, a broad band of emotions is required, far broader than a band that contains only the moral cheer of unbegrudgingly acting on moral principles. A stripped-down notion of moral gladness or cheer simply does not convey the richness of full emotional engagement characteristic of virtue rooted in the epistemic and attitudinal supports of ordinary emotions. On my reading of *The Doctrine of Virtue*, it is cultivating this more diverse palette that is especially important to the project of virtue. And the graciousness that follows from acting from duty without resentment itself depends on having these specific ordinary emotions as a general part of the practice of morality. Though perhaps possible, it would be peculiar to think an individual could do what is right "gladly" merely

---

[85] DV 456.

[86] For Kant's own statement of this notion of pleasure or cheer, see the famous response to Schiller in Rel. 23n/18n; also DV 485.

in the absence of opposing inclination, and not in the presence of
supportive emotions that alert her to moral occasions and that
convey affectively, to her and others, her moral concerns.

Along these lines, it is important to emphasize that in *The
Doctrine of Virtue*, Kant views the empirical supports of moral
interest not simply as the natural consequences of a commitment
to morality, but as ends we have a positive duty to promote.[87]
This strengthens the view found in the earlier *Lecture on Ethics*.
There, Kant says, somewhat paradoxically, duty *becomes*
inclination:

> The command to love our neighbor applies within limits both
> to love from obligation [practical love] and love from inclina-
> tion [pathological love]. For if I love others from obligation, I
> acquire in the course of time a taste for it, and my love, origi-
> nally duty-born, becomes an inclination.[88]

The claim in this early writing is that duty becomes naturalized. In acting from duty, an agent comes to develop the positive,
phenomenal supports that underlie duty – presumably both
context-specific emotions, such as benevolence and love, and the
overall sense of cheer – *ein fröhliches Herz* – that follows from an
integrated moral character. *The Doctrine of Virtue* (written some
twenty years later) appeals to these psychological principles of
habituation but strengthens the claim. It is not enough that benevolence or love be conceived of as the natural consequence of duty-
generated maxims of beneficence. In addition, we have a positive
duty to cultivate these emotions. We have a duty to promote them
actively as derivative duties of our general duty of beneficence.[89]
In short, we have a moral duty to "naturalize" our duty.[90] This is
no more and no less than the duty to perfect our nature as a

---

[87] Guyer emphasizes this point in his treatment (1993).

[88] LE 197.

[89] See Guyer (1993, 366). DV 402.

[90] Even G 399, in which Kant says that "love out of inclination cannot be commanded," is compatible with this interpretation. I take Kant to be repeating
here the familiar claim that we cannot be commanded to have certain natural
advantages. That is a matter of external lottery. But we can be commanded to
love out of inclination if this means cultivate what by nature we already have.

subpart of our duty of moral perfection. A program of morally habituating the emotions is something we must actively choose to engage in.

Thus, a central focus in *The Doctrine of Virtue* is on what we can do to become the sort of person for whom moral interest is abiding. The Aristotelian notion of a stable and reliable character rooted in appropriate emotions reemerges. But on the Kantian view, these emotions are regulated by an interest that looks beyond the narrow focus of ordinary emotions – beyond responses to need, loss, shared interests, attractiveness, and all the ordinary contexts to which we have emotional reactions. To be cultivated properly, emotions must ultimately be responsive to the demands of reason as the source of moral agency. So, for example, sympathy serves beneficence because recognizing others' frustrations or pain is a way of seeing how one can step in to support their sense of being an agent who can meaningfully set ends and bring them about. Sympathy helps get us to the moral claims others make on us, but it doesn't, on its own, constitute a direct or complete moral response. (Though, on the somewhat unorthodox view entertained earlier, it may itself have moral content if thoroughly cultivated in a way in which it fully internalizes moral principles.) On the Aristotelian view, in contrast, responding to others through pity, friendliness, generous feelings, and the like (in ways that are medial, i.e., properly delimited or "fine") just *is* to respond morally, for there are no other purer or more principled ways of grasping what makes action right. The emotions, when transformed through habituation in ways that harmonize with overall considerations of good living, themselves embody the moral response. Kant, too, recognizes that morality becomes efficacious and discriminating via the discernment of the emotions. But the values of the moral law, and the fundamental notion of free practical agency, shape and regulate ordinary emotions. In the Aristotelian scheme, in contrast, there is no comparable, higher-order value to be appealed to, abstractable from the circumstanced person and an agent's ability to respond to a person in those circumstances.[91] There is no moral interest that takes us to a person as

91 Pity and good will, for example, are altruistic emotions. They are directed at

such, independent of a shared conception of the good or context. This point is taken up in Chapter 5 in the discussion of friendship.

Before proceeding, let us pause to take stock. What we have seen so far is that emotions are *necessary conditions* for acting from the motive of duty. In some cases, they serve instrumental (epistemic) roles indispensable for acting from moral interest; in other cases, they are intrinsically valued as ways we act from and convey moral interest with a human face. In light of this last claim, especially, I would argue that emotions are constitutive of virtue in its human embodiment. More generally, we might say Kantian virtue, on this view, is a hierarchically structured composite whose primary constituent is the disposition to act from moral principles for their own sake and whose subordinate constituents include cultivated natural capacities, such as emotions, that support that disposition. To say that cultivated emotions are part of virtue is to expand upon Kant's own theme in *The Doctrine of Virtue* that emotions can become "practical" or "moral" and no longer be merely "pathological."

5 VIRTUE AS A STRUCTURED COMPOSITE: *RELIGION WITHIN THE LIMITS OF REASON ALONE*

The notion of virtuous character as a hierarchically structured composite with cultivated emotions forming a constitutive part finds some support in a central passage in the *Religion*.[92] The thrust of the passage is that good character has a regulative structure; it is an ordered composite in which incentives from inclination are not denounced, as the Stoics would argue they must be, but, rather, conditioned and transformed. Briefly put, Kant

another's benefit without ulterior motive. But they reach out to the person as one *I* can respond to. In the case of pity, I must think that I, too, to some degree, could suffer that sort of loss. (see Rh. 1385b12–15; NE 1167a18–20). The point is that the response goes out not to the person as such, but to the person in a local context to which I can connect. The point comes across most forcefully when we appreciate that civic friendship for Aristotle sets the boundary of those to whom we stand in relations of justice.

[92] Rel. 26–28/21–23; see also 36/31.

distinguishes three *Anlage* or predispositions to good that characterize human nature: the predisposition to animality (as a mere
living being), the predisposition to humanity (as a living *and* rational being), and the predisposition to personality (as a living
and rational being who is *accountable*). The predisposition to animality concerns self-love expressed in our impulses toward self-
preservation, propagation of the species, and basic sociality. The
predisposition to humanity is a form of self-love expressed in our
cultural strivings and social dependence upon and rivalry with
others. The predisposition to personality is the capacity to hold
ourselves morally accountable by justifying our actions in terms
of autonomously generated moral principles. All of these predispositions are "original" parts of our human nature that, when
properly transformed and ordered, are a part of a more inclusive,
composite conception of good character.

> All of these predispositions are not only *good* in negative fash-
> ion (in that they do not contradict the moral law); they are also
> predispositions *toward good* (they enjoin the observance of the
> law). They are *original*, for they are bound up with the possibil-
> ity of human nature. Man can indeed use the first two contrary
> to their ends, but he can extirpate (*vertilgen*) none of these. By
> the predispositions of a being we understand not only its con-
> stituent elements which are necessary to it (*Bestandstücke, die
> dazu erforderlich sind*), but also the forms of their combination,
> by which the being is what it is.[93]

Here again we have essentially the ancient project of ordering
and rendering harmonious the parts of the human psyche or soul.
A well-regulated soul is not simply a matter of the absence of
counterincentives. The goal is to transform our self-love so that it
promotes and advances compliance with the moral law. Moreover, Kant's language seems to suggest that cultivated natural
and social powers are not simply necessary *conditions* of moral
agency, but necessary, hierarchically structured *parts* (*Be-
standstücke*) of the overall character or fixed (original) disposition
(*Bestimmung*) of a human being to achieve the moral good. They

[93] Rel. 28 /23.

support moral personality within a wider, composite notion of what it is to be a morally good person. Natural powers and capacities that when untutored fall only under principles of self-love, when properly habitutated and ordered can be supportive parts of moral character as well. This is not to eliminate conflicts or to claim that a transformation of the passions is anything but difficult. Ours is an "unsocial sociability," Kant says pithily elsewhere,[94] and a decision to reorder one's incentives (a "revolution in one's cast of mind") makes one merely "susceptible" to goodness. "Only in continuous labor and growth" does one become a good person.[95]

> This change can be regarded as a revolution. But in the judgment of men, who can appraise themselves and the strength of their maxims only by the ascendancy which they win over their sensuous nature in time, this change must be regarded as nothing but an ever-during struggle toward the better, hence as a gradual reformation.[96]

As Kant suggests here, virtue requires not simply choosing character, but choosing the course of habituation that goes with it, however suspicious Kant sometimes seems to be of the Aristotelian idea of virtue as a habituated state.[97] A few words are in order here, especially given the comparative nature of our study. Kant, in criticism of Aristotle, often seems to think of habituation as producing mindless states that will lack the intellectual struc-

---

[94] *Idea for a Universal History from a Cosmopolitan Point of View*, 21.

[95] Rel. 47–48/43.

[96] Rel. 48/43.

[97] See Kant's remarks at DV 383, where he clearly fails to appreciate Aristotle's view that reliable and stable habituated states of virtue are themselves informed by and expressed through practical reason. Kant's neglect of the Aristotelian notion of practical wisdom is also evident in his characterization of the principle of the mean at DV 432. In the *Religion* passage we have been considering, however, he seems far more appreciative of a general notion of habituation. And certainly, in *The Doctrine of Virtue*, despite his criticisms of Aristotle, he appeals to a project of virtue that implicitly relies on the steady transformation of character over time through choice, experience, and critical practice.

ture necessary for sensitive moral judgment. So consider the following remarks, clearly directed at the Aristotelian view:

> But virtue cannot be defined and valued as a mere *aptitude* or
> . . . a long-standing *habit* of morally good actions, acquired by
> practice. For unless this aptitude results from considered, firm,
> and continually purified principles, then, like any other mecha-
> nism of technically-practical reason, it is neither armed for all
> situations nor adequately insured against the changes that new
> temptations could bring about.[98]

But there is no reason to assume that reliable and stable habituated states must lack the resources of practical reason, or that
those states can come to be habituated in the first place without
capacities for practical reason developing in tandem. Nor is there
anything Aristotle says about the way habituation takes place or,
more specifically, about the training of the emotions that implies
the absence of such capacities for discernment and judgment.
Indeed, Kant, like many commentators, has badly misconstrued
Aristotle's conception of habituation or *ethismos*. Literally, the
term means character formation. This will involve habituation
and practice, but always in a way that involves the use of practical
reason and the development of practical wisdom. Indeed, Aristotle's separation of the virtues of character and intellect in *Nicomachean Ethics*, Book II, should be viewed as little more than an
expository device for taking up these notions *ad seriatim*. It is not
meant to signal any great conceptual divide. In actual practice,
Aristotle doesn't even stick to the expository model. As early as
Book II, the key definition of virtue at 1105b makes significant
reference to the choice-making capacities of the person of practical wisdom, and in the discussion of the individual virtues reference is regularly made to choosing *hōs dei* ("in the right way"),
which again refers back to the exemplary sort of judgment characteristic of the person of practical wisdom. Again, at the conclusion
of *Nicomachean*, Book VI, Aristotle insists on the ultimate interde-
pendency of practical wisdom and full virtue: One cannot be
good without practical wisdom, or practically wise without good-

[98] DV 383–84.

ness.[99] These points are often missed in Kantian criticisms of Aristotelian theory. It is argued that the sort of emphasis Kant gives to the flexibility and resourcefulness of practical reason is simply lost on Aristotle. Kant himself says as much in his blunt criticism of Aristotle's doctrine of the mean. It is a useless doctrine, he says at one point, for getting at the modern notion of discretionary judgment required in the application of wide duties of end.[100] The problem is systematic, he suggests: The notion of a mean is rooted in a theory that ultimately lacks a concept of acting on reasons or maxims. "For who will specify for me this mean between the two outer limits? What distinguishes *avarice* (as a vice) from thrift (as a virtue) is not that avarice carries thrift *too far* but that avarice has an entirely *different principle* (maxim)."[101]

Whatever the merits or demerits of Aristotle's notion of the mean, Aristotle does have a notion of acting on intention or choice (*prohairesis*) that, as we have said, does in a limited way some of the work of the Kantian notion of a maxim. Later chapters will say more about how practical judgment fits into each theorist's conception of virtue. But for the moment, we can note that in the *Religion* passages we have been considering (and in the argument of *The Doctrine of Virtue* itself), Kant relies on a general notion of habituation as part of his conception of the perfection of virtue. Despite his critcisms of Aristotle, he appeals to a project of virtue that, like Aristotle's, relies on the steady transformation of character through choice, experience, and critical practice over time.[102]

To return to our earlier discussion, what can we say about the praiseworthiness of this more composite Kantian conception of virtue? Are cultivated virtuous feelings, and the structured conception of character that supports motivation from duty, themselves candidates for moral worth, or is moral worth itself still restricted narrowly to dutiful action done from the motive of duty?[103] I do not think there is a clear textual answer here, in part because the notion of moral worth is simply not central to *The*

---

[99] NE 1144b30.   [100] DV 432–33 and note.   [101] DV 404n.

[102] For a discussion of Aristotelian habituation, see Sherman (1989, ch. 5).

[103] In Herman (1993, ch. 1), she argues that the "attitude of virtue" will be expressed in cultivated emotions though moral worth will still rest narrowly in dutiful action motivated by duty.

Doctrine of Virtue or the *Religion* in the way that some have argued it is in the *Groundwork*. In these later works the shift is to the psychological constitution of the person for whom acting from duty is itself not an accidental sort of thing, but an interest stably rooted in character and its supportive structure. The shift is to moral anthropology, to how we can practice morality, and not merely to how morality is possible. This is the shift to virtue. But once virtue becomes the preeminent focus, the notion of moral credit ascribed to an action in virtue of good willing no longer has easy application. For virtuous character will include the effort and agency of virtue (i.e., strength and fortitude, in Kant's terms), and also the gifts and lucky breaks with which that attitude must work. Virtuous character is embodied, and thus, to some extent, always limited by stepmother nature's endowments. In contrast, true moral merit or worth (however difficult to determine, in practice, the conditions for its correct attribution) is, in principle, meant to zero in on the pure agency involved in the adoption of moral interest, independent of constitutional and external circumstances. Still, there is one passage from the conclusion of *The Doctrine of Virtue* worth recalling.[104] This is the passage, referred to earlier, where Kant says that duty done without emotion has no inner worth (*keinen inneren Wert*), and only with emotion can it become meritorious and exemplary (*verdientslich und exemplarisch*). Kant specifically refers the cheerfulness that accompanies virtue (*Frohsinn*) and does not mention the ordinary, context-specific emotions he emphasizes earlier. However, if we are guided by my earlier interpretation that a cheerful frame of mind is a matter not just of acting from duty in the absence of contrary inclination, but of acting in a way that is supported by context-specific emotions (in their various roles), then the presence of these emotions also might be required for the action to be truly "meritorious and exemplary." Granted, we are no longer working with the *Groundwork* notion of "moral worth." Even so, we have some conception of moral praiseworthiness that Kant is willing to put forth. And it is a notion that need not be devoid of a connection with credit; for the moral agent with a structured

---

[104] DV 484–85.

conception of character *cultivates* emotions in a way that is responsive to the conditions of the moral law. His emotional align-
ment is not just a matter of luck. As such, dutiful action done from
the motive of duty without the support of emotions that flow
from a structured conception of character would, on this interpretation, simply not be in the fullest sense morally praiseworthy.
Here again, the emotional aesthetic of morality seems more than
merely decorative.

6 IN WHAT SENSE ARE WE AGENTS OF
OUR EMOTIONAL EXPERIENCE?
ANTHROPOLOGY FROM A PRAGMATIC
POINT OF VIEW

To some, the *Anthropology* may be a strange text to appeal to for
evidence of Kant's positive evaluation of the emotions in the
moral project. For here Kant makes explicit the impulsive and
obsessive nature of certain emotions (what is translated as "emotional agitation" and "passion") and the ways both can resist the
dominion of reason. Taxonomically, passion (*Leidenschaft*) falls
under the general heading of inclination (*Neigung*) and inclination, under the more general notion of appetite (*Begierde*). Emotional agitation (*Affekt*) is not an appetite but a reactive feeling of
pleasure and pain (*Gefühl*).[105] As with Aristotle's general notion
of *orexis*, inclinations have to do with the appetitive pursuit of
objects represented by us. On Kant's view, inclinations become
reasons for action, when they are taken up into a maxim by our
power of choice (*Willkür*). We are practical agents in the sense that
we give ourselves reasons for action, for which, in virtue of our
capacities as moral lawmakers, we can be held morally accountable. (That is, we are practical agents in a two-tiered way: first,
insofar as we act under a subjective principle or maxim (and so,
unlike lower animals, are not moved brutely by affect or impulse); and second, insofar as we can ground those maxims in
objective moral law issued by our own will (*Wille*). Among Kant's
present claims is that passion is an inclination that is obsessive

---

[105] Anth. 251.

and not easily subject to choices that can be constrained by either moral or prudential reasoning. Agitation, too, resists the influence of circumspect reason.

In the grip of tumultuous and sudden emotion, an agent sees with blinders. She gets lost in the moment, missing the forest for the trees:

> Generally speaking, what constitutes a state of emotional agitation is not the intensity of a certain feeling but rather the lack of reflection that would compare this feeling with the totality of all the feelings (of pleasure or displeasure) that go with our state. A rich man whose servant awkwardly breaks a beautiful and rare goblet while carrying it around at a banquet will think nothing of this accident if, at the same moment, he compares this loss of *one* pleasure with the multitude of *all* the pleasures that his fortunate position as a rich man offers him. But if he isolates this one feeling of pain and abandons himself to it (without quickly making that mental reckoning), no wonder he feels as if he had lost his happiness completely.[106]

Kant makes similar remarks about passion – that it dwarfs other inclinations, that "it sweep[s] them into the corner just to please one," that the folly of the person gripped in passion is that he makes a *part* of his end the *whole*. Passion "is an enchantment that refuses to be corrected."[107] We are liable to these kinds of reactions when we experience what Kant calls natural and social passions. Natural passions are "ardent" passions connected with freedom (i.e., unrestrained movement) and sexual urges;[108] social or cultural passions are cooler passions for the external goods of honor, power, and possession.[109] Two significant points emerge in Kant's discussion of the cultural passions. First these passions reflect Kant's sour view of our sociality. Ours is an "unsociable

---

[106] Anth. 254.
[107] Anth. 266.
[108] On abuses of our freedom, see "Idea for a Universal History from a Cosmopolitan Point of View," 23. On the sexual instinct, see "Conjectural Beginning of Human History," 112–13.
[109] See Anth. 268 for the distinction between natural and cultural passions.

sociability," naturally beset by antagonism and rivalry.[110] Our social lot is to compare and contrast ourselves so that under the social gaze we inevitably sow the seeds of envy and greed. Our self-love feeds on competition; only morality, with its egalitarian basis of dignity for all, can be an antidote: "Envy, the lust for power, greed, and the malignant inclinations bound up with these, besiege his nature . . . *as soon as he is among men.* "[111] The shadow of Rousseau looms large. Second, these social passions feed on a more fundamental vulnerability to surrender our will to others. In an interesting departure from the Stoics, who also decry enslavement to the passions, Kant holds that our passional enslavement is not ultimately to the *objects* of our passions[112] – "fertile fields or cows" as Kant puts it[113] – but to other *persons* to whom we might surrender our wills in order to hold on to those objects. The grip of the passions must be understood not "according to the objects of the appetitive power . . . but rather according to the principle of the use or abuse men make of their person and of their freedom, when one man makes another a mere means to his ends."[114] Thus, the real problem is not attachment to *impermanent objects,* as the Stoics maintain, but surrender *to others* in virtue of that attachment. "Each of these manias is a slavish disposition by which others, when they have made themselves masters of it, have the power to use a man through his own inclinations."[115] The point underscores one dimension of Kant's break from eudaimonism: For the ancients, and especially the Stoics, the problem with passional attachment is that attachment ultimately entails loss and the reversal of happiness; it threatens our *eudaimonia.* For Kant, the problem with passional attachment is that satisfying its demands can make us the mere playthings of *other persons;* it threatens our dignity. According to both the Stoic

---

[110] "Idea for a Universal History from a Cosmopolitan Point of View," 20–21.

[111] Rel. 93–94/85; see 27/ 22.

[112] Though Kant does make the Stoic point elsewhere: "It is not by fortune but only by wisdom that life can acquire value for us: and its value is, accordingly, within our power," Anth. 239.

[113] Anth. 268.

[114] Anth. 269–70.

[115] Anth. 272.

and Kantian views, passion points to the limits of our rational agency, though this fact is registered differently within each theory.

The point of these colorful passages is that both passion and agitation threaten practical agency. "Emotional agitation works like water breaking through a dam: a passion, like a stream that burrows ever deeper in its bed."[116] Whereas "emotional agitation does a momentary damage to freedom and self-mastery; passion abandons them and finds its pleasure and satisfaction in slavery."[117]

But why draw attention to these particular emotional states? Why draw attention to this nosology of emotions, given our interest in establishing the role of emotions in the morally salubrious life? I do so to stress, as Kant himself does in this very work, that they are not representative of all emotional states. They are only a part of a wider range of emotional experience that Kant is eager to detail in this work. They are some of the ways we experience emotions, but not the only way. Indeed, on his view, they are extremes, maladies (*Krankheit des Gemüts*) that require therapy and spiritual doctors. Again, the Stoic influence is unmistakable. Following the Stoics, Kant argues that an effective therapy will promote a sense of "apathy." But he insists that by "apathy" he means neither "lack of feeling" nor "subjective indifference regarding objects of choice." In the truly tranquil mind there will be emotions, but none that are abject or lacking the sovereignty of reason. In this sense, a "noble character" will be freed from both the turbulence of affect and the desperate edge of passion.[118] For Kant more than the Stoics, *apatheia* really does become *eupatheia* – a state of good or wholesome emotions that support duty. These are the so-called practical emotions.

What I wish to emphasize about the *Anthropology* is that despite the negative rhetoric about certain emotions, what we see is Kant struggling to redraw the battle line between reason and emotion (and agency and passivity) in a more discriminating way. As part of this orientation he stresses that emotional states that are maladaptive are themselves often to be viewed not as

---

[116] Anth. 252.   [117] Anth. 267.   [118] DV 407–8.

permanent disabilities, but as malleable conditions that can be transformed through our practical agency. There are things that we can do, through our will and reason, to transform them. Though emotions, in general, are perhaps not states that can be directly willed, Kant insists in these lectures that emotions can often be affected gradually, by what we will and by how we understand the circumstances that surround us. There are steps we take toward gradually shaping them so that they become something more than impulse. Indeed, the general focus of the *Anthropology* is about psychological empowerment – how to heal mental weaknesses and how to enhance the scope and reach of effective practical agency. Setting out the spirit of this work, he states: "The ineradicable *passive* element in sensibility is really the source of all the evil things said about it. Man's inner perfection consists in his having control over the exercise of all his powers, so that he uses them *as he freely chooses*."[119] An underlying theme is that practical agency can extend into the domain of feelings as well.

The effect of practical agency on emotional experience emerges forcefully in a distinction Kant draws between "sensitivity" (*Empfindsamkeit*) and "sentimentality" (*Empfindelei*):

Sensitivity is a *power* and *strength* by which we grant or refuse permission for the state of pleasure or displeasure to enter our mind, so that it implies a choice. On the other hand, sentimentality is a weakness by which we can be affected, even against our will, by sympathy for another's plight; others, so to speak, can play as they will on the organ of the sentimentalist. Sensitivity is virile; for the man who wants to spare his wife or children trouble or pain must have enough fine feeling to judge their sensibilities not by *his* own strength but by their *weakness*, and his *delicacy* of feeling is essential to his generosity. On the other hand, to share ineffectually in others' feelings, to attune our feelings sympathetically to theirs and so let ourselves be affected in a merely passive way, is silly and childish.[120]

---

[119] Anth. 144.
[120] Anth. 235–36; on training emotions through more behavioral methods, see Anth. 252 and Anth. 151.

Embedded in this sexist passage is the important point that emotions need not be impulsive or resist reform. They aren't only agitations or passions. Many are quite easily susceptible to the influence of reason. With effort and guidance, they can be trained to become more discerning and supportive of endorsed ends. In particular, Kant suggests here that with effort, we can cultivate a sense of empathy that allows us to identify with those whose circumstances may be considerably different from our own. From this empathic perspective, we look at others not in terms of our own abilities or weakness, but in terms of theirs. We learn how to reach out to them in a way that doesn't merely project ourselves. Moreover, there is strength of will involved in this refined way of attending. In a perspicuous way, we cultivate *how* we will be affected. The emotion involves cognitive assent. As Kant says elliptically, undoubtedly in reference to the Stoic notion of emotion as involving an assent to belief, "it implies a choice." But here, in contradistinction to the Stoic analysis, Kant reserves voluntary assent only for "wholesome" or "practical" emotions.

Kant nicely illustrates in this passage the supportive roles emotions can play in the moral life. First, they record moral salience: The husband is able to make nuanced discriminations because of his emotional sensitivity. He sees what might otherwise go unnoticed, and sees with an alertness (and readiness to act) that a cooler registering of "the news" might not facilitate. Second, this sensitivity is a "delicacy of feeling," Kant says, essential to generosity. Conveying certain emotions (enhancing one's actions through accompanying emotions) may itself be a constitutive part of what it is to act generously in a virtuous way.[121]

As we have said, the excerpt above adverts to the idea that there is agency in how we stand toward our emotions. They do not merely happen to us. We assent to various ways of being affected, and to various forms of control. Some of this involves taking actions that make conducive certain emotional consequences rather than others. In homespun style, Kant says if one

[121] Contrast the more qualified claim at Anth. 158 in which fine sensitivity is said to be important for well-being, but doesn't necessarily make an individual morally better (*nicht eben moralisch-besser*).

wants to soften one's anger, then sitting rather than standing when one is angry might help to dissipate the tension.

> When an angry man comes up to you in a room, to say harsh words to you in intense indignation, try politely to make him sit down; if you succeed, his reproaches already become milder, since the comfort of sitting is [a form] of relaxation, which is incompatible with the threatening gestures and shouting one can use when standing.[122]

In a similar spirit, Kant says with a sexism that plagues the *Anthropology*, when a woman practices smiling, the facial gesture helps to promote a spirit of benevolence. Here, as in our discussion of Aristotle, the idea is that emotions can change from the outside in. We become by doing, behaviorally stimulating deeper, psychological changes. We prod ourselves through our own facial and gestural cues.

This notion of a behavioral therapy undergirds Kant's further remarks that the pretense of virtue can itself ultimately stimulate properly grounded virtue.

> Men are, one and all, actors – the more so the more civilized they are. They put on a show of affection, respect for others, modesty and disinterest without deceiving anyone, since it is generally understood that they are not sincere about it. And it is a very good thing that this happens in the world. For if men keep on playing these roles, the real virtues whose semblance they have merely been affecting for a long time are gradually aroused and pass into their attitude of will.[123]

Kant doesn't elaborate on the psychological or educational mechanisms at work. He doesn't tell us *how* we become by doing, how enactment gradually transforms one's dispositions and beliefs. In this sense he doesn't move us beyond Aristotle's similarly sketchy remarks about habituation. Still, what is significant for our purposes is Kant's commitment to the view that there are active roles we can take to cultivate emotions. Emotions are not merely passive states. We as agents influence how we are affected.

[122] Anth. 252.   [123] Anth. 151.

As we have already seen from the sensitivity passage, changes in how we think about circumstances also affect our emotions. Shifts in the beliefs and construals that ground emotions can sometimes help to change those emotions. Relevant here is a discussion entitled "On voluntary consciousness of our ideas." Here, Kant suggests that directing where and how one attends to sense representations, for instance, consciously "turning away from an idea" "even when the senses urge it on us," is a "strength of mind" acquired by practice.[124] In terms of the emotions, we can say that what they pick up and record is itself not a passive process but subject to the influence of persuasion and discourse. Still, Kant suggests that this can be an uphill struggle when particularly strong emotions are on board. Kant makes the point in terms of love, and in his hands the subject turns comical:

> The suitor could make a good marriage if only he could disregard a wart on his beloved's face or a missing tooth. But our power of attention is guilty of particularly bad manners if it immediately fastens, even involuntarily, on others' shortcomings: to direct our eyes to a button missing from the coat of someone we are face to face with, or a gap between his teeth, or to fasten our attention on a habitual speech defect not only disconcerts him but also spoils our own chances of social success.[125]

What is comical here is Kant's wistful attempt to deny that an important value of the testimony of the emotions is precisely its rawness. Emotions let us see ourselves and others with a certain immediacy and candor. They record values with an immediacy that more studied reflection often misses. If there is something called "love at first sight," then it would seem to depend more on this candor of the emotions than on learning how to direct one's eyes. All the same, sustained and mature love surely depends not just on mood but on will, and on how we learn to see the world and correct for our shortsightedness. That, too, is a part of loving. If we pair this passage with the earlier one about sensitivity, Kant is suggesting that attending through the emotions is not a passive

[124] Anth. 131; see also 128.   [125] Anth. 132.

or ineducable process. It often requires control and self-monitoring. It may require efforts at refocusing, in the very way that the loving husband takes efforts to see things so that he doesn't merely project onto his wife his own notions of virility and strength.

Still, not all our mental habits are worth dwelling on, Kant warns. In what seems to be a clear criticism of Pietist fanaticism, he urges that watchful attention to our involuntary mental wanderings – "to inner experiences (of grace and temptation)" if not already a form of mental illness leads to the lunatic asylum.[126] It is only voluntary mental efforts that merit our reflection:

> But the real purpose of this section is to give the strict *warning*, mentioned above, against occupying ourselves with spying out the *involuntary* course of our thoughts and feelings and, so to speak, carefully recording its interior history. This is the most direct route to Illuminism and Terrorism, by way of the confusion caused by alleged inspirations from on high and powers flowing into us, by none of our doing, from some unknown source . . . To observe in ourselves the various acts of the representative power *when we call them forth* merits our reflection.[127]

Without delving into Kant's criticisms of mysticism (or trying to puzzle out exactly how he means to distinguish between voluntary and involuntary thought), we can note it may be precisely by spying out the mind's meanderings that we manage to bring our thought and emotions a step closer toward control. To ignore certain thoughts and associations that pop into our heads unsummoned may be just to encourage their untended growth, leaving them unchallenged by more reliable beliefs or stories. Moreover, to make this point, we needn't import depth psychology or a Freudian method of association. For Kant's own notion of introspection and the self-monitoring of mental habits and modes of attending easily accommodates the point. Indeed, Kant's prevailing interest in cultivating our sensibilities – so that we attend in a way accessible to reflection – would seem to extend precisely to

[126] Anth. 134.   [127] Anth. 133.

those areas where we may now be unreflective but can ultimately cultivate greater awareness and control.

But even granting this, it is unclear how much we want to support Kant in this drive for control. We can get a glimpse of the problem by turning to his critical remarks about novel reading, a subject he briefly visits in the *Anthropology*. In a simplistic way, we might say Kant objects to novel reading for the very reasons that someone like Proust celebrates it – namely, that it encourages us to jump back and forth from fiction into our own lives.[128] It is an active transport from the literary page to our lives. Whereas for Proust this is the true empowerment of novel reading, for Kant it is a defect, a sign of a messy and jumpy kind of imaginative activity that fragments consciousness between what is fictitious and what is in the cracks and recesses of our own soul. The fact that we get derailed when we read a novel is for Kant a lamentable sign of mental disarray and disorder. It expresses lack of control: "*Reading novels* has the result, along with many other mental disorders, of making distraction habitual. . . . It permits our mind to interpolate digressions while we are reading it (namely, to interpolate other happenings we invent), and the course of our thought becomes *fragmentary.*"[129]

What we begin to see here are general worries about free-floating imagination. The meandering and falling required before the mental reins are tightened is not something with which Kant is comfortable. To focus without being distracted, to collect ourselves and "gather forces," to remove obsessions, stubborn gazes, annoying jingos and tunes that flood the mind – this is the goal of mental hygiene, he tells us.[130] The messiness that comes with flights of fancy and imagination in its free play are potential threats to self-mastery.

It is here that we might feel Kant's conception of practical agency becomes too heavyhanded. For if we eliminate certain experiences of passivity – moments of passion and imaginative

---

[128] See Nussbaum (1990a) and Sherman (1994a).

[129] Anth. 208.

[130] Anth. 207. I cannot help but call attention to the intense anti-Semitism in the note that precedes this section (205n).

transport – don't we give up too much? If we exercise a kind of mental control that purges us from the turbulences of emotion, we gain in mastery but at the cost of being alienated from the wounds and joys that humanly matter. Again, if we keep imagination even and orderly, then what becomes of the surprises and discoveries, the moments of peering into corners and cracks that depend upon a liberated and unblinded vision? Kant wants to rid us of the horror of falling, of being struck down without being able to stand again, of losing control in moments of terror or pity or mystical transport or imaginative revelry. On his view, pretenses of love might serve just as well as real love, and yet lack all the messy fumbling and vulnerability to betrayal. Here, what we lose for the sake of order becomes clear. Yet one might wonder at this point if there isn't a conception of practical agency that allows for greater risks. Isn't there a way of feeling the heights and depths of human experience such that we can become empowered by these moments, experience them and yet rebound in a way that puts them into perspective – just as Kant suggests a healthy emotional life requires? Perhaps a limited but instructive model here is that of Aristotle's tragic spectator, who experiences with shuddering fear and pity what could in fact happen to oneself, and yet having lived through those emotions, is now able to leave the theater empowered by the catharsis.[131] Here, of course, there is all the safety of the theater's stage and mythological story. There is literary distance. But still in that very safety there is a lesson we may be able to hold on to when tragedy strikes at home, or imagination and passion fix on events in our own lives. The literary experience is not just one of living out a plot through imagination and emotion. It is one of remembering the protection that comes from watching and understanding and being sufficiently detached so that one can put that experience into perspective with other events in a life. That very safety in distance is itself something to take home, something for the recovery in one's own life. It offers a kind of control that first tolerates some sinking and soaring. In a similar way, our nonliterary expe-

---

[131] On tragic catharsis, see Lear (1992). On the Aristotelian notion of tragic mistake, and the roles of pity and fear in the tragic response, see Sherman (1992).

rience of emotions might be thought of as both immersed and distanced. What might be worth striving for is a way of experiencing the intensity of passion while still having at hand the perspective of wise judgment.

A few words of summary might be in order before proceeding. We have seen that in the *Anthropology*, Kant warns against pernicious forms of emotion and the threats they pose to self-control. He points out various techniques for making them more responsive to our rational agency. Insofar as Kant is often viewed as silent on the issue of an *education sentimentale*, these texts constitute important counterevidence. They show ways that practical agency, or will, can inform, and in turn be strengthened by, habituated states of character. The parallel with the Aristotelian project is clear. However, we raised concerns that the transformation of emotions ought not be so thoroughgoing as to undermine the very capacity of emotions to record human values and concerns. Even intense passions and emotional agitations may play an important role here, and moreover, a role that is ultimately compatible with forms of control and practical agency. We have suggested that Aristotelian tragic pity and fear might provide an important model of how we learn through a process that includes both emotional immersion and distance. However, it is not clear if Kant would approve of this kind of relation between the literary and lived life, or would validate, in the first place, experiences of extreme emotional intensity. But whatever Kant himself would say, a *Kantian* conception of practical agency that allows more breathing room for moments of passivity and volatility may not be an altogether bad thing.

7 RESPECT AS A DISTINCTIVE MORAL EMOTION: *CRITIQUE OF PRACTICAL REASON*

Finally, we need to turn to the *Critique of Practical Reason* and the singling out of respect as *the* most genuine practical or moral emotion. In the section entitled "The Incentives of Pure Practical Reason," the explicit focus is on the effects of practical reason, that is, the source of the moral law on our phenomenal nature: "What happens to the human faculty of desire as a consequence of the determining ground" of morality.[132] Kant's claim is that practical reason motivates us directly (that is, we take a direct interest in principle of pure pratical reason), but in addition, insofar as we are affective creatures, we experience that determination affectively, as respect. Respect is not itself a separate sort of motivation. Rather, it is the effect of moral motivation on feeling. In a sense, it is a kind of epiphenomenon.[133] More specifically, it is the feeling of pleasure in appreciating oneself as author of the moral law and capable of reasons for action that meet the demands of the moral law, and yet of pain in having one's reasons for action based on self-love judged untenable and in conflict with morality.

> If anything checks our self-conceit in our own judgment, it humiliates. Therefore, the moral law inevitably humbles every man when he compares the sensuous propensity of his nature with the law. Now if the idea of something as the determining ground of the will humiliates us in our self-consciousness, it awakens respect for itself so far as it is positive and the ground of determination. . . . This effect is on the one side merely negative; but on the other, in respect to the restrictive practical ground of pure practical reason, it is positive.[134]

Kant goes on to claim that respect is *a priori*. His meaning is unclear, but one possible interpretation is something along the following lines: If there are *a priori* practical principles (by which rational agents, such as ourselves, are capable of being moved), and if in addition to being rational agents, we are also affective agents so constituted that we have desires that can always conflict with those principles, then there will always be present the ingredients for respect. There will always be present the conditions for the "painful" checking of reasons for action based on self-love, but also the conditions for the "pleasurable" feelings of mastery that come from appreciating our legislative status. Put more simply, respect is just the affective side of our ever available capacity to be moved by practical reason.

---

[132] KpV 73.
[133] On this point, I have learned from Andy Reath.
[134] KpV 75.

There is something else to notice in these remarks of Kant's, which is that respect seems to be an emotion that has clear connection with a cognitive content. The negative feeling, or pain, associated with respect arises when we *dwell on* the frustration of specific ends of self-interest (i.e., the striking down of self-conceit as one "*compares* the sensuous property of one's nature with the law" [italics added]); its pleasure is that stirred by *appreciating* our legislative authority and newfound mastery in its regulative agency. It is not just that the emotion has pleasurable and painful "feels." Rather, the pleaure and pain are directed at certain thoughts or construals. To feel respect is to see ourselves *as* inhibited and *as* governed by a supreme law whose source is our own reason. The pain and pleasure of the emotion are directed at those judgings and are the causal effects of them. If we generalize, emotions seem to involve cognitions that are productive of emotion and partially constitutive of them. Respect is that emotion which has *that* specific evaluative content. There is no quantitative feel we can identify as characteristic of respect that reliably sets it apart from other emotions. Rather, the emotion just is a particular intentional content and an affective feeling directed toward that content. Other emotions, too, would have a similar structure. Benevolence, for example, becomes a feeling that has to do with pain at the sight or thought of others' suffering and pleasure at the thought of their joy. Such emotions can be said to become "practical" (or properly conditioned by and supportive of duty within a structured conception of character) when they embrace increasingly more adequate appraisals, such as when we take to heart new relevant information: for instance, that this is not a worthy object of benevolence or love, or that this, too, is a case of a need and is a possible occasion for beneficence.

This is not Kant's official account, however.[135] In the case of ordinary emotions, he never develops the view that they are intentional – for example, about things that we judge to be good

---

[135] Though, as I have just suggested, in his account of respect one sees faint glimmers of the notion that pleasure and pain are connected with cognitions we dwell on – in his terms, with what we dwell on when we "compare" the sensuous property of our nature with the view of ourselves as authors of the moral law.

or bad. The view that emotions are intentional is, of course, Aristotle's view. Connecting emotion with evaulations is at the heart of an Aristotelian account of the emotions and at the heart of an Aristotelian view that emotions can be transformed by revisions of our evaluative beliefs and construals such that they come to embrace more adequately our judgments of what is overall good. As Aristotle puts it, emotion registers that something we care about looks good or bad to us. Taking pleasure or pain in certain circumstances (as we do in the case of emotions) involves a kind of judging; as we have said, it involves *phantasia* or *doxa*. This is the force of the *Rhetoric* account discussed in Chapter 2; it is the force of the more general remarks Aristotle makes in the *De Anima*: "To perceive then is like bare asserting or thinking; but when the object is pleasant or painful, the soul makes a sort of affirmation or negation, and pursues or avoids the object."[136]

Kant's own official theory of the emotions leaves out the conceptual connection of emotion with cognition. His view, essentially, is that emotions are sensations. They are a psychic quality of feeling. An emotion like anger may be typically caused by a belief that one has been injured, but it could be caused by a cognition quite different from this (such as the belief that there is a cantaloupe), or by no cognition at all, since the emotion is essentially an affective feel and only contingently connected with a cognition.[137] Consider the following remarks from the Introduction to *The Metaphysic of Morals:*[138]

> We call the capacity for pleasure or pain at a representation *"feeling"* because both of these comprise what is *merely subjective* in the relation to our representation and contain no reference to an object which could give us knowledge of the object (or even knowledge of our own state). . . . Pleasure or pain . . . expresses nothing at all in the object, but simply a relation to the subject.[139]

---

[136] DA 431a8–10. See MA 701a35; 702a15–21.
[137] For a good discussion here, see Oakley (1992, 22).
[138] I am grateful to Christine Korsgaard (1996) for calling my attention to this passage.
[139] DV 211–12.

As Kant puts it in the note that follows,

> if the subjective aspect of our representation cannot become *part of our knowledge* because it is merely the reference of the representation to the *subject* and contains nothing that can be utilized for knowledge of the object, then this receptivity to the representation is called *feeling*.[140]

The claim is that feelings themselves don't tell us much of anything about the world. They tell us that we have been affected, but give us no determinate news of those things or of our own state either. "Pleasure and displeasure do not belong to the cognitive power as it refers to objects; they are determinations of the subject and so cannot be ascribed to external objects."[141] All we get is a feeling – a feeling that, according to famous remarks in the *Critique of Practical Reason,* registers quantitative, not qualitative differences.[142] Of course, Kant might still hold that emotions are essentially sensations, and that cognitions nonetheless count among the typical causal antecedents. This may go some way to establishing a connection between cognition and emotions, but so long as emotions are essentially sensations, it is an inadequate position. For on such a view, the emotion is, as we said, no more than contingently connnected with a certain cognitive content. The emotion of respect could conceivably be caused by cognitions very different from the ones Kant lists, or again, could be caused by no cognition at all. For on the official account, emotion would just be a "characteristic feel."[143]

Now how damaging is this to Kant? After all, he thinks the emotions do give us important information about the world and direct our attention to action that reason judges we ought to do. Is there still a point in visiting the debtors' prisons and sickbeds in order to cultivate a discerning sense of sympathy, if feelings of sympathy are not themselves representations of objective features of the world (though caused by them)? Is there a point to perfecting our affective susceptibilities as ways of tracking "the news" if they are themselves not cognitive or epistemic capacities but, as

[140] DV 211n.   [141] Anth. 240.   [142] KpV 23–24.
[143] For a helpful discussion of a cognitive account of emotions, see Oakley (1992).

Kant puts it in the *Critique of Practical Reason*, brute receptivities of commensurable pleasure or pain?

I think Kant's position on the emotions is unsatisfatory, but that nonetheless his overall view of the importance of cultivating emotions can be salvaged.[144] In part, Kant seems to be relying on the idea that (a) though emotions themselves do not contain appraisals about the morally salient features of the world, nor (b) are themselvs a source of determinative reasons for moral action, in both cases they play a role (and with training, a more reliable role) in directing our attention to circumstances that are morally salient and to actions that are responsive to moral claims. So, for example, overcoming prejudice and understanding the neediness of a particular group of individuals can *evoke* or *cause* feelings of sympathy we previously did not have. In this case, emotions would give us some news, though they would not themselves be constituted by that evaluative "news" or determine its moral import, or be a source of reasons for action, without supplementation from judgments of reason concerning the demands beneficence makes.

Even so, we shouldn't minimize a certain instability in Kant's views when it comes to the emotions. An intentional or evaluative view of the emotions would better cohere with his appreciation of their epistemic function, while still not disturbing his view that emotions may not themselves be the source of determinative reasons (or motives) for moral action. To justify such choices, we may simply need additional and different information than emotions typically contain, (e.g., information that helps us grasp the claims of individuals in terms of their rational agency). In a sense, there is a failure of systematization here. Kant's treatment of the emotions always, at a certain level, remains episodic, keyed to the interest at hand. Even when he talks head-on about the role of emotions in the account of virtue, as he does in *The Metaphysic of Morals*, where he discusses natural and moral perfection, or in the Second *Critique*, where the topic is the effects of duty on our phenomenal nature, the discussion is never brought fully around to a systematic treatment of emotion. His solutions remain ad hoc,

---

[144] I am grateful to Andy Reath for helping me moderate my view here.

unsupported by a theory of the emotions that does full justice to his own view of their utility. In addition, there is the challenge of Kant's rhetorical style when he takes on the emotions.

But to return to the notion of respect for the moment, there is nonetheless something terribly important that Kant captures in this notion. And this is the notion that a conception of morality must find room for a feeling that is responsive to persons simply as persons, independent of contingent circumstances or stations. So while sympathy responds to need, affability to characteristics we find attractive in another, pity to undeserving tragedy or misfortune, respect is different in that its focus is not local or context-specific. It can plausibly be singled out as *the* moral emotion, not so much because rational agency generates it spontaneously in everyone, but because it is a response to rational agency itself. More strictly, it is a response, in the first instance, to the moral law, and secondarily a response to persons, insofar as they have the capacity to act from that law. Its evaluative focus is legislative agency as such.

8 A FEW COMPARATIVE NOTES

In the course of this chapter I have argued that Kant has more to say about the emotions than is typically acknowledged by friends and foes alike, and certainly a wider range of positive views about how emotions support morality. The common reading of Kant in which emotional experience is characterized primarily by immediate inclination, or by agitation and obsessive passion, is simply wrong. There is a far wider panoply of phenomena that goes under the broad heading of emotion or feeling. Included are *cultivated* emotions that form an habituated part of character. And the "cheerful heart" of virtue may implicitly refer to the presence of these. Many commentators concede that on a Kantian view emotional motivation or emotional expression is permissible so long as it is morally regulated by the constraints of the moral law (e.g., benevolence is fine so long as it is guided by honesty). Still, others go on to argue that the presence of inclination need not detract from a morally required action's having moral worth (e.g., a beneficent act done from duty can have moral worth even if it also happens to express sympathy). However, I have argued for something more than toleration. The cultivation of emotion is not merely tolerated, but is required as a part of moral perfection. It is a part of the human embodiment of virtue and the human empowerment of moral agency.

Thus, what I have pointed to throughout this chapter is a conception of *embodied* moral agency that helps us understand Kant's fuller view of moral practice. On such a view, cultivated emotional sensitivities would help us record moral relevance and express moral interest in the concrete circumstances of human life. Being callous while honest, or imperious but truthful, will be morally lacking. Granted, according to Kantian theory, action must ultimately be guided by and promote what is right, according to standards that respect our humanity and free practical agency. But the view I propose would underscore the fact that other aspects of persons and our responses to them are morally important, even if ultimately regulated by respect for agency. *How* we aim to respect rational agency, in terms of emotional attitude and affect, morally matters. To fail to cultivate affective sensibilities that support duty is, as Kant says, to neglect something that is "meritorious and exemplary" in the moral response.[145] It is a kind of moral weakness.[146] The relevant category is Kant's own notion of virtue, understood not simply as fortitude *against* obstacles, but as fortitude *in* transforming the material substrate of character in ways that ultimately strengthen practical agency. Again, virtue becomes embodied – a certain form in the material substrate of our natures whereby the whole composite becomes "virtue."[147] On this Kantian view, it would be derelict not to develop our affective natures as part of the fulfilling of our moral perfection and its subordinate ends. All this is to say that Kant takes seriously the project of the moral improvement of the

---

[145] DV 485.
[146] See DV 384; see DV 390 for a discussion that seems to elide lack of virtue with lack of moral worth..
[147] Here I have vaguely in mind an analogy with Aristotle's analysis of substance at the conclusion of Book VII of the *Metaphysics*.

self.[148] It is an obligatory end, alongside our duty of end to promote the happiness of others. In light of our duty to moral perfection, we are not to rest on the flaws and defects of our *given* nature. That we are surly or peevish won't do as an excuse for failing to make serious efforts toward developing a kinder spirit. Here, as elsewhere, a significant part of Kantian morality is striving to be better. The project filters down to the condition of our emotions. Emotional maturity is not a matter of moral indifference. Virtue is defective if it fails to aim to cultivate appropriate materials. It is important to remember here that for the Kantian, in contrast to the Aristotelian, moral assessment of virtue will remain primarily a matter of first-person evaluation. So whereas within Aristotelian theory, appraisal of character in terms of *to kalon* takes both a first- and a third-person perspective, within Kantian theory, assessing the progress of virtue remains a more private matter. But this makes the Kantian project of assessment no less important. The duty to moral perfection is just that – a duty, whoever is doing the appraising. And the cultivation of moral emotions falls under that vigil.

Still, Kant's view, I have suggested, is ultimately unstable because his conception of the emotions as psychic sensations is, at bottom, implausible and undercuts the very roles he assigns emotions in moral practice. The rhetorical and desultory style that characterizes his discussion of the emotions is perhaps a telltale sign of his own lack of clear systematization here. It seems to me that Aristotle's theory of the emotions, with its focus on evaluative appraisals, does better to explain the role of emotions in virtue, and perhaps it is not surprising that he, unlike Kant, accords emotions the unequivocal role he does in his moral theory.

There are a few final points of contrast between the Aristotelian and the Kantian that need airing, and that put some perspective on the more textual study in which we have been engaged. It might be argued that the real source of Kant's ambivalence about

---

148 In this regard, his views are quite different from the Stoics, who hold that virtue is an "all or nothing" thing. Hence, in one text "moral progress" (*prokopē*) is listed as an indifferent, albeit one that is intrinsically valued. See Diogenes Laertius 7.107 (SVF 3.135) = L and S 58m (reproduced only in vol. 2).

the role of emotion in the moral response comes to no more than this: that we cannot *ensure success* in *actually expressing* the emotions that we think are appropriate. For the Kantian, the most we can demand is good willing, that is, sincere effort in certain relevant endeavors, constrained by the principles practical agency itself generates. If an agent tries to be sympathetic because she realizes it is important for morality, but simply cannot make it happen – if she makes the attempt part of her sincere maxim of what is relevant to helping another, but can't bring it off – is she subject to moral self-criticism? Presumably, a Kantian would argue "no," especially if the agent is one who, on the whole, takes seriously a policy of developing sympathetic feelings, exhorts herself to do better when she fails, cultivates the right outward gestures, and monitors her behavior to see how she is doing. A moral defect in character, on this Kantian view, shows up not so much in the finished product as in whether or not there is adequate striving of a will toward the right ends.[149]

In contrast, it might be objected, Aristotle's notion of what is praiseworthy in action and emotion ultimately fails to separate out what is a matter of one's own effort and what is a matter of circumstance and the gifts of constitution. Also, in requiring that virtues be expressed in appropriate emotions that are perfectly harmonized with wisdom, Aristotle may be simply too optimistic about how the most virtuous humans will react to the circumstances that bring on emotion, too optimistic about how they will respond to reversal, wrenching loss, human despair, devastating betrayal, too optimistic that cultivated human efforts to show right emotions and feelings will be successful and in line with practical wisdom. The psychological reality in the very best persons is that they manage to make the right choice, but conflicting feelings may nevertheless sometimes leak through. Maybe Kant, in emphasizing willing rather than expression, whether it be in the sphere of action or of emotion, simply takes us back to ourselves as agents and to a well-circumscribed area where we can be agents in control. Through the notion of duty, he accepts the inevitability of conflict in the nondivine agent, however impor-

---

[149] See DV 433.

tant transformation of inclination (and not mere inhibition or extirpation) is as virtue's goal. Perhaps the difference between the two philosophers is as basic as this: Kant articulates the ordinary moral view that we can act from duty even when inclinations pull us in the opposite direction. We strive for psychic harmony and are meritorious when we achieve it (this is the force of the account of virtue we have been exploring), but even in the face of temptation we can summon duty as a reliable motive. Aristotle, in contrast, believes that psychic conflict leads to deep motivational instability, and that full psychic harmony, expressed in a transformed sense of self-love that reaches out to what is fine,[150] is the only real basis for reliably summonable and stable moral motives.

But to argue that duty can be summoned against competing inclinations is not to discount the role of supportive emotions, even in such cases. The role of the emotions as modes of attention or sensitivity enter here. I may do a good deed to another, not out of desire but out of duty, but even here, I may first notice this person as needy as a result of a report that works through the emotions. In emphasizing the reliability of duty in the face of contrary inclination, Kant may obscure this epistemic role of supportive inclination, which elsewhere he himself acknowledges is a part of full moral practice, and which we find more systematically developed by Aristotle, especially in the *Rhetoric*.

Still, in the notion of duty and particularly in the notion of respect, Kant points to something Aristotle does not adequately grasp. The point emerges if we focus briefly on Aristotle's discussion of friendship in the ethical works. Aristotle makes clear in this discussion that friendship is the most important forum for beneficence because it is the most deeply connected with moral development and with the conditions for sustaining moral character.[151] There are forms of good will (*eunoia*) toward strangers and the like, but we do not realize ourselves as fully in

---

150 This, I believe, is the point of remarks in NE IX.4 and IX.8, where Aristotle proposes a sense of *philautia* (self-love), which, through training in virtue, becomes nonegoistic. For a valuable discussion of these texts, see Annas (1993, 223–322). I take up the issue in the next chapter as well.

151 For the connection of friendship with self-development, see the remarks on self-knowledge in IX.9 and the closing remark at NE IX.12.

these forms of virtue. For we do not, in addition, share a life or common good with these beneficiaries. Significantly, on Aristotle's view, philanthropic feelings that go out to persons whom we do not know, such as in the case of pity or kindness, still reach out to others on the basis of some shared context – that we could suffer similar fates, or that the beneficiaries are those who have a characteristic we admire or to which we can relate.[152] In a sense, on the Aristotelian view, our moral interest must connect with others whom we can appreciate from our own corner of the universe, who are part of our lives, relevant to our conception of good living, in a set of circumstances that we broadly share. The idea of being morally interested in persons, simply as such, in virtue of a source of value that is not dependent on circumstance or shared context, is, I take it, at the heart of Kant's break with Aristotle. The dialogue continues in Chapter 5, with further reflection on the place of the shared life in Aristotelian and Kantian ethics.

[152] See esp. Rh. 1385b13–15 and NE 1167a18–20.

Chapter 5

The shared voyage

We have now discussed the role of emotions in Aristotelian and Kantian theories of virtue. Early on in the discussion of Aristotle's views, I touched on the intuitive idea that emotions are a kind of social fiber. They connect us with others in a way that cold reason or affectless action cannot. Moreover, certain emotions, attachment or affiliative emotions, are directed specifically at the cultivation and maintenance of relationships. These relationships, or *philiai*, as Aristotle would call them, are grounded in shared activity and interest. In this chapter, I explore the role of friendship or affiliation in Aristotelian and Kantian accounts of morality. The general topic of friendship has come under considerable discussion in recent years. Within political philosophy, communitarians have charged that the issue of community is not adequately addressed by a political liberalism, such as Rawls's, based in Kantian notions of the person; within moral philosophy, feminists have argued that the moral importance of family and friendship has been obscured by an overemphasis on the moral perspective of impartiality. These contemporary debates are too extensive to review here, though I hope what I have to say might shed some light on them. For the purpose of this chapter, my aim is straightforward and limited. I want to explore what it is we value about doing things together, and how it is morally significant. I begin by examining these issues more or less independently of Aristotle and Kant's writings in order to fix our own intuitions about why we are interested in the topic in the first place. In many ways, though, our own commonsense views about this topic are Aristotle's starting place too.

In Section 1, I begin with some general reflections about friendship and "doing things together," and then follow the debate as it unfolds in Aristotle and Kant's works.[1]

1 DOING THINGS TOGETHER

We tend to think of morality as caring about self and others, and as requiring the cultivation of capacities *in* self to take care *of* self and others. The goodness is in oneself, in excellences or virtues, exercised outward on appropriate objects. However, the goodness of friendship is not like this.[2] Unlike generosity or beneficence, it is not an internal state of character that then comes to be actualized on appropriate occasions. A friendship is relational, something between rather than in a person, however dependent it is on traits of character in each person and however dependent it is on each person's representation of the other. One couldn't have stable friendships without beneficence, generosity, compassion, and so on, exhibited toward one another. But friendship isn't the exercise (or reciprocal exercise) of these states, any more than it is the exercise (or reciprocal exercise) of some virtue such as friendliness. For friendliness does not depend upon attachments to the persons who are its object, nor, more importantly, does it depend upon mutuality.[3] Friendship, in contrast, is essentially relational and its specific value is in its forms of mutuality. (Note, this is not to imply that virtue itself is something absolutely stable inside that can survive any and all external conditions. On an Aristotelian view, for example, the emphasis on habituation

---

[1] Some of the themes were explored earlier in Sherman (1993b).

[2] Aristotle seems to point to this at NE 1155a1, where he hesitates from unqualifiedly calling friendship a virtue. In his more systematic classifications, he regards it as an external good (see NE I.8–10; Rh. 1386a10–11). Nussbaum (1986, ch. 12) usefully labels it a "relational good."

[3] NE IV.6. Self-regard has the attachment aspect of friendship: we do not view ourselves as simply an appropriate occasion for the exercise of specific virtues; we are *committed* to ourselves. But, of course, this attachment lacks the mutuality of friendship. See Aristotle's comparisons of self-love and love of others at NE IX.4 and IX.8.

makes clear that virtue is not merely *occasioned* by what is outside, but is developed or corrupted by the kinds of activities we engage in. Deprivation, war, torture, or poverty can force activities that eat away at the core of virtue.[4] In Kant's theory, too, virtue is conceived of as a progress,[5] and a struggle against temptations large and small. Kant emphasizes the independence of a good will from contingency, but presumably, he, too, would acknowledge that there are conditions humans face that strain the most virtuous commitment. These points notwithstanding, friendship, in contradistinction to virtue, is an activity that in an essential way is outside us, and subject to the contingencies introduced by its dependence on a person who is separate from ourselves.)

The general point is, however, that we value such relationships as part of moral living. It is not simply that we treat certain individuals in special ways, framed by the context and requirements of specific relationships. It is that we care about the fact that we do things together. And we care about that activity for its own sake. More limited points are often raised in connection with the notion of affiliation. Group effort produces group products that are valued and that couldn't be achieved in isolation. Equally, community requires cooperative virtues that we value as social beings. A willingness to compromise, to seek consensus, to be trustworthy and fair, all go with collective effort.[6] But the point I emphasize is the more basic one, yet one often missed in discussions about friendship. We simply value doing things together for

---

4 See Rh. 1386a4–12.
5 In this regard, it is distinguished from Stoic theory, which views virtue as an all-or-nothing matter. Moral progress, significantly, is an indifferent. See, for example, Diogenes Laertius 7.107 (SVF 4.135) = L and S 58m.
6 Compare Rawls's discussion of the "morality of association" (1971, sec. 71). As Rawls describes it, taking on the roles and values of the collectivity requires, among other things, the art of perceiving others, of understanding their intentions, and cooperating with points of view that are different from one's own. This comes close to the point I wish to make, though I emphasize mutual interaction and attunement less than cooperation. On Rawls's view, the morality of association fits into a three-staged scheme of moral development, adapted from Lawrence Kohlberg. The Kohlbergian scheme has been criticized in the work of Carol Gilligan (1982), essentially for marginalizing the morality of association, or what has come to be called "the caring ethic."

its own sake. Apart from valuing the benefits and virtues related to being a friend, we prize the give-and-take of mutual exchange. We value creating a shared world and expanding self through a sense of mutuality defined by our interactions. The pleasure of mutuality and the expansion of self that comes with it is a core part of human development and flourishing.

I come to this point through some examples:

Take deliberating together. We can deliberate together for personal or group ends. In the case of joint deliberation where we deliberate for a group end, there is the collective aspiration: improving the university, strengthening the department through its new appointments, working out American foreign policy in the Mideast. These are goals to which the group is devoted as its project. There is also group deliberation for personal ends. One can seek the values of stimulating dialogue and critique in order to promote one's own private ends, to formulate new ones, or to refine existing ones. It is true, to a greater or lesser degree, one's personal ends don't make sense except against a larger, shared background that goes well beyond the self. The use of language, of course, testifies to this. It is a shared conceptual scheme of the most fundamental sort. Less globally, specific goals are indebted to the traditions that give them meaning. To engage in philosophy as a personal end is still to subscribe to group values in significant ways, as defined through the standards of the profession and specific historical traditions. Still, it may be as a personal end that one seeks to do philosophy, though one conducts the dialogue always with past and present interlocutors.

But so far the examples have focused on joint activity as valued for an end separate from the social interaction itself, whether that end be joint or private. Yet independent of specific products and activities, there is the value of the group dynamic itself. Interaction that shows mutual interest and responsiveness is prized simply for that reason.

In this regard, consider conversation. In the ideal, and perhaps inspired, case there is the thrill of being in conversation with another, of seeing the other's point, of her seeing yours, of hitting on salience *together,* of acknowledging that the discovery is not mine or yours but ours, of realizing that even if it is more mine than yours, the real pleasure is in sharing it, in making it public to the other who acknowledges a comparable pleasure in its apprehension, and then, of going somewhere with it, together. There are, to be sure, the specifically intellectual benefits of such partnership: Two minds think better than one, dialogue corrects for the blind spots of monologue, the stimulus of others provides energy and continuity to our activity not easily mustered on our own. As Aristotle would say, we can think better, be more critical, have stamina when we are engaged with others. But these are not the joys of mutual interaction itself, though they are some of the advantages that accrue to each party. The joy of interaction – here, through conversation – is in creating shared terrain, in going on a voyage together, in taking a flight of fancy, in locating for ourselves a subject matter and focus that defines our joint excursion. We value being engaged in this sort of mutual interaction and value what makes it possible in ourselves and others. There is, of course, a limitation of scope here. Not just any two individuals can see eye to eye in this way. To call it "chemistry" is to put it too strongly. To point to common language is to put it too weakly. The terrain in between is murky. But the mutual tracking that goes on in good conversation need not presuppose the bonds of enduring friendship or previous affiliation. It itself can be a moment, suspended as it were, in mutual interaction.

This points us to a related kind of joint activity. When I play Legos with my son Jonathan, a certain devotion on my part to the activity, an ability to "get into it" and to be a responsive playmate is valued. If I am easily distracted, have my mind on my work, can't generate building schemes that capture his imagination or mine, can't respond to his cues for a certain kind of phantasy play, I am simply not a good playmate. I am lacking as a partner engaged in a common pursuit. Indeed, perhaps play, what children do so well, captures the bare idea best. In looking for a good playmate, a child isn't simply concerned with a boy or girl who is decent and fair, who doesn't abuse the rules and is sympathetic to one's needs. That is part of it and is an interest at a remarkably early age. But there are lots of other things that matter. Once beyond the age of parallel play, there is the relish in inventing made-up stories together, in inventing a myth about the team fort and the rules of membership, in going off on some spaceship to a secret planet that is jointly named by its young discoverers, in making up a game, in short, in inventing a shared world together, with spontaneity, enthusiasm, loyalty, and mutual enjoyment. Here the value of affiliation is conspicuous apart from the specific ends it promotes. Doing it together, with the right sort of devotion, matters. But this kind of mutual engagement is not mere child's play. Constructing a shared world, however brief or enduring, characterizes the best sort of adult interaction too.

Consider a different case, perhaps a somewhat strained case, one might think, of a face-to-face community. I am thinking of a stereotype of divorced parents and their coordinated activity of parenting. The two share responsibility for their daughter and agree upon common goals; their activities are highly orchestrated and part of an overall plan to promote their daughter's welfare. There is joint deliberation in the planning and reliability in its exercise; a devotion to a common cause and shared values in its realization. In addition, both benefit the other by being reliable parents who can be counted on to fulfill their mutual interest in caring for the child.

Still, certain values of shared activity are missing. It is not that they lack a common goal that makes reference to something other than their own personal advantages. The well-being of the daughter *is* their common goal, and to that they are unwaveringly loyal. And they deliberate collectively toward that end, just as they share other parenting activities together, in the same locale if not always under the same roof. All the same, they lack the dynamic valued in group interaction. They don't *interact* in a way that captures what is best in group activity. They lack the spontaneity and enthusiasm of sharing in each other's thoughts, even those related to their common end. There is a certain emptiness to the present moment, a resistance to letting the conversation go beyond necessities. In their case, the explanation may chalk up to lost love, a lack of enthusiasm *for each other* that makes them standoffish.

But whatever the cause, what the young playmates have, this couple lacks: namely, the mutual acknowledgment of pleasure in interacting and in sharing discoveries. It is not just formal features that are decisive – that they don't share their daughter at the same time, in each other's company, much of the time. For these formal criteria of "sharing" could easily be satisfied without the substantive facts of the case changing.[7] It is that they don't enjoy sharing the activity *with* each other. They may admire each other as fine and decent parents. But still, this is looked upon as something external to the other's project rather than as the fuel that rekindles his or her own efforts. What is missing is a delight in spending time together that energizes the shared activity and that in the best of cases, spills over into nonshared moments. To put it in the vernacular, they don't like "hanging out" together. Put more genteelly, "visiting" each other leaves them cold.

Much of this talk of mutuality may conjure up notions of intimacy and perhaps even romance. But mutuality can be understood also outside of intimacy. There are shared voyages we take simply by being drawn into casual conversation with others, by playing with another through verbal repartee, by singing together the same tune, by knowing that others endorse brand x over y, by putting weight on the same point and acknowledging it through a shared glance or head nod, by concurring about some matter of taste or fact, and acknowledging the consensus. However weighty or insignificant the subject, what is valued is mutual responsiveness and the ability to engage another and to be engaged in return. The mutuality of the moment is not lost.

Mutual responsiveness of this sort, particularly as it is sustained in relationships, is a human good rooted in the sociality of our natures. We needn't think of "nature" in this usage as something fixed by a value-free inquiry, nor again as something fully determined and merely awaiting expression. Much can be said

---

7 Think of two people reading the same joke book at the same time, perhaps in the same room, perhaps even hearing each other laugh. Reading the same joke book is a "shared activity," but hardly the sort that points to the value of community. Here, Kant's remark from the second *Critique* is relevant: "In this way a harmony may result resembling that depicted in a certain satirical poem as existing between a married couple bent on going to ruin, 'Oh, marvelous harmony, what he wants is what she wants'; or like the pledge which is said to have been given by Francis I to the Emperor Charles V, 'What my brother wants (Milan), that I want too'" (KpV 29).

about how to understand an appeal to human nature. But for the
moment, the point to stress is simply that our sociality is at the
core of a kind of an existence that is unmistakably human; it is
connected with a system of views about how we tend to live and
what matters to us, and how radically different our lives would
be if we were to abstract recognizable forms of mutual interaction
from it.[8] Finding pleasure in the mutuality of shared projects is
not simply a contingent end, like enjoying carpentry or dance or
music. Unlike these, the pleasures of common pursuit appeal to
psychological facts about human nature that are persistent and
that bridge local differences of taste and talent. Both Aristotle and
Kant recognize this, however differently it figures within their
theories and however differently they weigh its importance.
Without delving too deeply into the texts just yet, a few preliminary remarks are important. The significance of friendship within
the Aristotelian account is unmistakable. Two out of ten of the
books of the *Nicomachean Ethics* are devoted to the topic of *philia*,
as are correspondingly large portions of the *Eudemian Ethics* and
the *Magna Moralia*.[9] In the *Politics*, too, friendship is a persistent
theme. As Aristotle takes up the ancient debate, the question
posed is whether the complete and self-sufficient life, that is, the
ultimately good life lacking in nothing which could make it more
desirable, will include friendship. It is important to appreciate
that the question is not an idle one. Among the surveyed views of
the wise and many, the philosophical life of solitary contemplation is a strong contender for the good life,[10] and one Aristotle
himself is drawn to in the notorious discussion in Book X.7–8 of
the *Nicomachean*. There he seems to argue that contemplative activity, characteristic of the solitary life, may in an absolute way
best meet the critieria of a good life. Sorting out the text here is an
extremely complicated matter, and one that would take us far

8 See Nussbaum(1986, ch. 12), who takes this up in connection with the general
method of Aristotle's inquiry, and Annas (1993, chs. 3–9), who usefully analyzes the appeal to nature in the study of ancient ethics in general.
9 NE VIII and IX; EE VII; MM II.11–17.
10 The three candidates standardly offered for the good life are pleasure, contemplation, and virtue: NE I.5; EE 1215a35-b5; cf.1216a28–29.

beyond the scope of our present inquiry.[11] For our present purposes, it is important to note that however attractive and worthy
the life of contemplation and however noninstrumental its
value,[12] even it, Aristotle argues, may be best sustained by humans when they engage in the activity with others. "The wise
person, by himself, is able to engage in contemplation, and the
better, the wiser he is; and perhaps he can do so better with fellow
workers [*sunergous echōn*]."[13] Our most godlike and divine
pursuit – contemplation for its own sake, still characteristically
takes, in our hands, a social form. Aristotle doesn't pursue the
point, but even in solitude our contemplation often takes the form
of conversation in the conjured presence of another. We construct
audiences and interlocutors to move our thoughts along. The
more fundamental point, which Aristotle does pursue, is that self-
sufficiency for a human being itself needs to be understood as
taking a relational form. The *Magna Moralia* reminds us that "we
are not investigating the self-sufficiency of a god, but of human
beings" and that, as the *Eudemian Ethics* explains, our well-being
is relational, whereas in the case of a god he is himself his own
well-being.[14] In the *Nicomachean*, a similar gloss on the term "self-
sufficient" is introduced:

> Now by self-sufficient we do not mean that which is sufficient
> for a man by himself, for one who lives a solitary life, but also
> for parents, children, wife, and in general for his friends and

---

11 There is an extensive literature on this subject, and I mention only some of the
   relevant writings. For important studies that argue for consistency between
   Book X.7–8 and the rest of the NE, see Broadie (1991), Cooper (1987), Devereux
   (1981), Keyt (1983), and Kraut (1989); for doubts, see Ackrill (1980), Cooper
   (1975), Nagel (1980), and Nussbaum (1986).
12 This is Aristotle's emphasis at NE 1177b1–4. See Korsgaard (1986a) on comparisons of this notion of an intrinsic good with the unconditional goodness of
   the good will. The point I go on to make about the dependency of Aristotelian
   contemplation upon social forms of activity may undercut Korsgaard's notion
   that contemplation is an intrinsic end in the Kantian sense of bearing its value
   in itself, isolated from all contexts and conditions.
13 NE 1177a35.
14 MM 1213a8; EE 1245b18–19.

fellow citizens, since humans are by nature social and political.[15]

Again, he says, our virtue is most complete when it is exercised not merely toward ourselves, but in relation to others. As such, it is a most general kind of justice in which we view ourselves always in a community with others.[16] In all this, Aristotle is reminding us that we must direct the search for a good life to its specifically human application. We may strive to be most godlike and to transcend our own limits (it may even be important to exhort ourselves in these ways, and "not follow those who advise us, being human, to think [only] of human things or being mortal to think only of mortal things").[17] But social relations, more than not, frame the very way we think of our form of life. "For no one would choose to have all good things on condition of living alone."[18] Aristotle's task is to ground this reputed view within a more systematic account of good human living.

It is tempting to think that Kant's moral inquiry cannot accommodate the topic of friendship except in a peripheral way. The ancient question is, What is the good life? What are its constitutents? What makes for the most complete goodness over time? Friendship fits easily within this framework. Kant rejects *eudaimonia* or happiness as the central concern, turning instead to the grounding of moral obligation in practical rational nature.[19] With this move, friendship might seem to be squeezed out, becoming at best a subjective end in the nonmoral sphere of happiness that is conditioned by morality. However, as I have been arguing, Kant's grounding of obligation in practical rational agency is the beginning of a further story about what is required for promoting and maintaining such agency. Good willing (the

---

[15] NE 1097b8ff, with slight alteration of the Urmson translation.

[16] NE 1129b26ff.

[17] NE 1177b32.

[18] NE 1169b17ff.

[19] Though happiness, of course, enters, as a conditional set of ends regulated by the unconditional goodness of practical rational nature, or moral agency. The Highest Good is the composite good in which happiness is proportionate to morality; see KpV 111–14.

perfection of rational agency, or what Kant calls "humanity")[20] is not whistling in the wind but effort that depends upon the cultivation of further human resources and goods. The support and educational efforts of our friends will enter here, always carefully limited by an agent's own privileged role in taking primary responsibility for her own moral development as the perfection of her own rational agency.[21] The supportive role of friends enters in more extensive ways when we consider just how comprehensive the practice of morality is on a full Kantian view. On a full Kantian view, morality is exhibited not only at those moments when we act on reasons that are determined by us as sufficient (i.e., determined and justified by the constraints of rational agency itself, opposed to merely self-interest), but also in recognizing the moral significance of occasions and in formulating maxims that themselves bear the marks of that awareness. This, too, is the expression of moral character. It is a part of the account of moral agency. But to bring home the present point, acknowledging this further emphasizes the importance of both moral habituation in a full Kantian theory and the role of friends within that account. We need friends as supports and consultants in all the stages of moral development and practice – from the transmission of values, to the recognition of their relevance in particular occasions, to discussion and conversation about hard cases, to understanding the grounding of choices in what is unconditional about rational agency. Moreover, friends, attuned as they are to our habits and weaknesses, can be crucial monitors of the self-deceptions and exemptions that prey on the best moral lives. And they can help us to see how, in our construal of circumstances, we wear a lens that often distorts.

I have given a reconstruction. Kant's own classification of friendship is vague, and his discussion slim in comparison to Aristotle's. The sections on friendship are appended to duties to others and thus seem to fall among our duties to promote others' happiness. Respect and practical love, the most general headings under which our duties to others fall, have broad scope – to

---

[20] DV 392, 387. Cf. G 437; Rel. 27–28/22–23.
[21] DV 386.

humanity in general and in an extended way, to animals. Friendship is a special case, the "intimate union of love and respect."[22] In a more perspicuous way than beneficence, it is a way of partaking in others' ends as our own. Friendship "is an ideal of the emotional and practical concern which each of the friends united through a morally good will takes in the other's welfare."[23] It is a form of mutual benevolence. But what I have outlined as the role of friendship in the project of moral perfection does not easily fit within our duties to promote the happiness of others, at least as Kant conceives of happiness, as separate from moral perfection. Moreover, Kant's tone is often one of cynicism about the possibility of nonexploitative friendships. Mutuality and equality in friendship are in practice rare, he thinks, and friendship is always a teeter-totter of getting close, but then having to keep one's distance in order to preserve respect. We shall come to all this, but here the questions to keep in mind are: How much of what Kant says amount to theoretical limits on an accommodation of friendship within an account of moral life? How much of what he says are simply accent points, which like his negative remarks on emotions, need to be carefully assessed for their actual theoretical implications? Finally, even if they are only accent points, how much adjustment can one make before one loses the overall emphasis and direction of his account?

Before turning to the Aristotelian account, I want to recall again the feature of friendship I have been focusing on as valuable. And this is a sense of tracking something with another, of mutual attunement to each other's moves and of enjoying that process. The operative feature here is not respect for others, nor beneficence, nor even cooperation, though each may be important in doing things together, and friendship may be a place to cultivate those values. What I am pointing to is a sense of mutual engagement. At risk of being expansive, what is at stake is some measure of transcendence; it is a relaxing of one's own sense of boundaries

---

[22] Friendship takes on the modern gloss of close or intimate associations. As we shall see, Aristotelian *philia* includes this, but extends more widely.
[23] DV 469.

and control. It is acknowledging a sense of union or merger with another.[24]

Now, is this dimension of sociality discussed in Aristotle and Kant's writings, and if so, in what way? In the Aristotelian account of friendship, the importance of mutual activity is a central focus. In a rare and unparalleled way within philosophical discussions, Aristotle offers a detailed and concrete account of the various ways friendship expresses mutuality. In Kant's account, mutuality remains a necessary feature of stable friendship, though friendship itself is viewed as far less important than the cultivation of more general virtues, such as beneficence or gratitude, that do not depend upon attachment or mutual interaction.

2 ARISTOTELIAN FRIENDSHIP AND SHARED ACTIVITY

Philia is usually translated by our term "friendship," but the ancient concept is considerably broader than what we mean by friendship. It includes chosen relationships among intimates, as well as nonchosen relationships within family or *polis*. Equally, it can include casual acquaintances who come together through commercial associations or recreation. Paradigmatically, friendship, as I shall continue to translate *philia*, is characterized by mutual attachment, manifest by certain "attachment emotions," such as love and affection, and upon separation or loss, grief and mourning. But the full range of emotions find their home here too – pity, fear, joy, sympathy, anger, shame, hatred, and so on, often in intense form given the importance of certain relation-

---

24 Related points have been argued within contemporary psychological theory. Whereas earlier Freudian theory focused on separation and independence from the parental world (and internalization of those differences within the individual), the writings of contemporary psychoanalysts such as D. W. Winnicott (1971) and Jessica Benjamin (1988) focus on child development as requiring a dynamic between individuals, fostered by the pleasures of mutuality and connection. Interactive gazes, smiling, facial play, cooing matched and attuned to the child's own sounds, establish a pattern of mutual influence and adaptation that is perhaps the earliest mode of a sense of oneness and mutuality. For a detailed clinical study, see Greenspan (1989). For a discussion of mutuality in the sphere of love, see Person (1988).

ships in our lives. Equally, friendship involves commitment, manifest in a willingness to give priority to friends in terms of resources and time. It is accepted belief, Aristotle reports, that friends come first in terms of benefaction and care.[25] This does not rule out restrictions from justice or other virtues requiring more impartial exercise. However, Aristotle accepts the commonsense view that friends, in general, have priority on one's resources – this he takes to need no argument, and moreover, that it is fine and good to exhibit altruism, or other-regarding concern, in such spheres.[26] Indeed, according to Aristotle, friendship is the primary sphere of altruism. Although he also discusses good will and benefaction among strangers, friendship is nonetheless taken to be the most important place in which these states of character are manifest. And this has to do with the mutuality of friendship and its intrinsic value and importance for moral development throughout life.

Aristotle accepts the general Greek view that *philia* covers a broad range of relationships; his interest is in systematizing the discussion. To begin with, he classifies friendship as being of three major types, based on the reasons or grounds for which friends come together – that is, "the things through [*dia*] which they love."[27] One can seek in a friendship what is good, what is pleasant, or what is useful. Although the division is presented as exhaustive, his own later discussion includes a wide variety of friendships, such as those between family members and fellow citizens, which do not neatly fit into these pigeonholes.[28] Friendship based on what is good or, as he sometimes puts it, good character,[29] is the most stable kind of friendship, since good

---

[25] NE 1155a8–9; 1169b12.

[26] NE 1155a9.

[27] NE 1155b27ff.; see b18ff.

[28] In the *Eudemian Ethics* civic friendships are regarded as a species of utility friendship, whereas in the *Politics* (esp. Book III), they seem to be forms of virtue friendship crucial to an education in living well. In general, I prefer the latter classification and think there is also merit in regarding the friendship between parent and child as a kind of virtue friendship, or at least a friendship crucially involved in the development of the child's virtue. I discuss the training of virtue within the family in Sherman (1989, ch. 5).

[29] NE 1164a12,1165b8–9; EE 1242b36.

character tends to be a reliable condition and those interested in cultivating a union on its basis are committed in a stable way to the end of virtue. It is the most paradigmatic form of friendship, too, with respect to depth and level of mutual engagement. Second, Aristotle lists the necessary elements of all friendships. Whatever the ground of friendship, all friendships must involve reciprocation of affection, reciprocation of good will, and crucially, mutual recognition of that pattern of exchange. In other words, friendship involves mutual affection and mutual benefiting. Friends "do not fail to notice" (*mē lanthanontas*) the exchange of good will and good feeling.[30] They are not like distant benefactors, engaged in some exchange that may be equal and reciprocal and yet still lacking in mutual acknowledged interaction. Nor are they like distant admirers, formally exchanging a glance. The significant value is in the mutual recognition of the exchange. Like the reflection of one mirrored image in another, the exchange is reiterated but also deepened through mutual acknowledgment.[31]

> For many people have goodwill to those whom they have not seen but judge to be good or useful; and one of these might return this feeling toward another. These people seem to bear goodwill to each other; but how could one call them friends when they are unaware of how they feel toward one another? To be friends, then, they must be aware of bearing goodwill and wishing well to each other for one of the aforesaid reasons.[32]

I want to discuss the issue of mutuality more fully, but first we need to record that Aristotelian friendship requires benefiting another as a separate other, for his or her own sake. It is important to stress this point for it is often thought that the emphasis on friendship in Aristotle's writings points to a kind of other-regard that does not sufficiently recognize either the separateness of friends or the moral significance of a noninstrumental relation to

[30] NE 1156a4.
[31] Of some relevance here is Tom Nagel's (1979) intriguing remarks about the mutuality of the erotic glance, and also Sartre's famous discussion in Part III of *Being and Nothingness.*
[32] NE 1156a1–5.

them. The objections are Kantian in spirit. But it is clear that Aristotle recognizes both considerations, even though he certainly does not accord the place of another agent's good in the deliberative space of a practical agent in the way Kant does.[33] A friend is "another self," "another me," but as he aptly qualifies in the *Eudemian,* a friend is always a "separate self."[34] The point comes across clearly in the *Rhetoric* definition of friendship. There Aristotle reports the popular view that friendship is "wishing for another what you believe to be good things, for the sake of the other and not for your own sake, and being disposed, so far as you can, to bring these things about."[35] In the *Nicomachean Ethics,* for the most part, he takes for granted this commonsense view, though he does make the following explicit point: Loving a friend is not like loving some lifeless object. One may love wine, but "it is ridiculous to wish wine well; if one wishes anything for it, it is that it may keep, so that one may have it for oneself. But to a friend we say we ought to wish what is good for his sake."[36] Aristotle intends to preserve this point in the concise definition of friendship he goes on to give in the next few lines. But although Aristotle recognizes the Kantian point that we ought not treat persons as mere things, or as mere appendages of self,[37] he never accords this point a keystone place in his theory or sets out to ground it in some more fundamental fact about our capacity for end setting and choice. And this is so, even though he does argue that the capacity for authoritative reason, determinative of fine choice, is what is best in us and what is most deserving of self-love and praise.[38] The point bears on a more general one. Aristotle's theory is not systematic in the Kantian way – it does not

---

[33] In this regard, there remains a fundamental issue between Aristotle and Kant, even if it is supposed that the best life for an agent, on the Aristotelian view, includes activities in which the goods of others are valued for their own sake. I am grateful to the Press's reviewer for helping me formulate the point.

[34] MM 1213a13, a24; NE 1170b7; EE 1245a30; EE 1245a35.

[35] Rh. 1381a1; also NE 1166a5.

[36] NE 1155b29–31; cf. 1167a18; EE 1237b30–33.

[37] See MM 1194b11–20 on Aristotle's view that a child is not properly a subject of justice for she is not yet separate; she is like an appendage of a parent.

[38] Especially NE 1166a18–23; cf.1177a11ff.; friendship itself exhibits this capacity for choice. See EE 1236b3–7, 1237a30ff.

build up from a single capacity or good that we all are held to share (such as the setting of ends) and that in its perfection is taken to be the source of normative constraints on us. Aristotle's theory is not without its system or normative constraints, but it works in a different way. It posits ideal happiness as the ultimate good that normatively guides our pursuits. This will be a structured whole constituted by increasingly specified ends that mutually order and delimit each other.[39] A global grasp of the internal delimitation of the components of happiness (e.g., how generosity mutually fits with temperance, or honesty with kindness) guides us in our choice of what is fine. What is worth pursuing within that happiness will include virtuous activities and friendships, and these will take into account the good of others for their own sake. A further grounding of concern for others in a way separate from our own happiness is not viewed as necessary, for to pursue one's own happiness, in this overall way, is to pursue what matters to one, but never out of motives that reduce to ordinary self-love or egoism.[40] The point for now is that genuine other-regard is preserved in Aristotle's theory, though it is assumed more as a fact of our practice than as something that needs to be justified in terms of more basic ends.

It is sometimes thought that utility friendships cannot sustain genuine other-regard, for any mutual benefiting within such a friendship must ultimately redound to the individual utility that grounds the friendship. Aristotle's own views on this vary across different writings, though he is consistent throughout in regarding utility friendship as, at best, an attenuated form of friendship. He is overall less sanguine in the *Eudemian* than in *Nicomachean* about the possibility of commercial relations between persons establishing a context for mutually disinterested regard.[41] Still, it seems plausible to hold that while utility may bring individuals together, once so affiliated, they wish each other well for their

---

[39] For further discussion of Aristotle's notion of a structured whole, and for the idea of specification in guiding choice of ends, see Richardson (1992).

[40] See NE IX.8. Both Annas (1993, chs. 1–14) and Kraut (1982, ch.2) discuss the modern misinterpretation of Aristotelian eudaimonism as a kind of egoism.

[41] See EE 1241a5ff.; cf. EE 1242b33ff.

own sakes and not for personal utility.[42] Admittedly, the depth
and stability of this mutual disinterest may not be very great.
Utility friendship is transient, Aristotle insists, and, accordingly,
any altruism that is a part of it will survive only so long as the
friendship does.[43] Moreover, it is a friendship of limited dimensions, based not on a person's whole character but on a slimmer
set of features that may not bring into view a person's characteristic ways and habits. In general, the depth and level of altruism
will be limited by the superficiality of the tie. In contrast, character friendship typically involves a thoroughgoing familiarity with
another and a spending of time together that strengthens and
stabilizes feelings of trust, good will, and mutual benefit.

This takes us to the issue of mutuality. "There is nothing so
characteristic of friendship as living together." "Spending days
together" and "delighting in each other" is "what is thought to be
most characteristic of friendship."[44] True friends want to spend
time together and find pleasure simply in the mutual interaction
of shared activities. What is striking about Aristotle's account is
his insistence on this fact. Whatever the added advantages and
benefits of friendship, what draws us to friendship for its own
sake is its essential mutuality. As I said earlier, mutuality can be
captured in more transient interactions – in a great conversation,
in knowing glances, in a moment of shared repartee that lasts no
longer than an instant, yet captures in that moment the magic of a
special connection. But Aristotle's claim is that we appreciate
mutual activity in its fullest when it lasts – when it has a chance to
create its own history – and when it brings to bear the full dimensions of a person. Character friendship does this. The point is
captured in Aristotle's language. The oft-repeated phrases are
"spending days together," "spending time together," "living together," "acquiring experience of one another and becoming familiar with each other's habits."[45] "Friendship requires time and
familiarity with each other's characters." And it requires "know-

---

[42] See Cooper (1980) on the force of this in the NE definition.
[43] NE 1156a10–21.
[44] NE 1157b19; 1158a9–10.
[45] NE 1157b8, b15, b19–24, 1158a9, a15, a23, 1166a23; EE 1235a2.

ing the fact" that each finds the other likable. This is established not in the abstract but through shared activities, that take time, that establish trust, and that build on past interactions. "As the proverb says, 'persons cannot know each other until they have eaten salt together.'"[46] Friends share meals, but more importantly, "speech and reason" (for "that's what it means for human beings to live together, not just to pasture in the same place like cattle").[47] They share political pursuits, and critical reflection about the aspirations and achievements of living a good life. They perceive together and study together.[48] In general, they share activity (*sunergein*).[49] They do things *with* each other, where the "with" is not the "with" of parallel play, but the "with" of mutual engagement.

But equally, they share an emotional life together. And this is so on many planes. As virtuous persons, they express their virtue not simply in action but in a wide range of medial emotions. They communicate these to each other, and to others, about matters of importance in their lives. In a formal sense, they share a common core of well-cultivated emotions – there is a certain emotional consensus, we might say, about matters of importance. As Aristotle puts it, friends feel pleasure and pain at the same sorts of things;[50] with character friendship, this is not simply a matter of shared taste, but a matter of shared moral sentiments (pity, fear, hope, anger, and, in general, pleasures and pains in that sense) that are appropriate to circumstances. But once again, it is important to capture the mutuality of the consensus. Consensus, between friends, is never at a distance.[51] It is expressed not just in the fact that as a friend, you think certain feelings are apt and capture how you might respond. Something stronger often seems to be required – that you can become emotionally engaged in another's joy or sorrow, excitement or worry. Just as with sharing in activity, you partake and are present, and are not simply a

---

[46] NE 1156b26–31.   [47] NE 1170b1–14.   [48] EE 1245b5–25.

[49] Nussbaum (1986, ch.12) raises the important point that this best friendship Aristotle has in mind will be between adult males who, while married with families, choose male companionship to share activities from which women are excluded.

[50] NE 1166a7–8, a27.   [51] See NE 1167a21–25.

sideline observer. Essentially, this is empathy. A sense of oneness comes not from some tacit or abstract knowledge that a friend might be similarly affected, but by another's emotional expression of that fact to us through empathetic engagement. That is part of the pleasure of mutual interaction. It is part of its pain, captured also by the sense of shame that can spread beyond the boundaries of self to a friend. In the *Eudemian Ethics,* Aristotle points to a similar notion of "singleness of mind" (*mia psuchē*) characteristic of friendship: "A friend wishes most of all not only that he feels pain when his friend is in pain, but that he feels the same pain (for example, when he is thirsty, sharing his thirst), if this were possible, and if not, what is closest to it."[52] Whatever is "closest to it" must be something that signals a friend's emotional engagement in our lives. What is important, Aristotle implies, is that a friend convey in a palpable way that my joy or grief matters to her, too. This requires a willingness to devote attention to the concrete details of another's experiences and a capacity to imagine what is less accessible to one's own point of view. Aristotle emphasizes, as we have said, consensus and shared tastes. But the empathy he has just talked about needn't imply endorsement. Appreciating another's pain and conveying that to him or her can be quite a separate matter from believing one would or should respond similarly. True, Aristotle has in mind the context of character friendship, and here especially one expects to find the mature and fine expression of emotion. But even so, he never conceives of character friendship apart from the developmental journey of becoming good. Such a friendship is an arena for moral growth and not just a place for easy endorsement or praise. Virtue friends "become better by their activities and by correcting each other. For from each other they shape themselves in terms of the characteristics they approve."[53]

It is also worth commenting on the sort of equality that Aristotle says characterizes the best sort of mutual exchange.[54] With regard to virtue friendships, there is no suggestion in his writings

[52] EE 1240a36–39.
[53] NE 1172a11–14, my translation; cf. Rh. 1388a31–35.
[54] See NE VIII.4–7, 13–14.

regard to virtue friendships, there is no suggestion in his writings that equality involves an isomorphism of character traits or developed capacities. As just suggested, in the best of friendships there is emulation and learning from the strengths and wisdom of another. Though the mature moral agent will have all the virtues (i.e., Aristotle's thesis of the unity of virtues),[55] the pattern of unified virtues will inevitably take different shape in different virtuous individuals. In one individual, a sense of generosity may be preeminent, in another, the courage of battle. It is not that certain characterisitics are absent in the other or that an individual ignores the requirements of the full set of virtues. It is, rather, that different circumstances lead to different actualizations. Goodness has a different landscape in different, equally good persons. The majesty of friendship is, alongside the surprise and discovery in finding a kindred soul, the surprise (and at times consternation) in marking the distance that can still separate two like-minded souls.

The general discussion of shared activity and shared emotional lives should make clear that virtue friends do not simply prize each other for abstract qualities that could easily find their home in other individuals. It might be tempting to think Aristotle's notion of choosing another on the basis of virtue could be glossed in that sort of way.[56] But it should be amply clear by now that Aristotelian friendship is rooted in particularity and in the detail of daily living and interwoven activity. The mutual and ongoing interaction of a friendship builds on, but goes beyond, initial reasons for choosing a friend. Living together, spending time together, coming to know the intimate details of another's ways, are forceful counters against the tendency to idealize certain abstract qualities or, again, a whole person in his or her full particularity.[57]

---

55 NE 1144b30ff.
56 The view is, of course, best expressed by Diotema in the ascent passage of Plato's *Symposium,* and critically discussed by Vlastos (1973) and Nussbaum (1986, ch.6).
57 On this point about idealization of the particular, see my critique of Nussbaum in Sherman (1994a).

3 FRIENDSHIP AND ITS PLACE IN GOOD LIVING

We turn next to the placement of friendship within Aristotle's conception of good living, or *eudaimonia*. Friendship figures in Aristotle's scheme of goods as an external good, subordinate to virtue. In *Nicomachean* I.8–9, Aristotle suggests two classes of external goods, with friendship figuring in each. First, friends serve an *instrumental* role to the exercise of virtue. They are among things that are by nature "cooperative and useful as tools."[58] As he puts it at another point, they are among the "resources without which it is impossible or at least not easy to act finely."[59] Second, they are goods which on their own are intrinsically valuable. They belong necessarily to happiness (*huparchein anagkaion*),[60] and their absence takes something from it. The debate about the roles external goods play has attracted a good deal of discussion in recent Aristotelian literature. In light of this my own remarks will be brief with attention focused on friendship itself.[61]

The ways in which friends are instrumental are fairly clear. As Aristotle summarizes at the start of his account, we need friends in times of prosperity and times of poverty, in youth for guidance and in old age because of our infirmities, in our prime to stimulate us, so that with another mind we can think and act more effec-

---

[58] NE 1099b28.
[59] NE 1099a33–34.
[60] NE 1099b27.
[61] Cooper (1985) denies that there are two roles, assimilating Aristotle's distinction to two ways in which external goods are instrumental for virtuous activity. In one case, they are necessary for the performance of virtuous activity at all; in another, they allow for enhanced performance of virtuous activity. The view I have adopted (with some qualification) – that external goods can be instrumental for the performance of virtue or intrinsically valuable in enhancing it – is argued by Nussbaum (1986) and Irwin(1985c). For a concise discussion of the debate and its Stoic implications, see Annas (1993, 364–84). I leave aside discussion of the point that Richard Kraut (1989) argues, that while external goods are necessary conditions of happiness, they are not included as *parts* of it. I am assuming these two roles (of instrumentality and intrinsic value) are relevant whether external goods are included in or only conditions of happiness.

tively. In a most general way, friends provide objects and opportunities for our virtuous activities as well as support for our moral
development. This latter role is most important for Aristotle in his
own account. Of course, Aristotle recognizes that individuals
might be able to manage without friends during certain periods
of their lives and still live worthy lives. His general point, which
he finds supported in the *endoxa*, is that it is not easy to live
without friends given our limited capacities and limited self-
sufficiency. The point is no doubt helped by the fact that *philia*
ranges over a far wider variety of relationships than the modern
notion of friendship. Family and fellow citizens figure as friends,
and these friendships cannot easily be dissolved. Even if we don't
readily acknowedge their role, they are with us as background
supports in varying ways at different periods of our lives. But
Aristotle makes a stronger argument for the place of friendship in
the good life. Even if we didn't need friends for other ends or
were to believe that, on balance, friendship hurts more than it
helps (that through death and departure, for example, friends
expose our human vulnerability in the worst way), still friendship
would be valued as an intrinsic good. It is an intrinsic good, in the
sense that Aristotle outlines elsewhere, we would still choose it
for itself even if nothing further resulted from it.[62] It adds something in its own right to happiness, and the absence of it takes
something away. So, he says, there are some things, the lack of
which "mars" happiness, such as good birth, good children, and
beauty. "We don't altogether have happiness" if we are "solitary
or childless, or if our friends or children are thoroughly bad, or
are good but they die."[63] Similarly, Aristotle says, friendship in
general is "choiceworthy for its own sake"; "A friend is not for
use or help . . . for when we need nothing, we still seek others to
share our enjoyment."[64]

It is important to be clear about what kind of intrinsic good
friendship is. Picking up on Aristotle's language in his classification of external goods, some have characterized external goods in

[62] NE 1097b4–5.
[63] NE 1099b2–7. Cf. 1095b25–28; 1100b22–30.
[64] NE 1159a27 (cf.1155a29–32); EE 1244b15–20; Pol. 1278b20–24.

their intrinsic role as "enhancing" or "adorning" happiness.[65] With the addition of certain goods, our happiness is embellished; in their absence, it is marred.[66] But the notion of friendship as an embellishment understates the way it is an intrinsic value within happiness (though the notion that its absence mars it, does better). For what friendship adds of its own value to happiness is not some adornment, or accent touch that intensifies what is already reasonably complete. On Aristotle's view, friendship is a pervasive good, and indeed the predominant structure of much good living. Even if we try to separate out its instrumental role in promoting the exercise and development of virtue, we can appreciate that the pleasure of mutual interaction is not one intrinsic good among others. It is something that is ubiquitous and that runs through most of our forms of activity. The mutual interactions of the best sort of friendship structure our happiness, according to Aristotle, in a way that defines our happiness almost as something shared. As Aristotle puts it, it is "the greatest" and "most necessary" of external goods.[67]

We explored the intrinsic value of shared activity in the last section. It is easy to miss the force of Aristotle's remarks here. His many statements on the pleasure of spending our days together with others, of sharing the same tastes and interests, of feeling the same pains and pleasures, are just statements of the intrinsic value of common pursuit. We would pursue it even if no further advantage came with it. Aristotle's discussion of the way friendship is intrumental to virtue is more systematic. In *Nicomachean* IX.9 he isolates two primary roles. First, he develops the intuitive idea that friends play a pivotal role in our self-knowledge. We come to know ourselves through the mirror of another who is similar yet separate. As John Cooper has argued,[68] the *Magna Moralia* presents this argument more succinctly than the matching

---

[65] See Annas (1993, 378).

[66] NE 1100b26 – *kai gar auta sunepikosmein pephuken;* 1099b2 – *hrupainousi to makarion;* 1100b28 – *thlibei kai lumainetai to makarion.*

[67] NE 1169b10,1155a4; EE 1234b33.

[68] Cooper (1980). On his discussion of the relation of the MM to the ethical corpus, see Cooper (1973).

passage in the *Nicomachean*. The *Magna Moralia* text runs as follows:

> We are investigating the self-sufficiency not of a god, but of what is human, and whether the self-sufficient person will need friendship. Now if a person looks upon his friend and sees what he is and what sort of character he has, such a friend will seem to him to be another self, just as it is said, "This is my second Hercules, a friend is another self." Now to know oneself is very difficult, as even some philosophers have said, and most pleasant (for knowledge of self is pleasant). Moreover, direct study of ourselves is impossible (this is shown by the fact that the very things that we censure others for, we don't notice ourselves doing, and this comes about through partiality or passion, which in many of us blind our judgment of what is right). And so, just as when we want to see our own faces, we see them by looking in a mirror, similarly when we wish to know our own characters, we can know them by looking up a friend. For a friend, as we say, is another self.[69]

Aristotle makes it clear here, in a way that he does not in the corresponding *Nicomachean* passage, that we look outward to others because of our own tendency toward self-deception. It is not just that we want to contemplate worthy actions akin to our own (*oikeias*); rather, we want to see ourselves with greater accuracy, flaws and all. When others mirror back to us our feelings and attitudes, we see as if from outside ourselves. Aristotle's insight is simple but profound. Self-knowledge is pivotal in Aristotle's general account of virtue. According to his view, virtue is necessarily reflective; it has an intellectual structure. It cannot be exercised without *phronēsis* (practical wisdom) and the deliberative capacity for making justified or reasoned choices. But *phronēsis* enters not simply in moments of deliberative choice where, as Aristotle says, there is inquiry (*zētēsis*) about what to do and a question of justification.[70] It figures in background reflection about the general ends of good living as a whole, their interrelation, and their specification in a determinate way within that

[69] MM 1212b8–24.   [70] NE 1142a31ff.

structured whole. This is not abstract stuff, but systematized knowledge that works through the material of our own experience and practice. Practical wisdom, Aristotle notes, is related to the capacity of understanding (*sunesis*). This capacity concerns judgment or discernment about practical matters that here and now don't issue in choice, but that could become subjects of deliberation or inquiry. The very activity of filling in the outline of Aristotle's ethical inquiry, as we answer for ourselves the question of what is happiness, would presumably be an engagement of this form of practical understanding. But at a more informal and personal level, this sort of practical reflection is what Aristotle envisions as engaging character friends. They are interested in how the different claims of virtue and the demands to self and other can be structured and limited within the most completely good life. They are interested in how an exercise of a virtue, here and now, is fine and shows right judgment, though might not hit the mark in a slightly altered context. They are interested in whether one has recognized what is morally salient (i.e., perceives finely) or fails because of some disavowed but nagging desire that forces more noble concerns out of the foreground, as if they were "asleep," Aristotle might say.[71] In general, they are interested in coming to know themselves and to assess honestly whether their actions and emotions are indeed fine – whether they are objectively good specifications of happiness. I take it these are all ways of understanding the import of Aristotle's claim that friends contribute to each other's self-knowledge. They help to interpret these further claims as well: Friends live together not as cattle by grazing the same pasture, but "by sharing in argument and thought" (*koinōnein logōn kai dianoias*) about good living.[72] We choose as intimate friends "those who are honest with us, who can speak about their foibles (*ta phaula*)," and reciprocally, those before whom we are not ashamed of our own foibles and "conventional wrongs," but do feel deep "shame

---

[71] As in the discussion of *akrasia* at NE VII. 3. I intimate here at a notion of motivated ignorance, though Aristotle seems to diagnose *akrasia* as a more purely intellectual or perceptual failure. See Pears (1984) and Sherman (1995a).

about those things that are really wrong."[73] Friends support self-esteem[74] but also the honest self-appraisal that must go with it.

Aristotle indicates a second, more basic way in which friendship sustains us. It enables us to keep our activity alive and continuous (*energein sunechōs*), in a way that we find pleasant.[75] There is a sense of zest and energy when we do things with others, a robustness to our lives that solitary activity often lacks. Again, within Aristotle's scheme, the contribution to happiness is crucial. For a happiness is not a passive state of virtue-in-possession, but an active realization of our virtuous states. Sustained, excellent activity (*energeia*) is a defining feature of our happiness.[76] Its pleasure depends, in part, upon the unimpeded actualization of our developed abilities. Friendship, as a facilitator of activity, directly contributes to the mode our happiness must take. Just as it would be absurd to call a person happy who slept away her life,[77] so it would be absurd to think we could sustain the activity happiness requires in the full absence of friends.

These arguments emphasize the role of friendship as "means" to happiness, but it is well established that Aristotle's notion of what is pursued "toward" an end (*pros ta telē*) embraces constitutents and specifications as well as causal conditions.[78] The activities of friendship are often best thought of in the former way, as shaping and molding ends themselves through its activity. Thus, friends keep us active and alive, not like some vitamin pill

---

[72] NE 1170b11–12.   [73] Rh. 1381b28–31; 1381b18–22.   [74] NE 1172a12; Rh. 1381a33–b1.   [75] NE 1170a3–6; cf. 1177a22–35.   [76] NE 1098a14, 1098a16.
[77] NE 1098b30ff.
[78] There is an extensive literature on the notion of constitutive means that aims to counter the nineteenth-century utilitarian gloss on Aristotle's writings, in which all choice was thought to be instrumental toward some antecedently fixed end. The discussion centers on the translation of choice of *ta pros ta telē*, now commonly translated as choice of "the things with regard to the ends" and taken to accommodate constitutive as well as purely instrumental means (as suggested by reading NE II in light of NE VI). Important discussions of this topic are by Allan (1977), Greenwood (1973), Irwin (1975), Nussbaum (1978), Sorabji (1980), Wiggins (1980). I also take up the issue in Sherman (1989, chs. 2 and 3). For a contemporary discussion of the notion of constitutive means within an account of deliberation about ends, see Richardson (1994).

we might pop but, more often, by stimulating new interests and ends, and by introducing us to new activities that bear the mark and value of their transmission. There is a "transference," to put it in psychoanalytic talk. Friends may be antidepressants, "sustainers," in a more Aristotelian idiom. But it is not just that they fuel us. They fuel us with ideas and possibilities that were not on the horizon before. The activities "actualize" us; they don't merely keep us active. The mutual benefiting that is an element of friendship often works in the same way. What friends can offer, as opposed to distant benefactors, is a sharing in activity that defines the end to be promoted. So, for example, I may decide that the best way I can promote my daughter's interest in music is not by financing her tuition at conservatory. Grandparents or scholarships can do that. My place is to share with her my proficiency and love of music; music becomes a family activity, something we all care about and do together. This kind of engagement, with its mutuality and shared discovery, defines and puts value on an end in a way that benefiting at a distance typically cannot.[79] Again, the point is not that obligations to friends are often more stringent and take priority. It is that how we can help is different because of the medium of shared activity.

There is a further question that needs to be addressed about the place of friendship in Aristotle's account. Simply put: Why does friendship figure so importantly in a discussion that makes the excellences of character and intellect, that is, the goods of the soul and not external goods, the centerpiece? Even granting that hap-

---

[79] Note, I am not suggesting here that all forms of engagement positively support another's good. Clearly, some involvement is invasive or meddlesome, and an infraction of privacy. Equally, mutuality can be a partnership in self-destructive ends (sadomasochistic enjoyments might be considered here); in some cases, mutual consent is inadequate as a final arbiter of choice. The Kantian notion of respect is often introduced here as a constraint on permissibility. Aristotle does not have such a well-defined notion, nor a single value that universally constrains action in that way. Some have argued that the notion of shame or *aidōs* comes close to playing such a role (see Nussbaum 1980). I do not see it as comparable to the notion of respect for rational agency that underlies the Kantian list of virtues. Within Aristotle's theory, the notion of balance and constraint enters in a different way, with the notion of the "fine" indicating, in some sense, an objectively good choice.

piness is activity and friendship contributes in special, "most necessary" ways to that activity, why does the topic get more discussion than any of the individual virtues? The answer, I think, is
because friendship is on the border between agency and what just
happens to us. This, in many ways, is Aristotle's distinctive focus
in discussing happiness: to embrace the limits of our agency.[80]
Emotions display this in an interesting way. We can cultivate our
emotions and learn how to "stand well" toward them, but essentially they are ways of "being affected," and sometimes we are
just plain "stuck" or "struck." Kant, of course, is insistent upon
this. The point is clearer to Aristotle in the case of friendship – that
it involves our efforts and characters, but equally someone else's
separate choices and efforts, and all that just happens to them.
Although through friendship another is woven into one's own
life, the other remains separate and a source of external contingency in the deepest way. Thus, there is much that one can
control about one's friendships – whom one chooses and for what
reasons, and how one builds consensus and cultivates emotional
ties. Mutual choice as much as mutual affection is constitutive of
friendship.[81] But such choices are often framed by fateful encounters and tragic losses. Ultimately, the separateness of another's
will and life are firm limits with which one must always psychologically and morally contend. The Stoics emphasize the psychological costs, Kant emphasizes the moral limits imposed by the
separateness of another's will. Aristotle, like the Stoics, recognizes the lack of control that friends introduce, but he sees no
alternative but to include them among the central goods in a
conception of happiness. The Stoics do not rule them out from
selection, but they call them "preferred indifferents" to
distinguish them from what is "chosen" unqualifiedly as good in
the way that virtue alone is.[82]

---

80 I am not suggesting that Aristotle is always single-minded here or that his
discussions stably articulate this position. Discussions about external goods in
NE I.8–10 and NE X.7–8 are notoriously vague about just what position Aristotle is defending. For the unstability of his view, see Annas (1993, ch. 18).
81 EE 1236b2ff., 1237a31.
82 They coin this technical term to mark the difference. See, for example,
Diogenes Laertius 7.101–3 = L and S 58A; 7.104–5 (SVF 3.119) = L and S 58B;

Aristotle's frequent comparison of self-love to friendship is instructive in this regard. Aristotle often compares friendship to self-love in order to emphasize that what is so basic to our commitment to ourselves (and especially so for the good person, given her harmonious soul) is also a mark of true friendship. We wish ourselves to live, we wish to benefit ourselves for own own sake, we have a taste for our own ideas and pleasures, by and large we endorse our own choices, and enjoy spending time in our own company.[83] All this formally characterizes genuine friendship; it is just that the object now is outside us. The good person's relation to herself is analogous to the relation she shares with a friend.[84] But once these attitudes are redirected toward others, the game changes. Self-love has commitment, but it doesn't have mutuality; it is not a relationship. And, on Aristotle's view, it is relationships that introduce a heightened form of contingency.[85]

Stobaeus 2.84,18–85,11 (SVF 3.128) = L and S 58E. For further texts on the selection of indifferents, see L and S 58A-m.

[83] NE IX.4.

[84] NE 1166a30–33.

[85] According to Julia Annas's discussion(1993, 261ff.), self-love has psychological primacy in Aristotle's account of friendship. She holds that Aristotle takes its primacy to be a psychological fact commonly accepted, and that he endorses it without much argument. The thesis of psychological primacy, on her view, doesn't mean that concern for a friend is ultimately instrumental to one's own good; or that it is morally permissible to give my own concerns priority. It simply means that as a fact, we begin with concern for ourselves, and that similarly as a fact, we can move outward to concern for others. But it is important to add to this account that Aristotle primarily has in mind the connection between the good person's self-love and the love of others. I take this as suggesting two things: that not any self-love can be a condition for loving others, and also that healthy love of others is not something that just happens without habituation. In this sense, we move outward to others in the right way only with the proper ethical training. But also, loving ourselves in the right way requires proper ethical training. Still, one wishes Aristotle had said more about just why or how loving oneself in a nonconflictual way best prepares one to enjoy others. For further discussion of the relation of self-love to love of others, see Homiak (1981).

4 WIDER ALTRUISM

Aristotle makes a compelling argument for the central importance of friendship within a good life, both as an intrinsic good
and as a good indispensible for moral development. He stresses
the developmental features of adult friendships as well as those
features in family and civic friendships. However, what appreciation does Aristotle have for altruism that is not limited to contexts
of shared activity and common pursuit? Does a sense of other-
regard extend to those with whom we do not have some sort of
tie? Citing the common beliefs in the *Eudemian Ethics*, Aristotle
emphasizes again the importance of attachment to other-regard
in general. "The whole of justice is in relation to a friend."[86] This
forces the question, Can we be morally good to those who are not
part of our shared life? Again, in collecting the popular views,
Aristotle reports:

> There seems to be a natural friendship of parent for offspring
> and of offspring for parent, not only among humans but among
> birds and most other animals, and among members of the same
> species[87] for one another, and especially among humans, when
> we praise lovers of humanity.[88] One might see in travels how
> every human is familiar to and a friend to another human.[89]

However, when we turn to Aristotle's theoretical development
of friendship, we never really find a defense of the true lover of
humanity who can extend other-regard beyond some shared

---

[86] EE 1242a21ff.
[87] I follow Annas here in translating same species, rather than "same race," in
order to emphasize the connection with other creatures' behavior in the preceding phrases. See Annas (1993, 253, n.15).
[88] The term is *philanthropos*. Aristotle does not use the term much, though it does
appear in *Politics* II.2 in the discussion of Plato's attempt in the *Republic* to
foster *philia* throughout the whole city, and again in the *Poetics*
(1452b38ff.;1456a21) in discussing what motivates an audience to come to feel
the tragic emotions. The context there is obviously wider than friendship,
though pity, Aristotle emphasizes in Rh. II.8, will still be restricted to those
with whom we can identify.
[89] NE 1155a16–21.

community.[90] Nothing like the Stoic idea of extending one's self-love outward, in expanding concentric circles that stretch to the whole of humanity, can be found in Aristotle's remarks.[91] Other-regard is deeply connected with a sense of the common good that can stretch to the limits of the *polis,* but not easily beyond. The sort of general claims Kant introduces about respect for persons as such are simply not anticipated by Aristotle. In most general terms, the Kantian argument is that respect for persons is based on their legislative capacity as rational agents. We promote respect positively through beneficence, interpreted as a duty wide in requirement, that is, subject to our discretion about its application. The claims of attachment affect the discretionary application of this duty (to whom, and when and where),[92] but not the moral reasons for being beneficent in the first place. It is required of us and owed to others as rational agents. The Aristotelian view is that we are emotionally responsive to others as persons situated in particular circumstances and cultivate attachments, near and far, in order to strengthen and educate our responsiveness. When we respond to individuals in those circumstances, we benefit the individuals for their own sake. But an underlying, more abstract notion of practical interest in others' common humanity, as such, is not at all on the horizon. The response is to individuals in their circumstances, not to something in them that is unconditioned, and separable from context.

It needs to be stressed that what Aristotle fails to appreciate is *not* some intuitive notion of mutual disinterest or genuine other-regard. As I said earlier, Aristotle assumes we can extend our self-love to others, that we do so regularly, and that we do it without egoistic motive. In *Rhetoric* I.9, Aristotle perhaps pushes the argument too far, suggesting that genuinely fine action removes all

---

[90] Annas (1993, 253) makes this point.

[91] See Hierocles (Stobaeus 4.671, 7–673, 11, part) = L and S 57G, part. "The outermost and largest circle," according to Hierocles, "embracing all the other circles, is the circle of the whole human race." Also, Cicero, Fin. 3.62–68 = L and S 57F; and Anonymous Commentary on Plato's *Theaetus* 5.18–6.31 = L and S 57H. The closest one comes to finding Aristotle recognize the Stoic point is in the list of the *endoxa* at NE 1154b20.

[92] See DV 451; cf. 435 and 393.

benefit to self that might accrue from virtuous action to others. It is finer, too, he claims, if our beneficent acts aim to benefit others after our lifetime, for then there could be no question of mixed motives. In the *Nicomachean Ethics*, Aristotle begins to sort out more adequately the role self-love plays in virtuous action toward others. He makes it clear that we can add in self in a way that doesn't detract from genuine other-regard. First, following roughly the argument of IX.4, healthy self-love can be thought of as a primary psychological attitude concerned with liking and caring for an individual (namely, oneself), and this general attitude can extend to others. The extension begins in and is maintained by a healthy self-regard. This sort of self-love has primacy in the sense that it is a *condition* of other-regard. Such primacy does not entail that we give priority to our own wishes or choices.[93] Second, in IX.8, Aristotle says in a deliberately paradoxical way that self-love is not merely a condition of love of others but is most perfectly manifest in love of others, for insofar as appropriate acts of loving others are a matter of doing what is fine without inner strife, one is satisfying and loving the most authoritative and truest part of self.[94] Again, he says paradoxically, the good person in taking less of her share (of material goods) takes more of her share (*pleonektei*) (of what is fine).[95] *Pleonexia*, as Aristotle's listeners would know, refers to greed and selfishness. The virtuous person, in sacrificing for others, is "selfish" about what is fine.

But this still is not an argument for unlimited, genuine other-regard. It is true, we need to remember that Aristotle's list of virtues includes generosity, magnificence, and magnanimity. These will have more extended reach, as will altruistic sentiments such as good will, kindness, and pity. Kindness extends widely to those in need, where the occasion, and not the personal tie, is what is relevant.[96] Similarly, good will, Aristotle stresses, is not the same thing as friendship, "for one may have good will toward

---

[93] I am following Annas here.
[94] Summarizing the arguments in NE IX.8, and especially 1168b19ff.
[95] NE 1136b20–22; cf. 1169a29–35.
[96] See Rh. II.7.

people whom one does not know and without their being aware of it."[97] Yet the example Aristotle chooses suggests that we still extend the feeling in restricted ways – good will is what we feel toward a competitor, he says, whom we perceive as excellent or decent, or courageous or handsome. Like love, there is a moment of attraction or connection that sparks the feeling.[98] The response is to something we can connect with. As such, it doesn't quite capture the notion of a general love of humanity that makes any person, in principle, worthy of our moral regard. There is a comparable restriction on the notion of pity. We feel it toward those who suffer undeservingly, and who are like us in "age, character, disposition, social standing, or birth."[99] In the context of tragic response, these restrictions make good sense. The tragedian, intent on eliciting cathartic responses, heightens rather than relaxes points of identification between audience and character. It is important to note that Aristotle discusses tragic pity in the general context of *to philanthropon* – a "love of humanity," or general capacity to respond to other human beings.[100] But once again, the term is more or less restricted in Aristotle's usage. It does not have the far reach of the modern notion of moral concern that, in principle, extends to any person, independent of shared context.

We need to counter these remarks with the reminder that the boundaries set by Aristotelian friendship will themselves be wide. Friendship extends outward to the limits of the city. But, and this is the point, it does not go beyond.[101] A few further notes are important here. The city-state will be a partnership that includes smaller units of households and families aimed at the self-sufficiency of a good life. It will be a network of friendships, built on mutual support in both directions – families educating sons for full citizenship, the *polis* taking on the role of education through its laws and customs, music and tragic performances. Aristotle extends friendship throughout the city, but never conceives of its form of other-regard as directly mimicking the friendship of more

---

[97] NE 1166b31.   [98] NE 1167a18; 1167a3ff.   [99] Rh. 1386a25.
[100] Poet. 1453a2; 1452b38; 1456a21ff.
[101] Also see Pol. 1252b5–9, where Aristotle supports the view that barbarians are like slaves who lack their own capacities for internal leadership.

intimate unions. Fellow citizens shed blood on the battlefield for each other as kith and kin, and share in a common education and habituation in the virtues. But in *Politics* II, Aristotle rightly rejects Plato's notion that civic unanimity can be achieved by dismantling these smaller units of family and then trying to reproduce potent feelings of partiality across all citizens. What results from Plato's notion is a "watery friendship,"[102] a devalued attachment that does not in the end extend the original sympathy. When "my father" or "my son" is used, as in the *Republic*, "each of two thousand or ten thousand applying it to the same thing" the expressions die out, Aristotle says.[103] They lose their meaning, because one can't extend partiality to large numbers of people in a way that preserves the sense of priority and intensity of those original commitments. The notion of standing in a special relation to an individual becomes weakened, on the one hand by common ownership (for a son becomes only fractionally one's own), and on the other by having too many sons among whom to spread one's love. Similarly, one can say she's "my mother" over and over to women of the appropriate generation to whom one bears little personal tie, but the meaning depends on an original relationship (on some original model) that can be reproduced, only partially, with just so many people. To have that kind of relationship, you must feel toward another, Aristotle says, a sense that something is "one's own" (*to idion*) and "that one must be content with it" (*to agapēton*).[104] The second notion is difficult, but together with the first it implies the notion of a relationship that can endure and that has a certain exclusivity of focus. The point is that friendship needs to bind the city, but not as a stretched-out form of partiality. Our time and resources allow us to cultivate those sorts of ties with only so many people. Aristotle's alternative is not a local alliance of citizens who come together only for cooperative advantage.[105] He wants to hold on to the partiality introduced by a system of private property and separate families, but then nest it within a wider form of other-regard that is nurtured through common culture or *paideia*.[106]

---

[102] Pol. 1262b15–16.   [103] Pol. 1262a2–6 and 1262b17.
[104] Pol. 1262b23–24.   [105] The *summachia* of *Politics* III.5.   [106] Pol. 1263b36ff.

It is clear then that the city is not merely the sharing of a common locality for the sake of preventing injury and exchanging goods. These are necessary conditions of the city, but even if all of these conditions are present that does not make for a city; but a city is a partnership of families and kin in living well (*eu zēn koinōnia*), for the sake of a complete and self-sufficient life. . . . This sort of organization is the function of friendship, for friendship is for the purpose of living together. And thus the end of the city is good living (*to eu zēn*), and these things are for the sake of that end.[107]

On this model, there will be special concern for those with whom we are intimate, and a distinct form of other-regard that embraces wider loyalties. But what is important for our purposes is that other-regard is still restricted to those with whom one has some personal or civic tie. The notion of a concern for others in faraway lands with whom one shares only a common humanity, does not capture Aristotle's philosophical attention, even though it is among the pretheoretical views he entertains.

We have yet to mention anything about justice and its forms of other-regard. This has been deliberate, as the terrain here is vast. A proper treatment would include discussion of Aristotle's classification of types of justice in *Nicomachean* V, the different political constitutions discussed in the *Politics* and their suitability for achieving justice and good living in general, the relation of institutional justice to justice in the soul, the nature of civic education and its relation to private education in the family, and, in general, the congruity of Aristotle's views with modern insights about justice. Systematic discussion would take us well beyond our scope.[108] Still, in a most limited way, we can raise the question of whether there are features of Aristotelian justice that capture a purer form of other-regard than what we have been considering so far. In a qualified way, I believe there are. Several points need to be made. First, though justice is a virtue within Aristotle's scheme, its reference is less in terms of an agent's own inner

---

[107] Pol. 1280b30–40.

[108] For recent useful works on Aristotelian justice, see Crocker (1992), Miller (1989), Mulgan (1991), and Nussbaum (1988, 1990b), as well as Sen (1993).

perfection than of impingement upon others. General justice is virtue in relation to others, as our actions impinge upon others.[109] Unlike the other virtues, it has less to do with a motivating range of feelings, which produce wrong actions and which lie at the extreme of some mean, than with the external aspect of our action as it relates to another.[110] In this sense, it bears a relation to Kant's notion of juridical duties as marking out a class of duties whose point is action, not motivation. Second, the claim has been made with some plausibility that corrective justice reveals other-relatedness in a particularly pure way.[111] Unlike distributive justice within Aristotle's scheme, corrective justice depends not on merit as one of its criteria, but purely on the transactional nexus of the parties. The parties are doer and sufferer of the same injury.[112] They stand related to one another simply in the terms of their action. Corrective justice aims to restore the original parity before the injury.

> For it makes no difference whether a good man has defrauded a bad one, nor whether it is a good or bad man that has committed adultery; rather, the law looks to the difference of the harm alone and treats the parties as equals.[113]

Here we seem to have a purer sense of other-relatedness than one finds in Aristotle's other discussions. What is due others depends not on personal ties, character, and so on, but simply on interactions and impingements of persons on each other directly. The separateness of persons and the externality of relations to others come into fuller view. But once again, we need to remember that this sort of justice is nested within the political structure

---

[109] NE 1130a10–13.

[110] For the view that injustice in fact misses the mean in the same way as the other vices do, where this is conceived of as a kind of misorientation of aim rather than something caused by egoistic motive, see O'Connor (1988). Williams's view (1980) is that Aristotelian injustice, unlike the other vices, does not import a special motive, but the lack of one, namely an indifference to fairness. He criticizes what he takes to be Aristotle's own view, that the root of injustice is the egoistic motive of *pleonexia*.

[111] The argument is put forward by Ernest Weinrib (1987), whose broad position I here outline.

[112] NE 1132a5–6.   [113] NE 1132a2–5.

of a *polis*. Justice extends just so far to its limits and not beyond. It extends to those with whom we are, in some way or other, connected as friends.

> The whole of justice in general is in relation to a friend. For what is just is just for certain persons, and persons who are partners, and a friend is a partner, either in one's family or in one's life. For a person is not merely a political creature, but a creature who lives in households as well.[114]

Within Aristotelian theory, there is no conception of a law that in principle ties all human beings to justice. The notion of a kingdom of ends simply does not make sense when the boundaries of moral interaction are set by the *polis*.

I raise this point not to use Kant as the whipping boy of Aristotle. There is little value in that sort of dialogue. The project we are engaged in is one of exposing the vantage points that an ancient theory such as Aristotle's offers us and, in turn, the different horizons a modern moral theory, such as Kant's, opens up. Aristotle's theory insists upon, in a way virtually neglected by modern moral theory, the importance of shared activity and its place in moral development. The interactions of friends, family, and citizens become at once the home of moral development and the home of moral activity. But part of the problem is that the two spheres need not be one and the same. In particular the arena important for moral development need not be the exclusive arena for moral practice. The latter takes place on a wider stage, where our moral concerns range beyond the limits set by shared contexts and the personal ties that nurture.[115]

5 KANT AND FRIENDSHIP

When we turn to Kant's writings we find no huge tracts devoted to the discussion of friendship and shared living. The topics of intimacy and love get only marginal notice. The merits of social

---

[114] EE 1242a21ff.

[115] Moral practice within that sphere, of course, brings its own moral development. The two moments are never fully separate. But Aristotle is right to believe it is not the primary sphere of moral development.

rather than solitary dwelling are not debated. The special role of friends in moral development is not a primary concern. None of this is very surprising, however one-sided the legacy has been for modern moral theory. In Kant's philosophical world, there is no urgent debate in the air about the primacy of a contemplative life versus one that is social and civic. There is no theoretical interest in discussing the things we care most about and which make life self-sufficient or complete. Those issues are part of the eudaimonistic debate and arise in a pointed way when we ask what counts for our happiness. It is a mistake, Kant thinks, to make *that* question the focus of moral theory. But friendship, as we have seen, also arises when we ask a different question, namely: How do we become good and engage most wholeheartedly in the project of virtue? And this is a question that *does* interest Kant, since he is concerned not just with what a virtuous attitude of will is, but with how we cultivate and maintain it. Still, he rejects outright the idea that the moral sphere is one and the same as the sphere of moral development. The focus is on an ethical commonwealth that extends beyond the borders of happenstance and personal tie. And as a result, the topic of friendship no longer has pride of place.

Still, Kant does have some things to say about friendship, and it will be important to review the texts in order to see just what role he accords friendship within moral theory. Although his remarks are brief, I want to examine them carefully since they will point to a way Kant himself can be pushed to take more seriously the question of friendship's role in moral development. But the absence of his own argument in this direction is telling. His deliberate focus is on an ethical commonwealth in which the practice of morality extends well beyond the sphere of friendship, however important friendship might be for preparing us for that commonwealth.

The topic of friendship is addressed in two brief sections at the conclusion of *The Doctrine of Virtue* under the general discussion of our duties to others. The definition Kant proposes bears similarity to Aristotle's, although Kant has in mind a modern notion of friendship that has far narrower scope than the ancient concept of *philia*. Friendship, he tells us, is a union of mutual love between two persons and a commitment to each other's welfare. "It is an ideal of emotional and practical concern which each of the friends united through a morally good will takes in the other's welfare." But what is distinctive in Kant's account is the emphasis on respect. "Friendship (considered in its perfection) is the union of two persons through equal and mutual love and respect." The goal of friendship is to love in a way that neither compromises another's dignity nor diminishes one's own: "For we can regard love as attraction and respect as repulsion, and if the principle of love commands friends to come together, the principle of respect requires them to keep each other at a proper distance."[116] Friendship is a constant teeter-totter between getting close and keeping at bay. Its fragility lies precisely in the difficulty of striking the right balance between the two poles. Whereas Aristotle sees loss and departure as the vulnerabilities we face through forming attachments with others, Kant sees betrayal and failure of respect as the real danger.

I shall come to this in a moment, but first we need to note that despite the hazards and instability of friendship, Kant regards friendship as not merely a permissible end of our happiness, but a duty. It is a duty generated by reason, in which we are to strive to the extent that we can to cultivate within certain relationships the mutuality of love and respect:

> Even if friendship does not produce the complete happiness of life, the adoption of this ideal in men's attitude to one another contains their worthiness to be happy. Hence humans have a duty of friendship. – The striving for perfect friendship (as the maximum good in the attitude of friends to each other) is a duty imposed by reason – not, indeed, an ordinary duty but a duty of honour.[117]

This is important. For it might be thought that on a Kantian view friendship is merely an optional end that, like a wide range of contingent ends, is valued as a constituent of happiness, ultimately conditioned by morality. To the extent that particular acts of friendship do not violate the conditions of rational agency, in

[116] DV 470.   [117] DV 469.

other words, do not internally involve forms of manipulation or deception, or do not involve other violations of perfect duties, they are permissible. But this does not appear to be Kant's argument here. Though his remarks are brief and somewhat chatty, he appears to argue for friendship as an obligatory end on the model of the other duties of virtue he has discussed. On such a reading, a moral agent cannot, without some violation of her human rational nature, will a maxim in which she chooses to deny herself all engagement in forms of mutual love and respect characteristic of friendship. Here it is useful to recall the argument for the obligatory end of beneficence, as set out in the *Groundwork*.[118] The argument for this duty of end is that a policy of mutual indifference would fail to support rational agency in a way that a finitely rational being requires. As finitely rational natures we are necessarily limited in our ability to achieve the ends we set ourselves. Yet our dignity and unconditioned value rests precisely in our capacity to will ends. To sustain this capacity we need to be able to rely on the assistance of others. We depend upon others to implement our ends when we cannot, and in general to extend the limits of our rational agency. To deny ourselves their assistance is to thwart our rational natures.

One way the ends of mutuality and affiliation can be seen as obligatory is as specifications or more concrete forms of beneficence. Given our particular variety of rational nature, promoting another's ultimate good is often, as we have said, a matter of doing things together. Kant's placement of friendship at the conclusion of his discussion of duties to others lends support to this reading. Through friendship we promote the well-being of others to whom we have particular ties. We partake in the ends of their happiness in a particularly engaged and involved way.

But this classification may not be adequate, even on Kant's view. Though he has no drive to discuss friendship extensively in its own right in the way Aristotle does, still the remarks he does make suggest that friendship is not just an exercise of the virtue of beneficence. It is a mutual relationship, and it is precisely failures

---

118 For an interpretation of beneficence (the fourth example at G 423 and 430), see Barbara Herman's discussion (1993 ch. 3).

of mutuality that so capture Kant's attention in his discussion. Friendship involves another's will in a way that the exercise of virtue does not. A crucial duty of end within friendship may be to strive to embrace the attitude of beneficence in our relation to another, but the good of friendship is something more than that. It is something that stretches beyond one's agency and hence exposes one to risks in the way Kant is so aware of. Even in terms of the duties of end we are to cultivate in ourselves, beneficence doesn't quite capture what is required in friendship. Kant says what is involved is mutual love and respect. In addition to beneficence, this presumably includes attentive engagement in a shared activity. Learning how to see with another and from another's point of view – in ways that are empathetic – are, we might say, further duties of end within friendship. But beneficence is stretched in another way in the case of friendship. The point is this: Kant typically separates the end of beneficence from substantive participation in another's moral perfection on the grounds that moral perfection is the perfection of one's own capacity to set ends; to have someone else do this for oneself is, in his terms, "self-contradictory."[119] This is the basis of Kant's separation of duties to self from duties to others. In the case of self, we promote our natural and moral perfection; in the case of others, we promote the permissible ends that they set for their own happiness. Kant draws bold lines here and says little about how we are to understand this distinction in practice. His remarks force questions about the nature of moral persuasion and counsel and, in general, about the role others play in our education and moral development. Much can be said here, but what should be pointed out is that Kant himself clearly recognizes that friends can offer what distant benefactors cannot, and that part of that intense engagement of friendship amounts to participation in the project of another's moral development. There are opportunities for candor and mutual criticism that simply are not available in more attenuated relationships. And these exchanges are crucial for moral growth. Kant recognizes this, yet sees in such moments the pervasive threat of manipulation and violation of respect. The

[119] DV 385–86.

threats loom large and set the very tenor of his discussion of friendship. A true friend is something we desperately seek, but something, given the insecurity and meddlesomeness of human nature, we can rarely be sure to have found.

> From a moral point of view it is, of course, a duty for one of the friends to point out the other's faults to him; this is in the other's best interests and is therefore a duty of love. But his *alter ego* sees in this a lack of the respect which he expected from his friend and thinks either that he has already lost something of his friend's respect or that, since he is observed and secretly criticized, he is in constant danger of losing it; and even the fact that his friend observes him and finds fault with him will seem in itself an insult.[120]

Indeed as one goes on to read Kant's account, one cannot help but be struck by what seems almost a paranoia about the perils of union and the dangers of betrayal.

> A human is a being meant for society (though he is also an unsociable one), and in cultivating social intercourse he feels strongly the need to reveal himself to others (even with no ulterior purpose). But on the other hand, hemmed in and cautioned by fear of the misuse others may make of this disclosure of his thoughts, he finds himself constrained to *lock up* in himself a good part of his opinions. . . . He would like to discuss with someone his opinions about his associates, the government, religion and so forth, but he cannot risk it – partly because the other person, while prudently keeping back his own opinions, might use this to harm him, and partly because, if he revealed his failings while the other person concealed his own, he would lose something of the other's respect by presenting himself quite candidly to him.[121]

We want to open up to others, but we are afraid others might take advantage of our candor, or use the occasion to conceal their own faults and gain the upper hand. We want to love another, but if we are too ardent we may lose that other's respect. Intimacy always carries with it the possibility of betrayal: One must be

[120] DV 470. [121] DV 440–71.

aware "of secret falsity even in the closest friendship so that a limit upon trust in the mutual confidences of even the best friends is reckoned a universal maxim of prudence in intercourse."[122] These concerns about failed mutuality are not absent in Aristotle's account. He, too, worries about the slander that may sully utility friendships and about whether such friendships can indeed be maintained without firm external contracts enforcing the terms of the relationship.[123] He reminds us that the mutual pleasure of romanitic partnerships can sometimes last for no more than a day,[124] too that the elderly may be too churlish and plaintive to be good friends. But these truncated forms of friendship are discussed largely to show that they are just that – unstable friendships that bear the name "friendship" in only a qualified sense (*kata sumbebēkos*). The very purpose of his extensive discussion of character friendship is to detail an alternative, an ideal, so we might get a glimpse of what true mutuality among morally mature individuals might look like. But here Aristotle reminds us, in a way that Kant does not, that such mutuality is earned – that trust comes with days spent together in shared activity.[125] It is not just that some friendships have it and others do not. It is that the activity of certain friendships creates it as part of its commitment. Kant stipulates a form of friendship, "moral" friendship as opposed to "emotional" friendship, which in principle can secure a love adequately constrained by respect. But significantly, the issue of how respect or trust is cultivated is not itself raised. Kant's focus is not on the development of trust, nor really on the nitty-gritty of how we come to establish mutuality. As always, his overt concern is with moral practice and its failures, and less so with the issues of moral development and nurture.

The negative view of our sociality that emerges in this tract on friendship relates to a more persistent theme in his writing. In the early essay "Idea for a Universal History," he tells us ours is by nature an "unsocial sociability."[126] The condition is not just an

---

[122] Rel. 33/28.   [123] NE 1157a20–25; 1158b6–11; 1162b5–6.   [124] NE 1156b1–4.
[125] See esp. EE 1237b8–14.
[126] The notion is developed in the "Idea for a Universal History from a Cosmopolitan Point of View." The implications of this notion for a reading of the

early developmental moment. It is a natural way we relate to fellow humans, a predisposition to humanity, in the *Religion's* terminology. Our interactions are marked by rivalry and competition. We want "to acquire worth in the opinion of others" but harbor the persistent fear that others may be superior to us.[127] In both the *Religion* and early political writings, Kant goes on to argue that nature makes a virtue of necessity: It is the cunning of nature to use the competitive desire "as a spur to culture."[128] We cultivate rational powers as a response to social antagonisms and competition. It is in civil society, marked by freedom "and therefore [by] a continual antagonism among its members" (with "limits of this freedom" compatible with the "freedom of others") that humans most fully cultivate their natures.[129] But the cultivation is always fed by rivalry, even if at once kept in harness by a sense of equality and juridical duty. The empirical assumptions of the modern natural lawyers, such as Grotius and Pufendorf – that we are by nature rivalrous and depend upon law to mediate our differences – are shared by Kant.[130] For Kant especially, what is salient about our breed of social interaction is just how easily prey it is to manipulation. What is striking is not the pleasure of mutual attunement or the spontaneity of the shared voyage, but the fear of rivalry and antagonism. Given this characterization of our sociability, it is perhaps not surprising that Kant himself does not dwell on intimacy or affiliation as positive sustenance for our breed of rational agency. The Aristotelian idea that where there is friendship there is little need for justice seems to be inverted for Kant: Where there is friendship, one especially needs justice.[131]

But however dismal Kant may regard our social track record, still, in principle, healthy friendship should be able to find a place in a Kantian account of moral perfection. It is easy to find the

anthropological grounding of Kant's moral project are explored by Wood (1991).

[127] Rel. 27/22.   [128] Rel. 27/22.

[129] "Idea for a Universal History from a Cosmopolitan Point of View" 22/45; here I rely on H. B. Nisbet's translation, anthologized in Reiss's edition (1970).

[130] See Schneewind's important recent work on the natural law tradition and the origins of Kantian autonomy (1986; 1990a,b; 1991a,b).

[131] NE 1155a27; I am grateful to Ed Langarek for putting the point this way.

elements of such a reconstruction in his own account. In a programmatic way, it would appeal to the following evidence. Earlier
in *The Doctrine of Virtue,* Kant lists self-knowledge as "the first
command of all duties to oneself." It requires assessing "your
moral perfection, in relation to your duty."

> Impartiality in judging oneself in comparison with the law and
> sincerity in avowing to oneself one's inner moral worth or un-
> worth are duties to oneself that follow immediately from that
> first command of self-knowledge.[132]

The duty is a ubiquitous one. Where there are questions of
deliberative assessment, the command to know oneself requires
sincerity in proposing the maxims of one's actions and conscientious efforts in checking them against the impartial tribunal of
moral law. Where there are less urgent questions of action, still a
duty to self-knowledge requires an ongoing reflective attitude
about one's moral habits. This will involve an assessment of one's
habits of moral perception and capacities for recognizing what is
morally relevant. Bias and prejudice, as well as tendencies toward
rationalization and self-deception, need to be routed out. At bottom, one must "scrutinize, fathom" one's motives, however "un-
fathomable the depths and abyss of one's heart" ultimately are.
For this process, as Kant says, "is the beginning of human wisdom."[133] Indeed, morality, on the Kantian view, is largely a ferret-
ing out of one's attempts at self-deception and evasion. The true
enemy of morality is not inclination that runs contrary to duty,
but reason's attempt to veil such desires from its own view. It is
reason's misuse of its own power that is the real foe:

> Yet those valiant men [the Stoics] mistook their enemy: for he is
> not to be sought in the merely undisciplined natural inclina-
> tions which present themselves so openly to everyone's con-
> sciousness; rather is he, as it were, an invisible foe who screens
> himself behind reason and is therefore all the more
> dangerous.[134]

132 DV 441–42.
133 DV 441.
134 Rel. 57/50.

On the commonsense view Aristotle develops, friends supply us with the mirror that we lack on our own. As such, they figure crucially in our projects of self-knowledge. Kant himself points to a similar dimension of friendship in his discussion in *The Doctrine of Virtue*. Though he insists upon the hazards of candor, he never disputes the need for mutual disclosure and critical discourse. We long to find others with whom we can reveal ourselves with confidence, those with whom we can open up and come out of our prisons. In the rare, best sort of friendship, where one establishes mutual trust, there is a sharing of thought and confidences that is truly liberating: "He is not completely alone with his thoughts, as in a prison, but enjoys a freedom denied to him with the rank and file, with whom he must shut himself up in himself."[135] Intellectual camaraderie is the stuff of such friendships, but so, too, intimate and candid reflection about each other's characters and habits. We seek a mutual relationship in which we can reveal with confidence our failings and accept the appraisals of others as honest and well intended. Indeed, we have a moral duty, he says, to be honest with friends about their faults and weaknesses, and to offer such criticisms without intent to harm. As with all interactions, duties to avoid calumny and backbiting apply here. Kant is at pains to point out how competitive and defensive egos can creep in to undo these relations. But at the same time he cites the intense need for confessionals and the hunger for disclosure before a trusted audience. These points indicate, however tentatively, some appreciation on his part of the role of friendship in the projects of self-knowledge and moral development.

6 THE ETHICAL COMMONWEALTH AS A SOCIAL GOAL

As we have said before, Kant, in explicit contrast to Aristotle, characterizes the sphere of moral practice as extending well beyond those to whom we share personal ties or a cultural context. Membership in an ethical commonwealth is in virtue of our hu-

---

[135] DV 472; italics omitted.

manity, conceived simply as the capacity to set ends. Its perfection or truest realization is in a good will. Accordingly, Kant says at the end of his discussion of friendship, "the friend of humanity" is the person who can regard all persons ("that is, the whole race") with equality, whatever their station or walk, or relation to oneself.[136] The solidity of the moral bond rests in respect for others' moral capacities and not in the vagaries of affection or love. Even the term "friend of humanity" (*Freund den Menschen*), in contrast to the ancient term "lover of humanity" (*Menschenlie-benden; Philanthrop*) connotes, he claims, "thought and consideration for the *equality* among humans." But in what sense, if any, are we to think of this larger ethical commonwealth as something of a community? Does the question even make sense once we require that morality embrace persons far and near, simply in virtue of their rational nature? To pose a different but related question, to what degree does Kant acknowledge the developmental role small communities and friendships play in preparing us to exercise the virtues in this most extended sphere? In short, what of the ancient agenda remains as part of Kant's agenda as well?

To some extent, Kant takes up these issues in the *Religion Within the Limits of Reason Alone*. There he argues that moral practice requires conceiving of the dominion of the moral law as establishing a society in which the cause of virtue becomes a mutually acknowledged and collective effort. Like devotion to the common good within the *polis,* the moral good becomes the rallying point of this community:

> As far as we can see, therefore, the sovereignty of the good principle is attainable, so far as men can work toward it, only through the establishment and spread of a society in accordance with, and for the sake of, the laws of virtue, a society whose task and duty it is rationally to impress these laws in all their scope upon the entire human race. For only thus can we hope for a victory of the good over the evil principle. In addition to prescribing laws to each individual, morally legislative reason also unfurls a banner of virtue as a rallying point for all

---

[136] DV 472–73.

who love the good, that they may gather beneath it. . . . A union of persons under merely moral laws, patterned on the above ideal, may be called an . . . *ethical commonwealth.*[137]

Kant's claim is that parallel efforts at virtue are not sufficient to combat the temptations of evil that individuals face on their own. One needs "a society, enduring, ever extending itself, aiming solely at the maintenance of morality, and counteracting evil with united forces." Individual conscientiousness needs to be spurred on by the example of others rallying under the same banner. Here, the shared context is not family or nation, but rational nature. However impracticable unanimity is toward this goal, it is our duty to join such a commonwealth. In a most explicit way, Kant insists that the individual practice of morality be viewed as something we do with others, and something we regularly reaffirm in others' presence. Fraternal ties spread through this commonwealth not simply by some abstract aknowledgment of equality, but by imagining a political and social community that shares a goal and an educational mission. The ethical commonwealth is rational nature's version of the political commonwealth, and like the latter, it needs to be conceived in the concrete terms of sharing a common good. As Kant elaborates, the ethical commonwealth is the social embodiment of the Highest Good. The Highest Good, recall, is the composite unity of perfect virtue in the world and the happiness conditioned by it.[138] Though Kant regards that notion in the second critique as the goal of everyone's "moral wishes," it is cast there as primarily a theoretical end. It satisfies a philosophical or dialectical urge to find a most final totality for moral reflection. In the *Religion*, it becomes a practically regulative ideal, which depicts our moral practice as a social and communal project: "For the species of rational beings is objectively, in the idea of reason destined for a social goal [*gemeinschaftlichen*

---

[137] Rel. 94/86.
[138] KpV 114–15. For important recent discussions of the social character of the Highest Good, see van der Linden (1988) and Yovel (1989). My own discussion is especially indebted to Van der Linden's study, though I ultimately disagree with his conclusions. For a more general discussion of the Highest Good, see Wood (1970).

Zwecke], namely, the promotion of the highest as a social good [*gemeinschaftlichen Gut*]."[139]

There is a clear view here of the importance of a moral community as a lodestone for moral practice. We need to envision ourselves as not alone in our efforts, however unsure we may be of the ultimate contributions others make. But to what extent does Kant see this wide sense of community as itself dependent upon smaller communities that foster a sense of moral concern? Again, to what extent does he take into account the role of friendship as important in the project of moral perfection?

In the political essays,[140] Kant is quite aware that a moral world order is effective at the global level only if it builds on and sustains smaller communities of moral order lower down. A persistent theme of those essays is that the moral perfection of the human race is intergenerational and intercultural. It depends upon a web of actual, smaller communities committed, however imperfectly, to virtue.

But in the *Religion* we get less of a sense that the collective project of morality must be nurtured from the bottom up through a network of narrower affiliations. From Kant's point of view, the church is the historical and material forerunner of an ethical commonwealth, but it needs to be overcome precisely because it fails to embody the autonomy of reason. The historical or "visible church," as Kant calls it, must gradually yield to the "invisible church," the pure religion of reason that is internal to all of us. Ecclesiastical faith must make its transition to moral faith, and individuals must become united under the "invisible" banner of a commonwealth of good wills. I quote in full :

> In the end religion will gradually be freed from all empirical determining grounds and from all statutes which rest on history and which through the agency of ecclesiastical faith provisionally unite men for the requirements of the good; and thus at last the pure religion of reason will rule over all. . . . The integuments within which the embryo first developed into a human

---

[139] Rel.94/89.
[140] Especially "Idea for a Universal History from a Cosmopolitan Point of View" and "Perpetual Peace."

being must be laid aside when he is to come into the light of day. The leading-string of holy tradition with its appendages of statutes and observances . . . becomes bit by bit dispensable, yea, finally, when man enters upon his adolescence, it becomes a fetter. . . . Though each obeys the (non-statutory) law which he prescribes to himself, he must at the same time regard this law as the will of a World-Ruler revealed to him through reason, a will which by invisible means unites all under one common government into one state – a state previously and inadequately represented and prepared for by the visible church.[141]

This is a troublesome passage. On the one hand, Kant sensitively grasps here, as in the earlier essay "What Is Enlightenment," the urgent need to liberate humankind from repressive religious forms of his day. They are fetters that, even if once useful, need to be thrown away at the age of moral maturity. On the other hand, he does not indicate other *historical* (or material) vehicles through which the ethical commonwealth might better be prepared.[142] Indeed, in a discussion, such as the *Religion* presents, which so emphasizes the importance of a community to support individual virtue, one would expect to find provisions for moral community at other levels. But such an account is absent. It could be that Kant views such lower-level efforts as capable of fostering only partiality and parochial preference. But this is not the import of his remarks about friendship in *The Doctrine of Virtue*. Properly regulated friendship is compatible with more impartial concerns[143] and, in a general way, is an effective forum for self-knowledge and moral perfection. Indeed, it can be argued that if the ethical commonwealth is a goal we *must* seek, then we must imperfectly bring it about through individually willing ends, including the ends of association devoted to the more manageable pieces of that ideal goal. If we reasonably assume that the

141 Rel. 121–22/112. Compare the conclusion of the *Lectures on Ethics* passage in which Kant holds that "justice and equity, the authority, not of governments, but of conscience within us, will rule the world" (253). In the full context of this passage, Kant seems to imply that noncorrupt forms of government can properly promote the individual conscience.
142 Van der Linden (1988, 157) is sensitive to this point.
143 See Herman's helpful remarks on this in Herman (1993, ch. 9).

moral progress to the Highest Good is an arduous path, then we will need among those ends supportive associations to help us struggle against obstacles that stand in the way of unswerving virtue. We will need friends who help us to know the way of virtue.

Once again, Kant does not emphasize the developmental path. His preoccupation is with the end of mature moral practice, in terms of both its requirements and its grounds. But just as Aristotle presents a somewhat lopsided picture of morality, so, too, we might say, does Kant. Of course, one cannot expect any given theorist to do justice to all sides of a debate. The very advantage of a comparative discussion is precisely to bring to bear the perspectives of other theories that do not easily emerge in a more internal discussion. Still, if we were to combine some of the merits of the Kantian and Aristotelian points of view, what we might aim for is a comprehensive theory that at once recognizes the far reach of our moral concern and also the role of affiliation in cultivating that concern.

Chapter 6

Aristotelian particularism

Preceding chapters have discussed the role of emotions in Aristotelian and Kantian ethics, as well as the role of affiliation. In this chapter and the next, we turn to the notions of practical reason and moral perception. On the face of it and, indeed, on traditional tellings, our two accounts differ considerably on this subject. In Aristotelian ethics there is explicit emphasis on deliberating about the particulars of a case, with practical wisdom itself sometimes taking the form of perception.[1] We are reminded regularly by Aristotle of the limitations of rules and procedures, and of the shortfalls of misplaced rigor. We must seek only so much precision as is appropriate for the subject matter.[2] Practical wisdom is not scientific understanding (*epistēmē*), Aristotle insists.[3] Rather, it is a conjecturing and aiming (*stochazomai*) at the changing particulars.[4] We work with summary rules, at best – rules of thumbs that hold only for the most part. Along with a focus on the particulars, there is also an emphasis on the actualized achievements of virtue – on moral choice as it is realized in actual action and an embodied standard of practical reason captured by the example of the practically wise person. On the Aristotelian view, to learn about virtue and moral reasoning we need to turn to a concrete paradigm. There is no algorithm we can appeal to for general guidance, no procedure that formalizes our practice. In a certain

---

[1] NE 1142a23–30.   [2] NE 1094b11–22; 1103b34–1104a10.
[3] NE 1142a23–24.   [4] NE 1109a23, a30; 1106b15, b28; 1141b13.

palpable way, virtue is an embodied matter. Its subject matter is concrete particulars, its methods are those revealed in practice and exemplified in action.

In Kantian ethics, in contrast, the emphasis is on the universalizability of reason and on the availability of a formal principle for guiding moral judgment. More specifically, rational nature yields its own moral constraints and these can be generalized and abstracted in a formulaic way. Practical laws are laws of freedom (constraints) generated autonomously by the will. A certain weight is given to the presumptive moral rules that these constraints yield, though ultimately, it is emphasized in recent interpretations especially, moral deliberation must be more fine-grained than merely following rules.[5] Occasions for deliberation are precisely occasions when rules conflict or questions linger about the rightness of action. Still, in these cases, according to a standard view, the moral law, constructed by reason, supplies a procedure (the Categorical Imperative procedure) for deliberation.[6] Proposed maxims, or willings, are brought to the procedure and assessed for their moral permissibility. On the standard view, moral justification stands at a different level from the proposing of maxims. So whereas within Aristotelian ethics the moral moment sits squarely in the perception of moral salience and choice of action, according to most interpretations of Kantian ethics the moral moment is more the moment of insuring that one's maxims can function as a principle for others.[7] Again, in contrast to the Aristotelian view, it is not actions but specifically *maxims* of action that are the locus of moral assessment. In a certain way, Kantian virtue, following the Stoic conception of virtue, turns inward. The moral principle is an internal principle generated by reason; what is good and has unconditional value is the well-structured will, not something further it achieves in the world.

[5] See especially O'Neill (1989) and Herman (1993).
[6] In the next chapter I raise questions about just how formal a procedure this is.
[7] Though recently Herman (1993, ch. 10) has attempted to combine the perceptual and justificatory moments in the Kantian account, by suggesting that in the case of the good person, the values of the Categorical Imperative are themselves captured in the first order process of proposing one's maxim. I address her suggestion in the next chapter.

I want to assess these broad contrasts in light of a more systematic examination of each theorist's account of the role of practical
reason and moral perception within virtue. In particular, I consider whether some of the common charges leveled from each
side against the other can be sustained. So, for example, in the
absence of a criterion for right choice, does Aristotelian particularism reduce to an unacceptable form of intuitionism, as Kantians sometimes charge? Conversely, can it be fairly charged
against Kantian ethics that the focus on deliberative procedures
rules out a role for moral perception within the full account of
practical reason? Moreover, just how formal are those procedures
and what roles do they play? Admittedly, the range of material
here is extensive, and the valuable contemporary literature from
both Aristotelian and Kantian camps is impressive.[8] Still, I want
to bring the two philosophers into dialogue in a way that avoids
both oversimplification and caricature. As before, the hope is to
fine-tune the conversation by a return to the texts and the issues
they raise. I begin with Aristotle in this chapter; I then turn to
Kant in Chapter 7 and complete the Kantian picture in Chapter 8.

1 BRIEF REMARKS ON PRACTICAL REASON AND "HABITUATED" VIRTUE

In a certain way, it is easier to pinpoint the role of practical reason
in Kantian virtue than it is to pinpoint its role in an Aristotelian
account. For a start, on the Kantian view morality is grounded
only in our rational nature. Principles of practical reason, such as
those concerning universalizability and noncontradiction, are
taken to yield constraints on our willings. To have virtue is to be
effectively constrained by these principles. In Aristotle's account,
the role of practical reason in virtue is less straightforward, not
simply because Aristotle has no interest in grounding morality in
the priority of reason, but because of an artifice of his own presen-

---

[8] On practical reason in Aristotelian ethics, see Annas (1993), Charles (1984),
Cooper (1975), Dahl (1984), Engberg-Pedersen (1983), Nussbaum (1978, 1986).
On Kantian interpretations of the maxim and the various formulae of the
Categorical Imperative, see Bittner (1989), Herman (1993), Hill (1973, 1980,
1989, 1991), Korsgaard (1985, 1986b), Nell (O'Neill) (1975, 1989), Reath (1994).

tation. In *Nicomachean Ethics* I.13, Aristotle divides the soul into the rational and nonrational parts. Though he emphasizes that the nonrational part (the orectic part) is responsive to reason (i.e., it "shares in reason" in the way that a child obeys a parent),[9] he goes on to say that there are separate excellences of each part and that these can be taken up *ad seriatim*.[10] Excellence of the nonrational part is excellence of character, that is, moral virtue, which he will deal with shortly, excellence of the rational part is intellectual virtue (both practical and theoretical), which he promises to take up later. But though Aristotle does indeed postpone the extended discussion of practical reason until Book VI, his account of moral virtue in the earlier books makes it clear that moral virtue itself depends upon the capacities of practical reason and cannot be understood independently of them. The seminal definition of moral virtue in Book II makes this abundantly clear: "Excellence, then, is state concerned with choice, lying in a mean relative to us, this being determined by reason and in the way in which the person of practical wisdom would determine it."[11]

According to the definition, moral virtue is a *hexis prohairetikē* – a state concerning choice. That is, mature moral virtue is itself constituted by practical reason. Not surprisingly, the artifice of trying to discuss moral virtue independently of the excellence of practical reason is not one Aristotle himself can easily abide by. Practical reason, he goes on to claim, figures in virtue not simply through our choice-making capacities. The affective element of virtue itself embeds practical reason. This was, of course, the burden of our discussion of the emotions. On the Aristotelian view, emotions contain evaluations and construals that reveal what the emotions are about. It is these evaluations which change when emotions are genuinely transformed. In the case of moral transformation, the evaluative elements of the emotions must harmonize with the rational wishes and judgments of the rational part of the soul, insofar as these grasp the requirements of good living as a whole. Emotions must become "reasonable," we might

---

[9] NE 1102b25–1103a3.   [10] NE 1103a4–19.
[11] NE 1106b36ff. See NE VI.12 and 13 for further statements of the inseparability of practical wisdom and virtue.

say. Properly habituated emotions come to embed or internalize the judgments of mature practical reason. Still, the notion of habituation has suggested to many an absence of rational processes of argument and reflection. But as I have argued elsewhere, this is a misunderstanding of Aristotle's conception.[12] *Ethismos* (perhaps better translated as "character development" than "habituation") is not a mindless process of learning by repetitive skill and reinforcement, but a critical process of learning that involves judgment, inquiry, and a growing ability to make intelligible one's actions and to transform one's objectives and circumstances into right rational choices. If we do insist on a notion of habituated virtue as mindless, we need to be clear it is *our* notion of habituation, and not the Aristotelian notion of *ethismos*, that underlies the conception. As noted in Chapter 4, Section 5, Kant himself characterizes Aristotelian habituated virtue as mindless behaviorism, and no doubt contributes to our own modern misunderstanding.

2 ARISTOTELIAN PARTICULARISM: A START

A growing attraction of Aristotelian ethics among contemporary moral philosophers is its emphasis on the particularity of moral situations.[13] Notions of moral sensitivity and moral salience find a natural home in Aristotle's account of the perceptual aspect of practical wisdom, just as skepticism about the moral guidance of rules finds easy anchor in Aristotle's own skepticism about the possibility of codifying moral experience and even public law.[14] But even though Aristotelian ethics has become a rallying point for various expressions of particularism, Aristotle's own views about moral perception and the role of rules in moral agency are

---

[12] See Sherman (1989, ch. 5).

[13] For contemporary versions of particularism, see Blum (1994), Dancy (1993), Little (forthcoming), McDowell (1979, 1981), McNaughton (1988), Murdoch (1970), Quinn (1993, ch.12). For a well-stated and influential formulation of Aristotelian particularism, see Nussbaum (1985).

[14] Rh. 1374a25–35; NE 1137b20–25; see the important discussion at Pol. 1269a8–22 on the competing values of legal flexibility and stability.

still not all that clear. I revisit what are by now familiar texts and doctrines, to see just where Aristotle stands on some of the important issues that have spawned contemporary debate. I shall argue that Aristotle puts forth a *qualified* particularism in which general, but nonuniversal rules play a limited role.[15]

Perhaps a place to start is with the common reaction that often follows a modern-day reading of Aristotle's ethics. The reaction is that something is absent, and that that something is the moral perspective as a *general* perspective. To make a decision, on the Aristotelian view, is neither to subsume one's choice under some general principle or law nor to ask whether others *could* endorse the universalized maxim of one's action. Nor is there the move that others *should* act as we are acting.[16] Thus the *orthos logos* (right reasoning) of the person of practical wisdom does not involve transforming one's choice into some lawlike counterpart, despite a modern bias toward translating the phrase as "right rule."[17] Rather, the focus is always on the specifics of the case; wise judgment hits the mean not in the sense that it always aims at moderation, but in the sense that it hits the target for *this* case. As such, description and narrative of the case are at the heart of moral judgment. This is not to say Aristotle is blind to the fact, so urgent for the Kantian, that we regularly make exceptions for ourselves and that morality must be a matter of confronting

---

[15] Note also that Dancy (1993, 67–70), a standard-bearer for contemporary particularism, leaves room for an account of moral principles. "So it is important to see that is compatible with the constraints of particularism, though of course it represents particularism in a conciliatory rather than an aggressive mood" (70). His view of a moral principle, however, is extremely weak – it "amounts to a reminder of the sort of importance that a property *can* have in suitable circumstances." So, "it is wrong to hurt others" might be such a rule, but " it is wrong to hold a red shoelace" might also be a rule in less frequent, but suitable, circumstances (I am grateful to Maggie Little for discussion here). Through his notion that moral principles hold "for the most part," Aristotle's account of moral principles pushes toward more general claims.

[16] To ask if others *could* universalize one's maxim is a Kantian notion. To determine that others *should* so act belongs to Hare's (1963) notion of universalizability.

[17] See the standard Ross translation, as at 1138a10; it has been corrected by Urmson in the Revised Oxford Translation (1984).

squarely those rationalizations. On the contrary, Aristotle insists that the good life is a life studying one's actions, choices, and emotional responses, and studying them in a way in which one remains open to criticism and reform. This is the pressing agenda of the friendship among good persons. Still, it might be thought that an emphasis on the particulars of one's case invites precisely the sorts of rationalizations that a move toward generalizability (or an impartial procedural check) is meant to block. For in the details of our stories, we are able to secrete our partialities and distortions. Unless we pare down the story to some more basic moral shape, we cannot easily spot our excuses and self-exemptions. But here the Kantians are no more advantaged: Even though Kantian theory is undergirded by a deep appreciation of reason's deceptive ways, each individual is still left to the task of sorting out the duplicities in her actual maxims. To the extent that those maxims are contextually rich, the Kantian agent is susceptible to the same vulnerabilities facing the Aristotelian; she is no more or less advantaged in the business of isolating distorting habits. It is true, certainly, that testing one's action by hypothetical acceptance of its universal form introduces a distinct kind of monitoring. And under some interpretations this may force a certain amount of "paring down " that allows one to see the moral shape of a maxim more clearly. We come to these topics in Chapter 7. But for now, it seems clear that a move to the more general level of reflection still does not obviate the need for clarity in the case before one. We still need to see what is morally salient if we are to act in present circumstances. Put differently, the move to *what everyone could do* first depends upon an accurate and honest description of *what an agent herself would do* given a sensitive appraisal of the concrete circumstances. There is no way to avoid the first step. On the Aristotelian view, much of the achievement of moral practice is in the sorting out of the case itself. Here we need to remember that Aristotle often takes himself to be describing the moral judgment of the morally mature agent, in other words, the practically wise person. By and large, sensitivities will be developed and values stably internalized so that they are brought to bear in the very proposing of a choice. This does not eliminate the need for "reflective" perception that reaches back to more general values for guidance. Justifying the importance of a certain feature in a case may be precisely a matter of an upward appeal to some more general value. The perception is reflective in that we may go "back and forth" between the particular features of the case and the more general values, refining the latter through the narrative as well as grasping better the importance of the former by appeal to what is general. The values or ends themselves become fine-tuned by the case study.

We shall come to all this. For now the point is that Aristotle thinks of the development of moral character as continuous with the development of the capacities for moral perception. The point is perhaps clearest at *Nicomachean* III.5: If a person is somehow responsible for her character, so, too, will she be responsible for how things appear to her.

> Someone might say that everyone aims at the apparent good, but does not control its appearance; but the end appears to each person in a way that corresponds to his character. For if each person is somehow responsible for his own state of character, he will also be himself somehow responsible for its [namely, the end's] appearance [*tēs phantasias*].[18]

The claim is in reply to those who say we have no control over such matters. On that view, what appears good or bad is a passive taking in, divorced from character and values. Aristotle is notoriously vague here about how and at what point we become responsible for our characters. Still, at a general level he wants to argue that responsibility for character must include responsibility for what one sees and fails to see. Developing capacities for accurate appraisal and evaluation of circumstances relevant to virtue is a part of the perfection of virtue. However tempting it is to appeal to perceptual ignorance of ethical salience as external to character, the suggestion here, and certainly in the account of *akrasia*,[19] is that such ignorance is a failure of virtue. Character includes underlying patterns of seeing, as well as desires and

---

[18] 1114b1–3, my translation; cf. 1114b16–17.

[19] NE VII.1–3, in which *akrasia* is diagnosed as a failure to perceive properly the particulars relevant to one's best judgment of what to do.

emotions that affect one's seeing and evaluation of circumstances. One could not have a good character without an adequate attunement to the moral features of one's environment. And it is part of one's responsibility to cultivate that attunement.

(One needs to be careful here, however. Aside from this passage and the discussion of *akrasia* (at NE VII.1–3), Aristotle never squarely discusses the notion of perceptual errors that are a matter of reproachable ignorance. There has been a venerable tradition of commentators that has tried to detect such a standard of culpable negligence in Aristotle's account of wrongdoing because of mistakes (*hamartēma*) in *Nicomachean* V.8, and in particular in those mistakes, distinguished from mere accident, as unintentional but not contrary to reasonable expectation (*paralogos*).[20] The matter is complex, but as I have discussed elsewhere in greater detail,[21] Aristotle's usage of what is "not contrary to reasonable expectation" (or what cannot be reasonably unexpected) means simply that at some level, what happened is subject to coherent explanation in a way that sheer luck is not. That is, how the mistake happened is intelligible and can be rationalized or brought back to an account of agency. But to argue for the intelligibility of the mistake says nothing about what care and application could have then avoided. It does not directly illuminate the issue of negligence and avoidability. It simply says that a mistaken perception or action can be made intelligible from some point of view, not that the agent could have been so enlightened as to have known better at the time of action. The implications for understanding the *hamartiai*, or errors of dramatic tragedy, are clearest. Tragic mistakes based on misperception and mistaken judgment are made intelligible through the history and actions of the tragic character. As such, the mistakes are not just happenstance, but neither need they be outright cases of negligence or flaw. Circumstances can conspire to trap agents in ways that exac-

---

20 Thus, I do not accept the emendation of *aitias* to *agnoias* (1135b19) found both in Urmson's translation in the Revised Oxford Translation and in Jackson's translation of the fifth book. Implicit in that rendering is a sense of culpability I reject.

21 Sherman (1992). On broader issues of *hamartia* and culpability, see Bremer (1969) and Daube (1969).

erbate vulnerabilities. The fact that pity is often the appropriate response to tragic error points to the idea that the reversals wrought by tragic error are often disproportionate to an agent's own failure.)

3 EMOTIONS AS EVALUATIVE

There is a temptation to regard the discernment of the particulars as primarily the function of cognitive rather than affective capacities. Indeed, Aristotle himself takes up the notion of perception as a mode of practical reason in his discussion of the intellectual structure of virtue in *Nicomachean Ethics*, Book VI. As he puts it in a passage to which we will return, practical wisdom is concerned with the ultimate particular, "which is the object not of scientific understanding [*epistemē*] but of perception [*aisthēsis*]."[22] Aristotle's aim is to distinguish practical wisdom from scientific understanding while still characterizing practical wisdom and its subfunctions as cognitive states. But on a more comprehensive Aristotelian account, discernment of the particulars is not regarded as a purely cognitive function. Emotions will also serve epistemic roles crucial for perceiving salience. We can be alerted to occasions as threatening (and so a possible occasion for courage) or as marking others' need (and so a moment for beneficence) through emotions such as fear and compassion. Through their constitutive appraisals of particular circumstances, emotions help us gather information about our surroundings.

Quickly reviewing the epistemic functions of emotions may be helpful here. In Chapters 2 and 4, we talked about emotional sensitivities as *ways of attending to* and *communicating (or signaling)* values. In both capacities, emotions serve informational roles. We might say, they *record* and *convey* "the news." Aristotle does not himself articulate these roles for the emotions, but they help to make sense of his general view in the *Rhetoric* that emotions contain evaluations and, in turn, help connect that view with his conception of virtue as partially constituted by emotions. We can expand upon our earlier claims as follows: To take the second role

[22] NE 1142a23–30.

first, emotions signal or express valuations; through our affective attitudes, we often convey what we care about. In some cases, there may be a self-revelatory aspect to this; we learn what we care about by experiencing certain emotions. Independent of the affective experience, we may remain unaware that we hold these particular values.[23]

But equally, and perhaps more fundamentally, emotions enable us to attend to what we care about, however unacknowledged those concerns may be until we notice our emotional involvement. Put differently, we can *track* circumstances relevant to our concerns through emotional sensitivities. Emotions *lead us* to what we care about in addition to *telling us* (and others) that we care. They inform us of externalities relevant to our standing concerns. So, being capable of pity helps me notice another's undue suffering; a capacity for anger helps me to record an apparent and unjustified offense to self or those dear to me; a capacity for grieving helps me to appreciate that something valued has been lost. On Aristotle's view, an emotion is partially constituted by appraisals such as these. To take a more concrete example, it may be that I notice a child's quiet frustration in dealing with a more aggressive friend because I emotionally identify with that child and have a particular interest in empowering that sort of child. The emotional sensitivity helps me connect that concern to my present surroundings. Emotionally identifying with the child is a way I activate that concern, as well as possibly reveal it to myself and others.

The last example adverts to the idea that emotional engagement can hinder as well as help fine judgment of particulars. We are selective to features of our environment because of underlying affiliations, identifications, fears, hates, likes and so on, but not all these are well-modulated emotions, nor do they always promote other fine emotions. In Aristotelian idiom, good character depends upon *right* pleasures and pains. Yet some of our emotional responses lack just that quality and to that degree are epistemological handicaps. My identification with a child who is being bullied may be too emotionally engaged and identificatory.

---

[23] I have been influenced here by Stocker's (1996) stimulating discussion.

I may project my own memories or discomfort onto him, become too enmeshed to make correct moral judgments.[24] In the case of a family member, such involvement may be stifling and more a reflection of how *I* would feel and how threatened *I* would become than how the child actually feels. What is needed in this case may be an empathetic engagement that doesn't overproject my own anxieties onto the child. Empathy of this sort might better encourage the child's own development while still assuring the child that I care and am readily available for support.

The lesson to be learned here is not the old and tired one, that emotions should be distrusted. Rather, it is that they need to be educated in order to be reliable epistemic tools. We have emotional receptivities by nature, Aristotle suggests. They must be perfected by habituation and reflection in order to serve us well.[25] In many ways, Aristotle takes a similar, sensible stand toward reason: Reason, too, can distort, at times seeking a precision or systematization inappropriate to the complexity of its subject matter. However, to be aware of these tendencies is not to distrust reason's operations, but simply to be wise about how to use reason well.

How do we cultivate emotions as more reliable, epistemic tools? We have taken up related issues in Chapter 2, but a few words are in order here. First, as Aristotle puts it, we need to take stock of our predilections and impulsive leanings:

> But we must consider the things towards which we ourselves also are easily carried away; for some of us tend to one thing, some to another; and this will be recognizable from the pleasure and the pain we feel. We must drag ourselves away to the contrary extreme; for we shall get into the intermediate state by drawing well away from error.[26]

Aristotle begins by echoing our earlier point here – that we learn about our valuings through the report of the emotions (as he puts it here, what we tend toward is recognizable from pleasure and pain). His present point, of course, is that these valuings, as

---

[24] I owe thanks to Stocker (1996) for his discussion of enmeshment.
[25] NE 1103a25.   [26] NE 1109b1–5.

well as our sensitivities toward them, will often need to be modulated. His recommendation for how to modulate those excesses – essentially, by overcompensation in the opposite direction – may strike some as all too mechanical. But Aristotle's idea becomes more plausible when we appreciate that the extremes in either direction need not be viewed in a merely quantitative way. Modulation is not simply a matter of intensifying or reducing the volume of our emotions, though sometimes we speak loosely as if it were – as when we say we are trying to be more trusting and less cynical, or gentler and less angry. But here, of course, we mean to allow that being more trusting and less cynical still depends upon correct differentiation of cases – knowing when and to whom to be more trusting and less cynical, even if our general policy is to veer more toward one pole than the other. We want to allow that our emotional errors may simply rest on wrongheaded descriptions of what we see – for instance, getting angry because I see M. as trying to hurt me when she isn't, or as ignoring me when really she is just tired. But, note, in some instances there may indeed be an underlying pattern of emotional proclivities that helps explain why one tends to make such mistakes in the first place: perhaps, because one is *in general too* hungry for attention or *too* quick to see criticism as unjustified offense. This returns us to Aristotle's point: Grasping these sorts of underlying proclivities may stand an agent well for more accurate readings of her surroundings, and for more appropriate emotional responses at all levels. Moreover, a grasp that leads to this kind of change will not involve blindly following a general maxim of redirection. One drags oneself away from inappropriate leanings as a matter of resolve, but not without fine judgment about the specifics of each case.

We have been emphasizing that emotions are ways of evaluating and perceiving particulars (i.e., they are forms of appraisal), and that as such, they are important elements in Aristotle's account of discerning particulars. In some cases, they will be essential ways of obtaining information.[27] However, there are a few

---

[27] Presumably, emotions can involve evaluations of general or abstract ideas as well, as in the case of intellectual joy in the elegance of a mathematical theorem.

clarifications at this point. Some emotions seem considerably un-
focused and undiscriminating in their information gathering.
Moods, for example, can be diffusive; if they have intentional
content, it is almost at a meta-level – that a whole range of circumstances looks bright or black. In love, the world brightens; in
depression, a somber hue is cast and a sense of the inanimate
freezes what once breathed life.

These stand in contrast to other emotions – the emotions Aristotle champions in the pages of the *Rhetoric* – that are far more
specific in their evaluative range. Pity, on the Aristotelian view, is
not a general lens through which we see but an emotional sensitivity focused specifically on the disproportionate suffering of
some victim; the power of the reaction is in virtue of an identification that we, too, might someday endure a similar fate.[28] Fear, too,
is directed at specific sorts of circumstances we tend to find
threatening.[29] Much can be said here about the difference between moods and emotions, and the capacities for displacement,
idealization, and distortion that often are linked with moods.
Delving into these matters would take us well beyond our present
interests, and well beyond Aristotle's account.[30] But if there is a
point to bring home, it is that by and large Aristotle wants to
exploit the notion of emotions as focused, evaluative responses,
which, at their best, can collect detailed information about surroundings. In the *Rhetoric*, where the context is the orator's
arousal of emotions in the courtroom, emotional response depends on information conveyed verbally, that is, through persuasive discourse. But the fuller account of the *Rhetoric* makes explicit the obvious – that emotions are responses to nonverbal cues
as well, however cognitively they come to be represented by the
agent.[31] Shame is a response to the look and feel of others' eyes
upon us; anger is a response not just to verbal insult but also, as
Aristotle puts it, to others' inattention to the fact that "they fail to

---

[28] Rh. II.8.   [29] Rh. II.5.

[30] I discuss some of these issues (Sherman, 1994a) in reply to Martha
Nussbaum's remarks about love as a mode of perceiving the particulars in
their "uniqueness."

[31] Note here the Aristotelian view that even animals desire on the basis of a
representation of some good (i.e., a *phantasia*).

perceive our needs" or are "cheerful in the midst of our misfortunes."[32] These are simple points, but they remind us that emotions pick up on a wide range of cues, some more subtle and less
articulated than others. The more general point is that we
wouldn't have access to this information if we viewed discernment of the particulars as an emotionally disengaged process.
Constituted as we are, there is some information that we can get
only through an emotionally engaged process. Emotions are an
essential source of information.

These general remarks suggest that those who are unattuned to
their own or others' emotions will lose out on an essential information source, just as will those who see in such emotional reactions only impulsive, untrustworthy responses. In either case,
there is a splitting off of emotional engagement from critical
capacities that seems alien to an Aristotelian account (however
unworked out his view is of the actual realization of psychic
harmony in the soul). Granted, Aristotle sometimes does take a
more intellectualist stand. At *Nicomachean* IX.4, he identifies theoretical and practical reason with the true person, and love of
those features of the soul with fine and proper love of the self.
Similarly, in the account of *akrasia* in Book VII, he seems to sani-
tize incontinence as a misperception of the particulars indicative
of an intellectual failure – a breakdown in the cognitive
machinery – rather than as a "motivated" irrationality that reveals the work of desire's illicit hand.[33] Still, the overall tenor of
Aristotle's remarks on practical wisdom and character suggest
that the engagement and reporting of the emotions is an essential
source of information, without which we could not be practically
wise.

A final, more speculative note is in order. It may well be that
there is general benefit in openly acknowledging the reports of
the emotions, both when those reports are accurate, and also
when we have reason to suspect that they are not. In the latter
case, there is still educational benefit – we stand to learn how we
go astray. Aristotle makes this point in the text we have just
considered: It is important to know the excesses toward which we

[32] Rh. 1379b17.   [33] See Pears (1984).

veer. But we might want to go further. On a stronger reading, to be attentive to our misplaced emotions might require that we "own" them and openly acknowledge them, though without necessarily endorsing them. For "to own" them is to take a certain responsibility for them, to disavow them no longer or chasten them as alien. It is to "work through" them, in the hope that by reexperiencing those subversive voices, we can better understand them and go beyond them.[34]

4 PERCEPTION AND INTUITIONISM

We have been focusing on the emotion-laden content of much moral perception. There are other aspects to consider too. Perhaps most pressing is the characterization of Aristotelian moral perception as a kind of *immediate* intuition. Although Aristotle is often thought of as an intuitionist, just what is meant by that label is rarely explicit.[35] But if we understand intuitionism as implying a grasp of moral judgments that precludes more ordinary and reiterative processes of description, explanation, justification, or revision, then Aristotle is no intuitionist. No doubt Aristotle's famous formulation that "discernment rests with perception" and his notions of an expert's ability to see and judge with "the eyes of experience"[36] have contributed to the popular idea of virtuous moral judgment as a matter of simply "cottoning on."[37] But this

---

[34] On this psychoanalytic notion of "owning" disavowed mental contents, see Eagle (1988). By and large, Aristotle's notion of transforming emotions sidesteps this more conciliatory stage in favor of a straightforward chastening model. On his model, wayward emotions are transformed when they listen to reason from the top down, just as a child obeys the exhortations of a parent (NE 1103a2). Ears are turned upward to listen to the authority of reason, not downward to listen to the reasons of recalcitrant emotion. See Sherman (1995a).

[35] Though generally the association is with Ross and Moore. The standard criticism of intuitionistic ethics is put pithily by Nowell-Smith: "If I disagree with you" about a moral issue "you must charge me either with insincerity or blindness" (1954, 46). For a contemporary intuitionist position, see Platts (1979, ch. 10). For a useful general discussion, see Lovibond (1983, 11–22).

[36] 1109b23; 1143b11–14; 1144b8–13.

[37] I am most grateful to discussions with Alisa Carse in which she reminded me of the use of this term as part of an understanding of the Aristotelian model.

metaphor – of having eyes by which one sees aright – needn't suggest that the grasp of particulars is a mysterious, intuitive process that leaves to the side the usual processes by which we make sense of our experience, including description, reflection, and discourse. Nor should we think that the two principal elements of practical wisdom – a strong deliberative capacity and a grasp of particulars[38] – can be fully pried apart from the other in the way that a notion of intuitionism often suggests.

To be sure, Aristotle couples specific cognitive capacities, such as understanding (*sunesis*), judgment (*gnomē*) and insight (*nous*) with capacities for perceiving particulars.[39] And these sort of capacities he contrasts with the grasping of things through more general argument and account (*logos*). So, for example, consider the following passage:

> And *nous* is concerned with what is last in both directions; for about the first terms [*tōn prōtōn horōn*] and the last [*tōn eschatōn*] there is *nous* and not a rational account [*logos*]. And in demonstrations *nous* is about the unchanging and first terms while in practical reasoning *nous* is about what is last and changing, and hence is about the minor premise. For these are the origins of the ends to be aimed at, since the universals emerge from the particulars [through induction, cf. 1139b28]. And of these particulars, then we must have perception, and this is *nous*.[40]

Aristotle's point regarding practical reasoning is the simple one – that perception or apprehension (and not discursive reasoning) is involved in the final confrontation with the particular case. We must see the particulars under certain classificatory and evaluative descriptions (as Aristotle puts it, "the universals emerge from the particulars"). Recognitional capacities are central. But this does not quite capture the full process of judging the case. For typically, part of recognizing the importance of certain features in one's circumstances involves the mediated processes of description and redescription, talking the case over with another, ex-

---

38 For these two elements, see NE VI.9 and NE VI.11.
39 See NE VI.11.
40 NE 1143a35-b5, my translation.

plaining why and how you saw it this way rather than that way, in other words, trying to justify your "take." Here, the process is recognitional, but not well represented as perceptual. For at this stage we are not just perceiving things under certain evaluative and classificatory descriptions, but trying to catch their relative importance and relevance. Aristotle's perceptual idiom can tend to minimize this.[41] Admittedly, Aristotle is interested in indicating when intelligible action begins, and when preparation in thought (and perception) ends. The perceptual grasp of particulars is about what is "last" in this sense. But we needn't be forced into thinking that even the expert always comes to what is "last," that is, the "final" read, in a flash, without any interpretative sorting out. That "last" moment of "seeing aright" may itself be at times the culmination of considerable reflection and thought about the import of what one sees. Immediacy need not characterize all the stages of the full judgment of the case before one.

Still, one passage in particular seems to point to the immediacy of perception that critics associate with Aristotelian moral judgment. It will repay us to consider Aristotle's remarks in some detail.

> Practical wisdom is obviously not scientific knowledge [*epistēmē*] for it is about the last term [*eschatou*], as has been said. For the thing to be done is of this sort. And it is opposed to *nous;* for *nous* is about the first terms [*tōn horōn*] of which there is no account [*logos*], while practical reason is of the last thing [*tou eschatou*], which is an object not of science but of perception [*aisthēsis*]. This is not the perception of qualities peculiar to one sense, but of the kind by which we perceive that the last figure among mathematical figures is a triangle. For perception [*aisthēsis*] will come to a halt here too.[42]

The passage opposes the intuitive grasp (*nous*) of first terms in deductive, scientific accounts with the perceptual grasp of last terms or determinate particulars in action. The more restrictive use of *nous* here contrasts with our earlier passage in which the

---

41 I owe thanks to Jonathan Dancy for clarification here.
42 NE 1142a23–30, my translation.

perception of practical circumstances through *phronēsis* is itself regarded as an exercise of *nous* in the opposite direction. Putting terminology aside, the substantive question again is whether this grasp or perception must be viewed as an immediate apprehension cut off from a more discursive process. There is no reason to assume that it is. Aristotle's primary interest in pointing to the notion of perceptual grasp is to signal a capacity to recognize salience, whether it be geometrical salience or ethical salience. The analogue Aristotle has in mind is that of a geometer who is trying to figure out the basic compositional unit out of which a more complex geometrical figure is constructed. Perception "comes to a halt " at the triangle, not because it is absolutely speaking the ultimate geometrical figure into which the composition can be resolved (presumably, that would be a point), but because the geometer sees that in this case the triangle is salient for solving the particular problem at hand. So, for example, where the picture at hand is a series of connected octagons, the geometer may see that an equilateral triangle is the basic building unit for the compositional structure. To see this shape, or as we might say, to "gestalt it," is to see what is *salient* for knowing how to proceed.[43] Analogously, practical wisdom requires seeing the salient "shapes" embedded in complex scenes in a way that enables an agent to make choices relevant to action.[44] As in the case of the geometrical "gestalt," there is no special faculty or sensory mode for this kind of ethical perception, though it does require the relevant experience, as well as inductive capacities to learn from such experience and form proper concepts.[45] As Aristotle puts it in the *Poetics*, it is a matter of recognizing that "this is a that,"[46] however complex the process of becoming competent in the relevant set of concepts. But this may express the idea somewhat too simply again. For the recognition of shapes is not simply a descriptive process of classifying what one sees. Involved in recognizing shapes is another stage in which one relates these com-

[43] See my lengthier discussion (1989, 38–39). Also see Cooper (1975, 32–40); Engberg-Pedersen (1983, 206ff.).

[44] Dancy (1993, 111–16) develops this idea of salience as picking out the "shape" of the circumstances of choice.

[45] NE 1142a14–15, 1143b3–15.   [46] Poet. 1448b15.

257

ponent descriptions of a case to each other. Here, the idea is that by revealing their mutual interconnections, the practical shape of the situation emerges more fully.

But returning to Aristotle's above quoted text, does he view the recognition of shape, here symbolized by the triangle, as the exercise of a perceptual grasp (*aisthēsis*) that is nondiscursive? Aristotle suggests in the passage just quoted that there is a decisive moment when perception comes to a halt. Presumably he means that one must size up a situation, with relative fixity, if one is to be ready to act. But again, this doesn't mean that the description of the case is fixed forever, or immune to revision and justification.[47] Moreover, nothing he has said commits him to an account of just how one arrives at a description – in other words, whether it involves a quick apprehension or a fair bit of trying out of different alternatives. True, we tend to think of the expert as moving with ease, and as seeing quickly, with the ready eye. This may indeed be the image invoked by the expert geometrician. But Aristotle's actual remarks about perceiving salience do not commit him to the idea of "cottoning on" in a flash. It may well be that in some cases of "seeing aright," the ground has been laid quietly in advance, with experience organizing and preparing concepts in just the right way for this bit of selective seeing. But in other cases, the hand dealt may be a challenging one – even to an expert. Such an agent may have to go through various trials and errors, "conjecture" or "feel one's way" (*stochazomai*) toward the ends, as Aristotle puts it elsewhere,[48] before arriving at the most

---

[47] The *phronimos* is the measure of what is good. Gottlieb (1991) has urged that we understand this in non-Protagorean terms as a matter of "detecting" what is good rather than as "constituting" it. This either/or seems too restrictive. I would hold that the *phronimos* is the measure of what is good in virtue of a process by which values outside ourselves are sharpened and mutually supported through the dialectical activities of deliberation. For a more general discussion of the standard of *orthos logos*, see Gómez-Lobo (forthcoming).

[48] The term is usually translated "to aim" and occurs in connection with the process of hitting the mean. But the term also connotes a degree of conjecture and guessing. Cf. 1109a30; 1106b15,b28; 1109a23; 1141b13. For a fascinating account of mathematical "cottoning on" as itself often a belabored process that

accurate reading. Perhaps the point is that "seeing," no less than deliberative reasoning about a right or medial choice, may have its stages and trials. "Look at it this way," "emphasize this point now," "bring into the foreground that minimized detail," "see it from this kind of perspective so you can take this into account" – all this may be a part of getting the scene right. Here it is important to remember Aristotle's insistence that the practically wise person is good at deliberating and that deliberation is a matter of inquiry or figuring out.[49] Circumstances present varying degrees of complexity, and depending on the complexities, circumspect vision may require a fair amount of studying and figuring out, describing and redescribing the case. Equally, it may involve reframing one's objectives in light of the relevance of these particulars. Forcing too tight a distinction between that aspect of practical wisdom which is a matter of grasping the particulars (*aisthēsis*) and that aspect which is a matter of deliberation (*bouleusis*) and inquiry (*zētēsis*)[50] may be overly artificial and indeed highly misleading.

The critical aspect of seeing aright emerges in Aristotle's account of virtue friendship as a context for shared reflection on the requirements of the good life. Some of these issues were discussed in the last chapter; we can allude to them briefly in reference to our present topic of moral perception. Friends "study" or "contemplate" (*theorein*) each other's actions (*praxeis*), Aristotle says, as a way of coming to view their own conduct from a more critical perspective. "For we study better our neighbors than ourselves and their actions better than our own."[51] As Aristotle perspicuously puts it in the *Magna Moralia*, a friend is a mirror by which to understand oneself.[52] Two things are of note.

includes conjecture as well as flashes of insight, see the description of Professor Wile's work on the proof of Fermat's theorem, *New York Times*, January 31, 1995.

49 NE 1142b16–35; 1142a31–32.

50 These dimensions of practical reason are taken up respectively in NE VI.9 and VI.11.

51 NE 1169b33. See Cooper (1980).

52 MM 1213a12–25. The notion of character change in psychotherapy as involv-

First, we submit ourselves to become objects of self-study and not just of passive perception. Friendship is a context for active self-observation and self-knowledge. Second, Aristotle uses the general term *praxeis* here to designate what comes under critical review. But what comes under critical review might be broader, including not an isolated action but the construal of circumstances as part of the reason for one's action.

It is also helpful to recall that Aristotle views virtue friends as intense partners. Such friends spend their days together, living with one another, sharing in activities, discoursing, studying together (*suntheorein*), and as Aristotle says explicitly, "sharing the perceptions of each other" (*sunaisthanesthai*).[53] As noted in Chapter 5, this sharing in each other's perceptions, and in each other's pleasures and pains as well, needn't be taken always to imply endorsement. The more plausible interpretation is that friends, given their mutual involvement, appreciate how the other perceives matters and emotionally reacts. Of course, ultimately the pressing subject matter for such friends is the goodness of their lives. To modern ears this may sound stilted and overly intellectualized – a way of talking about the good life at a distance from one's own, and, too, in moralistic terms. But Aristotle's focus is profoundly practical and Socratic – it is about *my* life and its goodness, simply in the sense of *my living well*. Still, he goes beyond Socratic reflection, taking seriously the importance of emotional attachment to another as integral to the process of critical self-scrutiny and moral development. To live a good life requires an openness to profound and systematic reflection about its elements in the company of another whom one trusts and greatly admires for his or her own character and practical intellect. Having in place a collaborative life dedicated to this project suggests that at a most basic level, what one sees and how one sees will be part of that reflective review. Interpreting a situation and understanding its import may be open to the input of others, who may have seen things differently from up close, or who, from

ing the therapist empathically "mirroring back" the patient's remarks is developed by Kohut (1971, ch.11).
[53] EE 1245b23; see 1245b5–25.

a distance, may simply offer comparisons that help put matters into perspective. Friends "see together" – sometimes in unison but also in ways that supplement each other's finite vision. They are focused on the detailed particulars of each other's lives in ways that can help each other come to understand.[54]

We have been trying to capture the perceptual aspect of Aristotle's geometrical analogue, without losing sight of the descriptive, critical, and collaborative processes that can be part of seeing aright. The suggestion is that a notion of moral seeing, or "sensitivity" to salience, can make room for an interpretive process of coming to a description of a case and recognizing its import. I have suggested some evidence for this in Aristotle's overall remarks, although admittedly he does not outline the process as we have.

Matters are complicated, however, for there are still other ways that Aristotle's geometrical analogue of seeing the triangle might suggest a process that is too streamlined. In particular, if we take the metaphor too literally, it might be thought there is a *single* salient shape that typically stands out in circumstances and "silences" all opposing reasons.[55] But, of course, complex situations have complex contours and some of what is involved in seeing aright in our practical lives is the compositional structure of a scene and not just an isolated or dominant theme. To notice, for example, that circumstances call for generosity will be on its own inadequate unless implicitly included in that assessment is information relevant to how, to what degree, at what expense to oneself, and so on one should be generous here. The picture is multifaceted; salience might be better captured by the idea of "landscape" than "shape" if only because the latter seems to underscore that what we are after are the many shapes that go into

---

54 Note, "understanding" (*sunesis*) and "good understanding" (*eusunesia*), in Aristotle's cognitive vocabulary, are specific ways of being immersed in the particulars such that one can make informed practical judgments, even though one may not be in the position of having to act. In this sense, they are cognitive abilities distinct from *phronēsis*, which is more closely connected to a capacity for choice. See NE 1142b35–1143a18; 1143a6–9.

55 For a critical discussion of the notion of silencing (or defeating) competing views, see Dancy's discussion of McDowell (1993, 47–55).

an overall, structured composition. But even this won't capture it all. Tragedy presents not a fluid landscape, but conflicting and discordant landscapes. Two distinct pictures are salient. Here, one landscape or set of claims may ultimately prevail, but without fully silencing or defeating the other. To fail to be sensitive to both would itself be a kind of blindness. The fundamental point in all this is that reliance on the metaphor of "shape," suggested by Aristotle's geometrical analogue and echoed in some contemporary literature as well, should not be taken as encouragement for too streamlined a conception of either the content of a description of a case, or the descriptive process itself. A description may be compelling precisely because of its complex narrative strands and details. Certainly this is the lesson of literature. We become immersed in the particulars precisely through the narrative detail.[56] Perhaps a word of caution is appropriate here: The term "narrative" has become somewhat fashionable these days, not only within philosophy but in literary criticism circles and psychoanalytical theories.[57] Whatever the connotations of narrative in those various theories, what I mean by narrative is that a description of circumstances tells a story in that there is an order and interrelation, (i.e., shape) in the putting together of the components of the description. In this sense, the description is not a mere listing of elements or weighted factors.[58]

5 RULES AND PRACTICAL INSIGHT

We have been exploring the role of description in the notion of perceiving moral salience. Some contemporary particularists have been keen to minimize further the distinction between the activity of describing circumstances and that of justifying a choice

---

[56] See Nussbaum (1990a) for many of these themes.

[57] For psychoanalytic discussions of narrative, see Ricoeur (1977) and Schafer (1992).

[58] As Dancy notes well, descriptions such as these can have the vices and virtues of narratives, such that "features can be mentioned in the wrong order, and important relations without which the story does not make sense can be omitted, distorted or misplaced" (1993, 113). On the other hand, a narrative that holds together well can act as a persuasive argument for others seeing things in just the way one does.

in those circumstances. Jonathan Dancy makes the claim as follows:

> It is common to distinguish any description of this sort from a quite different activity, that of arguing for one's way of seeing the situation. . . . In part this is because of the view that, at least in the moral case, justification can only consist in the subsumption of this case under some general principle which commands rational support in some way or other. Since description is clearly not intended to achieve any such thing, description is one thing and justification another. I reject this account of justification, and with it the distinction between justification and description. To justify one's choice is to give the reasons one sees for making it, and to give those reasons is just to lay out how one sees the situation, starting in the right place and going on to display the various salient features in the right way; to do this is to fill in the moral horizon. In giving those reasons one is not *arguing* for one's way of seeing the situation. One is rather appealing to others to see it . . . the way one sees it oneself, and the appeal consists in laying out that way as persuasively as one can. The persuasiveness here is the persuasiveness of narrative: an internal coherence in the account which compels assent. We succeed in our aim when our story sounds right. Moral justification is therefore not subsumptive in nature, but narrative.[59]

In a similar way, Margaret Little has argued for a particularism that rejects the idea of lawlike generalizations having a justificatory role in morality. Moral principles still have a use in the moral life, but their use is pedagogic, as when a principle of fidelity is used in reference to particular paradigms, such as intentional lies. Moral justification itself is not ruled out, but it is not to be viewed as subsumptive. As with Dancy, and along the lines we have already suggested, moral justification is a matter of trying to persuade someone, often discursively, to see things in the right way, where a well-developed competency for discerning moral properties and for using moral concepts helps to delimit what is

---

[59] Dancy (1993, 113).

right.[60] What is crucial for these views is to describe the situation under the relevant concepts and to relate the descriptions achieved to each other so as to reveal mutual interconnections and overall import. What is *not* important is establishing the law-like nature of one's actions or lawful connections between the morality of one's actions and a particular state of circumstances.[61]

These are accounts broadly Aristotelian in spirit. They are useful springboards for reconsidering just how Aristotle does conceive of rules and moral principles and the role they play in moral reasoning, and moral practice, in general. Such considerations are especially important for our dialogue between Aristotle and Kant.

As has been routinely noted, Aristotle's discussion of practical reasoning in the ethical treatises or elsewhere, for that matter, never focuses specifically on the moral case. His examples are typically of ordinary practical reasoning, sometimes drawn from problem solving in skills (*technai*), sometimes from more mundane pursuits, such as figuring out how to slake one's thirst or satisfy one's need for a specific kind of clothing. To be sure, the analogy with *technē* is one Aristotle never uncritically embraces, and his own account of practical wisdom is meant to expose some of the critical differences between *technē* and practical wisdom.[62] Too close an analogy, he suggests, leads to running together the notions of production (*poiēsis*) and activity or practice (*praxis*), and with it, the notions of a good product and a good action. A good action (*eupraxia*) (even one of producing a good product) is good only in the particular setting, and one is responsible, to some degree, for understanding the circumstances of one's action. Timing and sensitivity to the particulars are crucial. Being an expert cabinetmaker, in contrast, does not require one to aim at a

---

[60] From Little (forthcoming).

[61] In challenging noncognitivists, particularists are eager to deny that there are hard-edged rules in ethics that can establish definitional mappings between moral and nonmoral properties. Their particularism is often a denial of the fact–value distinction. The debate between noncognitivists and cognitivists about the need to ground values in independent facts is obviously not one that concerns Aristotle or motivates *his* interest in particularism.

[62] See NE VI.5.

moving target in quite the same way.[63] Still, the analogy with *technē* is a starting point for Aristotle, as it is for Socrates and Plato before him, for a discussion of practical reasoning and competency in practical matters. If we assume, on Aristotle's part, some degree of reliance on the analogy, then his remarks in the opening pages of the *Metaphysics* about the role of general principles in *technē* may be a place to begin to understand their possible role in virtue:

> Experience seems to be very similar to scientific understanding [*epistēmē*] and skill [*technē*], but really scientific understanding and skill come to persons through experience; for experience made skill, as Polus says, speaking well, but inexperience made luck. And skill arises, when from many ideas gained by experience one universal judgment about similar things is produced [*mia katholou genētai peri tōn homoiōn hupolēpsis*]. For to have a judgment that when Callias is sick with this disease this benefited him, and similarly so with Socrates and also in the many individual cases, this is experience. But to judge that it has benefited all such persons with these symptoms, marking them off in one case, being sick with this disease this helps, such as in the case of phlegmatic or cholic persons burning with fever, this is skill . . . experience is knowledge of individuals, skill of universals [*tōn katholou*].[64]

The claim here is that medical skill, as opposed to a mere knack or lucky guess, is a matter of grasping a reliable pattern between the manifestation of a certain disease in individuals and the value of a particular cure. Skill is not just a matter of seeing the discrete cases – grasping what worked for Callias and also grasping what worked for Socrates. Rather, it is a matter of taking the next step – of inductively arriving at some general pattern from the particular cases that has predictive value for future cases. Since, on Aris-

---

[63] See Sarah Broadie (1991, 209) for discussion of the contrasts. Julia Annas (1993) has argued that the salvageable part of the analogy is that virtue, like a genuine skill, has a kind of intellectual structure. The expert can give an account (or *logos*) of what she does, in a way that the person who has a mere knack cannot.

[64] Meta. 981a1–16, my translation.

totle's view, skill can lead to scientific understanding, presumably the grasp of correlations may be a step toward a more substantive understanding of what mechanisms account for the effectiveness of specific cures for specific diseases.

Aristotelian rules of this sort have been thought of as *post facto* summaries of experience.[65] Similarities between cases are recognized and put under a single summary formulation (a rule), which becomes a shorthand for dealing with like cases in the future. As selective summaries of past experience, they presumably yield to more adequate summaries as the dissonances and novelties of new experience require. Elsewhere, Aristotle raises familiar problems about the impossibility of viewing rules as complete codifications of relevant cases. But for the moment we might note that even here, despite Aristotle's suggestion that there could be a universal judgment linking particular symptoms with a treatment, he never goes on to say that the competent doctor takes it to be a major premise in a deductive proof. Rather, his thought is simply this: that if we are to think of simple experience as a disjointed, serial taking in of individual cases, then we can think of a more skilled kind of experience as a competency in seeing patterns of relevant similarities and differences. To talk about universals is to draw attention to that competency without saying much about what it involves. The universal is simply a place holder to note that the expert *has* a recognitional competence that enables him to see and understand in a way that the inexperienced person or lucky guesser cannot. It is not a commitment to an absolute rule. It is, of course, true that Aristotle has little urge to express the Wittgensteinian point that the person competent in concepts simply "knows how to go on." But on the other hand, there is no obvious attraction to the picture Wittgensteinians are eager to criticize – that rule following is a matter of inexorably moving along rails that exist independently of the activity of the practice.[66] Aristotle will go on to claim in this passage that part of the competence of a skilled person is that she

<hr>

65 See Nussbaum (1978, essay 4; 1985) for discussion of this use of rules in Aristotle's account.
66 McDowell (1981, 145–46).

can transmit her skill through teaching and discourse. "It is a sign of the person who knows, that he can teach."[67] But significantly, he doesn't say what that teaching involves – in particular, to what degree it will involve rules or explanation or example. Presumably, once shorthand summaries (or rules of thumb) have been formulated in a certain area, these summaries can be passed on to apprentices as tools for their own practice. Still, Aristotle is tentative about just how much emphasis he wants to give to summary rules, even in the context of *technē* where rules may seem initially more formulatable than they are in ethics.

The passage just quoted from the *Metaphysics* leaves to the side Aristotle's well-known insistence on the variability of experience (so clear in the case of living well, where the "field of expertise" becomes the whole of life), and the consequent impossibility of codifying it by anything like exhaustive and comprehensive rules. This is a central theme of the *Nicomachean Ethics*, repeated in the familiar methodological caution against seeking a precision at the theoretical level inappropriate to the complexity of the subject matter. Ethical theory, on the Aristotelian view, is always a form of practical ethics. The ultimate concern is wise judgment about the particular case, not theoretical systematization or modeling for its own sake. Any theoretical refinement of normative ends is for the purpose of practice – as in the case of his own theory, to provide a "knowledge of the good that will have great influence on our lives. Like archers who have some target (*skopos*) to aim at, with this knowledge we shall be more likely to hit upon what is right."[68]

> But this must be agreed upon beforehand, that the whole account of practical matters must be given in outline (in type) and not precisely, just as we said at the outset that the accounts we demand must be in accordance with the subject matter: matters concerned with action and expediency have no fixity, any more than matters of health. And when our general account is of this nature, the account of particular cases is even more lacking in exactness; for they do not fall under any *technē* or set of pre-

[67] Meta. 981b9.
[68] NE 1094a22–24, my translation; cf.EE 1214b8.

cepts [*hupo paraggelian*], but the agents themselves must in each case examine what is appropriate to the occasion, as happens also in the art of medicine or of navigation.[69]

Here Aristotle is intent to distance both medical art and ethics from the oversimplifying and decontextualizing effects of hard-edged rules. His focus is on the difference context makes to what is relevant and, given the variability of context, the inherent limitation of viewing past cases as having clear predictive value. Still, it is important to recognize that Aristotle does not reject the role of rules altogether. Ethical competence will involve some push toward generalism, in the form of a grasp of principles that hold "for the most part."

> Our discussion will be adequate if its clarity matches the subject matter. For we should not seek exactness in all accounts alike, any more than we do in the products of different crafts. And fine and just actions, which political theory investigates, exhibit difference and fluctuation, so that it seems they exist only by convention, and not by nature. And goods also exhibit a similar sort of fluctuation because they cause harm to many people. For it has happened that some have been destroyed because of their wealth, and others because of their bravery. Thus we must be content, in speaking about and from such things, to indicate the truth roughly and in outline, and we must be content in speaking about things that hold for the most part [*hōs epi to polu*] and in drawing conclusions of the same sort from such things.[70]

The passage is suggestive but in need of interpretation. How are we to conceive of "for the most part" rules? Can we reconcile these less than absolute but nonetheless general rules, with the particularist's suspicion that rule formation is, on the whole, at odds with a narrative process of appreciating the shape of circumstances?

A natural way to read Aristotle's notion of "for the most part" rules is as a claim about what usually or generally holds, where the content of the claim is itself reasonably general and unspec-

---

[69] NE 1104a1–9, my translation.   [70] NE 1094b13–22, my translation.

ified with regard to full circumstances. In this sense, it is a rule of thumb, perhaps like "generally, facing the enemy is courageous" or "generally, giving to those more needy than oneself is an act of generosity." If we like, we can think of it as a correlation, which falls well short of entailment, between a thick moral property (represented by a virtuous state) and a particular action in generally conceived circumstances.[71] The qualification "for the most part" makes it clear that Aristotle means to deny that any action which is a matter of facing the enemy is necessarily courageous or, again, that because facing the enemy is morally relevant in one case (for determining courageousness), it will necessarily have the same relevance wherever it occurs. With regard to the first case, other factors can prevail; with regard to the second, relevance is always bound to context.[72]

These are negative points. But what more can we say positively about these kinds of "for the most part" rules? Aristotle does not further elaborate, but if we pursue the idea that the qualifying phrase means "usually" or "generally," then there might be some broad appeal to statistical or probabilistic evidence to support the claim – not in the sense that someone who says, "generally, to face the enemy is courageous" actually intends to establish her claim that way, but simply that it is frequency that she has in mind. Alternatively, "for the most part" rules might invoke a slightly different notion – that facing the enemy is a *typical* or *characteristic* example of being courageous, and that as such, in suitable circumstances this kind of action can be morally important. I think either suggestion captures the spirit of Aristotle's views. His point is that certain kinds of actions and circumstances generally or characteristically have moral importance and that we learn this sort of information from experience and go on to use it in future practice. While it is true any action (or property) can take on moral significance given a suitable context, Aristotle wants to say some sorts of actions or properties tend to be more commonly

[71] In contemporary noncognitivist–cognitivist debates, the discussion focuses on the possibility of a mapping between moral (thick or thin) and nonmoral properties. Aristotle is not interested in the fact–value distinction which that implies.

[72] See Dancy here (1993, 69).

morally important, others are paradigmatic in our minds when we think of what counts as courage and the like.[73]

In a certain way Aristotle does establish stronger rules. For at a more theoretic level, he will go on to suggest that each of the individual virtues is required for good living (on a version of the Unity of Virtue doctrine) and each is always correlated with certain spheres of experience – for instance, courage with the fear of important damages and losses, temperance with bodily appetites and their pleasures, or generosity with the stewardship of one's personal property where others are concerned.[74] (That is, courage always has to do with fear of loss, not, obviously, that all occasions of fear of loss will be courageous.) Even here, according to his view, to say certain virtues are required is simply to say certain *ends* are required, leaving wide latitude (now to borrow from Kantian terminology) as to the specific circumstances under which they are finely exercised and no fixed rankings among ends. It is a way of saying that "in your overall conception of good living, these must be among your commitments." This is to be distinguished from laying down prescriptive or proscriptive rules of action ("always tell the truth," "never intentionally deceive") that bring with them misleading assumptions about uniformity of context and, in the absence of antecedent priority rankings among them, stalemate as to how to sort out conflict.

While "for the most part" rules can be thought of as giving some common or characteristic examples of the circumstances in which required ends can be finely realized, they don't go substantially beyond that. To say they are even presumptive rules seems too strong. If anything, like the *endoxa* or received opinions that begin the dialectical process, they are an invitation to further discussion and qualification. They are starting points and illustrations of virtue more than hard-and-fast specifications of it. Indeed, the more stable Aristotelian commitment is to porous ends of virtue, though these may often be best grasped by various instantiations. Characteristic of ends is a plasticity that allows for

---

[73] For further discussion of "what happens for the most part" (*hōs epi to polu*) claims in the context of the Poet., see D. Frede (1992).

[74] For this list of correlations, see Nussbaum (1988a, 35–36).

sensitivity to the demands of context. To capture context requires a careful narrative of the overall landscape of a case in a way that highlights salient features. But still, suspicions may linger. Why isn't describing a case and pointing out something as salient still simply an intuitive settling of the case? What is the rational basis for seeing certain features *as salient*? If someone else doesn't see those features as salient, then is there nothing more to say to her other than that she is missing something important, that, in a sense, she is blind? Put differently, if in choosing reflectively, the Aristotelian strives toward a grasp of the whole of good living in terms of the connection of actions to more general ends and the mutual fit of general ends with each other, how can merely describing a case give one a rational argument for what to do? I think it can if the narrative process itself is viewed as helping to elaborate and specify general ends to which we are committed and as building mutual support among those ends.[75] So conceived, deliberation will involve a narrative of circumstances *as well as* a specification of ends. Both elements are implicit. An example should help. After much reflection and internal conflict, I have decided to give away a considerable amount of my moderate savings to a very close friend, who has become destitute after a sudden illness prevented her from working for a year and costly medical expenses wiped out her savings. My friend has two young children, and without my help and in light of new governmental social policies, she would have had to put them in foster care. I defend my decision to a critic (my alter ego) by saying, but look, I am well fed, have ample amount for the future, and no dependents to worry about. Moreover, I have enough to carry me through calamities of the sort that befell my friend. In contrast, my friend has other mouths to feed and no resources. True, the generous gesture means that I will probably have to alter the amount I am able to put into savings for the next years, and perhaps even work a year longer than I had anticipated. As such,

---

[75] I am relying here on Richardson's model of specification (1990, 1994), which draws on the notion of Rawls's wide reflective equilibrium. In proposing a hybrid narrative–specification model, I view myself as melding elements of Dancy's and Richardson's accounts.

I have to revise my long-term financial plan. But in so doing I don't see myself as acting imprudently, though I know the sorts of sacrifices that I am prepared to make I would have thought of as imprudent were I to think about my well-being more abstractly, and independently of this very case. Now, the point is that in describing the circumstances to myself, I am not simply seeing certain features as important in this context – that it is my friend who suffered a tragedy, that she has dependents, that I don't, that I am a healthy and steady earner, that I still can find ways to save, and so on. In addition, I see these as important in light of their bearing on my more general ends of prudential self-regard and generosity. My discourse implicitly includes that appeal. I examine the circumstances and talk my way through them, this way and then that, in order to figure out how and if I can be generous without financially crippling myself. In narrating this, I am simultaneously specifying those more general ends of prudence and generosity. Through the narrative I come to appreciate that generosity toward close friends can admit of certain sacrifices that still support a prudential sense of self-regard. Without appealing to some antecedent ranking among virtues, the conflict is settled by a specification benefiting from the considerations that emerge in a narrative process. The model is a hybrid of narrative and specification that takes seriously the rich context of our choices as well as the pull from more general values and formulations. The leading point is that what is salient may be contextual, but never free of appeal to more general or deeper values (albeit mutable) that help explain why something is important. Short of that appeal, contextual salience works in a vacuum. It is little better than intuition.

We have said that on the Aristotleian view there are no ranking orderings among ethical virtues and no absolute rules. But a few qualifications are in order. On some well-respected interpretations, the life of intellectual virtue, expressed in contemplation, ranks more highly than the life devoted to virtues of character, collectively characterized by a sense of general justice.[76] Equally,

---

[76] See Kraut (1989) for this view, but note also his rejection of a maximizing rule

though Aristotle doesn't have available the modern distinction Kant relies on between perfect and imperfect duties, or the presumptive rules perfect duties carry with them of "always" or "never" performing some action, he does single out adultery, theft, and murder as actions that can never be right (they never admit of a "mean").[77] But on my view, these qualifications do not mar the overall picture. "Generally and characteristically," Aristotelian virtuous action is conceived not as a matter of applying rules, but as a working out of ends in highly variable circumstances. Even on the view that contemplative activity is most highly valued, honoring that rank difference need not amount to following either a maximizing or a preemptive rule.

We have suggested that ethical rules of thumb are part of a web of background knowledge that gives us some clues and pointers as to how ends can be realized. There are other roles that rules serve in moral practice. Although Aristotle does not discuss these, we can supplement as follows. One would think rules would play a considerable role in the teaching of virtue, as a preliminary setting out of paradigms and examples but also as a way of verbalizing and bringing to mind the ends of virtue important in conduct – as in, "take care that you are temperate in your life" or "don't neglect generosity to others," "be kind even to those whom you don't like," and so on. These are rule-like setting of ends, rules of thumb – no more, but no less. Their point is to remind us of what can be important in suitable settings. They can serve as cajolings to the ethically immature, but also as self-exhortations to the relatively virtuous who also need occasional

---

as a way of "honoring" the importance of that rank difference in choices of action.

[77] NE 1107a11–12. In this context, it is worth noting that John McDowell's (1979) contemporary conception of virtue also does not seem to avail itself of the modern perfect–imperfect distinction. When McDowell speaks of "virtue imposing a requirement" (p. 26), he implies that an agent who perceives the appropriateness of certain ends on certain occasions *must* act to fulfill those ends. In contrast, an imperfect duty of virtue leaves latitude for an agent to act on some but not all of the occasions in which he perceives an end to be appropriate. On this last interpretation of Kant, see Hill (1971) and Baron (1995). I take up some of these issues in Chapter 8.

reminders in order to keep focused or resolute. (Here one might think of Seneca's exhortations to self upon the close of each day.) None of this is to deny that the exhortative power of rules is often wrapped up in the messenger who delivers them. Aristotle is eager to endorse this sort of point as evidenced in the pivotal role he ascribes to the *phronimos* as an embodiment of virtue, and, too, in the important role he ascribes to attachment relations to such a person and to the virtuous in general.[78] But it still needs to be emphasized that a rule may itself be a prod and guide for action.

Not all Aristotelian rules resist the deductivist aspiration. The tension between a particularist acknowledgment of the variability of circumstances and the aspiration for a deductive system of rules is nowhere clearer than in the law. Public order and stable expectation in social transactions push toward a rule-bound notion of adjudication; the variability in cases extinguishes all hope for a complete codification that would support deduction.

> In those cases, then, in which it is necessary to speak universally [*katholou*], but not possible to do so correctly [*orthōs*], the law takes the usual case [*to hōs epi to pleon*], though it is not ignorant of the error being made. But it is none the less correct; for the error is not in the law nor in the legislator but in the nature of the thing, since the matter of practical affairs is of this kind from the start.[79]

Aristotle adds to this in the *Rhetoric* that even if laws were to be formulated conditionally with bountiful hedging, any list of restrictions would still be an incomplete codification. Law "cannot be complete owing to the endless, possible cases"; "a lifetime would be too short to enumerate all of these."[80]

In *Nicomachean* V, the deductive aspiration is relaxed by an appeal to a method of equity (*epieikeia*) that relies on careful case-by-case inspection: "equity is better than the error resulting from

---

[78] See Rhet. II.4, 6, and 11 for a discussion of identificatory emotions, such as love, shame, and emulation, and their role in the transmission of values.
[79] NE 1137b14–19. For further discussion, see Sherman (1989, 13–22).
[80] Rh. 1374a33–35.

the rule being stated unconditionally."[81] However, Aristotle is quite clear that equity does not fully sidestep law. It still must take into account the legislative intention, considering "what the legislator would have said himself, had he been present there, and what he would have prescribed, had he known, in his legislation."[82] In this sense, equity is not a rejection of law but a "rectification of the law insofar as the universality of the law makes it deficient."[83] Still, it is a rejection of a deductive model of decision making in a practical domain in which the aspiration to use such a model is strong.

There is an obvious need for law in the public domain, however flexibly it is to be conceived. Civic governance requires public, written and unwritten, custom (*nomos*) to which citizenry can stably appeal. Equally, public governance requires the sanctions that law imposes and the impersonality of a source of rule that is separate from the will and whim of a ruler. All these are factors Aristotle well recognizes.[84] These contribute to the deductive drive. The model is less compelling from the start in the area of ethics. For one, it would be peculiar to think of the person of practical wisdom as correcting for deficiencies in some partial codification of virtue in the manner of the equity judge. To have practical wisdom is just to have virtue internalized in a non-codified way. However helpful moral rules of thumb, Aristotle doesn't think of them as expandable into explicitly statable rules or, in the absence of such rules, linked to a capacity that is analogous to following explicitly statable rules.[85] Nor does he think we make moral judgments by using some corrective notion of legislative intention. Here we might say that Aristotelian virtue ethics is

---

[81] NE 1137b24–5, my translation; 1137b9, also 1138a1–3; see Rh. 1374b18–22, 1374a30.

[82] NE 1137b23, Irwin translation; cf. Rh. 1374b11–13. I use the term "legislative intention" without implying the connotations it bears today of a narrow reading of the law.

[83] NE 1137b26–7, Irwin translation; see Nussbaum (1993) on equity and mercy in Stoic ethics and contemporary courts.

[84] See, for example, Pol. 1269a8–22.

[85] See McDowell (1981, 146).

275

simply not a legalistic ethics requiring the interpretation of law and tradition, in the way, say, Judaic ethics is.

6 THE PRACTICAL SYLLOGISM REVISITED

A discussion of the rationality of practical judgment in Aristotelian ethics would be incomplete without some mention of Aristotle's notion of the practical syllogism. Whereas many have viewed the syllogism as suggesting a deductive model of the application of norms, I believe this is misleading and that a more plausible interpretation supports the narrative–specification model illustrated in the earlier example. But I warn that my remarks are selective and brief. There is an extensive literature on the practical syllogism that includes considerable exegetical work and linkage with a wide range of topics in the philosophy of action. I cannot survey those discussions here.[86] My limited point is to show how we might plausibly see the broad lines of the syllogism as limning the narrative–specificatory process we took up earlier.

Through the notion of the practical syllogism, Aristotle proffers a now famous way of thinking about choice that makes explicit reference to desire and belief as starting points (premises) for deliberation.[87] Paradigmatically, the practical syllogism represents the moment of deliberative inquiry, where genuine questions arise about what to do.[88] Reason seeks an argument for what to do.[89] Though often the syllogism is cast as a justification for an action already decided upon, or alternatively as a way of *getting to* an action from fixed objectives and a fixed assessment of circumstances, on my view the syllogism represents practical ar-

---

[86] See, e.g., Annas (1993), Broadie (1991), Charles (1984), Cooper (1975), Dahl (1984), Kenny (1979), Nussbaum (1978, essay 4). For important criticisms of the syllogistic model, see Richardson (1994).

[87] In addition, he may also be saying desire and belief are components into which any final choice of action is analyzable. This interpretation may be particularly appropriate in thinking about animal action, where there is clearly no potential for deliberation. Broadie's remarks (1991, 232) are helpful here.

[88] "Deliberation is a particular kind of inquiry. . . . He who deliberates inquires and calculates." NE 1142a31-b2.

[89] My remarks in this paragraph have been influenced by Broadie (1991, 226–32).

gument in a more robust and fluid sense. It is not primarily a movement to a conclusion or, in reverse direction, to premises from a conclusion, but a more encompassing argument about how to understand objectives and the particular circumstances one faces so that a choice is rational. The work is not in drawing what follows from assembled premises, but in assembling those premises – in understanding what lies before one and what the nature of one's commitments are so that a practical choice is grounded.

Still, focusing on this aspect of the model leaves to the side many issues that a fuller account would want to answer. So it has been objected that there is the peculiarity of constructing an argument that moves to action rather than, say, to an intention or decision to act where the latter marks resolve rather than actual success in the world.[90] Just as problematic, some would hold, is moving to an intention from a desire (and belief) rather than from an antecedent intention. That is, is a desire the sort of thing that can carry one to an intention? For we can have all sorts of desires for things that are far removed from an interest in action. Equally, too, one can raise questions about the plausibility of separating belief from desire in a way that might imply that desire, on its own, can be free of evaluative and cognitive elements. That is, do I do well to conceive of a desire to drink as only externally structured by certain evaluations – such that it should be a drink that does not already belong to someone else or does not taste repulsive? Or has my desire in many cases already evolved so as to internally embed those sort of evaluative elements?[91] Does the notion of separate belief and desire premises encourage an artificial distinction that Aristotle himself would on consideration want to reject? I shall have to bracket these debates and others in order to focus on the narrower topic of how, and if, the practical

---

[90] See the *De Motu Animalium* formulation of the conclusion: "at once one acts." Aristotle's unified account of animal and human action is probably the cause for thinking of choice as immediate.

[91] I am grateful for Barbara Herman putting the question this way in an unpublished paper, "Making Room for Character in Kantian Ethics." This, of course, is the debate that appears in Rep. IV (426ff.), in Plato's questioning of Socrates' assumption that all desire must be for some apparent good.

syllogism, as an account of the rationality of practical choice, coheres with Aristotle's stress elsewhere on practical judgment (and choice) as a matter of seeing. Does the syllogism give us a way of expanding upon that notion of seeing that deflects some of the criticism of it as merely intuitionistic? Can we see it as lending support to the narrative–specification model suggested earlier?

Before beginning, though, there are a few preliminaries. First we need to keep in mind that Aristotle never offers explicit examples of practical syllogisms involving moral choice. Whereas Kant selects as maxims for theoretical consideration those that raise explicit problems for moral permissibility (e.g., false promising, failure of mutual aid) and thinks of moral justification as a variety of practical reasoning distinct from prudence,[92] Aristotle never takes up a notion of *moral* justification per se. Granted, he holds that cleverness and mere practical calculation are not the same as the practical wisdom required for morally fine living.[93] Practical wisdom, unlike those other cognitive activities, requires virtue and true or good starting points (*archai*).[94] Even so, Aristotle has no interest in representing the moral reasoning that might be part of practical wisdom in a formulaic way; to be wise is to reason and judge well in an ordinary way that characterizes practice in general. Moral content may be distinctive, but not method. It is, of course, true that practical wisdom is about the whole of one's life, not just some part; the reasoning must be global, not narrowly technical or split off from important pockets of experience. But while this will make such reasoning considerably complex, it will not be different in kind from more ordinary varieties of practical reasoning. This may go some way toward explaining why Aristotle does not single out moral reasoning as a special case deserving of special examples.

Second, again to mark a break with our modern expectations, Aristotle views the account of action that he offers as a *common* account, with application to all animals, humans and beasts alike.[95] To be sure, beasts will have more primitive forms of cognition and desire than are ascribed to us, but on Aristotle's view,

---

[92] See especially Rel. 26n/21n for a succinct statement of this.
[93] NE 1142b5.   [94] NE 1144a31–36.   [95] MA 698a4.

animals do not move in the world merely by instinct and blind drive. In some fashion or other they represent goods to themselves. As Aristotle puts it, the objects of their desire are at once objects of thought.[96] *Orexis* is object-directed. However, the unified account can be the cause of considerable misunderstanding. For in taking up the parallel with animals, Aristotle is forced to leave to the side much of the interesting detail about human practical argument – for instance, that practical argument need result not in immediate action but in future indexed intentions;[97] that practical argument is not a simple, linear movement but a discursive process that works out saliences and assesses the viability of different alternative means; that acting on objectives requires a reiterative process by which those objectives are sharpened and their connection with other ends clarified. There may be other reasons for the oversimplification,[98] but whatever they are, I think Aristotle's simplified model can be easily plumped up to capture the important lines of deliberative enterprise.[99]

As is often noted, Aristotle's examples of practical syllogisms fall into two varieties: some are cases in which the major premise represents a universal deontic premise and the working out is conceived of as a case of rule application on a deductive model (e.g., "whenever someone thinks that everyman should take walks, he is a man, at once he takes a walk").[100] Others are cases where the major premise is about a good or end that is sought (hence, the premise of "the good");[101] the minor premise is a working out of constitutive or productive means[102] that help to

96 MA 700b24.
97 See Bratman's (1987) interesting work on intentions as plans.
98 Though I am not persuaded by Broadie's defense (1991, 231) that if we were to give too much detail about what is relevant in the case, "one might well wonder whether those to whom the explanation is offered could understand it at all."
99 For some earlier thoughts about a more robust model, see Sherman (1989, ch. 3).
100 MA 701a13–14; also DA 434a16–21 and NE 1147a24–31.
101 MA 701a25.
102 There has been an extensive literature defending the view that deliberation is not restricted to means–end reasoning but also can involve deliberation about ends. Involved here would be specification and revision of ends, as

bring about the end in these or anticipated circumstances (hence, the premise of the "possible"). (The whole syllogism would take the form: "I have to drink," . . . "Here's drink," . . . "At once he drinks.")[103] On this latter model, action is explained by reasons that include a desire and belief or perception. Given Aristotle's general skepticism about viewing ethical choice as application that follows a deductivist model, it makes sense to suppose that the second model reflects his more considered views about the movement between generalist and particularist poles.

Generally speaking, it is the minor premise that locates what is salient in the circumstances – that there is something suitably potable here, that I am a person for whom taking a walk would apply or, more interestingly for our purposes, that these are circumstances which call for courage of this kind, toward this person, involving these sorts of resources, delivered in this sort of way. As we said earlier, it is strained to think of evolved desires as shorn of all such evaluations. My desire to drink, under most circumstances, is simply a desire for drink that doesn't taste nasty. In a more extensive way, the *bouleseis,* or rational wishes for ends that figure in the major premises of ethical reasoning, will already be considerably specified and cognitively rich. The minor premise carries information about present circumstances that helps to refine those ends further so that they bear appropriately on the specific case. Thus, a desire to be generous may already embed certain evaluations (e.g., that generosity does not involve first stealing from others, or too great a depletion of one's own resources, etc.), but just what constitutes "too great a depletion of one's resources" when it comes to a particular action requires that

well as deliberation about their constitution. The more inclusive view relies on a more literal translation of the phrase standardly translated as "means." The phrase is – *ta pros ta telē*, literally, "the things with regard to the end. " I have defended the view (Sherman 1989, 86–94). For important discussions, see Allan (1977), Irwin (1975), Sorabji (1980), Wiggins (1980). A most succinct statement of the point is made by the Stoic Arius Didymus (Stobaeus 2.72, 4–5): As he puts it, some goods are "productive" (*poiētika*) of an end such as happiness, others "fill it up" (*sumplērousi*). For an excellent account Aristotelian in spirit, see Richardson (1994).

103 MA 701a32–33. Or again, "I need a covering; a cloak is a covering. I need a cloak." MA 701a17–18; also 701a16–17.

that objective be specified through the exigencies of the case. In understanding the demands of the case, certain factors may stand out, but they stand out as part of a more general landscape that aims to capture the situation.

Here we begin to see the link between the practical syllogism and our earlier discussion of the deliberative process as including a narrative and specificatory component. In the case of reasoning occasioned by genuine practical quandary, the objectives that figure in the major premises of a practical argument are dynamically understood as commitments to be refined, revised, and sharpened (i.e., specified) by reference to the relevant details that emerge from a careful narration of the circumstances. The narrative, too, is conceived dynamically and dialectically, as a way of discursively understanding what is important or salient in the particular context *and* in the context of ongoing values and commitments. Certain saliences may be a matter of immediate attunement, others arrived at more slowly, with the help, perhaps, of the eyes of friends. Still other saliences emerge only by more careful reflection from the top down, by focusing on normative ends whose importance got buried in the details of the case or in a more culpable distortion. One is forced to take a harder and more honest look at one's initial sizing up, guarding against easy rationalizations and defenses. Of course, not all of life's moments give one the leisure for this back-and-forth motion in moral judgment. Nor would it be a fine thing always to have to rely on it. Some right choices ought not require too much consideration. Mature sensitivities must in many cases replace more cumbersome reasoning. Practice and habituation, and the steady work of trying to integrate the ends of virtues with the full range of one's desires, emotions, and habits of perception, all are ways the Aristotelian agent prepares for ultimately getting it right. But it would be a mistake to think any of this happens overnight, and a mistake to think that the virtuous person is ever without deliberative challenges.[104]

---

[104] See Annas's view (1993, 93) that the syllogism (and discussions of it in NE III) depict an early stage of moral reasoning, whereas the discussions in NE VI about practical insight and perception point to a more mature stage of practi-

The virtues of the narrative–specificatory process may begin to emerge. Insofar as narration is not simply a balance sheet of weighted factors, but an organizing of them with descriptive and nuanced detail, the relevant factors may already produce something of an argument that can be persuasive and hold together coherently. There is a way of stacking up and framing the story that matters. But that the descriptions reveal something salient – in the preceding example, that my friend has mouths to feed and I don't, or that I am still a healthy wage earner with ample income to save – is in part due to their appeal to more general concepts, such as generosity and prudence. Narrative – to have rational bite, to be an explanation of the rationality of an argument – needs to make appeal to more general and deeply held values that are part of the working knowledge of the mature agent. And the force of that appeal is that it impels us to tinker with those general ends – to make them responsive to the new data and responsive to refinement. Through its general and particular premises, the syllogism can be seen as preserving the dialectical movement of particularist and generalist poles in practical argument – a dialectic too easily obscured when we think only about narrative from a particularist's point of view or only about the application of ends from a more generalist's perspective. It restores some of the depth of reasons and justificatory resources the practically wise and sensitive agent has available to her.

As we prepare to shift our attention to Kant, it is significant to note that whatever limited role Aristotle does give to rules, it is not as a way of implementing the value of impartiality. The notion of turning one's choices into laws or rules one can follow at the same time others do is simply not something that strikes Aristotle as a part of virtuous practice or its theoretical conception. He sees neither the objectivity of reason as forcing that sort of formal move – that is, that what is reason for me is a reason for others similarly circumstanced – nor the content of our moral life as echoing that thought – that as a moral agent I see myself as one

cal reasoning, characteristic of the *phronimos*. I have been arguing that there is less of a division of labor here than she detects.

among others. An impartial perspective of that sort is simply not one that Aristotle has any aspiration to voice.

But how damaging is the absence of this conception? The absence of a procedural check on self-exemption does not mean that Aristotelian ethics neglects the importance of other-regard. Altruism is an inbuilt, internal part of particular virtues, such as generosity, kindness, magnanimity, and, in many cases, courage. More generally, an Aristotelian agent simply fails in her virtue if she uses altruistic regard merely instrumentally, to redound to honor or a priggish sense of *to kalon*. Indeed, Aristotelian eudaimonism is misconstrued if it is thought to be little more than a version of ethical egoism. Aristotelian ethical theory may begin with the primacy of self and one's own *eudaimonia,* but the content of *eudaimonia* is never simply one's own good.

Still, the Kantian is arguing not simply for the importance of impartiality as a part of the moral view, but for its fundamental place in all moral judgment. The structure of moral judgment is this: Insofar as a rational agent is constrained by reason's own standards, that agent is constrained by every rational agent's own standards. The community of reason is established around the moral law. But in addition, Kant maintains that reason's standards constitute an abstract procedure by which we can, depending upon the particular interpretation, generate background normative principles and/or deliberate about actions in particular cases. Aristotle does not view reason as providing any such procedures. The moral perspective remains embodied in good character. In the next chapter we turn to Kant, and consider in what sense practical reason is a legislative capacity.[105]

[105] I wish to express thanks to Alisa Carse, Maggie Little, Mark Lance, and Henry Richardson for conversations about ideas in this chapter. I am also grateful to the members of the Georgetown–University of Maryland moral psychology reading group for the helpful discussion of a draft of this paper in October 1995.

Chapter 7

Making room for practical wisdom in Kantian ethics

The last chapter discussed the notion of Aristotelian particularism, so called because of Aristotle's clear emphasis on moral judgment as a matter of assessing the particulars of a situation. Particularist theories, such as Aristotle's, have often been labeled intuitionistic, the tag bearing the implicit charge that focus on the particulars is incompatible with appeal to more general grounds or rules through which one's deliberation can be checked, and that such focus is characterized by an immediacy of discernment that bypasses discursive capacities. In the last chapter I countered both these charges.

First, despite Aristotle's own caution about reliance on rules, they nonetheless play a limited role in his theory, as summary guides that inform perception as well as heuristics and exhortatives useful for the practice of morality. What they are not, however, is either comprehensive or determinately guiding. As such, Aristotelian rules do not take the form of universal generalizations from which particular directives deductively follow. Rather, to the extent to which norms implicit in the virtues can be expressed by rules, those rules are qualified by the locution "for the most part" (*hōs epi to polu*). They hold generally and characteristically, but with no presumption that they will obtain across all conceivable cases. Even so, Aristotle more typically thinks of norms embodied in commitments to ends – "to be temperate," "to be courageous" – with latitude as to the circumstances of fulfillment.

Second, discerning the particulars often conjures up a notion of "cottoning on" to the salient features of circumstances in a direct and immediate way. But I have argued that within Aristotle's theory recognitional capacities are better thought of as continuous with discursive and deliberative capacities. We can see this most clearly in the case of hard choices, where understanding a situation may require active conceptual work, with reflection and dialogue as to just what the morally salient features of our circumstances and intentions are. Of course, there may be many cases of routine choices where there is little that causes conflict or puzzlement; here discernment may be more or less immediate. We may perceive things quite readily under appropriate classifications and evaluations, as well as grasp their relative importance. But even so, Aristotle's notion is that the person of practical wisdom is *ultimately* reflective, moved to understand both the specifics in light of the broadest and most integrating understanding of deeper values, and those deeper values in light of the concrete cases that specify them. Thus, certain situations may not present an intrinsically deliberative challenge or simply may not give one the time (as on the battlefield) to make it such an occasion. Yet, in the way that battlefield choices seem to live with soldiers long after those choices are made, choices made with immediacy can often open rather than settle discursive understanding. There is "potential discursiveness" in the choice.[1]

While rules may play a limited role in Aristotelian theory, one specific function they do not have is that of vehicles that connect us to a community of other reasoning agents. They are not thought of as ways we get beyond our own point of view to a viewpoint that others could take up. The following Kantian idea that captures the kernel of morality – that it requires "the thought to occur to [a person] (he can scarcely avoid doing so) of what sort of world he would create, under the guidance of practical reason, were such a thing in his power, a world into which, moreover, he would place himself as a member"[2] – is thoroughly foreign to Aristotle. Thus, Aristotelian rules are neither universal general-

[1] The term is Henry Richardson's (1994, 33).
[2] Rel. 5/5.

285

izations nor universalized forms of an agent's choice. True, rules, ends, and most especially the overall, integrated conception of the good life that is the ultimate end of Aristotelian practical reflection represent a constant pull toward a more discursive understanding of our practical lives, and in the best of cases, there will be a social aspect to this discourse; typically, it will take the form of shared discourse among intimate friends about living the good life. But I emphasize now that this mode of reflection (even its more social variety) is not conceived of as a process by which we check our reasons by those which could be adopted by all others in a community.[3] This is, of course, what Kant introduces in his notion that the form of our good willing must be lawful. To be permissible, the maxims of our willing must be such that other rational agents could (not "would" or "will") act on them. That is, lawfulness is meant broadly to reflect the shared status of our practical reason. The commonsense question "What if everyone were to do that?" points to the Kantian conception of viewing rational agency as constructive of a principle that could hold for other rational agents. This is, of course, expressed in the Categorical Imperative's requirement that maxims have the form of universal law. But so, too, is it expressed in the other formulae of the Categorical Imperative – in the Formula of Autonomy whereby we must view ourselves as the ultimate sources of that law; in the Formula of Humanity, which stipulates how we must treat ourselves and others in virtue of our legislative status; and in the Formula of the Kingdom of Ends, whereby we are to conceive of ourselves as part of a social community in which each person is regarded as an equal and autonomous agent. This notion of practical agency as the font of laws that regulates the pursuit of the good within a community of equal persons is simply not a part of Aristotelian theory.

But several questions arise when we think of practical reason

---

[3] Contrast Aristotle's position on our limited identification with others with Stoic texts in which the boundaries of our connectedness extend outward to include the entire human race: Cicero, Fin. 3.62–8 = L and S 57 F; Hierocles (Stobaeus 4.671, 7–673, 11) = L and S 57 G; cf. Anonymous Commentary on Plato's *Theatetus*, 5.18–6.31 = L and S 57 H.

as a lawmaking capacity. The first question is, does such an emphasis leave room for the idea of practical reason as a capacity for discernment and appraisal of the particulars? Bluntly put, does conceiving of practical judgment as issuing in laws accommodate sufficiently our commonsensical and Aristotelian notion that practical judgment is principally a matter of "judging" the specifics of individual cases? For if we are at all persuaded by the Aristotelian account of practical judgment, then we might worry that that sort of account, with its emphasis on the descriptive and evaluative aspects of judging the interconnected features of a present case, is given short shrift once one's eyes are directed beyond the case to what can be said more generally. The rich contours of the landscape become flattened out in the generalization. But suppose we were to avoid this result by viewing the construction of law not as the creation of universal generalizations, but as a matter of asking, whether others similarly circumstanced could act on my maxim. In other words, one asks if one could endorse the universalized form of one's maxim. The specificity of the maxim would be retained in the thought experiment. Yet even assuming we can universalize a highly specific maxim (a matter we take up shortly), a further question arises as to what we actually learn about the rightness or wrongness of action by asking whether others could act as we do. Presumably, we learn about the wrongness of making an exception of ourselves. But not all cases of exception-making are wrong, as we shall see, and the test may not finely discriminate which ones are and why they are. Nor is exception-making the only way in which any action can be wrong. These remarks point to a far more general question of what role universalizability is to play in the practice of moral judgment. If we assume a mature moral agent will see with a vision deeply informed by moral considerations, then we will want to know what additional work is accomplished by turning the maxim of one's action into a law. An obvious charge is that universalization is otiose, an application of normative standards additional and external to sensitive moral judgment. For if we have judged well the requirements of *this* case, and appreciated what morality requires here and now, then what more do we learn by testing to see if others could so act? Haven't we already done our moral work? Hasn't moral judgment already secured the results we are looking for?

The problem is this: If the Categorical Imperative is viewed as primarily an *external* test by which in hard cases we either prospectively deliberate or retrospectively justify a choice, then its normative role in the routine practical judgments of virtuous agents, which may neither call for prior deliberation or posterior justification, becomes obscured. What might promise greater explanatory power is the view of the Categorical Imperative, or perhaps more accurately, its results, as supplying normative principles that inform routine choice and, we might say, judgment of the particulars. The Categorical Imperative would generate the reasons for a choice as morally choiceworthy. This role would be in addition to whatever role, if any, it may have in actually testing, or deliberating about, a choice. While I think this "background normative view" of the Categorical Imperative goes some way to taking seriously the role of the Categorical Imperative in a Kantian theory of virtue, we need to be careful that it does not slide into a theory of general subsumptive rules that once again minimizes the importance of narrative activity in judging a case. We shall have to see if a Kantian reconstruction can avoid this danger. In addition we shall need to take up the case where judgment is not routine but a matter of deliberation at the actual time of choice and consider just what benefit a formal universalization procedure offers. I shall suggest that deliberation here follows a far less formalized procedure than many Kantian critics and proponents have supposed. In this regard, Kantian practical reasoning may stand somewhat closer to Aristotelian notions of moral discernment and deliberation than we would have initially believed.

There are a number of issues, then, to take up in these coming pages. Among these is the role the Categorical Imperative plays in informing background virtue, and then again its role in deliberation where conflicts and the like unsettle habit and make urgent the question of what is the morally right thing to do. Is the Categorical Imperative a formal procedure in either of these cases? A subsidiary issue will be the nature of maxims as reasons that make intelligible our action.

Practical wisdom in Kantian ethics

1 SOME ROLES FOR THE CATEGORICAL IMPERATIVE

The traditional reading of the Categorical Imperative is that of a procedure that generates duties.[4] Duties, in turn, are typically expressed as rules from which particular directives are deductively derived, given the right factual circumstances. The problems with this sort of strict, rule-based account are conspicuous and were dealt with at length in Chapter 6. Briefly, rules are rigid and noncomprehensive. We simply cannot classify within the content of a rule all the features of situations that may be relevant to application of that rule. This is not to disallow that rules can be used to guide in a general way (especially when supplemented by an adequate account of how we *interpret* rules in light of the particular case), but they cannot be conceived of as imposing strict or absolute obligations. The unattractiveness of this top-down deductive view of duties has led in recent years to the widely accepted view of the Categorical Imperative as a procedure for deliberation.[5] The procedure tests from the bottom-up individually proposed maxims of action. As Kant puts it in the Typic of the second *Critique*, "Ask yourself whether, if the action which you propose should take place by a law of nature of which you yourself were a part, you could regard it as possible through your will. . . . Such a law is . . . a type for the estimation of maxims according to moral principles."[6] The putative advantage of the deliberative conception is that it can take seriously the novel and special features of particular circumstances. For it is the maxim, as responsive to circumstances, that is being assessed.

However responsive the maxim, if we go with the general contemporary trend, then we still go with a picture of moral judgment in which what is most salient is something of a second-

---

[4] See G 421, though note that *The Doctrine of Virtue,* Kant's central text in which duties are enumerated, does not follow the procedure. See Herman's (1993, ch. 7) nice laying out of this generative role as well as the deliberative model we will take up shortly.

[5] The deliberative model has been influentially formulated by Nell (O'Neill) (1975) and by Rawls in unpublished lecture notes.

[6] KpV 70.

order justificatory procedure of asking whether one's actions are permissible, obligatory, or forbidden. We formulate a maxim and then think of the moral apparatus as working outside that discursive formulation. But in many cases moral judgment seems a more internalized process in which the apparatus of the Categorical Imperative already informs and shapes the articulation of maxims. Here, the Categorical Imperative might play something like its more old-fashioned role as generator of standing normative principles that when suitably internalized, can provide background values, informing and shaping moral judgment as well as our construal of the case. Put differently, if the Categorical Imperative is supposed to encapsulate the work of moral conscience, then won't we want its principles to be at work not only when there are deliberative challenges but also when moral judgment is more routine? Shouldn't its principles inform the very evaluative capacities we use in narrating a case and in making a judgment based upon the reasons that that narrative presents?

Along these general lines, Barbara Herman has proposed that the Categorical Imperative enter as part of the background of our moral judgment; not, however, as generative of duties, but as generative of something less rigid – what she calls "deliberative presumptions."[7] These are general principles generated by testing against the Categorical Imperative procedure "generic" maxims of self-interest, such as "deceitful promising for my purposes." (On her interpretation, the maxims we find in the *Groundwork* examples are best thought of as generic maxims.) Deliberative presumptions serve as standing rules against exemptions from self-interest, though they are more supple than rules in that they can be defeated in deliberation by moral considerations embodied in conflicting deliberative presumptions. Such cases represent what Kant calls "conflicting grounds of obligations": we may deliberate about lying to save a life in a way we may not deliberate about lying to promote self-interest. Insofar as deliberative presumptions can be overridden in deliberation by competing moral considerations, they are distinct from actual duties which hold absolutely. Moreover, the notion of a *delibera-*

---

[7] Herman (1993, ch. 7).

tive presumption is meant to bring into relief the idea that conflicts are settled by deliberation and nuanced judgment, not by a deductive application of a rule.

But note, this still leaves to the side important questions of how deliberative presumptions are used to guide in routine cases. Here, too, we would want to avoid a deductive model of rule application with its oversimplification of both general ends and present circumstances. Elsewhere Herman does think of recognitional capacities in terms of "rules of moral salience" that would instruct us about the "sorts of circumstances to which morality requires a response." She suggests that these rules would lack the justificatory weight of deliberative presumptions. But as rules, they still face challenges as to just what their nature is and in what sense they map a correlation between particular features of circumstances and moral responses.

Her notion of deliberative presumptions bear an obvious, close resemblance to Ross's notion of *prima facie* duties. On Ross's view a *prima facie* duty is one that states our actual duty so long as no other *prima facie* duty conflicts with it.[8] On Herman's view, a deliberative presumption is determinative unless it conflicts with another deliberative presumption. Deceitful promises for any aspect of one's self-interest cannot be sustained; deceitful promising to save a life can be. If there is an implicit contrast with the Rossian system, it is that Ross leaves the outcome of conflict to perception (here making famous Aristotle's dictum "the decision rests with perception" and giving momentum to an intuitionistic reading of Aristotle), whereas Herman insists that this is space not for intuitive judgment but for deliberation. It remains an open question at this point if the form deliberation takes will itself be an application of the Categorical Imperative procedure. If it turns out not to be, and if, too, we accept a more discursive model of Aristotelian decision making than Ross envisions, then we will want to know just what substantive differences exist between the Aristotelian and Kantian models in the account of deliberation.

But for the time being, a more restricted comparative point with an Aristotelian account might be helpful. Whereas an Aristo-

---

8 I borrow here from Richardson's (1994, 36) useful discussion of Ross.

telian might formulate a comparable normative principle such as the above one as, "for the most part (or by and large), don't make deceitful promises," leaving wide-open the circumstances of application and exemption, Herman's Kantian would restrict the conditions under which excusing or canceling situations apply to those of competing norms. This underscores the Kantian concern to reject exemptions from self-interest.[9] By contrast, the potential conflict between self-interest and morality does not frame the Aristotelian project in any comparable way.

The Kantian account just limned can be seen as contrasting with the Aristotelian model in another way, namely, in accounting for the source of moral norms in our own reason. According to the Kantian view, normative principles or ends, or we might say, the ends of virtue, are themselves the product of the operation of practical reason on certain maxims that express our attempts to make exceptions for ourselves. Accordingly, these principles are not conventional artifacts (a charge sometimes made against Aristotelian ethics that we shall address shortly), but products generated autonomously by the Categorical Imperative itself. In contrast, it is often objected, it seems unclear in an Aristotelian account either how the various virtues are generated or what their unifying theme is. One might claim other advantages for the Kantian Categorical Imperative. Having simplified the playing field of choice by ruling out from the start contest owing to self-interest (here, note, self-interest is not the same as true basic needs that would be grounds for contest), it purports to supply a formalized method of deliberating that guides choice between conflicting grounds of obligation. In contrast, leaving instruction for hard choices, as the Aristotelian does in the model of the *phronimos,* does not provide a repeatable and easily transmittable method for general use. I return to this second point in Sections 4 and 5 of this chapter. But first let us turn briefly to the point about the "source" of Aristotelian norms.

It is often charged that Aristotelian virtues represent little more than a conventional list reflective of the social climate of his times. Courage, generosity, greatness of soul (magnanimity), are said to

---

[9] To what extent we demand this of imperfect virtues is considered in Chapter 8.

bespeak a tradition's values and reflect more the admired local practices of a milieu than norms that have a deeper connection to what is objectively the human good. A way of generating Aristotelian virtues from both pervasive human conditions of experience and enduring and deeply shared human abilities does not seem either forthcoming or obvious.

But I think this is wrong. As Martha Nussbaum has argued compellingly, the enumeration of the virtues in the *Nicomachean Ethics* proceeds by "isolating a sphere of experience that figures in more or less any human life" and that represents a sphere of which it makes sense to ask, "What is it to choose and respond well within that sphere?"[10] The virtue is what corresponds to right choice and emotion in those circumstances. So in the sphere of fear of important damages, courage represents what it is affectively to stand well and choose well in those circumstances; in the case of bodily appetites and pleasures, temperance is the corresponding fine state; in the sphere of distributing limited goods, justice is the virtue; in the sphere concerning stewardship of personal property where others are concerned, generosity is the named virtue; in the sphere of social association where play is prominent, easy grace rather than coarseness or insensitivity is the virtue; and so on for such virtues as truthfulness, expansiveness, greatness of soul, mildness of temper, a nameless kind of friendliness, the intellectual virtues, practical wisdom. So conceived, the individual virtues represent good human functionings in specific, pervasive spheres of human experience. They are ways we use our rational and emotional abilities well in the circumstances of human finitude. It may be that some of the virtue names Aristotle chooses are indeed culture bound, as may be some of his own more concrete specifications of those virtues. But as Nussbaum argues, everyone has "some attitude and behavior toward her own death; toward her bodily appetites and their management; toward her property and its use, toward the distribution of social goods; toward telling the truth; toward being kindly or not kindly to others, toward cultivating a sense of play and delight; and so on."[11] The job of ongoing ethical theory

---

[10] Nussbaum (1988a, 35).   [11] Nussbaum (1988a, 36).

is to articulate what constitutes the best specification within these fixed spheres. But what is important for our purposes is that there is a way of generating the Aristotelian virtues in light of our human capabilities and conditions of experience that marches us, in Humean parlance, to the capital of human nature itself.[12] The enumeration is not an artifice of a particular culture's conception of the good.

As said in Chapter 4, Kantian virtues, too, can be seen as a working-out of our moral anthropology. The specific ways we perfect self and others as rational agents are the responses required to preserve our finitely rational natures in the face of pervasive conditions of human vulnerability – such as motives of self-interest that lead to temptations to lie or avoid helping others, or to allow ourselves to languish or bring an end to our lives, and so on. But note that although Aristotelian virtue operates in a choice sphere where there can be excess and defect as well as virtue, excess and defect do not specifically refer to illicit or unfair self-interest. Of course, it may be that excessive ego involvement or defensiveness is at the bottom of many Aristotelian vices such as being too angry, or being niggardly or cowardly or daring. But even if this is the case, Aristotle has no interest in unifying the source of vice in this way. There are many ways to fall short of virtue, he tells us. Cataloguing them all as owing to an unsociable ego is not a move he has the least interest in making.

Before more is said about the employment of the Categorical Imperative procedure in generating standing normative principles, we need to explore the nature of maxims that are to be proposed to such a test.

2 THE CONTENT OF MAXIMS

Maxims express the "willings" or principles of an agent's actions.[13] Loosely put, maxims are proposals or plans for action. They depend for their content upon what an agent posits as an apparent good (a good that appears desirable) and upon what an

[12] *Treatise*, XX.
[13] Some of the material in this section is a revision of Sherman (1993a).

agent takes as relevant for its fulfillment. "A *maxim*," Kant says in *The Doctrine of Virtue,* "is the *subjective* principle of action, the principle which the subject himself makes his rule (how he chooses to act)."[14] The maxim is subjective in the sense that it is the plan or rule *of a subject.* On Kant's view, actions, as distinct from mere bodily movements, become intelligible by the choice of maxims, by the rule (propositionally formulated) that an agent gives herself in determining her will (*Willkür*). We might say, thus, that maxims are the expression of voluntary agency, or in Kant's terms, practical freedom. They express practical freedom in that a will determined by maxims is not brutely moved or necessitated by sensuous impulse. Rather, such a will (an *arbitrium liberum* as opposed to an *arbitrium brutum*) is affected by sensuous impulse, but then gives itself reasons for action. The point emerges in the Canon of Pure Reason in the first Critique:

> For the human will is not determined by that alone which stimulates, that is, immediately affects the senses; we have the power to overcome the impressions on our faculty of sensuous desire, by calling up representations of what, in a more indirect manner, is useful or injurious. But these considerations, as to what is desirable in respect of our whole state, that is, as to what is good and useful, are based on reason. Reason therefore provides laws which are imperatives, that is objective laws of freedom, which tell us what ought to happen.[15]

Kant makes a similar point in the later *Religion Within the Limits of Reason Alone:* "Freedom of the will is of a wholly unique nature in that an incentive can determine the will to an action *only so far as the individual has incorporated it into his maxim* (has made it the general rule in accordance with which he will conduct himself."[16]

---

[14] DV 225. G 401n; 421n.

[15] KrV A802/B830.

[16] Rel. 24/19. Henry Allison calls this central claim the "incorporation thesis." He argues for a connection between the spontaneity of the "I take" in maxim formulating with the spontaneity of "I think" necessary for the possibility of experience (1990, 35–41). I do not follow Allison in holding that the spontaneity of deliberating somehow takes us into the noumenal world of metaphysical freedom.

Acting requires maxims, and maxims require the standpoint of choice. To act under a maxim requires viewing oneself as an agent capable of choice. Even when one acts to satisfy certain desires, one acts on reasons or principles that *dictate that* those desires ought to be satisfied.[17]

It is important to note that a maxim is not just a practical judgment that something to be done is good, though it is that. As a principle it is in addition a commitment to action – a judgment that commits one to trying to bring about some apparent good through action. To have a maxim is as if it were to have one foot in the action. Of course, one's will can change or be defeated. And in such cases we abandon our maxims for others. In this sense, maxims are defeasible plans. To the extent that we are free, they can be revised or rejected.[18]

Marking out some points of intersection with the Aristotelian view might be useful here. The counterpoint to the Kantian maxim is the Aristotelian notion of a *prohairesis* or "reasoned choice." Like a maxim, it represents an agent's intention in setting out to perform an action and, generally speaking, an agent's conception of the apparent good for the sake of which the action is undertaken. But a maxim captures, in a way that that of a *prohairesis* does not, the idea of acting on a reason that operates at a different level from the orectic pulls and tugs of our inclinations. Even when the Kantian agent acts to satisfy desires, it is on the basis of a principle that those desires ought to be satisfied. On the Aristotelian view, practical reason refines and evaluates the objects of desire, and an agent does not act on a desire without its somehow being represented through reason or thought *as good* to that agent. In this sense practical reason *mediates* desire. But this employment of practical reason still doesn't quite capture the Kantian idea of acting on a maxim. For the Kantian notion is meant to signal a form of motivation distinct from the causal pull of desires, however mediated they become. To be motivated is to take oneself to have good reasons to act on certain incentives.[19] A

---

[17] See Hill's (1989) lucid discussion of this point; also Bittner, (1989).
[18] See O'Neill,(1989, 84); Rawls (1980).
[19] See Herman (1993, 221 n) here. "Agents have incentives (*Triebfedern*); they act

similar concern to distance ourselves from the springs of our nature is not Aristotle's, however eager he is to transform and shape those natural springs.

Furthermore, it is worth keeping in mind that Aristotle is simply not as impressed as Kant is by the need to capture the intent of our action by a vehicle other than the action itself. One needs to be careful here, though. For the technical notion of a *prohairesis* is meant to sum up the potentially deliberative aspect of a choice (it sums up the idea of intelligible action implying a practical argument or syllogism of which a *prohairesis* is a part) as well as the belief and desire elements into which any *prohairesis* can itself be analyzed. In pointing us to both, *prohairesis* represents the motivational aspects of an agent in a way that simply cannot be determined by looking only at the outer husk of behavior. In this way, the modern problem of the description of an action is in some sense on Aristotle's mind.[20] But even so, there is a pervasive actional and outward orientation in his views: Character is realized most fully in the completed action. Actualization is the actualization of character. A *prohairesis* that lacks action is, to some extent, simply incomplete. And on a plausible interpretation of a key text, an unrealized *prohairesis* is not a proper candidate for what is truly fine.[21] The contrast with the Kantian notion – that good willing can be fully good when devoid of good consequences – remains striking.

Generally speaking and as a most literal interpretation of the *Groundwork*, maxims conform to lawlike standards (are objectively good) when they can be acted upon by others without making conceptually impossible the original maxim or without thwarting the purposive nature of the will of an agent. So when I try to make a deceitful promise at the same time that I make the maxim a law for others, I make conceptually impossible the no-

from motives. An agent's incentives are all the sources of reasons for action that apply to her in virtue of her own desires and interests *and* in virtue of her rational agency. We say that an agent acts from motive *m* when she has an incentive that supports *m* and she takes *m* to provide good reasons for action."

[20] See NE 1111b5–6 on assessing a character more finely through *prohairesis* than through action.

[21] NE 1099a3–7.

tion of promising; again, when I hold that no one should give resources to others unless it serves self-interest, I undermine my own nature as one who must rely on external sources to set ends and realize them. These are the so-called contradiction in conception and contradiction in will tests discussed in the *Groundwork*.[22] I have more to say about the contradiction in conception test shortly.

On standard interpretations,[23] a maxim is represented by a means/end relation: "to do Action *A* in Circumstances *C* in order to bring about End *E*." It is an articulation of an intention to bring about some apparent good through our agency. As with any account of practical agency, questions quickly arise as to how determinate the principle is upon which we act. Is a maxim best thought of as a relatively general intention to bring about an end (like the major premise in a piece of practical reasoning), or a more specific intention, more finely tailored to the particular circumstances and capturing more intentional features of one's actions than just that one is aiming to bring about a certain end through certain means?[24] There have been arguments in recent literature supporting both the broad and more determinate notions of maxims, as well as positions that include both.[25]

Kant sometimes suggests maxims are general in the sense of broad policies, or in his own terms, basic life rules (*Lebensregeln*). The "maxim to increase my property by every safe means" might be mustered as an example of such a life rule.[26] Equally, following Herman, the "generic" maxims of self-interest that appear in the *Groundwork* examples, for instance, to make deceptive promises

[22] G 424.
[23] Korsgaard (1989); Nell (O'Neill) (1975).
[24] On the content of maxims, see Kant's own remarks at KpV 27.
[25] For discussion of the broad view, see O'Neill (1989), esp. ch. 5; Bittner (1974); Herman (1993, ch. 7); Höffe (1977). For the more determinate notion of maxims, see Herman (1993, ch. 10), and Nell (O'Neill) (1975); for a view that includes both, see Allison (1990); Korsgaard, (1989, 324).
[26] It is less clear if maxims are also general in the sense of specifying *kinds* of circumstances to which they apply. Kant's own example of circumstances that fall under the case "I now have in my possession a deposit the owner of which has died without leaving any record" suggests individual rather than general circumstances to which the maxim applies.

out of self-interest or to fail to help others when it is not in my self-interest, would count as *Lebensregeln*. Recently, Onora O'Neill has suggested a maxim as a general policy that expresses an underlying motivational state:[27]

> Maxims are not to be equated simply with intentions, which may be multiple, some of them profound and others superficial. Rather, a maxim is the *underlying* or *fundamental* principle of an action in the sense that any other principles to which the act conforms are selected and explicable because that is what it takes to act on a certain maxim in that situation (as perceived by the agent). . . . (The maxim is the *maxima propositio* or highest principle of some piece of practical reasoning.)[28]

To cite her example, I may have a maxim to make my guest feel at home. If I am an ancient Greek, hospitality may require the ancillary principle of offering wine and conversation; if I am British, it may be expressed by an offer of tea and biscuits. The maxim, though, remains the broad governing principle that overarches these executions. There are several advantages for viewing maxims in this way. First, an underlying intention allows us to organize and unify what might seem an otherwise motley collection of disparate intentions. It gives meaning to a complex array of intentions – of why I pulled out a mug, why I poured the coffee, why I started to chat about the weather. It gives meaning by grouping them under an end or policy. In so doing, it lends coherence to the notion of practical agency. Other considerations have to do with ease of applying the procedural apparatus of the Categorical Imperative. In focusing on the more general features of principles for action one may avoid certain intractable problems that arise from trying to universalize overly specific intentions.[29] Deliberately "rigged" maxims notoriously slip through universalizing. The rigging can be a matter of using proper names and dates. The maxim "I, Nancy Sherman, intend to make a deceitful promise to Samantha Block on July 2, 1995, on the corner of Main and Chestnut," though obviously morally impermissible,

---

[27] She rejects the idea, though, of a policy that must be long-term or "for life," (the latter perhaps, a more literal meaning of *Lebensregel*).
[28] O'Neill (1989, 129).   [29] O'Neill (1989, 87).

seems to satisfy universality, though not generality.[30] Similar problems arise in the case of other kinds of highly specific maxims, some leading to fortuitous results (as we shall see shortly in the case of lying to a murder), others not so.

We escape some of these snags by testing the more general maxims under which our specific maxims fall. Thus, generic maxims of self-interest that adopt means such as deceitful promising or indifference to others can be rejected without difficulty. There are other potential evaders that O'Neill hopes to trap by identifying a maxim with the fundamental intention behind an action – in particular, those actions for which maxims can be given that accurately capture *some* features of what an agent is doing, but not the motivational features that contain the morally problematic content.

> By taking an agent's fundamental underlying principle or intention as the point of application of his universality test Kant avoids one of the difficulties most frequently raised about universality tests, namely that it seems easy enough to formulate *some* principle of action for any act, indeed possibly one that incorporates one of the agent's intentions, which can meet the criterion of any universality test, whatever the act.[31]

Thus she asks us to imagine the notorious example of a Nazi who gives as the maxim of his action that he is "doing his job" or "only obeying orders." So formulated, "to do one's job" or "obey orders" is morally unproblematic. It is only when we unpack the fundamental motivational structure to which the maxim is ancillary and discover what the agent really took himself to be doing – perhaps "to do one's job so long as it doesn't endanger me" or "to commit genocide against those who are not true Aryans" – that we come to the morally revealing (and unworthy) aspect of the intention. To focus on the underlying motivational structure of action is to "offer a solution to the problem of relevant descriptions"[32] of action.

---

[30] See Rawls (1971, 131–32) for similar considerations that apply to principles of justice.

[31] O'Neill (1989, 86–87).   [32] O'Neill (1989, 87).

But this particular solution, at least as an exclusive one, has its costs. For restricting maxims to the underlying and unifying principle of one's willing may have the unwelcome consequence of shielding from moral survey morally relevant content in other pieces of intentional action that are only superficial or incidental to the underlying maxim.[33] What if I am intending to be hospitable to my guest, and can read many of the intentional features of my action as falling under this unifying theme, but yet still, I snarl a bit as I pass her a delicious biscuit, or drop a barely audible comment about her cackling laughter? Oughtn't I include these intentional features of my action as part of the maxim of my action that falls under moral watch? Indeed, if these willings are allowed to fall through the cracks because they are not themselves means for implementing my overarching policy of hospitality, then I protect from moral scrutiny many of the details of my conduct that clearly bear on moral assessment. I overlook the nuances of my action that have moral relevance and that in many cases may reveal not a single, fundamental intention at work but conflicting underlying intentions. How I judge the present situation and the reasons for action implicit in that judgment may be complex, not neatly subsumed under a single motivating policy. To exclude relevant intentional aspects of my choice from the proper scope of the maxim primarily for the sake of preserving the machinery of the Categorical Imperative is to unduly tailor the data for the sake of the theory.

For reasons much like these, Herman has proposed that we give an account of a maxim that can accommodate a wider range of the choiceworthy features of an action for the sake of which we choose that action. It would include "all the aspects of the action and end that make them choiceworthy for her," including the internalized normative constraints that shape the choice of action as well as collateral effects and other incidental intentions to the action that recommend the overall choice. In this sense, the maxim's content is richer than the stripped-down model of a maxim as a means to bring about a fundamental intention, suggested by the standard schema – "to do Action *A* in Circum-

---

[33] Herman (1993, 220).

stances *C* in order to bring about End *E*." The intuitive idea is to open to moral assessment as much of the detail of a person's actions (and, I would add, construed context) as possible. I quote:

> If in willing an action an agent proceeds as she judges her action and her purpose to be good, then the maxim of action that represents her willing should contain *all* the aspects of the action and end that make them choice-worthy for her. The convention of regarding maxims of action as represented by schemata of the form "To do *a* in circumstances *c* in order to bring about *e* (where *a* is an action and *e* an end, a state of affairs) has made it appear that the only evaluative component represented *in* the maxim is in the supposed causal fit between action and end. There is no reason for this restriction. It is true that Kant believes that all actions are taken for ends; it does not follow that the only sense of an action's goodness (choice-worthiness) that we have is its suitability to promote an end. . . . An agent may choose to act for an end because of her interest in it or because the end contributes to some further goal. And she may choose to act in a particular way because that action produces collateral effects also of interest to her. . . . If her choice is made on the basis of this rich background of value, then her maxim should include all of the aspects that determine choice-worthiness."[34]

On this view, the maxim becomes a vehicle that can carry a thicker view of our reasons for undertaking a choice than the standard view allows. As Herman puts it, it "includes all aspects of both action and end that the agent would offer as justification for her acting as she intends to act."[35] I think this is an important step in opening to moral assessment a wider range of morally relevant reasons for action captured only in a rich narrative of our intentions. It represents an important way in which Kantian moral self-knowledge can become expanded. It is still worth noting, though, that the maxim on this account, as in traditional accounts, will not include the emotional features of action. On a Kantian account, we may have duties to cultivate certain emotions as instruments and accompaniments to action, and along the

---

[34] Herman (1993, 221).   [35] Herman (1993, 221).

lines proposed in Chapter 4, right action may be fully "meritorious and exemplary" only if it is attended by the proper emotions.[36] But the primary vehicle for moral appraisal, namely, a maxim, if it captures only the intentional features of action, does not itself easily accommodate these emotions. Those features slip through the maxim as an account of what I was intentionally doing. I do not have a better suggestion at this point for how to accommodate emotions formally within the rubric of a maxim, but I have suggested that a complete appraisal of the moral action of a character will require, on Kant's own view, that we take them into account.

We have seen in this section the need for a flexible conception of maxims that accommodates different levels of generality regarding an agent's action. For the reconstructive purpose of showing how the Categorical Imperative generates broad, background norms of the sort that inform virtue and shape choice, general maxims seem appropriate. But in actual practice, whether judgment is routine or actively deliberative, it makes better sense to think of agents acting on maxims that are thicker in their account of what makes a particular action choiceworthy to an agent. In the terminology of Chapter 6, a fuller and more descriptive narrative of the features of the action that combines salient circumstances and objectives is required.

In all this we have assumed that an agent can gain reasonable access to her maxims. But Kant notoriously warns of the opacity of the heart to fathom its motives. We are not transparent to ourselves, and our own capacities for self-deception stand as more serious threats to our moral progress than the brute fact that we have desires that can go against the authority of morality. The real threat, Kant says, is not our sensuous natures but the "invisible foe who screens himself behind reason"[37] in rationalization, denial, and the like. Kant is even more blunt in another passage: "This dishonesty, by which we humbug ourselves . . . extends outwardly also to falsehood and deception of others. . . . It constitutes the foul taint in our race."[38] Still, must this be viewed as

---

[36] DV 484–5; see the discussion in Chapter 4, sec. 4 of this volume.
[37] Rel. 50/50.   [38] Rel. 38/33.

an overwhelming obstacle to the sort of moral assessment we are trying to reconstruct?

I think not. The difficulties of introspection should be viewed as no greater than the epistemic limits on ordinary empirical knowledge elsewhere. While Kant is more than candid about the massiveness of our capacity for self-deception, the fact of that propensity, like our radical evil in general, is cause not for despair or misanthropy but for our vigilant and "incessant counteraction against it."[39] As I have argued elsewhere,[40] textual evidence from the *Religion* and *The Doctrine of Virtue* give the broad lines of a therapy of self-knowledge, suggesting on the whole that the duty to know one's heart can proceed in something more than a random or arbitrary way. To be sure, Kant is well aware there is no therapy that is fully exempt from the vulnerabilities it sets out to treat. There is no perspective outside of human reason by which we can hope to gain safe haven from reason's own trickery and perversions. But Kant seems to think that the habit of self-reflection, including ways of reading the heart through reflectiveness about one's emotions, give one a clue to motivations. The emotions, as we have said before, serve an important epistemic role of disclosing what we care about, and Kant seems to confirm this point in remarks such as the famous one to Schiller, that good progress begets "a joyous frame of mind, without which man is never certain of having really *attained a love* for the good."[41] Of course, we would be foolish to think that the affective aspects of character cannot themselves deceive. But even so, in a fallible way, they may give some access to values and concerns that might otherwise remain veiled from one's reports about what motivates one's action.

Thus far we have put aside the question of just how the universalizability test works and in what sense it reveals morally wrong features of our actions. That is, in what sense does it disclose to us the moral values that right action is meant to embrace? Discussion of this issue in the next section will prompt us to consider

[39] Rel. 51/46.   [40] Sherman (1993a, sec. 3).
[41] Rel. 23n/19n. See also 75n/69n.

how we deliberate when there are real worries about what is the right thing to do. As I have intimated before, I do not believe we deliberate in such cases by appeal to a formal procedure of deliberation, such as universalizability represents.

3 KANTIAN UNIVERSALIZABILITY

Maxims are tested for their moral permissibility most perspicuously by the universal law form of the Categorical Imperative. The intuitive idea of Kantian universalizability is that morality requires that we not make an exception of ourselves. We should not give special exemptions to ourselves on the basis of self-interest. We have aired one charge against Kantian universalizability. This is that it seems an external process of justification, independent of the process of making a choice properly constrained from inside. I have just suggested that this need not follow. The regulative work of the Categorical Imperative can lead rather than follow, when the Categorical Imperative is viewed as a constructive procedure for justifying the background norms that shape choice. If, following Herman, we see a maxim as including the choiceworthy features for which our action is chosen, then included among these features, especially in the case of the mature moral agent, will be that the action is constrained by and responsive to moral reasons. In Aristotelian idiom, that the action is for the sake of "the fine" will be among the virtuous agent's reasons for choosing it. The Kantian adds to this that the norms that shape what is fine are themselves the constructed  product of the Categorical Imperative, as it is reflective of the standards of our reason.

Still, I want to consider more carefully the role of universalizability in this process. More specifically, I want to ask, in what sense does the universal law formula reveal both the fact that an action is permissible and why it is so? To focus on the last part of the question, in what sense does it disclose what makes our action right?

The Formula of Universal Law requires that I regard my action as an action others could act on at the same time as I do. "Act only on that maxim through which you can at the same time will that it should become a universal law." Procedurally, I start with a maxim, which I then universalize. A maxim fails if it produces a contradiction: As it is standardly put, it will produce a "contradiction in conception" if it is impossible to conceive of the maxim as a universal law of nature, a "contradiction in will" if it contradicts, in the sense of thwarts, the essential nature of the will itself.

Much has been written on how these contradictions are to be understood and the sorts of maxims the tests have most and least difficulty correctly assessing. Herman has pushed forward the discussion by showing that a commonly accepted interpretation of the contradiction in conception test does not successfully pick out morally wrong maxims, and that even when, under a different interpretation, the test does successfully flag what we have pretheoretical reason to believe are impermissible actions, the test is "not by itself sufficient to pick out the wrongmaking characteristic of an impermissible maxim."[42] The term she uses is "didactic." The test does not "didactically" show *why* an action is morally wrong. The first point is an older one, that universalizing does not systematically produce the right results. The second is a newer point – that even when it is successful, it does not show on its face the moral relevance of its results. To anticipate, the intuitive idea behind turning one's maxim into a law – that one may thereby learn if one is being a free rider – does not pinpoint *why* being a free rider is in fact wrong in this case.

I want to pursue these points for they bring us closer to understanding what advantage, if any, the Kantian notion of asking oneself if others could act on a maxim of my action, has. Is recognizing the unconditional value of rational agency in self and others best captured by applying that procedural test? If not, by what method do we morally survey our actions, and how does it compare to what is available in an Aristotelian account?

According to one interpretation of the contradiction in conception test, usefully identified by Christine Korsgaard as the practical interpretation, we show a maxim to be immoral if in imagining our maxim in a world in which everyone acts on that maxim,

42 Herman (1993, 236).

we cannot achieve the purpose of our maxim.[43] The contradiction is a practical one: The "maxim would be self-defeating if universalized." It cannot achieve its intended outcome in a world in which everyone aims to bring about the same purpose. The test exposes well the idea of free riding. "For what the test shows to be forbidden are just those actions whose efficacy in achieving their purposes depends upon their being exceptional."[44] That is, the rationality of such maxims is that they depend upon others not acting as we do, for example, upholding the institution of promising when we make deceitful promises. When our maxims become standardized through legislation, the maxim becomes pointless. It no longer is a rational way of achieving success.

However, Herman has shown that this interpretation of the contradiction in conception test leads to counterintuitive results. For it makes morally impermissible what she calls "coordination" maxims that also depend upon others not acting as I do – such as planning to play tennis on a Sunday morning so that I can take advantage of others being at church or taking a route to work that is based on the knowledge that others go a different way – but which are not in any intuitive way morally problematic ways of taking advantage of others. The test shows that I cannot *succeed* when others act as I do, but not that there is something *morally wrong* in taking advantage of their acting differently.

As Herman shows, the logical interpretation of the contradiction in conception test, set out by Korsgaard as an alternative interpretation, does not produce false prohibitions in the same cases. And, too, the logical interpretation follows more literally what Kant spells out in his own formulation of the test, that our maxim is impermissible if the action it proposes is inconceivable in a world in which it is universalized. Applying the test, we can conceive of booking a tennis court when others do the same, even if it is the case that the point of our action – of playing tennis when the courts are not crowded – would be defeated. The maxim will be pointless but not impermissible. In this regard the logical inter-

[43] O'Neill (1989, 81–104) seems to rely partially on the practical interpretation as part of the idea behind "rational intending."

[44] Korsgaard (1985, 36).

307

pretation of the contradiction in conception test is able to distinguish coordination maxims from deceptive maxims. Thus, when we universalize a deceitful promise for the purpose of self-advantage, the result is inconceivability or, as Kant puts it, an inner impossibility. When we universalize a coordination maxim, we do not produce the same result. To be sure, the practice of deceitful promise-making is ineffectual as an instrument for advantage, but unlike coordination maxims, it is, in addition, inconceivable.

But still – and this is the point that should concern us – what do we learn about the immorality of the action by having our pre-theoretical views about these maxims confirmed through this interpretation of the test? The practical interpretation exposed that we were taking advantage of others' habits and practices, though it did not show that we were doing so unfairly. Does proving a maxim to be inconceivable when universally practiced show that through that maxim an agent takes "unfair" advantage of others? Does this kind of logical irrationality do any better than practical irrationality in making perspicuous why our action is wrong? It would seem not.

It is here that Herman appeals to the Formula of Humanity as instructive. For according to that formula, good willing requires that we respect the rational agency in ourselves and others as an end in itself. We are to treat self and others not merely as means, but always at the same time as an end. Deception is a form of manipulation. When I make a deceitful promise, I take *unfair* advantage of others by denying them access to information required for them to assess the status of my promise. My deception amounts to the withholding of information required to make an informed choice. I deny others the opportunity of openly assenting to the very end toward which I require their contribution.

This argument is familiar, but it makes more pressing the question of just what work universalizing does, even in the case of constructing background norms. We have seen that the intuitive idea – that a failure in universalization indicates an impermissible case of self-exemption or free riding – becomes problematic in light of the coordination maxims and other cases of false prohibitions generated under the practical interpretation. Although the logical interpretation does not generate false prohibitions in the same way, it still does not show why the maxims it has rightly flagged are in fact to be flagged as immoral. Moreover, it tests best on generic maxims, and has difficulty in showing contradictions in highly specific maxims. Yet, as we said earlier, we have good reason for wanting to assess detail-rich maxims insofar as immorality may sometimes lurk in the details of our reasons for actions, and not in some more unifying, simplifying description.

One might address some of these worries by holding that the demand for a didactic method is itself not compelling. For a procedure can do only so much, and that it produces results, as in the general deception cases under the logical interpretation, might be thought to be adequate. But this I believe belies the promise of the Categorical Imperative. The Categorical Imperative is meant to be a method of self-surveillance as well as self-knowledge.[45] Through its explicit formulations of practical reason, we guide against moral violations at the same time we come to understand why and how our commitment to the value of rational agency issues in these moral constraints. To have a test that indicates *that* something is wrong but not *why* it is, is to return to the idea of the Categorical Imperative as a mechanical and external device disconnected from our understanding and reflective practice of morality.

But even if we agree that the Formula of Humanity must have a central place in the interpretation of Kantian ethics[46] (let us assume both in terms of the construction of general norms, such as nondeception and beneficence, and in deliberation where those norms themselves are not determinative), questions still remain as to whether using that "formula" amounts to a procedural test on one's actions. Broadly speaking, if we assess maxims of our actions in terms of their respecting the rational nature of self or others, then in what sense does that constitute a "method" for assessment? While I think the *Groundwork* examples suggest how certain broad norms can be generated by appeal to the Formula of Humanity understood procedurally, I do not think that formula

---

[45] See DV 441.
[46] For a discussions of that formula, see Korsgaard (1986b) and Hill (1980).

provides a formal deliberative procedure in cases where we really have occasion to deliberate and not merely reconstruct norms.

Even so, in the section that follows I suggest a more robust role for the Formula of Humanity than that of didactically supplementing a universalizing procedure. I propose that in many cases in which we must deliberate about the morally right action, Kantian deliberation is not a matter of universalizing but, rather, a matter of reflecting on what respect for rational agency requires of us in the circumstances before us. This is to put it in the most general way and perhaps too abstractly. For occasions for moral deliberation will often arise because of a conflict between specific normative ends, such as beneficence and nondeception. Here deliberation is a matter of working out what each of these specific norms requires in a way that optimally helps to resolve the conflict. But even so, we can appeal back to the normative content of the Formula of Humanity insofar as a grasp of the grounding of specific norms in respect for the rational agency of persons can deepen our practical and concrete reflection about what to do. But the point I am most interested in making is that even for the Kantian, deliberation (understood as working out a choice where guidance by norms does not as a matter of habit or routine settle the decision) is best thought of as an informal mode of reflection and not so distinct from the narrative–specification process outlined in Chapter 6, Sections 5 and 6. Adapting the broad lines of specification Henry Richardson has developed,[47] the reflection moves in two directions: from the top down, toward more concrete specifications of general ends, including, in this Kantian application, the most general end of respecting humanity; and from the bottom up, toward a more reflective grasp of the import of the circumstances one faces. The bottom-up process can be conceived as a discursive process that works through various stages[48] – that of describing and classifying the circumstances

---

[47] I am indebted in my description of this process of deliberation to Henry Richardson's account of the deliberation of ends (1994).

[48] Here, I am grateful to Jonathan Dancy for informal comments to me on how he envisions the narrative process to proceed. I should note specifically, though, that his remarks were not offered in the context of understanding Kantian deliberation. I doubt he would support my view of Kant here.

before one (including giving evaluative descriptions), of relating these different classifications to each other in order to capture the overall landscape of the case, and of grasping the relation of this overall pattern to others that are familiar. The deliberation is "reflective" in that it moves back and forth between the general and particular poles of practical judgment.

4 KANTIAN "REFLECTIVE" DELIBERATION

It is often held that an important contrast between Aristotelian and Kantian moral theories is that Kantian theory provides a procedure for deliberation about right action in a way that Aristotelian theory does not. If a more fruitful deliberative question for the Kantian agent to ask is, Does my action preserve the rational agency of self and others? then Kantian moral reflection would seem to take on a more discursive tone. The idea of moral deliberation as algorithmic becomes less apt and the idea of working out the implications of respect of rational agency in the case at hand, more promising.[49]

Put this way, deliberation has a familiar Aristotelian feel. Accepting the now standard reading of Aristotle's ethics – that we can deliberate about ends and not only means – moral deliberation will often be a matter of figuring out the requirements of internalized virtues in the circumstances of action. We deliberate about how to specify an end of virtue, say, friendliness, in this specific case, where I am annoyed or disappointed with another's actions toward me. On the Aristotelian view, the *phronimos* provides guidance by serving as an embodied paradigm of one who can respond to such circumstances with excellence.

In a certain way, what Kant may be asking us to do is not so different, though the helpful notion of an embodied guide is by and large absent.[50] The virtues, recall, are, most broadly, imper-

---

49 See O'Neill (1989, ch.1), who here replaces the formal idea of reason providing an algorithm for thought and action with the more informal idea of trial and tribunal as the methods of reason's self-discipline.

50 For the qualification, see Chapter 8, sec. 3 of this volume.

fect duties in the sense of ends we have a commitment to work toward. They leave wide room for fulfillment. The project of virtue (even in the case of acting on the perfect duties that in some catalogues fall under virtue, for example, proscriptions against lying or stupefaction) requires discerning correctly the applicability of those norms in the circumstances of our action. This requires specifying or tailoring those ends (in supple though non-lax ways) to the case at hand.

On this view of deliberation, the Categorical Imperative functions not as a *formal* universalization procedure but, rather, as a more *substantive* norm prescribing positive and negative respect for rational agents generally, and more specifically, through specific norms such as nondeception or beneficence. The norms are supple in that they stand ready to be transformed and thickened by the circumstances themselves. In this sense they are porous. While the reflective process is not peculiar to Kantian deliberation, the norm that substantively guides the process and gives the underlying rationale for the other norms, namely, respect for rational agency, is. In what follows I elaborate on this process through the use of a few examples. They are meant to show in the first case a conflict between two imperfect duties – the duty to self-perfection and the duty to beneficence – and in the second, a conflict between a perfect and imperfect duty, the perfect duty not to lie and the imperfect duty to beneficence or mutual aid. On a full Kantian account, each of these duties is a way of respecting or promoting persons as rational agents.

Samantha has a growing sense lately that she is languishing in a marriage. She feels unfulfilled, both intellectually and spiritually. By her lights, she and Rob seem to have grown apart, their interests taking different turns – hers toward exploring a more spiritual and meditative life, his toward more mainstream culture in general. She hadn't considered leaving Rob, but lately, for reasons she can't quite articulate, it seems a confrontable choice that keeps rearing its head for consideration. There are conflicts, though, some of which she perceives as moral conflicts. There is the end of her own fulfillment to be taken into account, but also the happiness of her husband and the children. The children seem thriving at the moment, her own moments of malaise neither

public nor pronounced enough for them to notice. She manages
to keep her disaffection undercover, believing the public space,
particularly that shared with the children, is not a place to air
emotions. Nor has Rob noticed much of her discontentment, for
she's concealing and he avoiding. It is mostly in sultry moments
of diary writing that her negative feelings break through. From all
that Samantha can tell about Rob, he seems content with his lot,
not feeling the restlessness she's sensing. When she has thought
about the possibility of separating from Rob, she sees it as a path
for perfecting herself, but one that would be a sure way of ne-
glecting the needs of her children and husband.

The question for Samantha is how to make headway rationally
on the moral conflict, which in Kantian idiom we can relabel as a
conflict between a duty to perfect herself as a rational agent and a
duty to contribute to the ends of others as rational agents. Is there
a way she can think of her situation that preserves both her commitment to the ends of her own perfection and the happiness of
her family, while at the same time making them more mutually
supportive? The story could take various turns. Samantha could
see that what she envisions as the children's future unhappiness
(were she to separate from Rob) as largely her own projections of
her fears. She has forgotten that her children are getting older
(they are now eleven and nine), and they are increasingly up for
the adventure of moves and new homes. Many of their friends'
parents are divorced, so there is not the same stigma attached to
that status as when she herself was a child. Equally, she remembers her past inability to assert herself in ways that were self-
fulfilling and how supportive Rob himself had always been of her
continuing education. They had talked about her deferring her
career and development to his, and how it would be morally
wrong for her to deprecate her own interests in preference to his.
If staying in the marriage required her servility, then this
wouldn't do. When they were honest with each other, she knew
well that he wasn't fully happy with her present state. As she digs
deeper, her perfection and the happiness of her family seem less
disparate ends.

But the narrative could go another way as well. Samantha
comes to appreciate that her disaffection within the relationship

has to do with her own issues of romantic fantasy and nonconformism, and that these in turn are something of adolescent residues. Her self-perfection becomes a matter of working through these patterns, at the same time that she cultivates a greater sense of tolerance and empathy for others who, like Rob, don't precisely mirror her own familiar, developmental story. She can respect his own projects more if she sees them not as some flawed versions of her own, but as ends that reveal his interests and that she can positively support as his own choices. Equally, she comes to appreciate that there is a project of self-perfection to be found in cultivating her spiritual needs within the context of remaining within her family. Sharing her spiritual discoveries with her children and husband takes on importance to her, and seeing them appreciate her "new" self reinforces her view that she can achieve her ends within her family.

Now, in this unextraordinary set of narratives is an attempt to lessen a perceived moral conflict by specification and narrative. From the bottom up is an organizing and reorganizing of the landscape in a way that allows salient features to emerge and their interconnections to be grasped. In the opposite direction is an appreciation of why something is salient through a grasp of more general values. General values are tinkered with and thickened through the encounter with the particular case. There are several additional points to note about this case:

1. Deliberation here is prompted by a *deliberative occasion*. In this case, there is a breakdown in the routine or habitual choices because of a perceived conflict between what to do for oneself and what to do for others. Deliberative occasions might be prompted by other sets of circumstances as well – perhaps one can't find appropriate means for bringing about some settled end or perhaps the usual way of doing things doesn't work this time around. Circumstances such as these set me thinking how to proceed with my end.[51] Not all cases of moral judgment need be thought of as deliberative, even though they are "potentially deliberative" – that is, at some point down the line require explicit

---

[51] Richardson (1994, 161).

justification and active integration with other commitments and ends.

2. The narrative suggests that the ends to which we are committed and which constrain our action are not well thought of as either *fixed* or *abstract*. Rather, their justificatory force is understood best in their encounter with practice. In this sense, the Kantian ends of self-perfection and others' happiness, and the most general end of respecting rational agency, can be understood along Aristotelian lines as ends that are only outline sketches to be filled in by the deliberative process. In the above case, we already begin with the more determinate imperfect ends of self-perfection and beneficence generated or constructed, let us assume, by an application of the Categorical Imperative. As the third and fourth *Groundwork* examples suggest, they are generated by defeat of proposals of generic maxims of languishing and mutual indifference, respectively, and according to the most plausible interpretation, a defeat generated not by the contradiction in conception as application of the Formula of Universal Law, but by the contradiction in will test, as application of the Formula of Humanity. (Note, here we do have the Formula of Humanity providing a procedural test for imperfect duties. But my point has been that in cases where we are not reconstructing the source of norms, but deliberating about their implications, we do not do well to conceive of the formulae as providing procedures.) As it has been elaborated in the literature, these ends would contradict, in the sense of thwart, the nature of the agent's will (in the first case) and the recipient's will (in the second): That is, to follow a policy of self-languishing is to undermine the nature of an agent's will as a power to set and realize ends of all sorts. Correspondingly, to follow a policy of mutual indifference is to undermine the finite will of others who in fulfilling the ends of their choice often require the extended resources of others as supplements. The defeat of these maxims as impermissible results in the installment of their opposites, maxims of self-perfection and mutual aid, as obligatory. Though obligatory, as ends they are wide in requirement, with latitude as to where, when, why, how, toward whom, by what means, with what frequency, and so on they are to be fulfilled. (That ends are generally expressed by abstract

nouns ("self-perfection") or infinitives ("to perfect self") makes their latitude obvious.)[52] Hence, the question arises for Samantha, In what sense must I not let myself languish? Am I allowing myself to do so if I stay in this marriage? Am I failing to take seriously the happiness of my children if I turn my attention to myself? The Kantian notion of imperfect duties having latitude and the Aristotelian notion that theory can only present virtues in outline form, roughly parallel each other here.[53]

In asking herself these questions, there is no sense in which Samantha is deductively applying some absolute end to this case. For at very least, it would be hard to imagine a universal generalization at once substantive enough and sufficiently hedged to be of use in such reasoning.[54] If the norm's description were sufficiently hedged, the implicit norm would be too vague to be helpful; if it were substantively described, too many cases would be left out that might be relevant. Given the general unavailability of a deductive reconstruction of practical reasoning, the deliberative reasoning must proceed differently. Committed to the ends of self-perfection and beneficence, Samantha's task is simply to determine what specific form or forms they take in this case. What counts as self-perfection? Is it exploring her new interests? Or is it loosening the hold of old habits that stand in the way of a more cooperative spirit with her spouse? In addition, what light can be shed on these questions by reflecting back on the rationale for these norms as captured in the generative account of them? The issue here is not some conceptual analysis of the self-perfection or, more generally, respect for rational agency. For even if there were some consensus as to what self-perfection "means," the question would still remain as to whether that notion resonated with what Samantha herself was really after and committed to in virtue of other ends. Again, there is no straightforward application. The work of judgment cannot be evaded.

---

[52] Richardson (1994, 71).

[53] I shall qualify this shortly, since Aristotle sometimes uses a locution that suggests there is only one way to get virtuous action right.

[54] See Henry Richardson's (1994, 33–41) fine discussion of the implausibility of a deductive deliberative model.

The dynamic aspect of deliberation should be apparent here and cast skepticism on standard views of Kantian deliberation as involving either the clamping down of absolute norms or the mechanical application of a testing procedure. To review, let us assume that the Categorical Imperative generates norms (either by the contradiction in conception test as application of the Formula of Universal Law, as discussed earlier, or the contradiction in will test as application of the Formula of Humanity, as we just rehearsed). What follows from this is neither deductive application in routine cases of guidance by use of these norms, nor formalized universalization as a procedural check in cases where conflicts between norms create deliberative questions. In the latter case, deliberation proceeds reflectively and discursively, by progressively articulating specifications of more general norms at the same time as we try to grasp the relative moral import of the concrete narratives we describe.

3. In the above account much hangs on the *narration* of the case. For specification works upward as well as downward. We have seen that there can be fluidity in the narration. Gestalts can shift with certain issues taking foreground, while others recede. At first Samantha thinks only of the upheaval to her children wrought by a move; later she imagines the adventure they might find in setting up a new home. As we argued in Chapters 3, 4 and 5, our emotional reactions play an important role in the construction of such narratives, often alerting us to what we care about in a way that might otherwise escape us. So fear can clue Samantha to a vulnerability she hadn't accounted for, just as joy can disclose an interest that may not yet be fully acknowledged. In addition, emotions can imbue a particular thought or focus with a retentive power. Thoughts experienced or remembered affectively often have a "grip" that blander mental contents simply lack.

One important point of going through the messy details of the above narratives is to remind us that typically there is no "case" given to an agent in the way philosophy texts often suggest. Rather, moral deliberation, and judgment in general, require that an agent make intelligible the case to herself, and this by describing (and redescribing) and evaluating (and reevaluating) features of the circumstances before one, with an eye to the mutual interconnection of these features in the overall landscape. This interpretive process is itself a crucial moment in deliberating. By telling the story in different ways, different forests emerge from the trees. We build the story upward, inductively, at the same time casting different concerns downward that further influence the shape of the narrative. Understanding the deeper rationale of certain norms – that beneficence, for example, involves respecting another's choice-making capacities – affects Samantha's concrete view of how to promote her husband's interests.

4. Given that the specification process is not a matter of seeking a deductively valid conclusion, questions remain as to just where *warrant* comes from in moving to a conclusion of practical reasoning. One strong possibility, again developed by Richardson, is that it comes laterally from other norms that lend support to our conclusion and that we implicitly draw on in reasoning. Connections of support or coherence are built among different norms that reinforce the practical value of each. Sometimes the connections can be fortuitous, a matter of two birds killed with one stone. For example, joining a neighborhood swim/tennis club can satisfy an interest in both having a pool within walking distance of one's home and belonging to a club that, unlike many in the area, has its own tennis courts. In some cases, the ends reinforce each other more substantively. For example, in our earlier story Samantha has spiritual needs that at first she thinks cannot be well met within the existing family. But as she begins to cultivate those needs at home, she finds additional support for them there, both in the project of teaching her children and husband about aspects of her spiritual practice and, in turn, in their increasing admiration of her for her achievements.[55]

The case of conflict makes vivid an ordinary urge to find coherence or unity among one's norms. The urge is there in the daily planning of activities, in scheduling with an eye to fitting together ends without temporal conflict. To take a pedestrian

[55] Richardson's example may be more felicitous: I may pursue opportunities for contemplation in our bustling world by going into a religious retreat. Once there, I discover additional doctrinal reasons for pursuing a more contemplative existence. The world being as it is, the ends reinforce each other (1994, 149–50).

318

example, when the dental assistant gives me a host of times for an appointment, the thought that stirs is, How can I schedule it so that I have time for the dentist, ample time for work, and still be home in time for the children? Modern "juggling" expresses the simple idea that as practical agents we look for ways to avoid scheduling conflicts among our ends. Sometimes we don't have to look too far – we merely capitalize on fortuitous support that comes our way. Other times, we must change the world, or "stack the deck," as Ruth Marcus puts it, to ensure that certain conflicts are less likely to arise.[56] We don't abandon our ends, but plan so that mutual support is forthcoming.

In Samantha's case, what to do is in some measure guided by finding actions that establish connections between the two relevant norms of self-perfection and beneficence. Staying on and rebonding with her spouse and family is a way of fulfilling her duty to contribute to their happiness at the same time that it marks a way of tending to old bothersome habits that stand in the way of her own development. She also discovers there are ways of engaging in family activities that support her own spiritual interests. There is an attempt to unify her ends and make systematic connections between them. One can, of course, go overboard here and dilute the radical nature of some interests by seeking to blend them too fully with other ongoing interests. Similarly, the romantic desire for an aesthetically well-constructed narrative may compromise a more honest account of the lived life's homely pursuit of ends. But these sorts of cases aside, it makes good sense to see ends as pursued within a coherent conception of ends, and to see this as a constraint on deliberation. Kantian reflective deliberation can be seen as following this model. In this sense, it bears similarity to the Aristotelian notion that we deliberate not about separate ends, but about the good life as a whole. Though there are other elements of Aristotelian eudaimonism that Kant would surely reject, including its stress on actualized intentions and its requirement for a fair measure of prosperity, this idea of bringing ends together in a mutually supportive way seems not so foreign or unwelcome.

[56] Marcus (1980).

We have been considering the discursive nature of the deliberative process in the case of the conflict of imperfect duties. In the example we considered, there was latitude in the fulfillment of both ends. But what of conflicts where one of the deliberative norms is a perfect duty (where what is obligatory is not an end but a required action or omission)? Doesn't the perfect duty not to lie, for example, not only override lying out of expedience, but also lying for the sake of an imperfect duty, such as the duty of beneficence? Isn't this precisely the kind of conflict where Kantian deliberation retains its unattractive rigor? Or, can we find room for wisdom in these kinds of cases as well? Can we reconstruct a more discursive, deliberative process here too?

There is much that can be said here and much that has been written. For a full discussion, I refer the reader to that extensive literature.[57] The infamous case Kant gives is one of lying to the murderer at your door intent upon killing the innocent you are protecting. Kant's claim is extreme: You have a perfect duty to self not to lie even in the case of saving a life. Sympathetic interpreters have shown that one can overturn Kant's own conclusions by treatment under the Formula of Universal Law. Though a universalized, public practice of deception is conceptually incoherent, a maxim to lie to a murderer may escape universalizing attempts because the person who lies in self-defense can usually assume that the murderer does not think his interlocutor in fact knows she is talking to a murderer and hence, in these very circumstances, is lying.[58] Similar results seem to hold for lying to deceivers in general. Still, these encouraging results become diluted once we appreciate, as we pointed out earlier, that highly specific maxims, in general, tend to escape the machinery of universalization. In this sense, universalizability seems of little genuine guidance in conflict resolution.

For these reasons and for the more general didactic reasons Herman has cited, we need to turn to the Formula of Humanity. As we have said, the Formula of Humanity reveals what is wrong

---

[57] Bok (1978, 1983), Herman (1993, ch. 7), Hill (1991, ch. 3), Korsgaard (1986a), Paton (1953–54).

[58] See Korsgaard (1986a).

about deception: Put simply, deception uses another person's reason as a mere means. A person who is lied to cannot assent to the end of being lied to. The lie is a manipulation of her will. Along these lines, Korsgaard has claimed that the Formula of Humanity can provide its own criterial tests for perfect duties to others. "An action is contrary to perfect duty if it is not possible for the other to assent to it or hold its end."[59] This is to restate Kant's own comments on the Formula of Humanity treatment of the deceitful promise example – that by such a promise the other person "cannot possibly agree with my way of behaving to him" and "cannot himself share the end of the action."[60]

But how far are we to go with these criterial tests, especially in nonroutine, deliberative cases, where we are working out the implications of established norms? As Korsgaard points out, treatment of the infamous case by the Formula of Humanity will result in more rigid treatment than treatment of the case under the Formula of Universal Law. For to lie even to a liar is to manipulate her will and deny her the opportunity for assenting to the end to which she is contributing. According to that formula, it is impermissible. Thus, while the Formula of Humanity has the virtue of making clear the wrong-making feature of lying in general, when applied as a deliberative procedure in a hard case, it is too unyielding. Put simply, as a procedural test, it lacks precisely what more nuanced judgment has.

Where does this leave us with our discursive notion of deliberating in hard cases? If we want to say that moral decency may permit or indeed require lying to the murderer or liar, is there a way, as a Kantian, of deliberating to this conclusion? Or must we simply rest with our intuitions – that lying is less heinous than preventing a threat to life – and at this point concede that we abandon the Kantian construct, wedded as it is to the notion of strict, perfect duties?

Clearly, a sympathetic interpretation would want to restore the lying prohibition to the status of a deliberative *presumption* rather than an absolute norm. As such, there can be cases in which it can be rebutted. But how would that deliberation go?

---

[59] Korsgaard (1986a, 331).   [60] G 429–30.

There are by now familiar considerations that would inform such deliberation. The servility of accepting oneself as victim of a lie without taking active defense is raised. For to allow oneself to be servile to the manipulations of another's will would be to violate one's own self-respect.[61] Equally, there is the idea that in lying to a liar or murderer (note, in the case of the murderer, coerciveness rests not merely in lying but in aggressive threats), one is not initiating evil in the world, but deflecting or averting a threat that is already there.[62] The world has been corrupted, so to speak, and the norms that hold in the ideal or utopian world are no longer strictly applicable. The scope of the norm of nondeception needs to be redrawn. Obviously, too, there is the weight of the duty of mutual aid and the claims it makes on promoting others' rational agency. Though, generally speaking, this may come up against the limit of the negative, perfect duty not to lie, so that just as we cannot kill to save, so, too, we cannot lie even to save, the case of lying to a murderer, it is claimed, is different because it is not merely a case of saving, but a case of repelling or preventing an aggressive assault against an innocent. As Herman develops this line of argument, the deception in this case is not an assault on an individual's rational agency ("integrity," in her terms), but a manipulation "in the service of a morally necessary purpose: a manipulation of a will to bring it into conformity with its own defining principles."[63] Here again, it is a manipulation that is a deflection rather than a direct assault, but notably, in this interpretation of the case, the deflection is not for the sake of one's own defense or that of the murderer's intended victim, but for the sake of the murderer himself – to "save" his will.

I have run through these considerations to give a glimpse of how one would proceed discursively to deliberate in the case of a conflict between a perfect and an imperfect duty. These considerations suggest ways of refining the normative prescription against lying and imply that the norm need be considered neither absolute and universal nor deductively applicable. Nor will it

---

[61] See Hill (1991, chs. 1 and 2).
[62] Hill (1974; 1991, ch. 6), Korsgaard (1986a).
[63] Herman (1993, 157).

work to submit the maxim of lying to a murderer to a set of testing criteria, such as either the Formula of Humanity or the Formula of Universal Law can represent. The Formula of Universal Law ends up passing the maxim for accidental reasons and in general lacks import about the wrongness of actions. The Formula of Humanity exposes what is wrong with deception, but interpreted only as a test, it fails to provide a supple enough way to deliberate in cases where there are genuine conflicts. One might shrug one's shoulders here and say that judgment remains unguided, a matter of intuition only. But the above considerations attempt to show that judgment has not fallen into an abyss where reason gives out. Considerations about one's own servility when one tacitly accepts being a victim of lying, about the way being lied to corrupts one's environment and puts an evil in one's way, about responsibilities to repel aggression and manipulate a will against its own corruption, and so on, all point to discursive ways we specify more finely the norm against lying in cases where it is not simply our own convenience that is the competitor. If the force of the considerations is that we are not in fact illegitimately or "unfairly" taking advantage of the murderer by lying, then a duty not to deceive leaves some specificatory latitude. More precisely, it leaves latitude as to *when* and *whether* the principle is appropriate to a particular situation. As we shall see in the next chapter, imperfect duties admit of a wider range of types of latitude.

Lying to a murderer might seem an easy case in which to relax the Kantian rigor. But the reason here cannot be that Kantian ethics has an implicit scalar ranking such that failing to save the life of a rational agent is twice as bad as deceiving a rational agent.[64] The value of rational agency on a Kantian view is absolute. As Kant puts it, dignity has no "market price." As such, both deception and the coercion involved in murder threaten the non-relative value of rational agency. On one line of reasoning, deceiving is justified as a means to help a person at risk not because some wills (a murderer's) are less deserving of respect than others, but because a will (such as the murderer's) can, out of respect, be blocked from its own corruption.

[64] See Herman (1993, 155–56).

This suggests that there may be a broader range of cases in which lying as a means to repel harm may be deliberative Kantian options. Consider another hypothetical example, inspired by recent reports by midshipmen at the U.S. Naval Academy. David receives a copy of an examination that is in fact the one the "mids" are due to sit tomorrow, but he is unaware of that fact and indeed has not been told that the exam is the real thing. "Bilge," study copies of past exams, regularly circulate in the dorm and are regarded by officials as legitimate study material. David does not end up spending time with this "bilge," since he already studied amply for the exam before the unsolicited material arrived on his desk. When David takes the exam, one or two examples look vaguely familiar, but he assumes they are just variants of bilge examples or examples sufficiently like the practice ones he has worked on from past lectures. After sitting the exam, he learns from others that what was circulating in the dorm the evening before was indeed the real thing, and that there had been a compromise of the security of the exam. What follows are allegations of widespread cheating on campus. As part of the official investigation of the test compromise, David's friend, Jonathan, is called in to testify regarding David's cheating. The investigation involves methods of entrapment and lying of which Jonathan has become well aware through the reports of all those who have emerged from closed-door sessions before him. Now, alone in a closed-door session, he has been told to tell what he knows, with threats made against him; he is certain, again, from the reports of those who preceded, that if he explains his friend's case in the manner explained above – that David was unaware that he had the genuine test – the investigators will distort it as evidence that David did in fact cheat and that David will consequently be separated from the academy and banned from a career in military service.

The case is complicated. I have preserved the different strands as a reminder of the motley nature of our experience and narratives of it. As Jonathan perceives it, lying to the investigator is a means to prevent aggression against his innocent friend. Here, it is not lying to save a life, but lying to save a career. I shall not repeat the sort of deliberative considerations I have indicated in the preceding case of lying, but I think they are apt. Issues of servility, of blocking the corrupt principles of another, of the duty to mutual aid, raise substantive considerations that may, arguably, defeat the prohibition against lying in a case like this. But the general point of this and the preceding examples is that permissibility is determined not by a formalized procedure, but by narration of the case and specification of the competing moral ends. An effort to grasp how the more general value of respect for rational agency informs those ends marks the distinctive normative flavor of a plausible model of Kantian deliberation.

5 COMPARING ARISTOTLE AND KANT ON JUDGMENT AND DELIBERATION

Having now outlined some of the broad lines of the Kantian account of practical reason, I conclude the chapter by drawing some comparative lines with the Aristotelian account. I believe there is greater rapprochement between the authors than our initial sketch of traditional contrasts (in the beginning of the last chapter, say) suggested.

Perhaps the first thing to note is that the contemporary promise of the Categorical Imperative as providing a testing procedure for deliberating in hard cases – the sort of procedure noticeably absent in Aristotelian ethics – seems to be somewhat dimmed. I have argued that Kantian deliberation follows a more informal, reflective method involving a rich narration of the salient features of the case in conjunction with a progressive specification of the conflicting norms involved. The general deliberative question is, What do those norms require of me in these circumstances? Appeal to the ultimate value of rational agency and to treating persons in nonmanipulative ways underlies the ideal agent's general understanding of those norms. While this norm is distinctively Kantian, the account of the deliberative method shares much in common with an Aristotelian conception. Deliberation, for the Aristotelian agent, as I have described it in Chapter 6, is largely a matter of judging the particular features of a case, with strong emphasis given to the discursive business of narrating the circumstances before one. Justification is not a flatfooted matter of appeal to rules or criterial tests, but a "working through" of what specific virtues relevant to a case require of one here and now. That is, the virtues are porous, not given in rules or applied procedurally, but to be worked out and developed in light of present exigencies. They have discretionary latitude. In the virtuous agent they inform how circumstances are described at the same time that they figure as part of a deeper and integrated type of understanding about the good life in general. To have the virtues is to have an understanding that is both general and particular.

The procedural method of the Categorical Imperative still has a clear employment on my interpretation of Kantian ethics. It generates the norms that inform judgment and guide deliberation. That is, it gives a constructive account of their origin according to internal constraints of our rational nature. (Here it might be useful to think of the Categorical Imperative and its construction of the basic norms as loosely parallel to Rawls's notion of the Original Position and its construction of the basic structure of society.) For reasons cited earlier, I believe this construction is best brought out by using the Formula of Humanity and not the Universal Law Formula, at least conceived on its own. (So even here, the thought experiment, Could others act on my maxim?, is not sufficient, and the notion of practical reason as legislative may not capture all we hope for in the Kantian model.) Obligatory ends are generated negatively by detecting impermissible policies, deemed so because they contradict or violate our essential rational natures as choosers of ends. In the case of neglect of others, we deprive others of the interpersonal resources which as finitely rational beings they need in order to be meaningful choosers of ends; in the case of neglect of ourselves, we deprive ourselves of the cultivated powers which as finitely rational beings (who develop through education and effort over time) we require in order to be able to pursue a wide range of ends in the future. Actions are contrary to perfect duties to others if others cannot assent to the ends of those actions; so, for example, when we lie to others, we deny them the opportunity of assenting to the lie. What is noteworthy here is that the generation of the various norms is by and large constrained by our rational nature, *contingently construed*. We need the aid of others in order to promote our rational natures *in the permanent human circumstances in which our own resources are finitely limited.* We need to cultivate our various powers in order to promote our rational natures *in the human circumstances in which those powers are not given fully developed but require for their realization nurture and education.* It is only lying, perhaps, that thwarts our rational natures in a pure way (though, even here, as pointed out earlier, the impossibility of universalized lying depends, once again, upon our finite nature to remember past deceptions).

I do not believe Aristotle can generate the norms of virtuous action in quite the same way. For a start, the Aristotelian virtues do not appeal to the preservation of our rational natures as primary, but to our rational *and* affective natures as interlocked aspects of our humanity. As we said earlier in rehearsing Nussbaum's account, we are to use our rational and affective capacities well in the specific domains humans regularly operate within – in circumstances of fear, excessive desire, others' needs, and the like. To use our powers well or excellently is never defined negatively, in terms of either avoiding logical contradictions or practical self-defeat. What is excellent is measured not against that sort of abstract rule, but against the embodied standard of a *phronimos*. This has notoriously raised the charge of a vicious circle (that we grasp virtue by looking to the person of practical wisdom, but only know how to recognize such an exemplar if we already know what virtue is). I think the circle is hardly vicious, and simply makes good use of the abiding Aristotelian point – that abstract ideas need be deepened by a grasp of their exemplification, and that exemplification, in turn, can be better understood through a reflection back on the principles embraced by that model.

Still, as we said earlier, the virtues can be given a more general account than Aristotle is often thought to provide. The virtues can be defined as ways of preserving self in certain ways – that if we don't stand up to certain fears, we can't preserve ourselves in the face of frequent threats and vulnerabilities; that if we don't work toward temperance, we can't make long range goals and plans that take us beyond the immediate desires of brutish living; that if we are uncommitted to generosity, we fail to appreciate our nature as socially interdependent beings whose flourishing depends

upon the goodness of others, and so on. In each case, what is
excellent in the use of our human powers is not defined ar-
bitrarily by the example of some heroic individual, but by what it
is reasonable to require of a human being in order to cope well in
the pervasive conditions of this world. Still, several features
distinguish this rough outline of an Aristotelian account from a
Kantian one. First, the powers that form the basis of our "selves"
to be preserved and actualized are our rational *and* affective natures viewed in a more interdependent way than even our anthropological account of Kantian ethics easily accommodates. On the
Aristotelian view, both are parts of human nature and together
sources of normative value; emotion needs to be responsive to
reason, but reason is activated best when emotions are invested.
Second, the account depends centrally on an embodied model of
excellence. As we have said, this may have to do with Aristotle's
deep skepticism about the usefulness of overly abstract conceptions in conveying practical, normative values. But also, his ethical theory is meant to be a theory about moral development. It is
both about what virtue is and how we become virtuous. The role
of models – of embodied *phronimoi* – whom we can emulate and
become inspired by is key.

There is one final contrastive point to note. Although we have
argued for a degree of latitude in the conception of Kantian perfect duties, the overall distinction between imperfect and perfect
duties is still important to preserve, and one not readily available
to Aristotle. While the apparent absence of perfect (juridical)
duties in Aristotelian ethics is often noted,[65] what is less noted is
just how unclear Aristotle is about the latitude that virtuous ends
in fact allow. Fine action is right action that hits the target
(*skopos*).[66] Though this will not be determinable antecedently or

---

[65] Here a qualification is important. At NE 1107a11–13, Aristotle is eager to
distinguish adultery, theft, and murder as always wrong, and to this extent
proscriptions of them may resemble something like juridical (perfect) duties. I
am grateful to Richard Kraut for reminding me of this passage, in April 1991 at
an APA, Author Faces the Critics symposium on *The Fabric of Character*.

[66] That is, discerns the case right, according to *orthos logos*, and the action is fine
in virtue of that discernment. But there are other sorts of targets, as Martha
Nussbaum has reminded me, that Aristotle often seems to have in mind. There

by a set of rules, there is a sense that we can identify some determinate target at the level at which context dependency makes
itself felt. In the language of that metaphor, there are many ways
to go wrong, literally, "to miss the mark" (*hamartanein*), but only
one way to get it right.[67] How much to give, when, how, and to
whom can be answered: *this much,* on *this occasion,* in *such a way,* to
her.[68] Despite Aristotle's frequent reminders of the indeterminacy
of contingent situations, in the actual judgment of when and how
to act, there seems ideally some mean that the person of practical
wisdom would fix on. There seems little discretionary room
around the bull's-eye.

Kant's use of the perfect–imperfect distinction can be seen as
something of an attempt to clarify the notion of hitting a target.
The sphere of virtue (*ethica*) is separate from justice (*ius*) insofar as
only duties within the latter sphere (corresponding by and large
to perfect duties)[69] have an external outer aspect that can be more
easily specified and externally regulated or enforced. In the case
of imperfect duty, however, or virtue proper, there is an obligatory end that leaves considerable discretionary latitude in how

is, in addition, the target or end of *eudaimonia.* So at NE 1117b9 Aristotle says
one might lose one's life performing a noble action, and so lose one's ultimate
target of *eudaimonia,* even though still one's action, as a fine action, reaches its
target (see also NE 1094a20, EE 1214b8–10). Similarly, there are ends or targets
that are the more determinate objectives of one's actions, such as saving one's
country or vanquishing the enemy. One might fail to reach these targets,
though still hit the target in the sense of exercising one's judgment correctly.
Note, on a related point, although on Aristotle's view the fine can tolerate
failed outcomes, nonetheless it matters to an assessment of fineness that *some*
action actually ensue. To extend Aristotle's metaphor (NE 1098b3–99a15), the
Olympiast injured before the competition and relegated to merely imagining
himself competing in the race has failed to achieve the fine in some important
sense.

[67] NE 1106b29–31.
[68] I am most grateful to Chris Dustin (on the occasion of a Boston Area Colloquium in Ancient Philosophy, 1992, devoted to an ancestor of this chapter) for
helping me refine my thoughts in this paragraph.
[69] There are perfect duties, too, that fall under duties of virtue, for instance,
proscriptions against suicide, lying, and stupefaction, and that admit of a more
or less determinate range of omission and commission. But Kant typically
thinks of virtue proper as imperfect.

and when an agent chooses to satisfy that end. Here, there is no specific outer aspect to look for; there is no determinate limit or target that must be hit. There is just an end or policy without the suggestion, for example, that we do wrong when we fail to exercise that end on a particular occasion in which we may judge it to be appropriate. There is latitude in choosing our occasions. It may be that in Kant's notion of an imperfect duty we have a truer sense of the discretionary room we expect to find in Aristotelian virtue. In the next chapter, we turn to further thoughts about the discretionary nature of Kantian virtue.

Chapter 8

Perfecting Kantian virtue: Discretionary latitude and superlative virtue

In the last chapter we saw that Kant's notion of imperfect duties brings to bear the important idea of discretionary latitude: We have play-room (*Spielraum*) in how we fulfill our ends. The introduction of this notion seemed a helpful way of relaxing what can be an overly rigoristic feature in Aristotle's account – perhaps best expressed by the thought that while there are many ways to go wrong in fulfilling virtue, there is only one way to get it right. Put this way, "hitting the mean" gives the sense that virtue has a determinate manifestation relative to each person – toward *this* object, at *this* time, in *this* manner. The discretionary element of good judgment becomes obscured. Still, Kant's notion of latitude may leave us wondering just how demanding his own conception of virtue is.

In this chapter I want to explore the kind of latitude imperfect duties permit. We can locate our discussion within the context of a pair of familiar, though conflicting, criticisms often leveled against Kant's theory of virtue. On the one side, it is argued that Kantian virtue theory is too latitudinarian, giving *arbitrary* discretion to whether we fulfill duties of virtue. This is sometimes couched within a more general view that Kantian ethics, as a duty-based theory, is minimalist insofar as doing one's duty is conceived of as doing some minimal amount and no more.[1] It is following the letter of the law rather than its spirit. On the other side is the criticism that Kantian morality is overly rigoristic, demanding too much of an individual agent, especially in promoting others' welfare. In emphasizing our duties to others rather than our own happiness or fulfillment, Kantian morality, it is charged, devalues the self.[2] In the course of this chapter, I argue that both of these views are misconceptions. Kantian theory can be seen as neither marginalizing morality nor marginalizing the self. Neither need be a vice of Kantian virtue. Following Kant's own cues, I argue that a Kantian conception of virtue ought to be stern, avoiding both a lenient indulgence and a fanaticism that strains beyond the attainable.[3]

2 IMPERFECT DUTIES OF VIRTUE: LATITUDINARIAN AND RIGORISTIC READINGS

Before beginning, however, it will be helpful to review the defining marks of an imperfect duty of end, as Kant develops that notion in *The Metaphysic of Morals*. Forgoing a detailed exegesis of Kant's terminology, we can distinguish wide imperfect duties from perfect duties in two primary ways.[4] First, as emphasized in Chapter 7, imperfect duties are duties to adopt a maxim of end, not a particular action. In the case of imperfect duties, "reason gives no law for actions but only a law for the maxims of actions."[5] An imperfect duty to act on a maxim of end characterizes a duty of virtue: "imperfect duties . . . are only duties of virtue."[6]

---

[1] Heyd (1982); Urmson (1958).

[2] Most recently voiced by Slote (1992).

[3] For Kant's brief remarks about latitudinarian and rigorist interpretations, see Rel. 22/18–19. My own discussion in this chapter is indebted to Marcia Baron's excellent account of the latitude of imperfect virtue in her new book (1995a), which I have read in manuscript form.

[4] Here, and in the next two paragraphs, I follow very closely Baron's (1995, ch.2) discussion of Thomas Hill. For further exegetical detail on imperfect and perfect duties, see Gregor (1963, ch. 7).

[5] DV 392.   [6] DV 390.

Second, imperfect duties of end admit latitude not allowed to perfect duties. As maxims of ends, the prescription of imperfect duties is indefinite, leaving room for discretion or "play-room" (*Spielraum*), as Kant puts it, in the fulfillment of those ends. So Kant says, "If, [in the case of imperfect duties] the law can prescribe only the maxim of actions, not actions themselves, this indicates that it leaves a play-room (*latitudo*) for free choice in following (observing) the law, i.e., that the law cannot specify precisely what and how much one's actions should do toward the obligatory end."[7] There is play-room in the "kind and extent" (*Art und Grade*) of the actions themselves."[8] Tom Hill has suggested that we understand different kinds of latitude in roughly the following way: There is latitude (a) in the judgment of *when* and *whether* an end (or principle) is appropriate to a particular situation, (b) in the choice of *how* to fulfill the end, and (c) in the choice of *whether or not to act* on an end in a given occasion when that end has been judged to be appropriate, "provided that one is ready to perform acts of that sort on some other occasions."[9] What is of most interest to us in this chapter is latitude type *c* – the nature of latitude in the decision of whether to fulfill imperfect duties that we judge to be appropriate to given circumstances.

In addition to the distinction between perfect and imperfect duties is the distinction between juridical and ethical duties. Whereas juridical duties can be externally regulated and enforced, ethical duties are a matter of inner sanction. In the case of ethics, others cannot compel us to fulfill our duties; they are a matter of self-constraint.[10] In the case of justice, corresponding to our duties are rights to exercise compulsion. But in addition to these different sources of sanction, juridical and ethical duties can often, though not always, be distinguished in the way that perfect and imperfect duties can be, by reference to whether the laws

---

[7] DV 390.   [8] DV 446.

[9] Hill (1971). Type *a* latitude (judgment of the occasion) will be required for the deployment of juridical virtues, as well as narrower imperfect duties of virtue such as those Kant in fact refers to as perfect virtues (e.g., duties of respect falling under imperfect duties to self and other).

[10] DV 379.

prescribe particular actions or only ends,[11] and by reference to the latitude allowed in fulfilling those laws.

However, this way of putting it doesn't quite get the distinction right, for perfect and imperfect are not mutually exclusive categories and perfect duties are, in fact, not restricted to the sphere of justice.[12] There are nonjuridical perfect duties in addition to nonjuridical imperfect ones. Put differently, there are perfect *and* imperfect ethical duties, or duties of virtue. Perfect and imperfect ethical duties are not mutually exclusive in that Kant views certain perfect (ethical) duties as derivative of more general imperfect duties toward self-perfection. So, for example, there are perfect duties to self with regard to one's physical nature (e.g., to avoid suicide, sexual defilement, gluttony, and stupefaction) and with regard to one's moral nature (e.g., to avoid lying, avarice, and servility) that fall under the more general heading of imperfect duties toward self-perfection, just as there are narrow duties of respect (to avoid contemptuousness, as well as backbiting and ridicule) that fall under wider imperfect duties to promote the happiness of others. In addition to these, there are "vices . . . opposed to love of man" which again include negative attitudes toward others, such as envy, ingratitude, malicious joy, as well as a general lack of charity in one's assessment of others' abilities and an absence of a conciliatory spirit.[13] It is not clear why Kant does not include the avoidance of these as narrow duties of respect, but perhaps he means to emphasize the positive, more transformative measures that would be typically coupled with their avoidance. In any case, although Kant does not label these or duties of respect as perfect duties, he does emphasize that duties of respect are nevertheless to be considered as "*narrow* in comparison with a duty of love" (by which we also fulfill our duties of virtue to others) and in their narrowness, "analogous to the juridical duty" we have in not encroaching on the outer freedom of others.[14] Still, the idea of perfect or narrow duties within the ethical sphere might seem odd, since Kant so often elides ethical

---

[11] See DV 381: "Ethics can also be defined as the system of the *ends* of the pure practical reason."

[12] See Gregor (1963, 115–116), and Hill (1971, 60).

[13] DV 458–64.   [14] DV 449.

duties of virtue with imperfect duties of wide obligation.[15] But Kant's idea behind a perfect (or narrow) ethical duty seems to be this: Just as juridical duties place *external* constraints on our imperfect duties of beneficence to others, so with regard to our own imperfect duty of self-perfection there are proscriptions (the negative duties characteristic of juridical duties) that place *internal* constraints on how we promote our moral and physical natures. So it will turn out in the case of imperfect duties to others, that in addition to there being juridical perfect duties that externally constrain fulfillment, there are narrow or strict ethical duties that restrict not so much actions (since these would fall under juridical duties) but emotional and intellectual attitudes including contempt, mockery, and probably what we would today label "hate speech." The general point is that in duties toward both self and others, there are narrower ethical duties of proscription that constrain wider imperfect duties. It is important to add, though, that even these narrower duties allow certain forms of latitude insofar as determining *when* and *whether* proscriptions apply requiring discretionary judgment. This also would hold of perfect juridical duties.

With these distinctions in hand, we can return to the question of the evidence for a latitudinarian or rigoristic reading of Kantian imperfect duties of virtue. In the passage just quoted in which Kant introduces the notion of latitude, he includes the following restrictions:

> But a wide duty is not to be taken as a permission to make exceptions to the maxim of actions, but only as a permission to limit one maxim of duty by another (e.g., love of one's neighbor in general by love of one's parents) – a permission that actually widens the field for the practice of virtue.[16]

There has been considerable discussion of how to interpret these qualifications. What seems clear is that Kant wants to guard against a "free for all" interpretation of wide imperfect duties of virtue. That imperfect duties admit latitude does not entail that there be "exceptions to the maxims of actions" in the sense that

15 As at DV 392. 16 DV 390.

one can fail to honor the obligatory end prescribed by the maxim. Promoting the happiness of others is a duty, omission of which is blameworthy, just as breaking a promise is. There is no permission to abandon an end of virtue. What there is permission to do, is to limit one duty by another (perfect or imperfect, as we have seen in Chapter 7), as well as one specification of an imperfect duty by another – for instance, helping parents rather than neighbors. In limiting an imperfect duty in this last way, one opens the possibility of forgoing action now in order to meet the demands of other claims of duty, which may not themselves require present action but which still compete for one's time. In this there is recognition that one's time and resources are ultimately finite. Kant's remarks are not meant to invite laxity. Quite to the contrary: Limiting one imperfect duty by another serves to "widen" or expand the field for the practice of virtue in that it does not restrict the fulfillment of an obligatory end to one specification that may be infrequently relevant. There are many ways to fulfill an imperfect duty such as that of promoting others' happiness. One cannot fail to help others simply because one is waiting for a time when parents, say, and not strangers will need one's services. Still, on a plausible interpretation of the above view, one would be permitted to "limit" one's time in community projects, say, because of the more stringent and ongoing demands of family, even though those family demands may not require attention at the very moment one is asked to help elsewhere.

Even so, these restrictions on the latitude of imperfect duties of virtue might seem to introduce an unwelcome rigorism. On the strictest reading of that passage we can pass over opportunities for fulfilling virtue only if there are conflicting grounds of obligation or, in Herman's terms, competing deliberative presumptions. We can't simply say "no," "not now," "some other time," on grounds of convenience. In this sense, the passage does not seem to support Hill's notion of latitude of type c, whereby an agent may pass over occasions for the fulfillment of obligatory ends "provided one is ready to perform acts of that sort on some other occasion." Kant seems to require that there be a more stringent claim from a competing ground of duty.

Some commentators, including Hill, have argued that grounds

for rejecting a rigoristic reading of Kant's restrictions are implicit in Kant's rejection of moral fanaticism, or what he calls, "fantastic virtue."[17] Here the following text from *The Metaphysic of Morals* is relevant:

> That man can be called fantastically virtuous who admits *nothing* morally *indifferent (adiaphora)* and strews all his steps with duties, as with man-traps; it is not indifferent, to him, whether I eat meat or fish, drink beer or wine, supposing that both agree with me. Fantastic virtue is a micrology which, were it admitted into the doctrine of virtue, would turn the sovereignty of virtue into a tyranny.[18]

Marcia Baron has pointed out correctly that Kant's criticisms here are in fact directed not against a rigoristic conception of virtue but against "phony virtue." The indictment is not of superlative virtue, but of a common misconception of it: As she puts it, "the fantastically virtuous man is someone who sees virtue (or the possibility of being virtuous) where it isn't. . . . He is not someone who takes imperfect duties too seriously but someone who makes a fetish out of trivial things (what to eat and drink, and when) wrongly thinking them to be morally non-trivial."[19] In short, this moral fanatic makes a fetish of the morally indifferent. (The Stoics make the point vividly: There are certain kinds of values that are of pure indifference to moral well-being, such as whether we have an odd or even number of hairs on our head or whether our finger happens to be contracted or stretched. They are entirely "equal with respect to choice and avoidance " and indifferent with regard to a morally good life.)[20]

This is not the only misconception of superlative virtue Kant indicts. In the second *Critique*, he repeatedly condemns the notion of pursuing supermeritorious action out of self-love rather than duty. What follows is part of Kant's broad-sweep attack on what he views as romanticized, high-flown morality:

> The mind is disposed to nothing but blatant moral fanaticism and exaggerated self-conceit by exhortation to actions noble,

[17] Hill (1971, 59) implies this.   [18] DV 409.   [19] Baron (1995a, 91).
[20] Diogenes Laertius 7.104–5 (SVF 3.119) = L and S 58 B.

sublime, and magnanimous. By it people are led to the illusion that the determining ground of their actions is not duty, i.e., respect for the law. . . . This law always humbles them when they follow (obey) it, but by this kind of exhortation they come to think that those actions are expected of them not because of duty but only because of their own bare merit . . . ; they produce in this way a shallow, high-flown, fantastic way of thinking, flattering themselves with a spontaneous goodness of heart, needing neither spur nor bridle nor even command, and thereby forgetting their obligation, which they ought to think of rather than their merit. . . . Certainly actions of others which have been done with great sacrifice and merely for the sake of duty may be praised as noble and sublime deeds, yet only insofar as there are clues which suggest that they were done wholly out of respect for duty and not from aroused feelings.[21]

This passage takes us closer to what Kant holds to be the marks of genuine, superlative virtue. Moral worth (and *genuine* moral merit) derive from the motive of duty, not from feeling ungrounded in moral interest, and least of all, not from motives that betray self-conceit. Moreover, this text underscores the notion that for Kant, superlative virtue is to be conceived of *within* imperfect duty, and not beyond or outside it, in the way a strictly supererogationist model requires: "Actions . . . done with great sacrifice and merely for the sake of duty may be praised as noble and sublime deeds, yet only insofar as there are clues which suggest that they were done wholly out of respect." If there is an arousal of wonder and the sublime, it is properly toward the disposition to obey the moral law itself.[22] This will be a point to which we return.

But while the above two passages just quoted caution against what Kant takes to be false conceptions of rigorous virtue, in their own right they do not tell against a more plausible rigorism. However, there are other passages that serve this end and that temper significantly the suggestion of rigorism in the passage from *The Metaphysic of Morals* (390) with which we began our discussion.

[21] KpV 85–86.   [22] See, in this context, Rel. 48–49/44–5.

Principal here is the notion Kant introduces in that work of "true needs" as limiting our imperfect duty to promote the happiness of others.

> [The law says] only that I should sacrifice a part of my well-being to others without hope of requital, because this is a duty; it cannot assign determinate limits to the extent of this sacrifice. These limits will depend, in large part, on what a person's true needs consist of in view of his temperament, and it must be left to each to decide this for himself. . . . Hence this duty is only a *wide* one: since no determinate limits can be assigned to what should be done, the duty has in it a play-room for doing more or less. – The law holds only for maxims not for determinate actions.[23]

Against the criticism that Kantian ethics is unduly directed toward the welfare of others,[24] this passage reminds us that the Kantian agent's happiness and needs are not a matter of moral indifference. Although on Kant's view we do not have a direct duty to our own happiness (since we are moved toward it naturally and thus don't require the compulsion of duty), we do have an indirect duty to promote it where neglect of our needs (as in the case of avarice or servility) threatens fulfillment of our moral ends and ultimately undermines our moral integrity. "To seek prosperity for its own sake is no direct duty, but it can well be an indirect duty" as in the duty to ward off poverty so we are not liable to temptation nor at the constant mercy of others' charity.[25] Kant stresses this limitation on beneficence over and over in *The Metaphysic of Morals*: "To provide oneself with such comforts as are necessary merely to enjoy life . . . is a duty to oneself. The contrary of this is to deprive oneself of the essential pleasures of life, whether from avarice (of the slavish kind) or from exaggerated (fanatical) discipline of one's natural inclinations."[26] These remarks, like the statement about true needs, are introduced as

---

23 DV 393. See KpV 62. Cf. KpV 161, in which he recommends that as a part of moral development, the moral learner try to relieve himself "of the constraints even of his true needs."
24 This is the force of Slote's criticism (1992).
25 DV 388.   26 DV 452; see also 455.

restrictions on the fulfillment of our ethical duties to others, though they can be cross-referenced with our perfect duties to moral self-perfection, which include in their catalogue, avoidance of avarice and servility.[27] The general point is that direct and indirect duties to self limit the latitude of our duties to others. Of course, assessment of how much we need to fulfill our duties to self itself allows of latitude, and thus while Kant represents the avoidance of avarice and servility as perfect duties, their deployment allows, as we have said earlier, for discretion. As Kant expresses the point in the true needs text, there will be latitude relative to the individual and determined by the individual on the basis of the agent's assessment of his own temperament: "These limits will depend, in large part, on what a person's true needs consist of in view of his temperament (*nach seiner Empfindungsart*), and it must be left for each to decide this for himself." In a general way, Kant's notion is reminiscent of Aristotle's view of virtue as a disposition to choose a mean or intermediate state "relative to us," that is, relative to the tendencies and needs of the individual choosing.[28] Kant might be allowing that varied and wide differences in the development of natural talents and modes of life frame different views of what count as bottom line necessities. How much warmth, food, education, companionship, or psychological support one needs will vary from subculture to subculture, and within that, from individual to individual, in terms of both temperament and cultivated habits. Of course, there is more than ample room for self-deception about the extent and urgency of our basic needs, as well as room for resisting reassessment. But as always, we have a stern duty to submit our appraisal to the sincere and conscientious review essential to a morally

---

[27] DV 432–37.

[28] NE 1106b36ff. What Milo the wrestler requires for a moderate diet will be different from what a lighter-weight charioteer needs. In this explicit metaphor, the limit is set relative to the weight and physical constitution of the individual. (Note, this metaphor may emphasize again the narrow range, for each person, of "hitting the mark right.") In a similar way, Aristotle suggests that what is appropriate to give away through liberality must be relative to one's own means and guided by a desire to avoid the extremes of leaving too little or too much for oneself (NE IV.1).

vigilant life. The duty to self-knowledge is "the first command of all duties to oneself," Kant reminds us. Included here is a duty to seek out the ways we deceive and protect ourselves through less than candid disclosures.[29] The problem of honesty is no different here than in other areas.

The claim about true needs is essentially a claim that beneficence must not involve devaluing the self. The self is one among equals, and with regard to dignity, which is after all the ground of our interest in the happiness of persons, each person can "value himself on a footing of equality" with others.[30] The promotion of my own happiness can, on grounds of my equality with others, limit my duty to promote others' happiness: "Legislative reason . . . *permits* you to be benevolent to *yourself* under the condition of your being benevolent to every other man as well."[31] Thus there is latitude to promote one's own well-being, as well as obvious latitude in the choice of *to whom* and *to what degree* one devotes one's beneficence: "In acting I can, without violating the universality of my maxim, vary the degree greatly according to the different objects of my love (one of whom concerns me more closely than the other)."[32] This fills out earlier remarks about the limiting of one specification of duty by another. The implication is not that friends and loved ones are the only ones deserving of beneficence, but that there is permissible latitude to do more for those we know. There are obvious reasons for this kind of preferential treatment within beneficence. As we have argued in an earlier chapter, bonds of intimacy and attachment allow us to help in substantive and deep ways often unavailable to others less well placed. Also, time is a nonrenewable resource. While we may be able to help others substantively through money and proxy participation, more costly time expenditures, through active engagement in the welfare of others, may be more severely limited, especially if we are not to ride roughshod over the true needs that support our own moral agency. This is not an argument to neglect beneficence in wider circles but one that recog-

---

29 DV 441; Rel. 50/50; 77/71. I touch on the issue in Chapter 7, sec. 2 of this volume, and more extensively in Sherman (1993a).
30 DV 435.   31 DV 451.   32 DV 452.

nizes the variety of means and degrees by which we can be beneficent to different persons. Kant holds that we are not abandoning
the end of beneficence in allowing this discretionary room, even if
it can be argued that we act more meritoriously when we cultivate
efforts to heal substantively a community that includes but is
larger than our immediate circle.

To sum up the textual evidence so far, we have considerable
latitude in the deployment of our wide imperfect duties, including latitude in choosing to pass over a helping situation in circumstances we judge appropriate to helping when there are opposing
grounds of obligation or when our own true needs or, more
loosely put, our own happiness, demand attention. But does the
evidence support the view of latitude Hill has suggested, in
which we may pass over occasions for fulfilling an imperfect
duty, such as beneficence, provided merely that we are committed to doing something some other time? As Hill puts it at one
point, a wide imperfect duty requires only that an individual "act
accordingly, at least sometimes, if he gets a chance."[33] Is there
evidence for this more relaxed latitudinarianism?

Baron has raised significant worries about this formulation.
Put briefly, her concern is that it tolerates tokenism – it permits us
to fulfill our duties to others by helping *only from time to time.*
Indeed, it seems compatible with Hill's view that beneficent acts
be kept at a minimum, though they should not diminish to zero.
We might also add there is a more general worry about the *spirit*
of minimalism it seems to tolerate. There is something too
calculating in fulfilling our duties to others by drawing on either
credits from the past or promissory notes for the future. It is true,
one migh sincerely say, I gave already this year to charity X,
suggesting by this some kind of budgeting not incompatible with
respecting one's own true needs. In Aristotelian language, liberality requires that we act as a steward of our inflow and outflow –
typically of wealth, but we might also add, of time. I have contributed time already to my child's classroom, I might say; there is
a self-check of my record that needn't be niggling or ungenerous.
But in asking this sort of question there is a decided difference

[33] Hill (1971, 58).

342

between asking have I done *something* and have I done *enough*. "Something" connotes a minimal amount. "Enough" leaves room for more and suggests a more serious responsibility. It is the minimalism of doing merely *something* that is problematic. Finally, general concerns about weakness of will, moral procrastination, frequent yielding to whim and pleasure over the fulfillment of virtue, point to ways that Hill's gloss undercuts Kant's own insistence that virtue requires fortitude and a serious commitment to the unending progress of moral perfection. As Kant might put it, virtue must be unindulgent, and not just ideally possible.

For these sorts of reasons I agree with Baron that we require a *sterner* latitudinarianism. We want some occasions for not fulfilling imperfect duties in the absence of both opposing grounds of obligation and unsatisfied bottom-line needs, but we want something more than mere convenience or past tokens to weigh in as good reasons for not helping others. Perhaps the simplest way to capture this is in a general formulation in which "sometimes" is replaced with "most of the time" in Hill's formulation that wide imperfect duties of end such as beneficence require that we act to promote those ends, at least "sometimes." This would insure that future opportunities for action come to more than merely *the last opportunity* before time runs out.[34] The point is to give clear emphasis to virtue in a conscientious moral life without requiring that an agent do *all* she can, or maximize. *Every* occasion that is not a morally indifferent one need not be devoted to virtue, but the emphasis should be on doing more rather than less over the long run.

Baron hopes to refine the view by arguing that the sterner latitudinarianism might best be captured in an interpretation that gives considerably less latitude to the duty to moral self-perfection than to the duty to promote my natural perfection and the duty to promote the happiness of others. If there is rigorism, it is in the notion that we must do, as she suggests, as much as

---

34 Hill suggests that we avoid the zero point in fulfilling virtue by making sure we are not nearing the last opportunity for virtuous action. Though one sometimes has this sense of urgency in high-risk situations, overall this seems a strange way of viewing most of life's occasions for virtue.

possible to perfect ourselves morally (without understanding this to mean, once again, on every occasion).[35] Her claim is that textual evidence bearing against rigorism in our duty to promote others' happiness does not seem to tell against the promotion of our own moral self-perfection.

There is something intriguing about Baron's suggestion, but a notion of differential rigorism may end up obscuring rather than clarifying the special and complex nature of our duty to moral self-perfection. To make this point, we need to consider briefly the end of moral self-perfection. What seems clearest in Kant's writings is that the duty to moral self-perfection operates on a different level than our imperfect duties to self as a natural being or our imperfect duties to others.[36] It is a more fundamental duty, in that what we aim to cultivate through moral self-perfection, namely, an abiding interest in acting not merely in compliance but from the motive of duty, is a condition for fulfilling all other duties in a morally estimable way. Cultivating moral interest is at once a way of cultivating a nonaccidental interest in other duties. In this sense, the end of moral self-perfection is something of an executive end that distributes over other ends. In the introduction to *The Doctrine of Virtue,* Kant expresses this hierarchical role, stating that the general duty to self-perfection requires the cultivation of natural powers and at the same time "includes the cultivation of one's *will* (moral attitude) to fulfill every duty as such. . . . Man has a duty of cultivating his *will* to the purest attitude of virtue, in which the law is the motive as well as the norm for his actions and he obeys it from duty."[37] The duty of perfecting oneself morally is concerned "subjectively" with "the purity of one's attitude in duty" and "objectively" "with performing all one's duties."[38] Kant's discussion of our moral self-perfection in *The Metaphysic of Morals* is episodic, but culling together the scattered segments, we can say that the general obliga-

---

[35] Baron (1995a, ch. 3).

[36] For a clear explanation of Kant's duties to self as they are catalogued in the DV, see Guyer (1993, 373–82).

[37] DV 387; also 392.

[38] DV 446.

tion to act from duty[39] will include these several sub-ends: as its first command, that we strive to know ourselves and our motives, scrutinizing the depths of our hearts as best we can; and that we judge ourselves conscientiously and impartially before an inner court, sharpening "our attentiveness to the voice of the inner judge."[40] It is easy to see how these are general, subsidiary requirements for fulfilling duties from an interest in the moral law: Strengthening moral motivation will require an introspective stance toward our past and present efforts, as well as the cultivation of an impartial attitude in putting forth morality's claims. Also listed under moral self-perfection are the negative perfect duties we commented on earlier, namely, duties to avoid avarice, lying, and servility. These support not so much our general end to be motivated by duty, but a further general end of our moral development: namely, the end of viewing ourselves as having equal dignity among other persons. This duty to self places permissible limits on our duties to others, as we have said before.

Beyond this, the duty to moral self-perfection requires cultivating, out of duty, the various natural powers that are especially useful for moral agency, such as emotional, perceptual, and affiliative capacities. Moral self-perfection requires that we pay serious attention to the psychological elements of our moral development, so that from moral interest we can transform our natures to support that interest. As we have remarked before, Kant does not list emotional capacities under the duties to advance our natural perfection, restricting that category primarily to intellectual powers, such as mathematical and logical skills, and memory and imagination. Instead, we find the cultivation of feelings of gratitude and sympathy catalogued as duties under our general duty of practical love or beneficence, just as avoidance of negative emotional attitudes of envy, ingratitude, and malice, on the one hand, and attitudes of imperiousness and derision, on the other, are also listed under duties of practical love and respect. Insofar as negative feelings are paired with more positive feelings

---

[39] Paul Guyer (1993, 373–76) introduces the term "the general obligation to act out of the motive of duty" as a translation of *Tugendverpflichtung*.

[40] DV 438–41; 401. See Rel. 77/71–72.

(e.g., ingratitude with gratitude, malice with benevolence) we can conjecture that Kant probably assumed that we most successfully override unwanted emotions not simply by controlling them, but by transforming them into more positive and gracious attitudes. The discussion of the virtues of friendship follow upon the discussion of these feelings as a special case of how the "push and pull" of respect and love operate in the case of attachment emotions. But the point I stress now is that in whichever niche emotional sensitivities end up being catalogued, they, no less than cognitive powers, are among the capacities to be developed as a part of the project of moral self-perfection. To take the perfection of oneself as an end is to cultivate one's agency *and* the supportive structure of one's agency in one's nature. This includes one's emotional susceptibilities, even if Kant often minimizes the point. Although Kant himself holds that emotions such as sympathy or gratitude are not themselves expressive of moral interest, there is no reason to think they could not be if cultivated to involve a concern for the rightness of action and the claims others make on us in virtue of their agency.[41]

We can now return to the issue of rigorism. In what sense, if at all, does the priority of moral self-perfection mean that we should be tougher on ourselves in promoting our moral self-perfection than in promoting, for example, others' happiness? In what sense do we have less latitude here? It can't mean that duties focusing exclusively on my moral perfection rather than others' well-being are to be given preference, or are to be worked at harder. For this misrepresents moral self-perfection as one duty among many. As we have seen, the sternness of effort directed toward moral self-perfection is not something apart from how we fulfill our other duties; it informs the attitude by which we fulfill our duties. One can, of course, imagine instances of apparent conflict – perhaps between an engrossing discussion with an intimate friend about my moral character *and* a call for help from a colleague. But there is no presumption that the first activity, because of its explicit focus on my moral development, takes precedence. It is absurd to

---

[41] I owe thanks to Andy Reath for helpful discussion of this point. I discuss the point at greater length in Chapter 4, sec. 4.

think of the importance of promoting my virtue as dictating specification in that way. In choosing to help, one takes no less seriously the cultivation of one's moral strength. So the rigorism
cannot be one that restricts our choice of *how* to fulfill duties of
moral self-perfection or our recognition of *when* occasions are
relevant. Moral self-perfection is not a separate end or value that
competes for our time in the way that contemplation, for example, in the Aristotelian scheme competes with practical activity
for primacy in the conception of the best life.

In a related way, restricted latitude cannot mean that I take care
of moral self-perfection *before* I turn to others. Virtue is a condition
of the virtues, but it is not a precondition in the sense that there
are powers to be developed *temporally* before helping others or
cultivating our natural talents. Developing a virtuous attitude is a
constitutive and concomitant part of fulfilling these actions from
the right spirit. While there may be some point to exercises that
develop powers before full actualizations – as in focusing on
shining examples of virtue from which to gain inspiration – on the
whole, Kant doesn't think of this as sideline training in lifting
moral dumbbells. Again, Kant may hold that we develop a certain
threshold level of strength before we can fulfill other duties in
morally worthy ways; however, there is no suggestion that this is
ever a matter of an ascetic retreat that would be done in isolation
from our duties to others or would systematically and routinely
compete with the performance of these other duties. The notion of
contemplative moral retreat, emphasized in certain moral and
spiritual traditions, is not something for which Kant has much
sympathy.

So it is not by isolating moral self-perfection that we accord it
differential status with regard to rigorism. But this is not to give
up on the notion of a sterner latitudinarianism. The kernel of
sternness is simply in the idea that we must strive unceasingly to
fulfill our duties from an interest in duty. We must utilize "every
means" to cultivate a conscience that can adequately motivate.
Ascribing a *wide* conscience to someone would amount to thinking of that person as unconscientious. But Kant is quick to qualify
that the frailty of our nature introduces its own form of width or
latitude, in that as human (and not holy) wills we can only strive

for and not fully achieve perfection.[42] Worries that this sternness will lead to equally stern and unabating requirements that we help others are minimized once we recall textual evidence that (a) discounts for morally indifferent occasions for helping (in the way that fantastic virtue fails to), (b) allows for great latitude in how we may help others, and (c) allows that, as equals among others, we cannot let our own happiness be a matter of moral indifference.

We might also note at this point that there seems to be textual evidence for relatively greater latitude in duties to promote those natural talents that don't specifically relate to our moral perfection. So Kant says: "It remains for us to choose, according to our rational deliberation about what sort of life we should like to lead and whether we have the powers necessary for that way of life (e.g., whether it should be manual labor, commerce, or scholarship)."[43] Here, an agent is free to rely on personal preference in the choice of *which* talents to realize, largely because there is much that is simply a matter of moral indifference in cultivating abilities in a nondegrading way: Whether one earns one's living by scholarship or carpentry need not be a matter of moral import. Our preferences and native dispositions can lead the way. Kant does hold that early on in our lives we have a duty to cultivate the widest range of powers possible so that we are best fit to realize whatever ends we may come upon in life. But in the refinement of these powers, in the selection of career or livelihood, we can leave much to subjective preference and natural ability. By contrast, a comparable permission to specialize according to natural ability does not hold in the moral sphere. Whether or not we cultivate sympathy, for example, as a subsidiary end of fulfilling our duties to moral self-perfection and beneficence, cannot depend merely upon our natural leanings and arbitrary preferences. We cannot be complacent with our natures here.

There is one final thought. This sterner view of virtue might seem to be obscured by Kant's own remark that neglect in the fulfilling of imperfect duties does not bring guilt or demerit to an

---

[42] DV 446.   [43] DV 445.

agent, but only an absence of moral worth.[44] This might sound as if omissions of acts in fulfilling imperfect duties are in general a matter of moral indifference, leaving no trace on character. However, this is not Kant's point. Moral worth has to do with dutiful actions performed from the motive of duty. Failure to perform a duty from the motive of duty lacks positive moral worth. So far these remarks don't speak to the question of the impact of omissions on an agent's overall character.[45] Elsewhere Kant does connect transgressions of imperfect duty more directly with the state of an agent's character. "To neglect . . . duties of love," he tells us, "is *lack of virtue* (*peccatum*)."[46] Neglect does not mean rejection of an end of virtue altogether. That would be a more serious failing amounting to vice, just as it would be on an Aristotelian theory.[47] But neither is neglect a matter of a single omission or action. Lack of virtue or moral weakness (*Untugend*), like virtue or moral strength (*Tugend*), is a cumulative affair. In this sense, Kant's notion of moral weakness is akin to Aristotle's notion of *akrasia* (literally, lack of control), which also refers to character states that fall off from excellence. True, Aristotle analyzes *akrasia* in terms of the practical reasoning involved in a given akratic choice.[48] Even so, the akratic is a character type, who doesn't simply occasionally fail to be motivated by what she knows to be best. It is a characteristic way of standing and acting in those circumstances. Again, there are degrees of *akrasia*, as there are degrees of strength, but character describes a pattern of action, not simply a discrete action or omission.

However we understand the latitude a sterner view of virtue

---

44 DV 390; some take this passage as evidence that Kant can accommodate something like the category of the supererogatory. I discuss Kant's accommodation below.

45 Although it is easy to think they might, since Kant uses the same notation of "+a," "0," "–a" at one time to refer to merit (worth), lack of moral worth, guilt, or demerit, and at another to refer to virtue, lack of virtue, and vice. (Contrast DV 390 with 384.)

46 DV 464.

47 DV 390; see Sherman (1992) on issues of culpable neglect.

48 NE VII.3.

tolerates, it is to character, and not to a single action, that on the whole we should focus. Weakness is not a matter of an occasional omission but a policy or pattern of omission on grounds of convenience or procrastination. As such, an omission of a duty of virtue may not be morally indifferent (it may be a bad thing), but it may not itself amount to dereliction of duty. Virtue is a "continual progress," Kant tells us, "from one perfection to others."[49] It reflects a policy or maxim of actions over time.

3 SUPERLATIVE VIRTUE

I now want to ask, In what sense is sacrifice a part of the perfection of virtue? If true needs and an indirect duty to one's own happiness set certain limits on beneficent action, then in what sense may the end of beneficence be fulfilled by actions that go "the second mile" and show a certain kind of selflessness or willingness to takes risks often characteristic of exemplary virtue? Selflessness is, of course, here used as a metaphor that need not entail sacrifice of body or needs required for survival; sacrifice of time can be a form of selflessness that undermines the satisfaction of needs. But the thrust of the question about the extent of sacrifice should be clear. Some have formulated the concern by asking if Kantian morality can accommodate the supererogatory.[50] Understood as good acts that go beyond what is required, supererogatory acts are morally worthy, but their omission is not blameworthy. It is often said that Kantian moral theory cannot accommodate the supererogatory and that this tells against the theory's capacity to capture the moral facts. There have been different responses to the challenge. Tom Hill has argued that Kant leaves room for the supererogatory as a subset of wider imperfect duties. Marcia Baron has questioned the supererogationist thesis itself, on grounds that it puts too much emphasis on discrete, extraordinary *acts*, and as such deflects from a more

---

[49] DV 446; italics omitted. See Rel. 77/71 for the notion of virtue as spanning a whole life.
[50] In a classic article, Urmson (1958) charges that Kantian ethics is inadequate in being unable to accommodate this class of actions. For an overview, see Heyd (1982).

plausible conception of superlative virtue that emphasizes superlative *character* and a superlative pattern of action *over time*. Moreover, this latter conception, she argues, better captures the ideal of
moral virtue implicit in the Kantian notion of imperfect duty.
Richard McCarty has argued for finding a purer analogue of the
supererogatory in the Kantian scheme, in the form of a quasi-
moral category that is *beyond* and not *within* imperfect duty. My
own view is that Kant gives importance to the notion of superlative virtue, particularly in the context of moral education at the
end of the second *Critique*,[51] and that formally, superlative virtue
can be accommodated within his account of imperfect duties in
The Metaphysic of Morals. I shall say something about this accommodation, but my primary focus will be on Kant's own focus –
namely, the educative role of superlative virtue.

First, I begin with the issue of sacrifice. Kant generally means
by sacrifice (*Aufopferung*) a renouncing of some material resource
or value in order to promote another's well-being. There are several passages to consider. We can start with the following from
The Metaphysic of Morals :

> The *subjective degree of responsibility (imputabilitas)* for an action
> must be judged according to the magnitude of the obstacles
> which had to be surmounted in the action. In proportion
> as the natural obstacles (of sensibility) are greater and the
> moral obstacle (of duty) is smaller, so much the more is a good
> action accounted to one's merit, as when, for example, with
> considerable self-sacrifice I rescue a total stranger from great
> distress.[52]

We can pair this with another passage from *The Metaphysic of
Morals* in which Kant warns that the rich person should not view
his beneficence as truly meritorious since it "costs him no sacrifice." In contrast,

> virtue is greater when the benefactor's means are limited and
> he is strong enough quietly to take on himself the hardship he

---

[51] Most explicitly at KpV 152 -63.
[52] DV 228; also on sacrifice, see DV 393.

spares the other. Then he can really be considered morally
rich.[53]

Various questions arise, including to what degree an action's
moral praiseworthiness depends upon obstacle. Virtue, in general, is strength in the face of vulnerability, and there are certainly
greater and smaller challenges to one's strength. Although Kant is
probably assuming a first-person assessment of sacrifice as he
does of true needs, he may nonetheless also have in mind the
perspective of spectator and the thought that as outsiders we may
get our best glimpse of an action done from duty when it is
against the backdrop of obstacle. As Kant puts the familiar point
in the second *Critique,* "it is in suffering that they [the moral
incentives] most notably *show themselves.*"[54] But also we need to
be reminded that what appear as obstacles or great risks from the
third-person point of view are not necessarily viewed that way by
the agent. Kant doesn't explicitly develop the point, but it may be
behind his statement that action is accounted praiseworthy "in
proportion as the natural obstacles (of sensibility) are greater and
the moral obstacle (of duty) is greater": that is to say, superlative
acts of beneficence may often involve a first-person perception
that removes much of the negativity of sacrifice and focuses on
the positive act of doing what one must. We needn't invoke im-
ages here of *fantastic* or holy virtue. The point is not *delusion* about
real loss but, rather, a perception in which relative loss is
diminished simply in virtue of the relative importance of virtue.
Moreover, this sort of comparison need not be a matter of actual
deliberative assessment – of downgrading the value of the sacri-
ficed goods upon assessment of the importance of beneficence.
Persons of exemplary virtue may not typically view their sacrifices as involving extraordinarily hard choices. Such persons may
respond to the demands of beneficence with relative equanimity.
How they see and judge things already diminishes the conflict.[55]

---

[53] DV 453.   [54] KpV 157; italics added.

[55] Here the example of French Huguenots who sheltered large numbers of Jews
in the village of Le Chambon in Nazi-occupied France comes to mind. See
Haillie (1979) and Blum's (1994, ch. 4) discussion of it.

Where we see Kant's most explicit discussion of sacrifice is in the *Critique of Practical Reason*. In a famous example in the beginning of that work, Kant asks whether we could imagine overcoming our love of life, if the cost of staying alive involved making a false deposition against an innocent man whom a sovereign wished to destroy under a false pretext.[56] An even more dramatic example of trying to induce calumny against an innocent occurs at the end of that work (here Kant asks us to imagine an honest man, on pain of his life, being threatened to join the calumniators of Anne Boleyn accused by Henry VIII).[57] But, significantly, in both cases, sacrifice of life is not in the service of beneficence, but in the avoidance of a lie that would be used as a tool of murder. The notion of true needs as setting a limit on what I must do to promote others' happiness isn't at issue. Rather, at stake is the violation of a perfect duty, which Kant presents in these cases as an "inexorable duty" to which "we give our most perfect esteem . . . sacrificing to it everything that ever had value to our dearest inclinations."[58] In another example in this last section of the second *Critique*, where Kant does explicitly raise the issue of risking life in a rescue effort,[59] he didactically uses the example more to argue that our moral esteem is weakened by consideration of possible violation of an agent's own duty to himself, than to emphasize how such action might be a noble fulfillment of duty.

Even so, the rescuing cases of the later *Metaphysic of Morals* suggest that Kant clearly held that we may take on risks and threats to our true needs in the service of beneficence. We may overlook our needs in the assistance of others, though such sacrifice is not required as a part of the fulfillment of beneficence. Imperfect duties of virtue may stretch in this way to accommodate the heroic, or what we might call the supererogatory. But we need to use the term cautiously. As we noted earlier, the idea of supererogatory acts has often been seen as something of a misfit in Kantian ethics, for such acts require going beyond duty

---

[56] KpV 31.   [57] KpV 156–57.

[58] KpV 159. I discuss the rigorisitc interpretation of the proscription against lying in Chapter 7, sec. 4 of this volume.

[59] KpV 159.

whereas Kantian ethics requires that we be guided by duty. As it is sometimes put, the supererogatory requires doing more than the *merely* obligatory. But once we appreciate that imperfect duties of end are neither narrow nor necessarily minimal in their demands, much of the force and appropriateness of this challenge is quickly deflated. Still, if the supererogatory is a matter of extraordinary moral *acts* rather than superlative *character* over time, then again this is not Kant's focus in his account of imperfect duties of virtue. As we have seen, imperfect duties of virtue require maxims of ends, not of specific actions. Moreover, to fulfill such duties in a conscientious way is to fulfill them with a commitment to regular and continuous action over time. The notion of the supererogatory as an indulgence that buys one credit against lesser kindnesses or more regular good deeds becomes suspect on this view.[60] Kant's emphasis is squarely on virtue as a "continual progress" over time, not on the single, extraordinary or uncommon praiseworthy act.

The claim, then, is that there is room for superlative virtue in the account of imperfect duty; one needn't look beyond it for a separate category. Although imperfect duties have lower limits, they seem to be open-ended at the upper limits. Indeed, Richard McCarty's view that imperfect duties of virtue set indeterminate upper limits that allow us to recognize efforts surpassing those limits as having a different moral status[61] – is simply not substantiated in the text of *The Metaphysic of Morals*, and indeed forces a strict analogue of the supererogatory onto that text in an unnatural way. Nor is there support for a separate category in the second *Critique*. In a passage we have already cited from that work, Kant insists that "noble and sublime deeds" performed at great sacrifice to self can be done "wholly out of respect for duty." He continues: "For all actions which are praiseworthy, if we only search we shall find a law of duty which commands and does not *leave us to choose* what may be agreeable to our propensity."[62] Kant is not here explicit about the kind of latitude that he will go on to

---

[60] See Baron (1988) for stimulating discussion of this point.
[61] McCarty (1989).
[62] KpV 86; italics added.

emphasize in his discussion of imperfect duties in *The Metaphysic of Morals,* but his point is compatible with that view – that the most magnanimous acts still must be viewed, on his scheme, as guided by duty or the moral law; praiseworthiness rests in its being recommended (however narrowly or widely) by moral principle. Although the terminology of imperfect duties is not used, it would be strange if Kant were restricting his remarks here to the performance of only perfect duties from the motive of duty. A similar point emerges in the *Religion.*[63] All the goodness one can ever perform, Kant insists, is still one's "simple duty." It is in "no way deserving of wonder. Such wonder is rather a lowering of or feeling for duty, as if to act in obedience to it were something extraordinary and meritorious." Kant's point is that duty itself can motivate the kind of uncommon moral action that other theories are forced to explain in terms of grand sentiments alone.

Thus, I don't believe we have to look outside the rubric of imperfect duty to accommodate superlative virtue. But this still leaves unaddressed the educative role superlative virtue plays in the Kantian scheme. Not a small part of the importance of the saintly and heroic in a commonsense conception of morality is its inspirational role. Kant, as we have said, is skeptical about the models we tend to elevate. But he doesn't disagree that the right kind of hero is someone who can inspire. Thus, his repeated insistence that we need to stay away from heroes of romance is not a discrediting of all heroes. It is not idealization that he is worried about, but simply idealizing the wrong model of virtue:

> It is entirely proper to extol actions which display a great, un-selfish, and sympathetic disposition and humanity. But in them we must attend not so much to the elevation of soul, which is very fleeting and ephemeral, as to the subjection of the heart to duty, from which a more lasting impression can be expected as it entails principles and not just ebullitions, as the former does.[64]

Of essence, then, is depicting an example that can illustrate, with inspiration and clarity, duty-based virtue. Kant's example of

[63] Rel. 48–49/44.   [64] KpV 156n.

resisting calumny paints one vivid portrait. We can now look at that text more carefully:

> Tell him the story of an honest man whom someone wishes to induce to join the calumniators of an innocent but powerless person (say, Anne Boleyn accused by Henry VIII of England). He is offered advantages, e.g., great gifts or high rank; he rejects them. This will cause only applause and approval in the mind of the hearer, because they represent mere gain. Now come threats of loss. Among the slanderers there are his best friends who now renounce his friendship; near-relatives who threaten him (who is without fortune) with disinheritance; powerful persons who can persecute and harass him in all places and in every circumstance; a prince who threatens him with loss of freedom and even of life itself. But that the measure of his suffering may be full, so that he may feel the pain which only the morally good heart can very deeply feel, let his family, which is threatened with extreme need and want, entreat him to yield; think of the man himself, who, though righteous, has feelings which are not insensible or hardened to either sympathy or his own needs, at the moment when he wishes never to have lived to see the day which brings him such unutterable pain – think of him without any wavering or even a doubt remaining true to his resolution to be honest. – Thus one can lead the young listener step by step from mere approval to admiration, and from admiration to marveling, and finally to the greatest veneration and a lively wish that he himself could be such a man (though certainly not in his circumstances). Yet virtue is here worth so much only because it costs so much, not because it brings any advantage. All the admiration and even the endeavor to be like this character rest here solely on the purity of the moral principle, which can be clearly shown only by removing from the incentive of the action everything which men might count as a part of happiness. Thus morality must have more power over the human heart the more purely it is presented.[65]

[65] KpV 156–57.

Here, in an example familiar in its general content though striking in its detail, Kant zooms in on a choice motivated by duty, which elevates an agent above the urgent demands for his own physical survival and for that of his family. The example focuses on the unconditional value of the freedom of the agent to rise above inclination and attachment, including the most basic attachment to life. Although the heuristics of this example, in contrast to the notorious sympathy example of the *Groundwork*,[66] do not require that we imagine all sympathy be extinguished in order to behold the motive of duty at work (this agent, while righteous, "has feelings which are not insensible or hardened to either sympathy or his own needs"), nonetheless, what we are directed to see as morally praiseworthy is the freedom to overcome these feelings and attachment emotions. Such feelings are not the ground of morality, nor the proper source of moral inspiration: "morality must have more power over the human heart the more purely it is presented." Even less so should we think of moral merit as located in the "transcendent feelings of greatness" that heroes take to "release themselves from observing the common and everyday responsibility as petty and insignificant."[67] The warning reminds us that superlative virtue, even if it involves resisting false defamation at great sacrifice, is not best thought of as self-contained in such moments, nor do such moments excuse a life in which common moral acts are systematically ignored.[68]

But although the above example doesn't require the absence of sympathy in a model of superlative virtue, it nonetheless does represent it as a conflicting motivational pull that stands in the path of duty. However, as argued throughout these pages, we need not view this as Kant's final or considered word on the subject. As we have seen in the chapter on Kantian emotions, and more recently in my brief remarks on moral self-perfection, there is basis for a composite picture of virtue in which the motive of duty is supported and enhanced by emotion and affiliative senti-

---

[66] G 398.   [67] KpV 156.
[68] See Sherman (1988), in which I discuss this theme in connection with Aristotle's notion of *megalopsuchia*.

ments. On that account, emotions are viewed as neither inherently passive nor outside the influence of practical agency and
freedom, but, rather, as subject to the regulation and cultivation of
reason in a way that can ultimately support rather than detract
from moral interest. Within that composite picture of virtue, to
fulfill duties from the motive of duty requires, for example, recognizing occasions for duty, where the input of the emotions is an
essential source of information. Equally, it may require communicating an emotional tone of action that is morally significant
to agent as well as recipient. Here, properly regulated and cultivated emotions, such as sympathy, amiability, and gratitude, enter as well as feelings of respect more directly responsive to our
status as autonomous agents. Although Kant regularly restricts
the notion of moral worth to compliance to duty out of duty, he
extols the more complete picture of virtue as an aesthetic model
that makes virtue attractive and accessible to its adherents. In a
passage from the *Anthropology* I have quoted before in the course
of these pages, the position is explicit:

> No matter how insignificant these laws of refined humanity
> may seem, especially in comparison with pure moral laws, any-
> thing that promotes sociability, even if it consists only in pleas-
> ing maxims or manners, is a garment that dresses virtue to
> advantage, a garment to be recommended to virtue in more
> serious respects too. The *cynics's purism* and the *anchorite's mor-
> tification of the flesh* without social well-being, are distorted fig-
> ures of virtue, which do not attract us to it. Forsaken by the
> graces, they can make no claim to humanity.[69]

These remarks make clear that by the time of the writing of the
Anthropology (in 1798, a decade after the second *Critique*), Kant
well recognized the educative importance of a more embellished
model of superlative virtue. But these are not isolated remarks. In
The Metaphysic of Morals written a year earlier than the *Anthropology,* and in the *Religion,* written four years before that, there is
clear emphasis on the aesthetic appeal of the moral sentiments.[70]

---

[69] Anth. 147.
[70] Equally, there is clear support from the *Critique of Judgment.* For a systematic

In *The Methaphysic of Morals,* Kant poses the following casuistical question:[71]

> Would it not be better for the welfare of the world in general if human morality were limited to juridical duties and these were fulfilled with the utmost conscientiousness, while benevolence were considered morally indifferent?

He answers in the negative:

> A great moral ornament, love of man, would be missing from the world. Accordingly, benevolence is required for its own sake, in order to present the world in its full perfection as a beautiful moral whole.

It is important to remember that by "benevolence" Kant means specifically feelings (as opposed to actions) by which we promote others' permissible ends of happiness. As humans we have certain natural susceptibilities, however limited they may be in some individuals, to react to the pain and joy of others. In cultivating these natural tendencies, we can apply our *"power* and *will* to *share* in others' *feelings, "* thus partially fulfilling, in our display of these feelings, our positive duty to promote others' happiness. Cultivating these feelings, becomes a "conditioned duty" that ultimately may express a moral interest, if we fulfill it, as our obligation to duty requires, from a motive of duty.[72] A similar story can be given for the cultivation of other feelings that support practical love and respect. We have duties to avoid derisive and imperious attitudes, best fulfilled not simply by suppression or control but by the development of more gracious emotions that represent alternative ways of reacting. "Pleasantness in our relations with others, good-naturedness, mutual love and respect (affability and propriety, *humanitas aesthetica et decorum)"* are ways "we associate virtue with the graces, and to effect this is in itself a duty of virtue."[73] Thus, the full perfection of virtue by no means excludes the emotions but, quite to the contrary, is palpably expressed in reason's effect on them. In the fullest and most effec-

study of the connection between Kant's ethical and aesthetic writings, see Guyer (1993).
[71] DV 458.   [72] DV 456.   [73] DV 473.

tive illustration of virtue, one would expect to see the emotions embellishing the work of virtue.

In addition to the appeal of these emotions, there is the overall grace of virtue itself, sensibly experienced by an agent and accessible to a spectator, in the pleasure of achieving compliance with the law. A "cheerless, morose, and surly" attitude "makes virtue itself hated and drives away its followers." The cultivation of virtue "can become meritorious (*verdientslich*) and exemplary (*exemplarisch*) only by the cheerfulness that accompanies it.[74] The point is repeated in the oft-quoted note from the *Religion* in which Kant essentially endorses Schiller's exaltation of the beauty of virtue:

> Now if one asks, What is the *aesthetic character*, the *temperament*, so to speak, *of virtue*, whether courageous and hence *joyous* or fear-ridden and dejected, an answer is hardly necessary. This latter slavish frame of mind can never occur without a hidden *hatred* of the law. And a heart which is happy in the *performance* of its duty (not merely complacent in the *recognition* thereof) is a mark of genuineness in the virtuous disposition.[75]

Essentially, then, we have pulled together elements of a more complete picture of virtue that show the effects of acting in compliance with the moral law on the deeper emotional fabric of the embodied moral agent. In a perspicuous way, this psychological project of showing the way the motive of duty is supported, implemented, and manifest in our phenomenal natures is a central task of *The Metaphysic of Morals* and the *Anthropology*, and to a certain degree, the *Religion*. With regard to our purposes in this chapter, it becomes clear that this more fully dressed picture of virtue can in principle exemplify the best in virtue, and that Kant himself argues that virtue so dressed is aesthetically attractive and inspiring. Consequently, we need not turn from these features in looking for models of superlative virtue in the figures of history and literature, or in models of emulation closer to home. Emotions play an important role in completing the picture of virtue – in presenting "the world in its full perfection as a

[74] DV 485.   [75] Rel. 23n/19n.

beautiful moral whole" so long as their subordinate role to duty is not obscured. While Kant insists throughout his writings that emotions do not stand on their own as having inherent value or moral usefulness, he also is clearly arguing that once regulated by the moral law and shaped by the duty to fulfill the moral law, they are a central feature of the best in human moral perfection. Kant may often emphasize the heuristics of duty elevating itself against inclination as well as the shining examples of pure virtue that show no trace of nonmoral incentives,[76] but he also recognizes the aesthetic grace in emotions that support duty in a more than merely ephemeral way. This transformative process, too, can be a picture of moral strength and certainly a picture of what is involved in full moral perfection. Thus, the depiction of duty rising against the interests of happiness, which is essentially Kant's focus in the calumny examples, is only a part of the truth about morality. The fuller story, which captures morality's perfection, is that while duty may run counter to our most enduring natural interests, even in such cases it may be experienced not only with dignity but with grace and with a panoply of emotions that support duty. It may well require a careful artistic brush to depict the contours of virtue in just the right way so that benevolence and a cheerful heart are not competitors to duty-based virtue but an expression of its grace. But Kant's own argument is that this is the exemplary form (the beautiful moral whole) virtue takes in the world, and that we are inspired and palpably charged by our encounters with it. It now becomes the task of philosophy, in its didactic role and perhaps with the help of literature, to capture what we already experience as the inspiration of moral perfection.

[76] As at Rel. 48/44.

Bibliography

Ackrill, J. L. 1980. Aristotle on *eudaimonia*. In *Essays on Aristotle's ethics*, ed. A. O. Rorty, 15–33. Berkeley and Los Angeles: University of California Press.

Adams, Robert Merrihew. 1988. Common projects and moral virtue. In *Midwest studies in philosophy*, vol. 13, ed. P. French, Th. Uehling, and H. Wettstein, 297–307. Notre Dame: University of Notre Dame Press.

Allan, D. J. 1977. Aristotle's account of the origin of moral principles. In *Articles on Aristotle: 2 Ethics and politics*, ed. J. Barnes, M. Schofield, and R. Sorabji. London: Duckworth.

Allison, Henry. 1990. *Kant's theory of freedom*. Cambridge: Cambridge University Press.

Ameriks, Karl. 1987. The Hegelian critique of Kantian morality. In *New essays on Kant*, ed. B. den Ouden and M. Moen, 179–82. New York: Peter Lang.

  1989. Kant on the good will. In *Grundlegung zur Metaphysik der Sitten: Ein Kooperativer Kommentar*, ed. O. Höffe. Frankfurt a.m.: Vittorio Klostermann.

  1992. Kant and Hegel on freedom: Two new interpretations. *Inquiry* 35:219–32.

  1995. On Paul Guyer's *Kant and the experience of freedom*. *Philosophy and Phenomenological Research* 55:361–67.

Annas, Julia. 1992. The good life and the good lives of others. In *The good life and the human good*, ed. E. Paul, F. D. Miller, and J. Paul, 133–48. Cambridge: Cambridge University Press.

  1993. *The morality of happiness*. New York: Oxford University Press.

  1995. Virtue as a skill. *International Journal of Philosophical Studies* 3:227–43.

Bibliography

Arnold, Magda. 1960. *Emotion and personality*. New York.: Columbia University Press.
Averill, James. 1974. An analysis of psychophysiological symbolism and its influence on theories of emotion. *Journal of the Theory of Social Behavior* 4:147–90.
  1976. Emotion and anxiety: Sociocultural, biological, and psychological determinants. In *Explaining emotions*, ed. A. O. Rorty. Berkeley and Los Angeles: University of California Press.
Barker, Andrew. 1984. *Greek musical writings*, vol. 1. Cambridge: Cambridge University Press.
Barnes, J., M. Schofield, and R. Sorabji. 1977. *Articles on Aristotle: 2 Ethics and politics*. London: Duckworth.
Baron, Marcia. 1984. On the alleged repugnance of acting from duty. *Journal of Philosophy* 81:179–219.
  1987. Kantian ethics and Supererogation. *Journal of Philosophy* 84:237–62.
  1988. Remorse and agent regret. In *Midwest studies in philosophy*, vol. 13, ed. P. French, Th. Uehling, and H. Wettstein, 259–281. Notre Dame: University of Notre Dame Press.
  1995a. *Kantian ethics almost without apology*. Ithaca, NY:Cornell University Press.
  1995b. Sympathy and coldness: Kant on the stoic and the sage. In *Proceedings of the Eighth International Kant Congress*, vol. 1, part 2, 691–703.
Belfiore, Elizabeth. 1992. *Tragic pleasures: Aristotle on plot and emotion*. Princeton: Princeton University Press.
Ben-Ze'ev, Aaron. Unpublished. *Frankly my dear, I do care: Analyzing emotions*.
Benjamin, Jessica. 1988. *The bonds of love*. New York: Pantheon.
Benson, Paul. 1987. Moral worth. *Philosophical Studies* 51:365–82.
Bittner, Rudiger. 1974. *Maximen*. In *Akten des 4. Internationalen Kant-Kongresses*, ed. G. Funke, vol. 2, 485–98. Berlin: Walter de Gruyter.
  1989. *What reason demands*. Cambridge: Cambridge University Press.
  1991 (fall). *How to act on principle*. Paper presented at the Onora O'Neill conference, University of Notre Dame.
Blum, Lawrence. 1980. *Friendship, altruism and morality*. Boston: Routledge & Kegan Paul.
  1994. *Moral perception and particularity*. Cambridge: Cambridge University Press.
Bok, Sissela. 1978. *Lying*. New York: Vintage.

1983. *Secrets*. New York: Vintage.

Bonitz, H. 1870. *Index Aristotelicus*. Berlin.

Boswell, J. 1934. *Boswell's life of Johnson*, vol. 3, ed. G. G. Hill; revised, L. F. Powell. Oxford: Oxford University Press.

Bratman, Michael. 1987. *Intention, plans, and practical reason*. Cambridge, MA: Harvard University Press.

Bremer, J. M. 1969. *Hamartia*. Amsterdam: Adolf M. Hakkert.

Brenner, Charles. 1982. *The mind in conflict*. Madison, CT: International Universities Press.

Broadie, Sarah. 1991. *Ethics with Aristotle*. New York: Oxford University Press.

Brunschwig, Jacques, and Martha C. Nussbaum. 1993. *Passions and perceptions: Studies in Hellenistic philosophy of mind*. Cambridge: Cambridge University Press.

Buchanan, Allen. 1977. Categorical imperatives and moral principles. *Philosophical Studies* 31:249–60.

Budd, Malcolm. 1985. *Music and the emotions*. Boston: Routledge & Kegan Paul.

Burnyeat, Myles. 1980. Aristotle on learning to be good. In *Essays on Aristotle's ethics*, ed. A. O. Rorty, 69–92. Berkeley and Los Angeles: University of California Press.

Calhoun, Chesire, and Robert Solomon. 1984. *What is an emotion?* New York: Oxford University Press.

Campbell, Colin. 1987. *The romantic ethic and the spirit of modern consumerism*. Cambridge, MA: Blackwell.

Cannon, Walter. 1927. The James–Lange theory of emotion: A critical examination and an alternative theory. *American Journal of Psychology* 39:106–24.

Caston, Victor. 1992. Aristotle on intentionality. Dissertation, University of Texas at Austin.

Charles, David. 1984. *Aristotle's philosophy of action*. Ithaca, NY: Cornell University Press.

1988. Perfectionism in Aristotle's political theory: Reply to Martha Nussbaum. In *Oxford studies in ancient philosophy*, supplementary volume, 185–206. Oxford: Oxford University Press.

Cohen, G. A. 1993. Equality of what? On welfare, goods, and capabilities. In *The quality of life*, ed. M. C. Nussbaum and A. Sen. New York: Oxford University Press.

Cooper, John. 1973. The *Magna Moralia* and Aristotle's moral philosophy. *American Journal of Philology* 94:327–49.

1975. *Reason and human good in Aristotle.* Cambridge MA: Harvard University Press.

1980. Aristotle on friendship. In *Essays on Aristotle's ethics,* ed. A. O. Rorty, 301–40. Berkeley and Los Angeles: University of California Press.

1985. Aristotle on the goods of fortune. *Philosophical Review.* 94:173–97.

1987. Contemplation and happiness: A reconsideration. *Synthese* 72:187–216.

1989. Greek philosophers on euthanasia and suicide. In *Suicide and euthanasia,* ed. Baruch A. Brody, 9–38. Dordrecht: Kluwer.

1993. *Rhetoric, dialectic, and the passions.* In *Oxford studies in ancient philosophy,* vol. 11, 178–84. Oxford: Oxford University Press.

1995. Eudaimonism and the appeal to nature in the morality of happiness: Comments on Julia Annas, *The morality of happiness. Philosophy and Phenomenological Research* 55:587–98.

Crocker, David. 1992. Functioning and capability: The foundation of Sen's and Nussbaum's development ethic. *Political Theory,* 20:584–612.

Dahl, Norman. 1984. *Practical reason, Aristotle, and weakness of will.* Minneapolis: University of Minnesota Press.

Damasio, Antonio. 1994. *Descartes' error.* New York: Grosset/Putnam.

Dancy, Jonathan. *Moral reasons.* 1993. Cambridge, MA: Blackwell.

Darwall, Stephen.1988. Self-deception, autonomy, and moral constitution. In *Perspectives on self-deception,* ed. B. P. McLaughlin and A. O. Rorty. Berkeley and Los Angeles: University of California Press.

Darwin, Charles. 1872. *The expression of emotion in man and animals.* In *What is an emotion?,* ed. C. Calhoun and R. Solomon, 115–24. New York: Oxford University Press.

Daube, David. 1969. *Roman law.* Edinburgh: Edinburgh University Press.

Davis, Wayne. 1987. The varieties of fear. *Philosophical Studies* 51:287–310.

1988. A causal theory of experiential fear. *Canadian Journal of Philosophy* 18:459–83.

De Sousa, Ronald. 1987. *The rationality of emotion.* Cambridge, MA: MIT Press.

1988. Emotion and self-deception. In *Perspectives on self-deception,* ed. B. P. McLaughlin and A. O. Rorty, 324–41. Berkeley and Los Angeles: University of California Press.

Devereux, Daniel T. 1981. Aristotle on the essence of happiness. In *Studies in Aristotle,* ed. Dominic J. O'Meara, 247–60. Washington, DC: Catholic University Press of America.

Dillon, Robin S. 1992. How to lose your self-respect. *American Philosophical Quarterly* 29:125–39.

Bibliography

Eagle, Morris. 1983. Anatomy of the self in psychoanalytic theory. In *Nature Animated,* ed. Michael Ruse. Boston: Reidel.

1984. *Recent developments in psychoanalysis.* New York: McGraw-Hill.

1988. Psychoanalysis and the personal. In *Mind, psychoanalysis and science,* ed. Peter Clark and Crispin Wright. Cambridge, MA: Blackwell.

Eden, Kathy. 1986. *Poetic and legal fiction in the Aristotelian tradition.* Princeton: Princeton University Press.

Ekman, Paul, ed. 1973. *Darwin and facial expression.* New York: Academic Press.

1982. *Emotion in the human face.* 2nd edition. Cambridge: Cambridge University Press.

Engberg-Pederson, Troels. 1983. *Aristotle's theory of moral insight.* New York: Oxford University Press.

1987. Discovering the good: *oikeiōsis* and *kathēkonta* in Stoic ethics. In *Norms and nature,* ed. M. Schofield and G. Striker, 145–83. Cambridge: Cambridge University Press.

Erb, Peter. 1983. *Pietist selected writings.* Ramsey, NJ: Paulist Press.

1989. *Pietists, Protestants and mysticism: The use of late medieval spiritual texts in the work of Gottfried Arnold (1666–1714).* Metuchen, NJ: Scarecrow Press.

Fairbairn, W. R. D. 1952. Repr. 1992. *Psychoanalytic studies of the personality.* New York: Routledge.

Fisher, John Martin, ed. 1986. *Moral responsibility.* Ithaca, NY: Cornell University Press.

Flanagan, Owen. 1991. *Varieties of moral personality.* Cambridge MA: MIT Press.

Flanagan, Owen, and Amélie O. Rorty, eds. 1990. *Identity, character, and morality.* Cambridge, MA: MIT Press.

Forschner, Maximilian. 1985. Das Gute und die Güter. Zur aktualität der Stoischen ethik. In *Aspects de la philosophie hellenistique.* Geneva: Vandoeuvres, 325–50.

Fortenbaugh, William. 1975. *Aristotle on emotion.* London: Duckworth.

Frankfurt, Harry. 1988. *The importance of what we care about.* Cambridge: Cambridge University Press.

Frede, Dorothea. 1992. Necessity, chance and "what happens for the most part." In *Essays on Aristotle's* Poetics, ed. A. O. Rorty, 197–219. Princeton: Princeton University Press.

Frede, Michael. The Stoic doctrine of the affections of the soul. In *Norms of nature,* ed. M. Schofield and G. Striker, 93–110. Cambridge: Cambridge University Press.

Bibliography

French, P., Th. Uehling, and H. Wettstein, eds. 1988. *Midwest studies in philosophy*, vol. 13: *Ethical theory: Character and virtue*. Notre Dame: University of Notre Dame Press.

Freud, Sigmund. [1886–1938] 1953–1974. *The standard edition of the complete psychological works of Sigmund Freud* (SE), ed. J. Strachey, vols. 1–24. London: Hogarth Press.

    1894. The neuro-psychoses of defense. SE 3:45–61.

    1896. Further remarks on the neuro-psychoses of defense. SE 3:162–85.

    1917. *Introductory lectures on psychoanalysis*. Lecture 25: Anxiety. SE 16:392–411.

    1926. *Inhibitions, symptoms and anxiety*. SE: 20:77–172.

Frijda, Nico. 1986. *The emotions*. Cambridge: Cambridge University Press.

Gay, Peter. 1966. *The enlightenment: An interpretation*. New York: Knopf.

Gewirth, Alan. 1978. *Reason and morality*. Chicago: University of Chicago Press.

Gilligan, Carol. 1982. *In a different voice*. Cambridge, MA: Harvard University Press.

Goffman, Erving. 1959. *The presentation of self in everyday life*. New York: Doubleday.

Golden, Leon. 1962. "Catharsis." *Transactions of the American Philological Association* 93:51–60.

Gómez-Lobo, Alfonso. 1988. A new look at the ergon argument in the *Nicomachean Ethics*. *Proceedings of the Society for Ancient Greek Philosophy*. Forthcoming. Moral excellence and right reason in Aristotle. *Apeiron*.

Gottlieb, Paula. 1991. Aristotle and Protagoras: The good human being as the measure of goods. *Apeiron* 24:25–45.

Gordon, Robert. 1987. *The structure of emotions*. Cambridge: Cambridge University Press.

Greenberg, Jay, and Stephen Mitchell. 1983. *Object relations in Psychoanalytic theory*. Cambridge, MA: Harvard University Press.

Greenson, Ralph R. 1965. The working alliance and the transference neurosis. *Psychoanalytic Quarterly* 34:155–81.

Greenspan, Patricia S. 1988. *Emotions and reasons: An inquiry into emotional justification*. New York: Routledge.

Greenspan, Stanley I. 1989. *The development of the ego*. Madison, CT: International Universities Press.

Greenspan, Stanley I. and George Pollack, eds. 1989. *The course of life*. Vol. 1: *Infancy*. Madison CT: International Universities Press.

Greenwood, L. H. G. 1973 reprint (1909: Cambridge University Press). *Aristotle, Nicomachean Ethics, Book Six*, with essay, notes, and translation. New York: Arno Press.

Bibliography

Gregor, Mary. 1963. *Laws of freedom*. Cambridge, MA: Blackwell.

Guenther, Herbert V. 1989. *Tibetan Buddhism in western perspective*. Berkeley, CA: Dharma.

Guyer, Paul. 1992. Book review of *Kant's theory of freedom* by Henry Allison. *Journal of Philosophy* 89:99–110.

　1993. *Kant and the experience of freedom*. Cambridge: Cambridge University Press.

　1995. Moral anthropology in Kant's aesthetics and ethics: A reply to Ameriks and Sherman. *Philosophy and Phenomenological Research* 55:379–91.

Haight, M. R. 1980. *A study of self-deception*. New York: Humanities Press.

Haillie, Phillip. 1979. *Lest innocent blood be shed: The story of the village of Le Chambon and how goodness happened there*. New York.

Halliwell, Stephen. 1986. *Aristotle's* Poetics. Chapel Hill: University of North Carolina Press.

　1992. Pleasure, understanding, and emotion in Aristotle's *Poetics*. In *Essays on Aristotle's* Poetics, ed. A. O. Rorty, 241–60. Princeton: Princeton University Press.

Hardie, W. F. R. 1977. Aristotle's doctrine that virtue is a "Mean." In *Articles on Aristotle*, vol. 2, ed. J. Barnes, M. Schofield, and R. Sorabji, 33–46. London: Duckworth.

　1978. "Magnanimity" in Aristotle's ethics. *Phronesis* 7:63–79.

Hare, R. M. 1963. *Freedom and reason*. New York: Oxford University Press.

Henson, Richard. 1979. What Kant might have said: Moral worth and the overdetermination of dutiful action. *Philosophical Review* 88:39–54.

Herman, Barbara. 1993. *The practice of moral judgment*. Cambridge, MA: Harvard University Press.

Heyd, David. 1982. *Supererogation: Its status in ethical theory*. Cambridge: Cambridge University Press.

Hill, Thomas, Jr. 1971. Kant on imperfect duty and supererogation. *Kant-Studien* 62:55–76. Reprinted in Hill (1992).

　1973. The hypothetical imperative. *Philosophical Review* 82:429–50. Reprinted in Hill (1992).

　1974. Kant's utopianism. *Akten des 4. Internationalen Kant-Kongresses*, ed. G. Funke, vol. 2, 918–24. Reprinted in Hill (1992).

　1980. Humanity as an end in itself. *Ethics* 91:84–90. Reprinted in Hill (1992).

　1984. Autonomy and benevolent lies. *Journal of Value Inquiry* 18:251–67. Reprinted in Hill (1991).

　1985. Kant's argument for the rationality of moral conduct. *Pacific Philosophical Quarterly* 66:3–23. Reprinted in Hill (1992).

1989. Kant's theory of practical reason. *Monist* 72:363–83. Reprinted in Hill (1992).

1991. *Autonomy and self-respect.* Cambridge: Cambridge University Press.

1992. *Dignity and practical reason.* Ithaca, NY: Cornell University Press.

Höffe, Otfried. 1977. Kants kategorischer Imperativ als Kriterium des Sittlichen. *Zeitschrift für philosophische Forschung* 31:354–84.

Hoffer, Axel. 1985. Toward a psychoanalytic neutrality. *Journal of the American Psychoanalytic Association* 33:771–96.

Homiak, Marcia. 1981. Virtue and self-love in Aristotle's ethics. *Canadian Journal of Philosophy* 11:633–51.

Hudson, Stephen. 1986. *Human character and morality.* Boston: Routledge & Kegan Paul.

Hume, David. 1888. *A treatise of human nature,* ed. Selby-Bigge. New York: Oxford University Press.

Hursthouse, Rosalind. 1991. Arational actions. *Journal of Philosophy* 88:57–69.

Inwood, Brad. 1985. *Ethics and human action in early stoicism.* New York: Oxford University Press.

1986. Goal and target in Stoicism. *Journal of Philosophy,* 83:547–57.

1993. Seneca and psychological dualism. In *Passions and perceptions,* ed. J. Brunschwig and M. C. Nussbaum, 150–83. Cambridge: Cambridge University Press.

Inwood, Brad, and L. P. Gerson. 1988. *Hellenistic philosophy: Introductory readings.* Indianapolis: Hackett.

Irwin, Terence. 1975. Aristotle on reason, desire, and virtue. *Journal of Philosophy* 72: 567–78.

1984. Morality and personality: Kant and Green. In *Self and nature in Kant's philosophy,* ed. A. Wood. Ithaca, NY: Cornell University Press.

1985a. *Aristotle's Nicomachean ethics,* translation and notes. Indianapolis: Hackett.

1985b. Aristotle's conception of morality. In *Proceedings of the Boston Area Colloquium in Ancient Philosophy* 1:115–43.

1985c. Permanent happiness: Aristotle and Solon. In *Oxford studies in ancient philosophy,* vol. 3, 89–124. Oxford: Oxford University Press.

1986. Stoic and Aristotelian conceptions of happiness. In *Norms of nature,* ed. M. Schofield and G. Striker, 205–44. Cambridge: Cambridge University Press.

1988. Disunity in the Aristotelian virtues. In *Oxford studies in ancient philosophy,* supplementary volume, 61–78. Oxford: Oxford University Press.

1990. Virtue, praise and success: Stoic responses to Aristotle. *Monist* 73: 53–96

Izard, Caroll. 1977. *Human emotions*. New York: Plenum.

James, William. 1899. *The will to believe*. New York: Longmans Green.

James, William, and Carl Georg Lange. 1884. What is an emotion? *Mind* 19:188–205. Reprinted in *What is an emotion?*, ed. C. Calhoun and S. Solomon, 127–41. New York: Oxford University Press.

Kennedy, George, tr. 1991. *Aristotle: On rhetoric*. New York: Oxford University Press.

Kenny, Anthony. 1963. *Action, emotion and will*. London: Routledge & Kegan Paul.

1979. *Aristotle's theory of the will*. New Haven: Yale University Press.

Kernberg, Otto. 1976. Object relations theory and clinical psychoanalysis. New York: Jason Aronson.

1995. *Love relations: Normality and pathology*. New Haven: Yale University Press.

Keyt, David. 1983. Intellectualism in Aristotle. In *Essays on ancient Greek philosophy*, vol. 2, ed. J. P. Anton and A. Preuss, 364–87. Albany: State University of New York Press.

Kidd, I. G. 1978. Moral actions and rules in Stoic ethics. In *The Stoics*, ed. J. Rist, 247–58. Berkeley and Los Angeles: University of California Press.

Kivy, Peter. 1984. *Sound and semblance*. Princeton: Princeton University Press.

1990. *Music alone*. Ithaca, NY: Cornell University Press.

Klein, Melanie. 1975. *Love, guilt and reparation and other works 1921 – 1945*. New York: Delta.

Kohut, Heinz. 1971. *The analysis of self*. Madison CT: International Universities Press.

Korsgaard, Christine. 1985. Kant's formula of universal law. *Pacific Philosophical Quarterly* 66:24–47.

1986a. The right to lie: Kant on dealing with evil. *Philosophy and Public Affairs* 15:325–49.

1986b. Kant's formula of humanity. *Kant-Studien* 77:183–202.

1986c. Aristotle and Kant on the source of value. *Ethics* 96:486–505.

1989. Kant's analysis of obligation: The argument of *Foundations* I. *Monist* 72: 311–40.

1996. From duty and for the sake of the noble. In *Aristotle, Kant and the Stoics*, ed. S. Engstrom and J. Whiting. Cambridge: Cambridge University Press.

Kosman, L. A. 1980. Being properly affected: Virtues and feelings in Aristotle's ethics. In *Essays on Aristotle's ethics*, ed. A. O. Rorty, 103–16. Berkeley and Los Angeles: University of California Press.

Kraut, Richard. 1989. *Aristotle on the human good*. Princeton: Princeton University Press.

1993. In defense of the grand end. A review of Sarah Broadie, *Ethics with Aristotle*. *Ethics* 103:361–74.

1995. *The morality of happiness* by Julia Annas. Book symposium. *Philosophy and Phenomenological Research* 55:921–27.

Kuehn, Manfred. 1987. *Scottish common sense in Germany, 1768–1800*. Kingston and Montreal: McGill–Queen's University Press.

Lazarus, R. S. 1966. *Psychological stress and the coping process*. New York: McGraw-Hill.

Lear, Jonathan. 1988. *Aristotle: The desire to understand*. Cambridge: Cambridge University Press.

1990. *Love and its place in nature*. New York: Farrar, Straus & Giroux.

1992. Katharsis. In *Essays on Aristotle's Poetics*, ed. A. O. Rorty, 315–40. Princeton: Princeton University Press.

Little, Margaret. Forthcoming. Particularism and moral justification.

Lloyd, A. C. 1978. Emotion and decision in Stoic psychology. In *The Stoics*, ed. J. Rist, 223–46. Berkeley and Los Angeles: University of California Press.

Loewald, Hans. 1980. *Papers on psychoanalysis*. New Haven: Yale University Press.

Long, A. A. 1974. *Hellenistic philosophy*. London: Duckworth.

1983. Greek ethics after MacIntyre and the Stoic community of reason. *Ancient Philosophy* 3:184–97.

1988. Stoic eudaimonism. In *Proceedings of the Boston Area Colloquium in Ancient Philosophy* 4:77–101.

Long, A. A., and D. N. Sedley. 1987. *The Hellenistic philosophers*. Vols. 1 and 2. Cambridge: Cambridge University Press.

Lord, Carnes. 1982. *Education and culture in the political thought of Aristotle*. Ithaca, NY: Cornell University Press.

Lovibond, Sabina. 1993. *Realism and imagination in ethics*. Minneapolis: University of Minnesota Press.

Lyons, William. 1980. *Emotion*. Cambridge: Cambridge University Press.

MacIntyre, Alasdair. 1981. *After virtue*. Notre Dame: University of Notre Dame Press.

Marcus, Ruth. 1970. Moral dilemmas and consistency. *Journal of Philosophy* 77:121–36.

Bibliography

Martin, Mike W. 1986. *Self-deception and morality.* Lawrence: University Press of Kansas.

McCarty, Richard. 1989. The limits of Kantian duty, and beyond. *American Philosophical Quarterly* 26:43–52.

McDowell, John. 1979. Virtue and reason. *Monist* 62:330–50.

———. 1981. Non-cognitivism and rule-following. In *Wittgenstein: To follow a rule,* ed. S. Holtzman and C. Leich. Boston: Routledge & Kegan Paul.

McLaughlin, Brian, and Amélie O. Rorty, eds. 1988. *Perspectives on self-deception.* Berkeley and Los Angeles: University of California Press.

McNaughton, David. 1988. *Moral vision : An introduction to ethics.* Cambridge, MA: Blackwell.

Meerbote, Ralf. 1984. Commentary: Kant on freedom and the rational and morally good will. In *Self and nature in Kant's philosophy,* ed. A. Wood. Ithaca, NY: Cornell University Press.

Mendus, Susan. 1985. The practical and the pathological. *Journal of Value Inquiry* 19:235–43.

Meyerson, Denise. 1991. *False consciousness.* New York: Oxford University Press.

Miller, F. D. 1989. Aristotle's political naturalism. In *Nature, knowledge and virtue, Essays in memory of Joan Kung,* ed. T. Penner and R. Kraut. *Apeiron* 22:195–218.

Mistis, Phillip. 1986. Moral rules and the aims of Stoic ethics. *Journal of Philosophy,* 86:556–57.

———. 1993. Seneca on reason, rules and moral development. In *Passions and perceptions,* ed. J. Brunschwig and M. C. Nussbaum, Cambridge: Cambridge University Press.

Modrak, Deborah. 1987. *Aristotle: The power of perception.* Chicago: University of Chicago Press.

Mulgan, R. G. 1977. *Aristotle's political theory.* New York: Oxford University Press.

———. 1991. Aristotle's analysis of oligarchy and democracy. In *A Companion to Aristotle's Politics,* ed. D. Keyt and F. D. Miller, 307–22. Cambridge, MA: Blackwell.

Murdoch, Iris. 1970. *The sovereignty of the good.* London: Routledge & Kegan Paul.

Nagel, Thomas. 1979. Sexual Perversion. In *Mortal questions,* 39–52. Cambridge: Cambridge University Press.

———. 1980. Aristotle on *eudaimonia.* In *Essays on Aristotle's ethics,* ed. A. O. Rorty, 7–14. Berkeley and Los Angeles: University of California Press.

———. 1986. *The view from nowhere.* New York: Oxford University Press.

Nell (O'Neill), Onora. 1975. *Acting on principle*. New York: Columbia University Press.

Nowell-Smith, P. H. 1954. *Ethics*. Harmondsworth, UK: Penguin.

Nussbaum, Martha C. 1978. *Aristotle's "De Motu Animalium": Text with translation, commentary, and interpretive essays*. Princeton: Princeton University Press.

1980. Shame, separateness, and political unity: Aristotle's criticism of Plato. In *Essays on Aristotle's ethics*, ed. A. O. Rorty, 395–46. Berkeley and Los Angeles: University of California Press.

1985. The discernment of perception: An Aristotelian conception of private and public rationality. In *Proceedings of the Boston Area Colloquium in Ancient Philosophy* 1:151–201.

1986. *The fragility of goodness: Luck and ethics in Greek tragedy and philosophy*. Cambridge: Cambridge University Press.

1988a. Non-relative virtues: An Aristotelian approach. In *Midwest studies in philosophy*, vol. 13, ed. P. French, Th. Uehling, and H. Wettstein, 32–53. Notre Dame: University of Notre Dame Press.

1988b. Nature, function, and capability: Aristotle on political distribution. In *Oxford studies in ancient philosophy*, supplementary volume, 145–84. Oxford: Oxford University Press.

1990a. *Love's knowledge: Essays on philosophy and literature*. New York: Oxford University Press.

1990b. Aristotelian social democracy. In *Liberalism and the good.*, ed. R. B. Douglass, G. Mara, and H. Richardson, 203–52. New York: Routledge.

1993. Equity and mercy. *Philosophy and Public Affairs* 22:83–125.

1994. The therapy of desire: Theory and practice in Hellenistic ethics. Princeton: Princeton University Press.

1996. *Upheavals of thought: A theory of the emotions*. Gifford Lectures 1993. Cambridge: Cambridge University Press.

Nussbaum, Martha C., and Amartya Sen, eds. 1993. *The quality of life*. New York: Oxford University Press.

Oakley, Justin. 1992. *Morality and the emotions*. New York: Routledge.

Oatley, Keith. 1992. *Best laid schemes: The psychology of emotions*. Cambridge: Cambridge University Press.

O'Connor, David K. 1988. Aristotelian justice as a personal virtue. In *Midwest studies in philosophy*, vol. 13, ed. P. French, Th. Uehling, and W. Wettstein, 417–27. Notre Dame: University of Notre Dame Press.

O'Neill, Onora. 1989. *Constructions of reason*. Cambridge: Cambridge University Press.

Parrot, Gerald, and J. Sabini. 1989. On the "emotional" qualities of certain types of cognition: A reply to arguments for the independence of condition and affect. *Cognitive Therapy and Research* 13:49–65.

Paton, H. J. 1953–54. An alleged right to lie: A problem in Kantian ethics. *Kant-Studien*. 45:190–203.

Pears, David. *Motivated irrationality*. 1984. New York: Oxford University Press.

Person, E. 1988. *Dreams of love and fateful encounters*. New York: Penguin.

Peters, R. S., and C. A. Mace. 1962. Emotions and the category of passivity. *Proceedings of the Aristotelian Society* 62:117–142.

Piper, Adrian. 1990. Higher-order discrimination. In *Identity, character, and morality*, ed. O. Flanagan and A. O. Rorty, 285–309. Cambridge, MA: MIT Press.

Platts, M. 1979. *Ways of meaning*. Boston: Routledge & Kegan Paul.

Price, A. W. 1989. *Love and friendship in Plato and Aristotle*. New York: Oxford University Press.

Quinn, Warren. 1993. *Morality and action*. Cambridge: Cambridge University Press.

Rawls, John. 1971. *A theory of justice*. Cambridge, MA: Harvard University Press.

———. 1980. Kantian constructivism in moral theory. *Journal of Philosophy* 77: 515–72.

———. 1989. Themes in Kant's Moral philosophy. In *Kant's transcendental deductions*, ed. E. Förster, 81–113. Stanford: Stanford University Press.

Reath, Andrews. 1989. Kant's theory of moral sensibility: Respect for the moral law and the influence of inclination. *Kant-Studien* 80:284–302.

———. 1994. Legislating the moral law. *Nous* 28:435–64.

Reiss, Hans, ed. 1970. *Kant's political writings:* Cambridge: Cambridge University Press.

Richardson, Henry. 1990. Specifying Norms as a way to resolve concrete ethical problems. *Philosophy and Public Affairs* 19:279–310.

———. 1992. Degrees of finality and the highest good in Aristotle. *Journal of the History of Philosophy* 30:327–52.

———. 1994. *Practical reasoning about ends*. Cambridge: Cambridge University Press.

Ricoeur, Paul. 1977. The question of proof in Freud's psychoanalytic writings. *Journal of the American Psychoanalytic Association* 25:835–72.

Rist, J. 1969. *Stoic philosophy*. Cambridge: Cambridge University Press.

———. 1978a, ed. *The Stoics*. Berkeley and Los Angeles: University of California Press.

Bibliography

1978b. The Stoic concept of detachment. In *The Stoics*, ed. Rist, 259–72.

Roberts, Robert C. 1984. Solomon on the control of emotions. *Philosophy and Phenomenological Research* 44: 395–403.

1988. What an emotion is: A sketch. *Philosophical Review* 97:183–209.

Robinson, Daniel, and Rom Harré. 1994. The demography of the Kingdom of Ends. *Philosophy* 69:5–19.

Rorty, Amélie O., ed. 1980a. *Essays on Aristotle's ethics*. Berkeley and Los Angeles: University of California Press.

1980b, *Explaining emotions*. Berkeley and Los Angeles: University of California Press.

1992. *Essays on Aristotle's* Poetics. Princeton: Princeton University Press.

Ross, W. D. 1988. *The right and the good*. Indianapolis: Hackett.

Schachter, Stanley, and Jerome Singer. 1962. Cognitive, social and physiological determinants of emotional states. *Psychological Review* 69:379–99. Reprinted in *What is an emotion?*, eds. C. Calhoun and S. Solomon, 173–83. New York: Oxford University Press.

Schafer, Roy. 1992. *Retelling a life: Narration and dialogue in psychoanalysis*. New York: Basic Books.

Schneewind, Jerome. 1986. The use of autonomy in ethical theory. In *Reconstructing individualism: Autonomy, individuality, and the self in western thought*, ed. T. Heller, M. Sosna, and D. Wellbery, 64–75. Stanford: Stanford University Press.

1987. Pufendorf's place in the history of ethics. *Synthese* 72:123–55.

1990a. *Moral philosophy from Montaigne to Kant*. Vols. 1 and 2. Cambridge: Cambridge University Press.

1990b. The misfortunes of virtue. *Ethics* 101:42–63.

1991a. Natural law, skepticism and method. *Journal of the History of Ideas* 52:228–301.

1991b. Classical republicanism and the ethics of virtue. Paper presented to the Riverside Philosophy Conference on virtue ethics.

Schofield, M., and G. Striker, eds. 1986. *The norms of nature*. Cambridge: Cambridge University Press.

Sedgwick, Sally. 1988. On the relation of pure reason to content. A reply to Hegel's critique of formalism in Kant's ethics. *Philosophy and Phenomenological Research* 49:59–80.

1990. Can Kantian ethics survive the feminist critique? *Pacific Philosophical Quarterly* 71:60–79.

Seidler, Michael. 1981a. Kant and the Stoics on the emotional life. *Philosophy Research Archives*.

1981b. The role of stoicism in Kant's moral philosophy. Dissertation, St. Louis University.

1983. Kant on the Stoics on suicide. *Journal of the History of Ideas* 44:429–53.

Sen, Amartya. 1985. Rights and capabilities. In *Morality and objectivity: A tribute to J. L. Mackie.* Boston: Routledge & Kegan Paul.

1993. Capability and well-being. In *The quality of life,* ed. M. C. Nussbaum and A. Sen, 30–53. New York: Oxford University Press.

Shapiro, Theodore, and Daniel Stern. 1989. Psychoanalytic perspectives on the first year of life: The establishment of the object in an affective field. In *The course of life,* ed. S. I. Greenspan and G. Pollack, 271–92. Madison, CT: International Universities Press.

Sherman, Nancy. 1980. Hegel's two dialectics. *Kant-Studien* 71–238–53.

1985a. Character, planning, and choice in Aristotle. *Review of Metaphysics* 39:83–106.

1985b. Commentary on T. Irwin's *Aristotle's conception of morality.* In *Proceedings of the Boston Area Colloquium in Ancient Philosophy* 1: 144–50.

1987. Aristotle on friendship and the shared life. *Philosophy and Phenomenological Research* 47: 589–613.

1988. Common sense and uncommon virtue. *Midwest studies in philosophy,* vol. 13, ed. P. French, Th. Uehling, and H. Wettstein, 97–114. Notre Dame: Notre Dame University Press.

1989. *The fabric of character: Aristotle's theory of virtue.* New York: Oxford University Press.

1990. The place of emotions in Kantian morality. In *Identity, character, and morality,* ed. O. Flanagan and A. O. Rorty, 158–70. Cambridge, MA: MIT Press.

1991a. Excellence. In *Encyclopedia of ethics,* ed. Lawrence Becker, 342–44. New York: Garland.

1991b. Practical wisdom. In *Encyclopedia of ethics,* ed. Lawrence Becker, 996–98. New York: Garland.

1992. Virtue and *hamartia.* In *Essays on Aristotle's* Poetics, ed. A. O. Rorty, 177–96. Princeton: Princeton University Press.

1993a. Wise maxims/wise judging. *Monist* 76:41–65.

1993b. The virtues of common pursuit. *Philosophy and Phenomenological Research* 53:277–99.

1994a. The heart's knowledge. An essay on Martha Nussbaum's *Love's knowledge. Internationale Zeitschrift für Philosophie* 2:204–19.

1994b. The role of emotions in Aristotelian virtue. *Proceedings of the Boston Area Colloquium in Ancient Philosophy* 9:1–33.

1994c. Review of *Sovereign virtue* by Stephen White. *Philosophical Review* 103:178–81.

1995a. The moral perspective and the psychoanalytic quest. *Journal of the American Academy of Psychoanalysis* 23:223–41.

1995b. The emotions. In *Encyclopedia of bioethics,* ed. Warren Reich, 664–71. New York: Macmillan.

1995c. Reason and feeling in Kantian morality. Book symposium on *Kant and the experience of freedom* by Paul Guyer. *Philosophy and Phenomenological Research* 55:369–77.

1995d. Ancient conceptions of happiness. Book symposium on *The morality of happiness* by Julia Annas. *Philosophy and Phenomenological Research* 55:913–19.

1995e. Kant on sentimentalism and stoic apathy. Comments on Marcia Baron's Sympathy and coldness: Kant on the Stoic and the sage. *Proceedings of the Eighth International Kant Congress* vol. 1, part 2, 705–11.

Simmons, Keith. 1989. Kant on moral worth. *History of Philosophy Quarterly* 6:85–100.

Skinner, B. F. 1953. *Science and human behavior.* New York: Free Press.

Slote, Michael. 1983. *Goods and virtues.* New York: Oxford University Press.

1984. Morality and self–other asymmetry. *Journal of Philosophy* 81:179–92.

1990. Some advantages of virtue ethics. In *Identity, character, and morality,* ed. O. Flanagan and A. O. Rorty, 429–48. Cambridge, MA: MIT Press.

1992. *From morality to virtue.* New York: Oxford University Press.

Solomon, Robert. 1973. Emotions and choice. *Review of Metaphysics* 27:20–41.

1984. I can't get it out of my mind: (Augustine's problem). *Philosophy and Phenomenological Research* 44:405–12.

Sorabji, Richard. 1980. Aristotle on the role of intellect in virtue. In *Essays on Aristotle's ethics,* ed. A. O. Rorty, 201–20. Berkeley and Los Angeles: University of California Press.

Sorell, Tom. 1987. Kant's good will and our good nature. *Kant-Studien* 78:88–101.

Stocker, Michael. 1976. The schizophrenia of modern ethical theories. *Journal of Philosophy* 73:453–66.

1987. Emotional thoughts. *American Philosophical Quarterly* 24:59–69.

1990. *Plural and conflicting values.* New York: Oxford University Press.

1996. *Valuing emotions*. Cambridge: Cambridge University Press.

Striker, Gisela. 1986. Antipater on the art of living. In *The norms of nature: Studies in Hellenistic ethics*, ed. M. Schofield and G. Striker, 185–204. Cambridge: Cambridge University Press.

1996. Emotions in context: Aristotle's treatment of the passions in the *Rhetoric*. In *Essays on Aristotle's Rhetoric*, ed. A. O. Rorty, 286–303. Berkeley and Los Angeles: University of California Press.

Sullivan, H. S. 1953. The interpersonal theory of psychiatry. New York: Norton.

Taylor, C. C. W. 1987. Hellenistic ethics: A discussion of Malcolm Schofield and Gisela Striker, *The norms of nature: Studies in Hellenistic ethics*. In *Oxford studies in ancient philosophy* vol. 5, 235–45. Oxford: Oxford University Press.

Thera, Nyanaponika. 1986. *The vision of dhamma*. London: Rider.

Thurman, Robert. 1984. *The central philosophy of Tibet*. Princeton: Princeton University Press.

1990. *The holy teaching of Vimalakirti*. University Park: Pennsylvania State University Press.

Urmson, J. O. 1958. Saints and heroes. In *Essays in moral philosophy*, ed. A. I. Melden. Seattle: University of Washington Press.

Van der Linden, Harry. 1988. *Kantian ethics and socialism*. Indianapolis: Hackett.

Van Fraassen, Bas. 1988. The peculiar effects of love and desire. In *Perspectives on self-deception*, ed. McLaughlin and A. O. Rorty, 123–56. Berkeley and Los Angeles: University of California Press.

Vlastos, Gregory. 1973. The individual as object of love in Plato. In *Platonic Studies*, 3–42. Princeton: Princeton University Press.

Wallace, James. 1978. *Virtues and vices*. Ithaca, NY: Cornell University Press.

Wallwork, Ernest. 1991. *Psychoanalysis and ethics*. New Haven: Yale University Press.

Watson, J. B. 1929. *Psychology from the standpoint of a behaviorist*. 3rd ed. Philadelphia: Lippincott.

Weinrib, Ernest. 1987. Aristotle's forms of justice. In *Justice, law and method in Plato and Aristotle*, ed. Spiro Panagiotou, 133–52. Edmonton: Academic Printing and Publishing.

White, Stephen. 1992. *Sovereign virtue*. Stanford, CA: Stanford University Press.

Wiggins, David. 1980. Deliberation and practical reason. In *Essays on Aristotle's ethics*, ed. A. O. Rorty, 221–40. Berkeley and Los Angeles: University of California Press.

Williams, Bernard. 1973. *Problems of the self.* Cambridge: Cambridge University Press.

1976. Persons, character and morality. In *The Identities of persons,* ed. A. O. Rorty, 197–216. Berkeley and Los Angeles: University of California Press.

1980. Justice as a virtue. In *Essays on Aristotle's ethics,* ed. A. O. Rorty, 189–200. Berkeley and Los Angeles: University of California Press.

1981. *Moral luck.* Cambridge: Cambridge University Press.

1985. *Ethics and the limits of philosophy.* Cambridge, MA: Harvard University Press.

Winnicott. D. W. 1971. *Playing and reality.* London: Penguin.

Wood, Allen. 1970. *Kant's moral religion.* Ithaca, NY: Cornell University Press.

ed. 1984a. *Self and nature in Kant's philosophy.* Ithaca, NY: Cornell University Press.

1984b. Kant's compatibilism. In *Self and nature in Kant's philosophy,* ed. A. Wood, 73–101.

1989. The emptiness of the moral will. *Monist* 72:454–83.

1990. *Hegel's ethical thought.* Cambridge: Cambridge University Press.

1991. Unsocial sociability: The anthropological basis of Kantian ethics. *Philosophical Topics* 19:325–51.

Woods, Michael. 1982. *Aristotle's Eudemian ethics,* translated with a commentary. New York: Oxford University Press.

Yovel, Yirmiahu. 1980. *Kant and the philosophy of history.* Princeton: Princeton University Press.

ed. 1989. *Kant's practical philosophy reconsidered.* Dordrecht: Kluwer.

Index

Ackrill, J., 195n.11
activity, as requirement of *eudaimonia*,
  5–6, 9–20
affective memory, 47; *see also*
  psychoanalysis
Agamemnon, 44
akrasia, 43n.36, 212n.71, 349
Allan, D. J., 213n.78, 279n.102
Allison, H., 19n.40, 21n.43, 295n.16,
  298n.25
Ameriks, K., 21n.43, 126n.14
Anaxagoras, 111
Andronicus, 104n.10
anger, 57, 66, 108–9, 170, 159–60
Anlage, 159–60
Annas, J., 7n.4–7; 49n.47, 68n.88,
  97n.142, 140n.45, 203n.40, 208n.61,
  210n.65, 215n.80, 216n.85, 276n.86,
  281n.104
Anne Boleyn, 353, 356
Anonymous Commentary on *Theatetus*,
  218n.91, 286n.3
apatheia, 112, 117, 167; *see also* apathy;
  Stoics
apathy, 116–20, 151, 155, 167; *see also*
  apatheia; emotions, Stoic; senti-
  mentalism
Aristoxenus, 89
Arius Didymus, 100n.1, 117n.45,
  279n.102; *see also* Stobaeus
Arnold, M., 55n.55, 57n.61, 67n.87
autonomy, 1, 138–9; *see also* Categorical
  Imperative; legislative reason
Averill, J., 26n.3,n.5

background norms, 288, 291–2; *see also*
  Categorical Imperative; deliberative
  presumptions; rules

Barker, A., 89n.129
Baron, M., 30n.13, 116n.43, 118n.47,
  332n.3–4, 337, 342–4, 350–1, 354n.60
Belfiore, E., 89n.129, 109n.26
beneficence, 129, 131–2, 142
Benjamin, J., 199n.24
Bett, R., 100n.1
Bittner, R., 241n.8, 296n.17, 298n.25
blessedness, as happiness, 10n.12,
  13n.21
Blum, L., 30n.13, 39n.28, 243n.13,
  352n.55
Boeri, M., 100n.1
Bok, S., 320n.57
Boswell, J., 153
Bratman, M., 279n.97
Bremer, J., 247n.21
Brender, N., 139n.43
Brenner, C., 26n.3
Broadie, S., 21n.43, 195n.11, 265n.63,
  276n.86,n.89, 279n.98
Brown, J., 7on.92
Brunschwig, J., 100n.1
Buchanan, A., 130n.20
Buddhism, 85n.122, 113–15

Campbell, C., 124n.9
Cannon, W., 54
Carse, A., 254n.37, 283n.105
Caston, V., 59n.68
Categorical Imperative, 8–9, 128–35,
  138, 141, 240, 284–330; as Formula of
  Humanity, 133, 286, 308–10, 315, 317,
  320–3, 326; as Formula of Universal
  Law, 286, 305–6, 315, 321–3, 326; for-
  mulae summary, 286; as Kingdom of
  Ends, 138, 224, 286; as method of self-
  knowledge, 146, 232–3, 309, 341, 345;

Index

and reflective deliberation, 311–25;
and role as deliberation procedure vs.
generator of background norms, 33,
289–94, 304, 305–11, 312, 315–17,
325–6; *see also* duties; moral perfection; narrative–specification model of
deliberation
catharsis, 91n.133, 174n.131
character, 11–12; *see also* habituation;
moral development; virtue, Aristotelian conception of; virtue, Kantian
conception of; virtue, Stoic conception of
Charles, D., 241n.8, 276n.86
Charles I, Emperor, 293n.7
Chrysippus, 101–2, 107
Cicero, 3, 17n.32, 82, 104, 106, 107, 111,
117n.45, 218n.91, 286n.3
Clinton, W., 70n.92
community, 189, 192, 236–8, 285–6; *see
also* ethical commonwealth; friendship; *philia; polis*
conflict, 318–19; *see also* moral conflict;
narrative–specification model of
deliberation; psychic conflict; regret
contemplation, 194–5, 272; *see also* theoretical reason
contradiction in conception and contradiction in will tests, 298, 306–8; *see
also* Categorical Imperative;
universalizability
Cooper, J., 46n.38, 49n.47, 53n.50,
100n.1, 195n.11, 208n.61, 210, 241n.8,
257n.43, 259n.51, 276n.86
courage, 96
Crocker, D., 222n.108

Dahl, N., 241n.8, 276n.86
Damasio, A., 40n.30
Dancy, J., 243n.13, 244n.15, 256n.41,
257n.44, 261n.55, 262n.58, 263,
269n.72, 271n.75, 310n.48
Darwin, C., 42n.34
Daube, D., 247n.21
Davis, W., 26n.5, 58n.66
de Sousa, R., 26n.5, 40n.29, 54n.52, 58,
83n.120, 111
deliberative presumptions, 290–2, 321,
336
Descartes, R., 26, 39n.28, 73n.97
Devereux, D., 195n.11
Diogenes Laertius, 17n.33, 117n.45,
183n.148, 189n.5, 215n.82, 337n.20
Diotema, 207n.56
Dustin, C., 329n.68

duties: ethical, 131, 136, 329; imperfect,
131, 348–9, 352–61; juridical, 136, 223,
329; perfect vs. imperfect, 131, 138,
273, 273n.77, 312, 320–3, 326, 329–30
332–6, 336; *see also* virtue, Kantian
conception of
duty, as motive, 126, 150, 358

Eagle, M., 254n.34
Eden, K., 92n.135, 109n.26
Ekman, P., 42n.34
emotions: alternative accounts of as
sensations, proprioceptions of viscera, and behavior, 53–5; Aristotelian
account of as intentional and evaluative states, 55–74; as attachment, 113–
15; characteristic ambivalence toward, 25–6; and control, 50–1; as
evaluative, 31, 36; habituation of, 32–
3; as intrinsically valuable, 48–50; as
modes of attending value, 28, 39–40,
50, 248–9; as modes of communicating value, 40–2, 50, 248–9; as modes
of creating value, 48, 50; as modes of
gesture, 41–2; as modes of self-
knowledge and self-disclosure, 47; as
moral motives vs. duty motive, 33; as
motivational, 49–50; orthodox objections to and Aristotelian inspired rep-
lies, 28–34, 38; and roles in morality,
39–52; *see also* emotions, Aristotelian;
emotions, Kantian; emotions, Stoic
emotions, Aristotelian, 24–98; and
change through evaluative shifts, 84–
9, 93; and choice, 75–83; compared
with Kantian conception, 177–8; and
constitutive affects, 64–5; and cultivation of through music and tragedy,
89–93; defined, 57–8; and empathy,
205–6; as evaluative, 53, 55–64, 68,
248–54; general account of, 52–74;
and habituation and cultivation of,
78–83; 83–8, 111–12, 250–4 (*see also*
moral development); as motivational,
66–73, 97–8; and objectless emotions
and sensations, 62–4; and practical
wisdom, 68–9; and praise and blame,
75, 77, 79; and psychic harmony and
conflict, 93–8, 253–4; and rhetoric,
55–7, 61; as right pleasures and
pains, 52–3; and roles in morality,
73–4, 97–8, 248–54; *see also*
emotions
emotions, Kantian: as attractive and
recommended aesthetic in virtuous

382

person, 147–9; characteristic ambivalence about moral significance of, 148–9, 151–2; compared with Aristotelian view, 177–8; duty to cultivate as supports of duty, 141–58; as evaluative, 119, 248–54; general roles of in morality, 144–51, 169 (*see also* emotions); habituation of compared with Aristotelian account, 157–9; as modes of attention, 145–46, 185; as modes of conveying moral interest, 147–8; and moral agency, 164–75; as motivational, 119, 149–51; as practical and pathological, 33, 100, 119, 158; as sensations, 178–81; and Stoic sage and antisentimentalism, 151–5; some terminological distinctions, 121n.1, 164–7; *see also* emotions; emotions, Aristotelian; emotions, Stoic

emotions, Stoic: contrasted with Kantian view, 149n.72; defined, 87, 103–7; and doctrine of *eupatheia*, 117–20; four types of, 106–7; as judgment, 103–7; and Kantian account of Stoic apathy as antisentimentalism, 116–20; and objections to Aristotelian moderate emotions in terms of unreliability and vulnerability, 101–7; and therapy of, 82, 85n.122, 87–9, 107–15, 116, 167; *see also* emotions; emotions, Aristotelian; emotions, Kantian

empathy, 48n.45; 259n.52; *see also philia*

ends, and their specification, 213–14, 271–2, 279n.102, 279–80, 317–18; *see also* narrative–specification model of deliberation

Engberg-Pedersen, T., 241n.8, 257n.43

enkratēs, 38

Epictetus, 108n.23

epistēmē, 239, 248

Erb, P., 124n.9

ethical commonwealth, 233–8; *see also* Categorical Imperative

ethical egoism, 7–9, 203n.40, 283

eudaimonia, 5–7, 283, 328n.66; defined, 9–10; as involving activity vs. mere possession of state, 11–15; as lived emotionally, 49; Stoic conception of, 17–19; *see also* eudaimonistic ethics; happiness; virtue, Aristotelian conception of; virtue, Stoic conception of

eudaimonistic ethics, 4–9; compared with Kantian framing question, 8–9; Kant's critique of, 6, 16–20, 118, 196, 225, 283; role of emotions in, 36–7;

Stoic conception of, 103–7

eupatheia, 100, 107n.21, 112, 117–20, 167; *see also* Stoics

external goods, 2, 5–6, 103, 128, 128n.18, 142n.52; instrumental vs. noninstrumental, 6, 208–10; Kantian conception of, 15–19, 144; and place in Aristotelian *eudaimonia*, 9–20; Stoic view of, 17–18, 103, 107; *see also* indifferents; *philia*

Fairbairn, W., 26n.3

fantastic virtue, 337

fear, 67, 96

fine or *to kalon*, 77, 219–20, 283, 328n.66

Forschner, M., 100n.1

Francis I, 193n.7

Frede, D., 270n.73

free rider, 133

Freud, S., 46n.42, 111, 114, 199n.24; and drive theory, 26, 55n.56

Friedman, M., 114n.41

friendship, 185–6, 187–238; as external good, 12; valued for its mutuality, 188–99; *see also* mutuality; *philia*

friendship, Kantian conception of, 224–38; compared with Aristotelian views, 226; defined, 225–6; and duty to cultivate, 226–8; and mutuality, 228; and our competitive natures, 230–1; and role in moral perfection, 236–8; and self-knowledge, 232–3; and vulnerability, 229–30; *see also* community; mutuality; *philia*

Frijda, N., 26n.5, 55n.55, 57n.61

Galen, 101.n5, 104n.9, 106n.16

Gay, P., 3, 121, 122n.6,n.7

gestural articulation, 41–2

Gilligan, C., 189n.6

Golden, L., 109n.26

Gómez-Lobo, A., 100n.1, 258n.47

good life, *see eudaimonia*

good will, 18–19, 189; *see also* Categorical Imperative; moral worth; virtue, Kantian conception of

Gordon, R., 26n.5, 76n.99

Gottlieb, P., 43n.36, 258n.47

Greenberg, J., 26n.3,n.5

Greenspan, P., 26n.5, 58, 63–4

Greenspan, S., 40n.32, 41n.33, 42n.34, 63n.76, 199n.24

Greenwood, L., 213n.78

Gregor, M., 130n.20, 135n.31, 332n.4, 334n.12

Index

Guenther, H., 85n.122
Guyer, P., 21n.43, 29n.8,n.10, 35n.21, 126n.14, 142n.53, 344n.36, 358n.70

habituation, 6, 32–3, 67, 78–83, 86, 111–12, 143, 170; and Aristotelian practical reason, 241–3; in Kantian account, 197; Kantian critique of Aristotelian conception of, 160–2; *see also* emotions, Aristotelian; emotions, Kantian; emotions, Stoic; moral development; psychogogy
Haillie, P., 352n.55
Halliwell, S., 89n.129, 109n.26
hamartia, 247
happiness: as distinct from morality, 16–20; duty to promote, 138, 142; virtue as sufficient for, on Stoic view, 17–19; *see also eudaimonia*; eudaimonistic ethics; external goods; indifferents
Hardie, W., 96n.141
Hare, R., 244n.16
Harré, R., 130n.21
Hellenists, 3; *see also* Stoics
Henry VIII, 353, 356
Herman, B., 29n.7–8, 30n.13, 35n.21, 39n.28, 130n.20, 133n.27, 134n.29, 141n.50, 143n.57, 150n.73, 162n.103, 237n.143, 240n.5,n.7, 241n.8, 277n.91, 290n.7, 296n.19, 298n.25, 301, 302n.34–5, 306, 307, 320n.57, 322, 323n.64, 336
Heyd, D., 332n.1
Hierocles, 218n.91
Highest Good, 19, 196n.19, 235–8
Hill, T., 241n.8, 273n.77, 296n.17, 309n.46, 320n.57, 322n.61–2, 332n.4, 333, 334n.12, 336–7, 342–3, 350
Höffe, O., 298n.25
Horace, 3
Huegenots, 352n.55
Hume, D., 113, 123
Hursthouse, R., 71
Hutcheson, F., 122, 123n.7

idealization, 207, 252
impartiality, 187, 282–3; *see also* Categorical Imperative; rules; universalizability
inclination, 125–6, 128, 141; *see also* emotions, Kantian
incompatibilism, 21n.43
incorporation thesis, 295n.16

indifferents, 17, 103, 215, 337; *see also* external goods; virtue, Stoic conception of
intuitionism, 254–62; *see also* moral perception; moral salience; particularism; practical wisdom
Inwood, B., 100n.1, 105n.13,n.15
Irwin, I., 17n.34–5, 100n.1, 213n.78

James, W., 65, 83
justice, 222–4

kathēkon, 107
Kenny, A., 25n.1, 26n.3, 92n.134, 276n.86
Kernberg, O., 26n.3
Keyt, D., 195n.11
Kivy, P., 40n.30, 91n.132
Klein, M., 26n.3
Kohlberg, L., 189n.6
Kohut, H., 259n.52
Korsgaard, C., 132n.26, 195n.12, 241n.8, 298n.23,n.25, 306–7, 309n.46, 320n.57–8, 321, 322n.62
Kosman, L. A., 77n.103
Kraut, R., 7n.6, 8n.8, 10n.9, 195n.11, 203n.40, 208n.61, 272n.76, 328n.65

Lagarek, E., 231n.131
Lance, M., 283n.105
Lange, C., 83
latitude, 326, 331–61; Aristotle and Kant compared, 328–32, 340
law, 274–6; *see also* Categorical Imperative; particularism; rules; universalizability
Lazarus, R., 26n.3,n.5, 57n.61
Lear, J., 91n.133, 109n.26
legislative reason, 6, 20, 128, 287–8; *see also* Categorical Imperative; law; universalizability
Little, M., 243n.13, 244n.15, 263, 283n.105
Loewald, H., 96n.141
Long, A., 100n.1
Lord, C., 89n.129
Lovibond, S., 254n.35
lying, 131–3, 320–5, 327, 353, 356
Lyons, W., 26n.5

Mace, C., 76n.99
Marcus, R., 319n.56
maxim, 137, 240, 245, 278, 287; compared with *prohairesis*, 296–7; defined, 294–5, 298; and its content, 294–305; and opacity, 303; *see also* Categorical Imperative

Index

McCarty, R., 351, 354
McDowell, J., 39n.28, 243n.13, 261n.55,
 266n.66, 273n.77, 275n.85
McNaughton, J., 243n.13
mean, 162, 328–30, 331, 340
metaphysic of morals, 2, 123, 127–35;
 see also moral anthropology
Miller, F., 222n.108
Milo, the wrestler, 340n.28
mimēsis, 48n.45, 90–2
Mistis, P., 100n.1
Mitchell, S., 26n.3,n.5
Modrak, D., 59n.68
moods, 251–2
Moore, G. E., 254n.35
moral anthropology, 1, 4, 6, 120, 123,
 127–35, 294
moral conflict, 43–5, 95–6; *see also*
 hamartia; tragedy; tragic mistakes
moral development, 80–93, 214, 217,
 224, 225, 325, 328, 345–6; *see also* emotions; friendship; habituation; moral
 perfection; *philia*
moral judgment, *see* Categorical Imperative; legislative reason; moral perception; particularism; practical
 reason; practical wisdom
moral perception, 238–3; and intuitionism, 254–62; as mode of practical reason involving emotions, 248–54; and
 responsibility for appearances, 246–7;
 see also moral salience; particularism;
 practical wisdom
moral perfection, 138, 141–3, 345–50
moral praise, 184, 75, 77, 79
moral psychology, *see* moral
 anthropology
moral salience, 2, 243; *see also* intuitionism; moral perception; particularism;
 practical wisdom
moral worth, 18, 67, 125–6, 162–4,
 182n.46, 349, 350, 358
Mulgan, R., 222n.108
Murdoch, I., 39n.28, 243n.13
music, 89–93; ancient modes of, 80; as
 narrative, 91
mutuality, 190–1, 201, 204–8; *see also*
 friendship; *philia*

Nagel, T., 195n.11, 201n.31
narrative, 262, 288, 303, 313, 317–18
narrative–specification model of
 deliberation, 271–2, 278, 281–2, 310,
 314–25
Nell, O., *see* O'Neill, O.

Novatus, 108
novel reading and imagination, 173–5
Nowell-Smith, P., 254n.35
Nussbaum, M., 15n.27, 25n.1, 30n.13,
 36n.24, 39n.28, 53n.50, 59n.68, 60n.73,
 68n.89, 82n.117, 100n.1, 102n.6,n.8,
 108n.24, 109n.26, 115n.42, 188n.2,
 195n.11, 205n.49, 207n.56–7, 208n.61,
 213n.78, 222n.108, 241n.8, 243n.13,
 252n.30, 262n.56, 266n.65, 270n.74,
 275n.83, 293n.10–11, 327, 328n.66

Oakley, J., 26n.5, 27n.6, 30n.13, 34n.19,
 56n.57, 66, 73n.97, 75n.88, 126n.13,
 179n.143
O'Connor, D., 223n.110
O'Neill, O., 130n.20, 240n.5, 241n.8,
 289n.5, 296n.18, 298n.23,n.25,
 299n.28–9, 300n.31–2, 307n.43,
 311n.49
Original Position, 326
orthos logos, 244, 258n.47, 328n.66

Parrot, G., 26n.5
particularism, 238–83, 284; overview of
 Aristotle and Kant on generalizability, 243–5; rules and their
 place in, 262–76, 284–6; *see also* moral
 perception; practical wisdom; rules
Paton, H. J., 320n.57
Pears, D., 212, 253n.33
Person, E., 199n.24
Peters, R., 76n.99
phantasia, 59–62
philanthropic feelings, 186, 217n.88, 220,
 234
philia: Aristotelian conception defined,
 199–201; and attachment, 199, 217–
 18; and critique of *Repbublic* V, 221;
 and empathy, 205–6; as energizer,
 213; and equality, 206–7; as external
 good, 208–16; and moral development, 80, 214, 224; and mutuality,
 204–8; and noninstrumental other-
 regard, 201–3; and role in *eudaimonia*,
 194–6, 208–16; and self-knowledge,
 210–13, 260–1; and self-love, 216,
 218–19; and utility, 203–4; and wider
 altruism, 217–24; *see also* community;
 external goods; friendship; mutuality
philosophes, 3, 121
phronimos, 9, 94, 258n.47, 327–8
Pietism, 123–5, 154, 172
Piper, A., 48n.44
pity, 67, 157n.91, 186, 175

Index

Plato, 2, 4, 63, 66, 92, 105, 128, 207n.56, 217n.88, 265, 277n.91
Platts, M., 254n.35
pleasure, as supervenient, 94
Plutarch, 104, 110n.31
polis, 220–4
Posidonius, 105n.13, 115
practical freedom, 295; *see also* Categorical Imperative; legislative reason
practical reason, Kantian and Aristotelian compared, 137–8, 278–9, 283, 311–12, 325–30; *see also* Categorical Imperative; legislative reason; particularism; practical wisdom; universalizability
practical syllogism, 69–72, 276–83
practical wisdom: inseparable from full virtue, 161, 278; as involving emotions, 68–9; in Kantian ethics, 284–330; and self-knowledge, 211–12; *see also* Categorical Impertative, moral perception; particularism; universalizability; virtue, Aristotelian conception of
prima facie duty, 291
prohairesis, 11, 137, 162; *see also* practical syllogism
Proust, M., 46n.42, 173
psychic conflict, 96–8, 136–7, 184–6
psychoanalysis, 47, 114, 259n.52; *see also* empathy; transference
psychogogy, 82, 108, 113; *see also* emotions; habituation; moral development; Stoic therapy of emotions

Quinn, W., 243n.13

rationalization, 134, 245; *see also* self-deception
Rawls, J., 187, 189n.6, 271n.75, 289n.5, 296n.18, 300n.30, 326
Reath, A., 150n.74, 176n.133, 180n.144, 241n.8, 346n.410
reflective deliberation, 311–25; *see also* narrative–specification model of deliberation
regret, 43–5
respect, 175–81, 214n.79, 218, 228–9; and practical love, 197–8
Richardson, H., 112n.40, 213n.78, 271n.75, 276n.86, 279n.102, 283n.105, 285n.1, 291n.8, 310, 314n.51, 316n.52,n.54, 318n.55
Ricoeur, P., 262n.57
Rist, J., 100n.1

Roberts, R., 26n.5, 76n.99
Robinson, D., 71n.96, 130n.21
Ross, W. D., 254n.35, 291
Rousseau, H., 122n.6, 166
rules, 239–41, 262–76, 284–6; and deductive aspirations, 274–6; holding for the most part, 268–71, 284; and Kantian and Aristotelian conceptions compared, 248–8; as pedagogical, 273–4; as summaries of experience, 266–7, 284; *see also* background norms; Categorical Imperative; moral perception; particularism; practical wisdom; universalizability
Ryle, G., 55n.5

Sabini, J., 26n.5
sacrifice, 351–5; *see also* virtue, Kantian conception of
Sappho, 54
Sartre, J. P., 201n.31
Schacter, S., 54n.53
Schafer, R., 262n.57
Schiller, 155n.86, 360
Schneewind, J., 231n.130
Schofield, M., 100n.1
Sedgwick, S., 130n.20
Sedley, D., 100n.1
Seidler, M., 100n.2, 121n.3
self-deception, 46, 211, 245, 304; *see also* lying; rationalization
self-knowledge, 146, 232–3, 341, 345; *see also* Categorical Imperative; *philia*
self-love, 218–19; *see also* ethical egoism; *philia*
self-sufficiency, 116, 211, 195–6; as criterion of *eudaimonia*, 10, 107, 225
Sen, A., 222n.108
Seneca, 17n.34, 102, 105n.13, 108–10, 111, 118n.47, 122n.6
sentimentalism, 116–20, 153–5; vs. sensitivity, 168–9; *see also* apathy; emotions, Kantian; emotions, Stoic
Sextus Empiricus, 17n.33
Shapiro, T., 80n.110
Sherman, N., 10n.9, 25n.1, 26n.4, 39n.28, 46n.38, 68n.88, 70n.90, 80n.110, 83n.119, 91n.131,n.133, 97n.142, 116n.43, 126n.14, 144n.58, 162n.102, 173n.128, 174n.131, 188n.2, 200n.28, 212n.71, 213n.78, 243n.12, 252n.30, 254n.34, 274n.79, 279n.99,n.102, 294n.13, 304n.40, 341n.29, 349n.47, 357n.68
Singer, J., 54n.53

386

Index

Skinner, B. F., 55n.55
Slote, M., 332n.2, 339n.24
Socrates, 3, 5, 18, 265, 277n.91
Solomon, R., 26n.5, 76n.99
sōphrōn, 38
Sorabji, R., 213n.78, 279n.102
soul: as rational and monistic in Stoic account,104–5; and rational and non-rational parts in Aristotelian conception, 38
Stern, D., 80n.110
Stobaeus, 17n.33, 105n.14, 106n.17,n.19, 107n.20
Stocker, M., 30n.13, 43n.36, 45n.37, 48n.44, 58n.66, 249n.23, 250n.24
Stoic sage, 116–19, 152–2
Stoic therapy of emotions, 82, 85n.122, 87–9, 107–15, 116; see also emotions, Stoic
Stoics, 1, 3, 5, 14–15, 99–120, 128, 166, 218; see also emotions, Stoic; eudaimonia; indifferents; virtue, Stoic conception of
Striker, G., 53n.50, 66n.84, 100n.1
Sullivan, H. S., 26n.3
supererogatory, 350–1; see also virtue, Kantian conception of
superlative virtue, see virtue, Kantian conception of
sympathy, 67, 126, 135, 142, 357; see also emotions; emotions, Kantian

technē, 264–7
theoretical reason, 10n.9, 12n.19; see also contemplation
Thera, N., 85n.122
Thurman, R., 85n.122
tragedy, 89–93
tragic mistakes, 247–8, see also hamartia; moral conflict; regret
transference, 73, 214; see also Freud; psychoanalysis
true needs, 339–42

unity of virtues, 207; see also virtue, Aristotelian conception of
universalizability, 130–3, 240, 241, 244–5, 285–8, 297–8, 305–11; see also Categorical Imperative; legislative reason; rules
Urmson, J., 332n.1

van der Linden, H., 235n.138, 237n.142
virtue, Aristotelian conception of: and conflict, 93–8; and constitutive role of emotions, 24–98; defined, 5; as inseparable from practical wisdom, 242–3; as involving action and emotion, 24; and stability, 95; see also character; emotions, Aristotelian; habitutation; moral development; particularism; practical wisdom; virtue, Kantian conception of
virtue, Kantian conception of, 121–86; compared with Aristotelian conception, 137–8, 139–40, 183, 184–6, 292–3, 326–8; defined, 16, 137, 140; and derivative pleasure, 155–6; duties of virtue to cultivate emotions,141–58, 182–3; duties of virtue to promote rational agency, 139–40; duties of virtue vs. juridical duties, 135–6, 138, 333–5; and inspirational role models, 355–61; and meritorious and exemplary virtue requiring emotion, 154–5, 163–4, 357–61; place of within Kant's overall ethical theory, 135–40; restricted to nonholy wills, 130–5; and sacrifice, 351–5; Stoic influence on, 16–20, 99–120, 121–2; as structured composite, 24, 158–64, 182; and superlative virtue, 337–8, 350–61; see also duty; emotions, Kantian
virtue, Stoic conception of, 99–120; as consistency of reason, 108; as sufficient for happiness, 17, 103; see also apatheia; emotions, Stoic; eudaimonia; indifferents; Stoics
Vlastos, 207n.56

Wallwork, E., 26n.4
Weinrib, E., 223n.111
White, S., 15n.27, 49n.47
Wiggins, D., 213n.78, 279n.102
Williams, B., 30n.13, 43, 223n.110
Winnicott, D., 199n.24
Wittgenstein, L., 55n.55, 70n.92, 266
Wood, A., 235n.138

Yovel, Y., 235n.138

Zeno of Citium, 18, 106
Zeus, 108